STUDENT LEARNING GUIDE

Principles of Marketing

Third Canadian Edition

Philip Kotler
Northwestern University

Prentice Hall Canada Inc.
Scarborough, Ontario

Canadian Cataloguing in Publication Data

Kotler, Philip
Student learning guide for principles of marketing, third Canadian edition.

1. Marketing. 2. Marketing – Management. I. Armstrong, Gary. II. Warren, Robert, 1964– . III. Title. IV. Title: Principles of Marketing.

HF5415.K636 1997 Suppl. 1. 658.8 C96-931494-9

Prentice-Hall, Inc., Englewood Cliffs, New Jersey
Prentice-Hall International (UK) Limited, London
Prentice-Hall of Australia, Pty. Limited, Sydney
Prentice-Hall Hispanoamericana, S.A., Mexico City
Prentice-Hall of India Private Limited, New Delhi
Prentice-Hall of Japan, Inc., Tokyo
Simon & Schuster Asia Private Limited, Singapore
Editora Prentice-Hall do Brasil, Ltda., Rio de Janeiro

ISBN 0-13-267261-8

Acquisitions Editor: P. Ferrier
Developmental Editor: M. Tsombanelis
Production Editor: A. Wallace
Production Coordinator: D. Starks
Permissions: M. Leupen
Cover Design: G. Robertson
Page Layout: L. Blank

2 3 4 5 WC 01 00 99 98 97

Printed and bound in Canada

We welcome readers' comments, which can be sent by e-mail to
collegeinfo_pubcanada@prenhall.com

Contents

Section One

Section Two

Section Three

Preface

The purpose of this Learning Guide is to help students learn and apply the concepts and ideas presented in the 3rd Canadian edition of Kotler's and Armstrong's Principles of Marketing.

The Learning Guide should be viewed as a supplement rather than as a substitute for the text. The objectives are to allow the student to (A) focus on the key terms and main topics of each chapter, (B) apply the concepts by analyzing brief cases in marketing, and (C) demonstrate an understanding of the material through self-testing with multiple-choice and true false questions.

The Learning Guide is divided into three (3) sections. The first section is divided into twenty-two (22) chapters with each chapter corresponding to a chapter in the text. Each chapter in the Learning Guide contains the following:

A. Chapter Overview
B. Chapter Objectives
C. Lecture/Student Notes
D. Key Terms
E. Applying Terms and Concepts
F. Testing Terms and Concepts
G. Answers

The first part of each chapter, "Chapter Overview," is designed to familiarize the student with the important topics presented in the chapter.

"Chapter Objectives," comprises the second part of each chapter. This is designed to focus the students' attention on the major points covered in the text. This section identifies what should have been learned after the chapter has been thoroughly studied.

The third component of each chapter, "Lecture/Student Notes" is provided to facilitate the learning process. It is intended for the student to keep notes and record information as the text is read and/or as the professor discusses text material. Selected charts, diagrams and other visuals are provided to draw attention to the main topics identified in the chapter.

The fourth part of each chapter, "Key Terms" is provided to focus attention on important marketing terminology. After the student has read the text; it is suggested that they cover the term, then read the definition and see if they can identify the term. “Key Terms” are referenced to the textbook.

The fifth segment of each chapter, "Applying Terms and Concepts," is designed to illustrate and apply topics in marketing. Each case in the section is a synopsis of a recent article in marketing, or has been adapted from an article or broadcast in marketing, or has been drawn from the author's experiences. After reading the case, the student is encouraged to answer the questions which follow. Suggested answers are provided in the answers section of the chapter.

The "Testing Terms and Concepts" portion of each chapter is made up of multiple-choice and true-false questions designed to test the student's understanding of the material presented in the text. Many questions call for knowledge of the factual information, others, however, call for an application of the factual information. The level of difficulty has been designated for each question (E for easy, M for medium and D for difficult). Suggested answers are listed in the answer section of the chapter.

The second section of the Learning Guide provides outlines for research papers and/or class projects. These activities are designed to reinforce learning which has taken place throughout the course. They are intended to be a practical application of the marketing theory presented in the text. Specific guidelines concerning topics, length, due date, method of presentation, grading and so on, will be provided by the course instructor.

The third section of the Learning Guide contains information about selected careers in marketing. Its intent is to demonstrate the great variety of employment opportunities which exist within the discipline of marketing. Information is also provided about trade associations and professional publications which will allow the student to gain additional information about various careers in marketing. This section compliments Appendix III of the text which also provides information on developing job search strategies, preparing a resume and cover letter, interviewing techniques and otherwise preparing for a successful career in marketing.

Studying Marketing

To better appreciate marketing and its role within the organization and society, the student is encouraged to personalize marketing by considering it from the perspective of the consumer, the marketer and the member of society. The student is also encouraged to periodically review the various topics studied in marketing to develop a greater appreciation of their inter relatedness. The intent is to have the student realize that the topics are not separate and disjointed, but rather flow together in a synergistic fashion. It is then that the student will appreciate the importance of marketing and how it interacts and coordinates with the other business functions.

This conceptual view of marketing will reinforce the need for a societal marketing orientation providing a greater opportunity for a consumer satisfaction and the achievement of organizational and societal objectives.

Acknowledgments

It is always important to acknowledge those people who make the final product possible. For this Learning Guide, this includes Professors Kotler and Armstrong who wrote the original text and Professor Cunningham at Queen's for her superb job in Canadianizing the text. The text is an exciting and practical book that fully covers all areas of marketing. Thomas Paczkowski deserves credit for developing the original layout of this Learning Guide for the US edition. A special thanks to Lesley Mann and Maria Tsombanelis at Prentice Hall. Without their support and advice this Learning Guide would not be possible. Finally, I would like to thank all the people that contributed to the production of the Learning Guide by either proofreading the text or offering encouragement. These include Kim Coghill, Glen Ismond and the University of Manitoba's Small Business Consulting Program, Culver and Mary Warren.

Robert Warren
Department of Marketing
University of Manitoba
Winnipeg, Manitoba

CHAPTER 1

MARKETING IN A CHANGING WORLD: CREATING CUSTOMER VALUE AND SATISFACTION

CHAPTER OVERVIEW

This chapter lays the foundation for the rest of the book. It defines marketing and several core marketing concepts, such as needs, demands, products, exchange, and markets. Marketing management involves the management of demand, and different views of what stimulates demand lead to different marketing philosophies. Because marketing affects everyone, and because people disagree on what goals the marketing system should try to accomplish, marketing has been adopted by businesses and nonprofit organizations in countries around the world. Marketing operates within a dynamic global environment. This poses challenges for marketers including a changing world economy, a call for more ethics, social responsibility, and a changing marketing landscape.

CHAPTER OBJECTIVES

When you finish this chapter, you should be able to accomplish the following:

1. Define marketing and outline the concepts of needs, wants and demands.
2. Discuss marketing management and express the basic ideas of demand management and building profitable customer relationships.
3. List the marketing management philosophies and be able to distinguish among the production concept, product concept, selling concept, marketing concept, and societal marketing concept.
4. Analyze the key marketing challenges in the next century, including growth of nonprofit marketing, rapid globalization, the changing world economy, the call for more ethics and social responsibility, and the new marketing landscape.

LECTURE/STUDENT NOTES

I. What is Marketing?

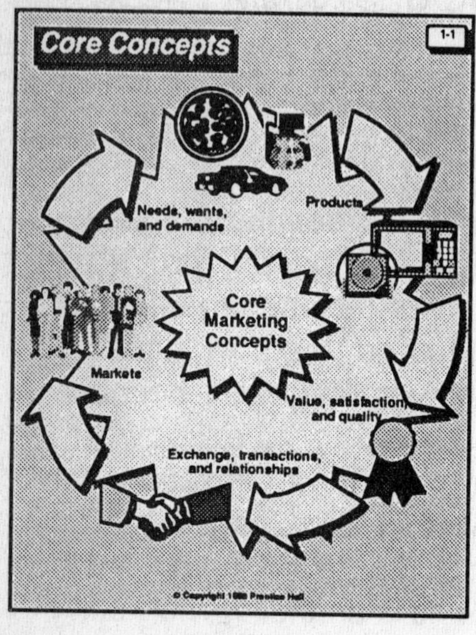

A. Needs, Wants, and Demands

B. Products

C. Value, Satisfaction, and Quality

D. Exchange, Transactions, and Relationships

E. Markets

Demand Management
1-4
Marketing Management
Demand Management
Key Concepts for Managing Marketing
Customer Lifetime Value

F. Marketing

II. Marketing Management

A. Demand Management

B. Building Profitable Customer Relationships

III. Marketing Management Philosophies

A. Production Concept

B. Product Concept

C. Selling Concept

D. Marketing Concept

E. Societal Marketing Concept

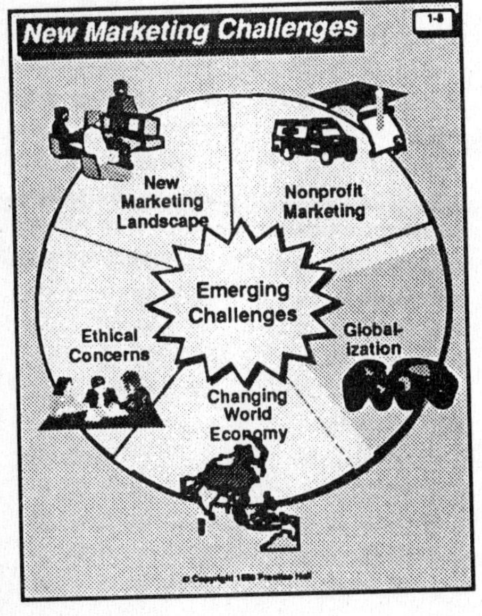

IV. Marketing Challenges into the Next Century

A. Growth of Nonprofit Marketing

B. Rapid Globalization

C. The Changing World Economy

D. The Call for More Ethics and Social Responsibility

E. The New Marketing Landscape

KEY TERMS

The consumer's assessment of the product's overall capacity to satisfy his or her needs.

Customer value (p. 10)

That which depends on a product's perceived performance in delivering value relative to a buyer's expectations.

Customer satisfaction (p. 11)

Human wants that are backed by buying power.

Demands (p. 8)

Marketing in which the task is to temporarily or permanently reduce demand.

Demarketing (p. 14)

The act of obtaining a desired object from someone by offering something in return.

Exchange (p. 11)

The set of actual and potential buyers of a product.

Market (p. 12)

A social and managerial process by which individuals and groups obtain what they need and want through creating and exchanging products and value with others.

Marketing (p. 6)

The marketing management philosophy that holds that achieving organizational goals depends on determining the needs and wants of target markets and delivering the desired satisfactions more effectively and efficiently than competitors do.

Marketing concept (p. 19)

The analysis, planning, implementation, and control of programs designed to create, build, and maintain beneficial exchanges with target buyers for the purpose of achieving organizational objectives.

Marketing management (p. 14)

A state of felt deprivation.

Needs (p. 7)

Anything that can be offered to a market to satisfy a need or want; it includes physical objects, services persons, places, organizations, and ideas.

Product (p. 9)

The idea that consumers will favor products that offer the most quality, performance, and features and that the organization should therefore devote its energy to making continuous product improvements.

Product concept (p. 16)

The philosophy that consumers will favor products that are available and highly affordable and that management should therefore focus on improving production and distribution efficiency.

Production concept (p. 15)

Building mutually beneficial long-term relationships with valued customers, distributors, dealers, and suppliers by promising and consistently delivering high-quality products, good service, and fair prices.

Relationship marketing (p. 12)

The idea that consumers will not buy enough of the organization's products unless the organization undertakes a large-scale selling and promotion effort.

Selling concept (p. 17)

The idea that the organization should determine the needs, wants, and interests of target markets and deliver the desired satisfactions more effectively and efficiently than competitors in a way that maintains or improves the consumer's and society's well being.

Societal marketing concept (p. 20)

Programs designed to constantly improve the quality of products, services and marketing processes.

Total quality management (p. 11)

A trade between two parties that involves at least two things of value, agreed-upon conditions, a time of agreement, and a place of agreement.

Transaction (p. 12)

The form taken by human needs as they are shaped by culture and individual personality.

Want (p. 8)

APPLYING TERMS AND CONCEPTS

To determine how well you understand the materials in this chapter, read each of the following brief cases and then respond to the questions that follow. Answers are given at the end of this chapter.

Handyman Hardware and Lumber

Thomas Steenburgh began Handyman Stores in 1979 after determining that a huge do-it-yourself market existed for hardware and building supplies. His research showed that as plumbers, electricians, carpenters, and others began charging more in the mid-1970's, many homeowners decided to do their own repairs and remodeling. And if their work wasn't quite perfect, homeowners could at least take satisfaction in knowing they had done the work themselves and that they had saved money. Steenburgh's research was consistent with the findings of the Do-it-Yourself Research Institute, based in Indianapolis, which estimated that do-it-yourself sales would grow from $6.4 billion in 1970 to $63.5 billion by 1990, thereafter increasing by approximately 8 percent per year.

Steenburgh's concept of retailing was to stock a wide variety of name-brand hardware and building supplies in what is essentially a warehouse. He spends virtually no money on fixtures and allows customers to use hand carts to select their own merchandise, which they bring to a centralized check-out area. The stores are open from 7 a.m. to 10 p.m., Monday through Saturday. Handyman's main form of advertising consists of flyers as inserts in local newspapers. When a Handyman Store is opened in a city, its prices are reduced to a minimum. The usual practice is to post a local competitor's catalog or flyer at the store and offer customers the same or comparable goods for 20 percent less. Prices are kept low because Handyman buys direct from the manufacturer and sells for cash or approved check only. It also saves money because its store serves as its own warehouse; each store is between 75,000 and 100,000 sq. ft. What merchandise does not fit on a shelf or rack is stacked on the floor, sometimes up to the ceiling.

One area where Steenburgh will not skimp is personnel. Since 85 percent of his sales are to do-it-yourselfers, he typically hires 30 to 40 salespeople for each store and trains them in do-it-yourself tasks. These salespeople liberally dispense free Handyman how-to pamphlets and practical advice on projects from start to finish.

Steenburgh's philosophy of selling quality products at a low price with good advice has served Handyman well. Sales per square foot have averaged between $250 and $275 this year at each of its 19 stores, with projected profits this year of $22 million.

Questions

_____ 1. Which of the following were involved in marketing activities?

A. Handyman
B. store personnel
C. customers
D. only (A) and (B)
E. All of the above

_____ 2. Steenburgh's analysis, planning, implementation and control of programs designed to create, build and maintain beneficial exchanges with target customers for the purpose of achieving organizational objectives is an example of __________ management.

A. exchange
B. production
C. marketing
D. selling
E. sales

_____ 3. Which of the following items should be considered Handyman's product?

A. hardware and building supplies
B. How-to-pamphlets
C. free how-to advice
D. only (A) and (B)
E. all of the above

_____ 4. Wallace Berry went to a handyman store and, without purchasing anything, simply collected several how-to pamphlets (to help him complete project he was working on) and left the store. This would constitute a(n):

A. exchange.
B. barter.
C. transaction.
D. theft.
E. none of the above

5. Identify Handyman's marketing philosophy and list the reasons for your decision.

____

____

____

____

____

____

____

Pet Insurance Company of America

George Smrtic founded the Pet Insurance Company of America (P.I.C.A.) three years after the death of his shetland collie, Priscilla. It seems that the 11 year old Priscilla developed heart and lung trouble and rather than spend the estimated $1,200 for treatment he had Priscilla put to sleep.

Smrtic reasoned that since Americans are inclined to insure themselves and many of their possessions, they might also be inclined to insure their pets. Especially since pets are seen by many as an integral part of the family - in some cases more loyal, obedient and loving than certain family members.

Smrtic researched the concept of pet insurance and found there are in excess of 110 million dogs and cats in approximately 65 million households. He also found that Americans spend 15 billion dollars a year on pets for everything from air-conditioned dog houses, to designer clothing, to toys, to vacations and more recently, beefy flavored beverages and ice cream treats. Smrtic's research, including data collected from the American Veterinary Society, pet owners, and individual veterinarians, indicates that dog owners spend $95 per year on veterinary care while cat owners spend $78 per year. Smrtic also found that not only are people's attitudes toward pets changing, but also that increasingly sophisticated and expensive medical treatments including chemotherapy, cataract operations and heart pacemakers are now available.

The basic policies which are underwritten by the Black Hawk Data Group of Dallas, sell for $49 with a $300 deductible clause. For $90 per year the deductible falls to $100. Each policy insures the pet against catastrophic illness and/or accident. Not covered are routine procedures such as examinations, office visits, inoculations and neutering.

The policies currently available only on dogs and cats, are sold only through veterinary offices with the veterinarian acting as an agent for P.I.C.A.

Sales to date have been excellent with over 70,000 policies providing $3,000,000 of coverage on approximately 100,000 dogs and cats. Competition from two other firms is minimal in that the market is expanding by 20-30% per year. P.I.C.A., which is licensed in 47 states, expects to begin offering policies on pets other than dogs and cats within a year.

Questions

_____ 1. The marketing management philosophy exhibited by P.I.C.A. in their research and design of insurance polices indicated they have adopted the marketing concept.

(True or False)

_____ 2. The insurance policy offered by P.I.C.A. should be considered a product even though it is an intangible -- a service which may never be used -- because it is capable of providing customer satisfaction.

(True or False)

_____ 3. The market for pet insurance is made up not only of current policy owners but also of potential policy buyers.

(True or False)

_____ 4. A veterinarian who provides pet care and products (food, shampoo, flea collars, bedding, clothing, etc.) is an example of a decentralized exchange market.

(True or False)

Change comes to the Soviet Union

The shortages of consumer goods in the former Soviet Union were legendary. Meat, poultry, detergents, toilet paper, razor blades, gasoline, automobiles, fashionable clothing and decent housing were in chronic short supply. An ordinary citizen would wait in line an average of two hours each day to buy what was available. Over a lifetime, that amounted to five years wasted standing in line. The Soviet currency, the ruble, until recently, was virtually worthless in international trade because it was not freely exchangeable with world currencies. This along with restrictive trade policy severely limited the average citizen's access to foreign goods.

It was easy to assume that the reason so few consumer goods were available was that soviet leaders simply decided to devote more of the nation's resources to military production and less to the production of consumer goods. But the problem was more complex than that and was partly based on how decisions were made in the USSR.

In our capitalistic society with its market-directed economy, the public has the major say about what gets produced because they "vote" with their dollars. If people like a product, they will buy more of it. The manufacturers will quickly make more if it because they want to make money, and the only way to make money is to give the public what it wants.

Things didn't work that way in the Soviet Union. The Soviets had a planned economy which meant that central planers in Moscow decided what it was the people want, or should want, and then ordered it produced. Decisions that were made in the market place in the United States were made by central planners in the Soviet Union. Sometimes the central planners were right; more often they were wrong. When they were wrong, shortages occurred and a black market arose to allocate the scarce goods and services.

In the effort to address certain problems within the Soviet Union, former President Mikhail Gorbachev instituted two revolutionary policies, Perestroika (Economic Restructuring) and Glasnost (openness and political democracy). Glasnost allowed Soviet citizens the opportunity to say what was on their minds while Perestroika allowed economic reform.

Government officials realized that the satisfaction of consumer needs, wants and demands, and the flexibility to accommodate changing market conditions was critical to raising the standard of living of the Soviet people. Government officials also realized that the average Soviet citizen had long enjoyed considerable security with guaranteed employment, health care, schooling and housing. But the movement to a more market directed economy would exact a considerable price in the form of lower security, higher inflation, unemployment and crime, and the need to institute unemployment and welfare programs.

These are problems that the former republic, now a collection of independent states, are grappling with.

Questions

1. What are the main characteristics of a market directed economy?

2. What role does marketing play in providing customer satisfaction in a market directed economy?

3. How does a market-directed economy differ from a planned economy?

4. Not all decisions in a market-directed economy are made in the marketplace. Some critical decisions are made by government officials elected by the people. Identify the types of goods and services resulting from these decisions and explain why they cannot easily be made in the marketplace.

Sources: "Holding a Bad Hand," *Newsweek* June 4, 1990, pp. 16-17; "Why He's Failing," *Newsweek* June 4, 1990, pp. 18-21; "Too Little and Too Late?"

TESTING TERMS AND CONCEPTS

Part One — To test your understanding of the concepts presented in this chapter, write the letter of the most appropriate answer on the line next to the question number. Answers to these questions may be found at the end of this chapter.

_____ 1. Marketing is best understood as the process of:

A. making a sale.
B. creating customer needs.
C. satisfying customer needs and wants.
D. promoting products and services.
E. generating a profit.

_____ 2. Marketing includes which of the following functions or activities?

A. selling, advertising and public relations
B. needs assessment and product development
C. pricing and distribution
D. only (A) and (C)
E. all of the above

_____ 3. A person's want becomes a demand when backed by:

A. needs.
B. products.
C. purchasing power.
D. desire.
E. exchange mechanisms.

_____ 4. For a voluntary exchange to take place, which of the following conditions need not be satisfied?

A. There are at least two parties.
B. Money must be exchanged between the two parties.
C. Each party is capable of communication and delivery.
D. Each party is free to accept or reject the other party's offer.
E. Each party believes it is appropriate to deal with the other party.

_____ 5. A market is a set of ____________ buyers of a product.

A. actual
B. potential
C. latent
D. both (A) and (B)
E. both (A) and (C)

_____ 6. The ____________ concept holds that all consumers will favor those products which offer the most quality performance and features and, therefore, the organization should devote its energy to making continuous product improvements.

A. production
B. product
C. service
D. marketing
E. selling

_____ 7. The selling concept is typically practiced for ____________ goods.

A. convenience
B. shopping
C. specialty
D. unsought
E. industrial

_____ 8. The societal marketing concept calls upon marketers to balance which of the following considerations in setting their marketing policies?

A. company goals
B. consumer satisfaction
C. society's welfare
D. only (B) and (C)
E. all of the above

_____ 9. ____________________ Programs are designed to constantly improve the quality of products, services and marketing processes.

A. Marketing service
B. Marketing audit
C. Physical distribution
D. Total quality management
E. Market review

_____ 10. The marketing concept expresses the company's commitment to:

A. organizational goals.
B. an integrated company effort.
C. consumer sovereignty.
D. only (A) and (B) above
E. all of the above

_____ 11. The production concept may be appropriate when:

A. supply exceeds demand.
B. the price is high and needs to be lowered through improved productivity.
C. a superior product has been produced by the competition .
D. all of the above
E. none of the above

_____ 12. When a merchant appears in a central location called a market place, the total number of transactions required to accomplish a given volume of exchange:

A. increases.
B. decreases.
C. remains the same.
D. fluctuates over time.
E. unable to determine from the information given.

_____ 13. The ____________________ concept holds that consumer will favor products that are available and highly affordable. Therefore, management should focus on improving production and distribution efficiency.

A. production
B. selling
C. marketing
D. product
E. societal marketing

_____ 14. Customer ____________________ depends on a product's perceived performance in delivering value relative to a buyer's expectations.

A. value
B. satisfaction
C. quality
D. service
E. demand

_____ 15. The marketing management philosophy that focuses primarily upon an attempt to understand the needs and wants of the firm's target market is the:

A. societal marketing concept.
B. profit maximization concept.
C. product concept.
D. selling concept.
E. marketing concept.

Part Two To test your understanding of the concepts presented in this chapter, respond to the following questions by writing the letter T or F on the line next to the question number if you believe the statement is true or false, respectively. Answers to these questions may be found at the end of this chapter.

_____ 1. Selling is only one of several marketing functions, but is often the most important function.

_____ 2. Marketing is human activity directed at satisfying needs and wants through the exchange process.

_____ 3. Intangible items such as a stockbroker's advice should not be considered a product as defined in the text.

_____ 4. Exchange, which is the act of obtaining a desired object from someone by offering something in return, is a tangential concept in the discipline of marketing.

_____ 5. Barbara Calvert recently donated $25 to her church's annual fundraising campaign. Barbara's donation should be considered a transaction.

_____ 6. Marketing activities may be performed not only by sellers, but also by potential customers.

_____ 7. The production concept may be an appropriate philosophy when demand exceeds supply and/or when product cost is high and improved productivity is needed to bring it down.

_____ 8. The National Parks Service has recently raised park fees, limited access to certain locations and reduced the length of the season in an effort to reduce the number of visitors to certain parks. These efforts designed to reduce the environmental impact of the visitors on the parks can be described as demarketing.

_____ 9. Marketing management is, in reality, demand management.

_____ 10. Selling focuses on the needs of the seller; marketing focuses on the needs of the buyer.

_____ 11. Customer value is the difference between the values the customer gains from owning and using a product and the cost of obtaining the product.

_____ 12. Transaction marketing is part of a larger idea or relationship marketing.

_____ 13. Managing consumer demand means managing production.

_____ 14. Many domestically produced goods and services are "hybrids," with design, materials purchases, manufacturing and marketing taking place in several countries.

_____ 15. Given the increased level of competition in today's marketing environment, there is a decreased need for companies to take responsibility for the social and environmental impact of their actions.

Applying Terms and Concepts

Handyman Hardware and Lumber

1. E
2. C
3. E
4. E
5. The market concept because Steenburgh believes that the key to success consists of determining the needs and wants of target markets and delivering the desired satisfaction more effectively and efficiently than competitors. As such, he offers the following: low prices, quality merchandise, name brand merchandise, convenient hours, large selection, free advice from knowledgeable personnel and free how-to pamphlets.

Pet Insurance Company of America

1. True
2. True
3. True
4. False

Change Comes to the Soviet Union

1. In a capitalistic society with its market-directed economy, the people have the major say about what gets produced because they "vote" with their money. If they like a product, they will buy more of it. The manufacturers will quickly make more of it. The manufacturers will quickly make more of the product because they want to make money, and the only way to make money is to give the public what it wants. Therefore, supply and demand are allowed to interact and businesspeople are rewarded for producing popular goods and services. Also, competition helps to improve product quality and reduce prices.

2. In a market directed economy, consumers have the greatest opportunity to obtain what they want, when they want it, where they want it, to obtain the use of the desired goods and services and to acquire knowledge about them.

3. In a planned economy, decisions about what will be produced, who will produce it, when and where it will be produced, and the prices that will be charged are all made by government officials. In a market-directed economy, as the answer to the previous question pointed out, those types of decisions are made in the marketplace through the interplay of the profit motive, supply and demand, competition, and the pursuit of customer satisfaction.

4. Elected officials in the United States recognize that some decisions either cannot or should not be made in the marketplace. Decisions related to national defense, police and fire protection, primary education, welfare, and pollution control are obvious examples. Decisions to provide for the common good are not easily made in the marketplace because what one person would be willing to "pay" for national defense, for example, is likely to be different from what another person would be willing to "pay." Therefore, government officials make these decisions for us and we are taxed to "pay" for them.

Testing Terms and Concepts

Part One

1. C - M The term marketing must be understood not in the old sense of making a sale -- "selling" -- but rather in the new sense of satisfying customer needs. With increasingly stiff competition, rewards will go to those marketers who can best understand customer needs and wants and deliver the greatest value to their target customers.
2. E E
3. C E
4. B M
5. D E
6. B M
7. D M
8. E M
9. D D
10. E - M The marketing concept implies that all elements (departments) within the organization will work in a coordinated fashion to provide the desired level of customer satisfaction, thereby achieving organizational goals.
11. B D
12. B D
13. A M
14. B D
15. E D

Part Two

1. F - M While selling is an important function of marketing it is often not the most important one. If a marketer does a good job of identifying consumer needs, understanding consumer wants and demands, developing good products and pricing, distributing and promoting them effectively, these goods will sell very easily.
2. T E
3. F M
4. F D
5. F D
6. T D
7. T M
8. T M

9. T - E The organization has a desired level of demand for its products. At any point in time, there may be no demand, adequate demand, irregular demand, or too much demand, and marketing management must find ways to deal with these different demand states. Marketing management is concerned not only with finding and increasing demand, but also with changing or even reducing it. Thus marketing management seeks to affect the level, timing, and nature of demand in a way that will help the organization achieve its objectives. Therefore, marketing management is demand management.

10. T M
11. T D
12. T D
13. F D
14. T M
15. F M

CHAPTER 2

STRATEGIC PLANNING AND THE MARKETING PROCESS

CHAPTER OVERVIEW

This chapter discusses the importance of strategic planning and marketing's role in the development and implementation of plans. An organization must define its mission -- what it wants to accomplish in a broad sense -- and its objectives and goals -- what specific aims it has in a defined time period. By analyzing the units in its business portfolio and considering its various units in its business portfolio and considering its various marketing opportunities, the organization can determine where it is strong, where it is weak, and where it should be developing new products and markets to help it grow. Marketing management helps coordinate the sometimes -- conflicting goals of different functional areas to achieve organizational goals by providing customer satisfaction. Marketing management also helps to define and select specific customer segments, develops marketing programs to achieve better positions in the minds of customers, implements these plans, and exercises control procedures to ensure that the organization stays on the right track for accomplishing its objectives.

CHAPTER OBJECTIVES

When you finish this chapter, you should be able to accomplish the following:

1. Explain strategic planning and discuss how it relates to the company mission, objectives and goals.
2. Identify and define methods for designing the business portfolio, developing growth strategies and planning functional strategies.
3. Outline the marketing process explaining the concepts of target consumers, using marketing strategies for competitive advantage and developing the marketing mix.
4. List the elements involved in managing the marketing effort, including marketing analysis, the key elements of the marketing plan and the primary tasks of marketing implementation and control.

LECTURE/STUDENT NOTES

I. Strategic Planning

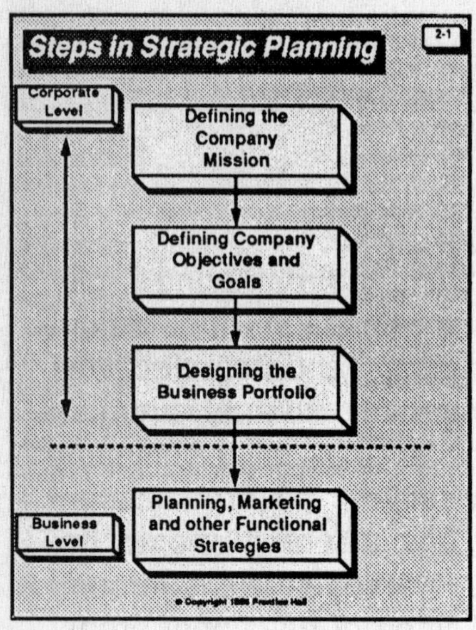

A. Overview of Planning

B. Defining the Company Mission

C. Setting Company Objectives and Goals

II. Designing the Business Portfolio

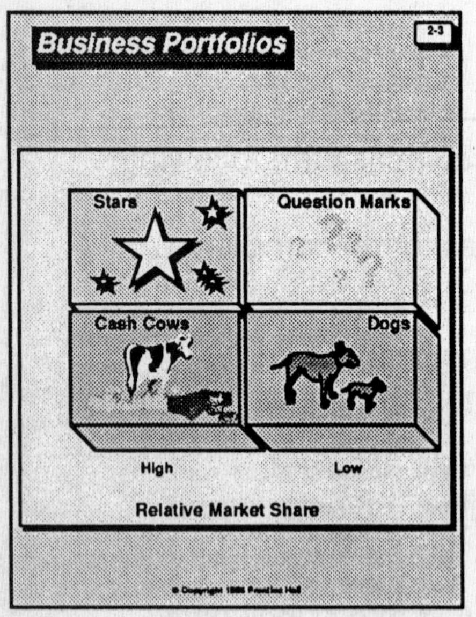

A. Analyzing the Current Business Portfolio

1. The Boston Consulting Group Approach

2. The General Electric Approach

3. Problems with Matrix Approaches

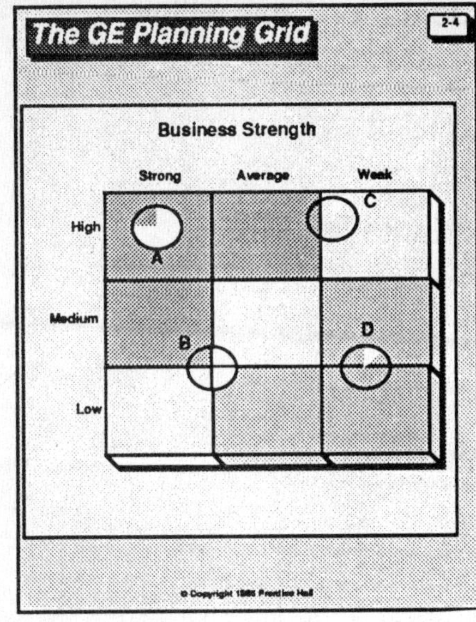

B. Developing Growth Strategies

C. Planning Functional Strategies

1. Marketing's Role in Strategic Planning

2. Marketing and the Other Business Functions

3. Conflict between Departments

III. The Marketing Process

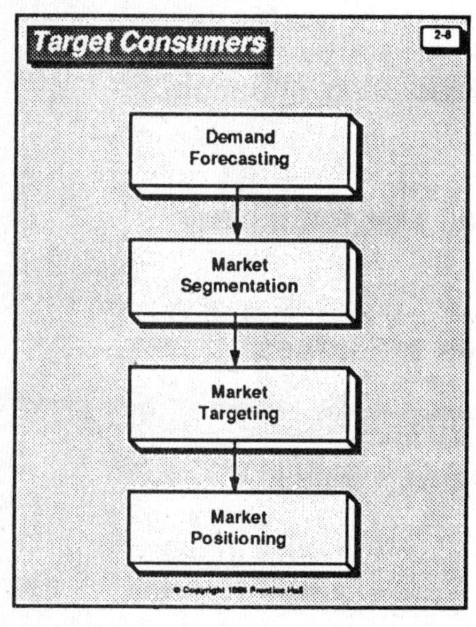

A. Target Consumers

1. Demand Measurement and Forecasting

2. Market Segmentation

3. Market Targeting

4. Market Positioning

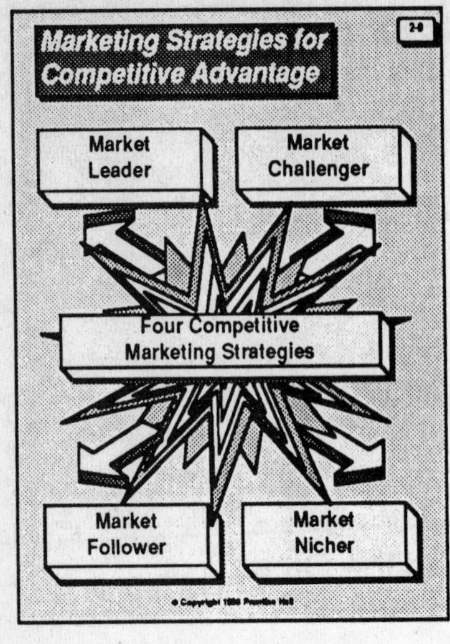

B. Marketing Strategies for Competitive Advantage

C. Developing the Marketing Mix

IV. Managing the Marketing Effort

A. Marketing Analysis

B. Marketing Planning

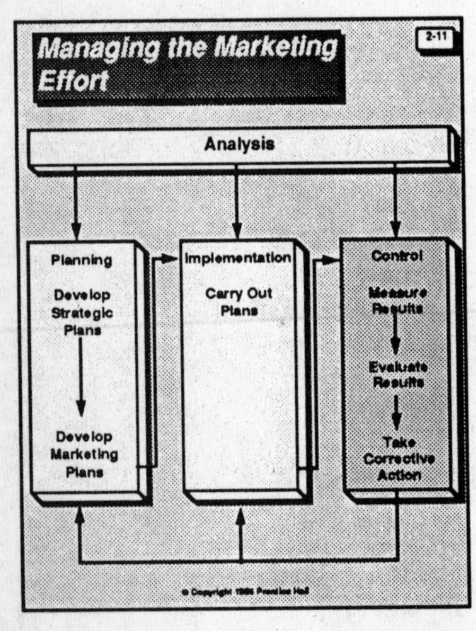

1. Executive Summary
2. Current Marketing Situation
3. Threats and Opportunities
4. Objectives and Issues
5. Marketing Strategies
6. Action Programs
7. Budgets

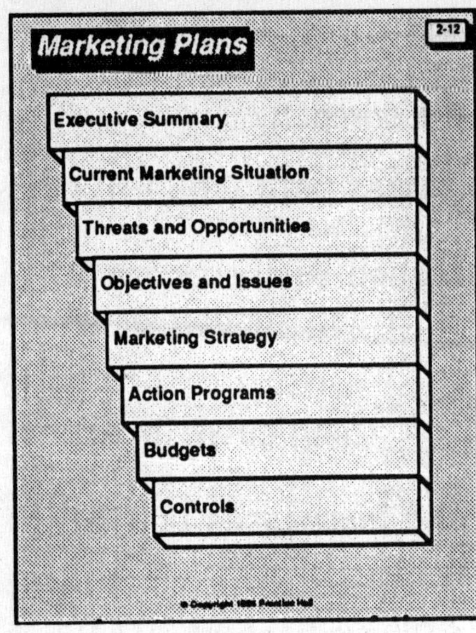

8. Controls

C. Marketing Implementation

D. Marketing Department Organization

E. Marketing Control

F. The Marketing Environment

KEY TERMS

The collection of businesses and products that make up the company.

Business portfolio (p. 41)

Low-growth, high-share businesses or products--established and successful units that generate cash the company uses to pay its bills and support other business units that need investment.

Cash cows (p. 42)

A strategy for company growth by starting up or acquiring businesses outside the company's current products and markets.

Diversification (p. 44)

Low--growth, low-share businesses and products that may generate enough cash to maintain themselves but do not promise to be large sources of cash.

Dogs (p. 42)

The opening section of the marketing plan that presents a short summary of the main goals and recommendations to be presented in the plan.

Executive summary (p. 54)

A portfolio-planning method that evaluates a company's strategic business units in terms of their market growth rate and relative market share. SBUs are classified as stars, cash cows, question marks, or dogs.

Growth-share matrix (p. 42)

A strategy for company growth by identifying and developing new market segments for current company products.

Market development (p. 44)

A strategy for company growth by increasing sales of current products to current market segments without changing the product in any way.

Market penetration (p. 44)

Arranging for a product to occupy a clear, distinctive, and desirable place relative to competing products in the minds of target consumers. Formulating competitive positioning for a product and a detailed marketing mix.

Market positioning (p. 49)

A group of consumers who respond in a similar way to a given set of marketing stimuli.

Market segment (p. 49)

The process of divising a market into distinct groups of buyers with different needs, characteristics or behavior who might require separate products or marketing mixes.

Market segmentation (p. 48)

The process of evaluating each market segment's attractiveness and selecting one or more segments to enter.

Market targeting (p. 49)

A comprehensive, systematic, independent, and periodic examination of a company's environment, objectives, strategies, and activities to determine problem areas and opportunities and to recommend a plan of action to improve the company's marketing performance.

Marketing audit (p. 62)

The process of measuring and evaluating the results of marketing strategies and plans, and taking corrective action to ensure that marketing objectives are attained.

Marketing control (p. 62)

The process that turns marketing strategies and plans into marketing actions in order to accomplish strategic marketing objectives.

Marketing implementation (p. 57)

The process of (1) analyzing marketing opportunities, (2) selecting target markets, (3) developing the marketing mix, and (4) managing the marketing effort.

Marketing process (p. 47)

The set of controllable tactical marketing tools--product, price, place, and promotion--that the firm blends to produce the response it wants in the target market.

Marketing mix (p. 51)

The marketing logic by which the business unit hopes to achieve its marketing objectives.

Marketing strategy (p. 56)

A statement of the organization's purpose--what it wants to accomplish in the larger environment.

Mission statement (p. 38)

A tool by which management identifies and evaluates the various businesses that make up the company.

Portfolio analysis (p. 41)

A strategy for company growth by offering modified or new products to current market segments.

Product development (p. 44)

A portfolio-planing tool for identifying company growth opportunities through market penetration, market development, product development, or diversification.

Product/market expansion grid (p. 44)

Low-share business units in high-growth markets that require a lot of cash in order to hold their share or become stars.

Question marks (p. 42)

High-growth, high-share business or products that often require heavy investment to finance their rapid growth.

Stars (p. 42)

A unit of the company that has a separate mission and objectives and that can be planned independently from other company businesses. An SBU can be a company division, a product line within a division, or sometimes a single product or brand.

Strategic business unit (SBU) (p. 41)

The process of developing and maintaining a strategic fit between the organization's goals and capabilities and its changing marketing opportunities. It relies on developing a clear company mission, supporting objectives, a sound business portfolio, and coordinated functional strategies.

Strategic planning (p. 37)

APPLYING TERMS AND CONCEPTS

To determine how well you understand the materials in this chapter, read each of the following brief cases and then respond to the questions that follow. Answers are given at the end of this chapter.

Don Seville Rum

In 1859, Don Jorge Seville began distilling and selling rum in Kingston, Jamaica. Initially, the townspeople carried his rum away in pails and tubs. Later, when Don Jorge began to bottle the rum, he had the labels marked with the likeness of a seagull, to assist illiterates in identifying his brand.

The seagull is still on each bottle of Don Seville Rum, and the company is now run by descendants of Don Jorge. The rum's secret formula hasn't changed, but just about everything else about the company has. Seville is now a worldwide operation with sugar cane plantations in Jamaica and bottling plants in Puerto Rico and Martinique, ocean-going cargo ships based in Trinidad, office buildings, warehouses and advertising agencies in Mexico and the USA, and a trucking firm in Spain. While most operations were somehow originally connected with the production and distribution of the rum, others, such as the development of a 124-acre luxury resort on the island of Antigua, are totally unrelated. The 11 semi-autonomous firms making up the Seville empire have sales estimated at $1 billion.

Don Seville is the world's largest selling rum, with an estimated 60 percent of the market. In the United States, Don Seville accounts for 75 percent of total rum sales. Although, impressive, Miguel Serrales, a great-great-grandson of the founder, has found the sales and profitability figures to be disappointing. While hard liquor sales in the USA decreased by 4.5 percent in recent years, rum sales increased by 2.3 percent. In view of this trend, Serrales had hoped that sales and profitability would have been higher. However, Serrales noted that increased competition from two firms, who promoted their product as premium rums, have recently begun to erode Don Seville's sales.

After considerable study, Serrales ordered the development and ultimate distribution of Caribe as Seville's own entry into the premium rum market.

Caribe will sell for $3 more per bottle than Don Seville. Projected sales this year are for 85,000 cases of Caribe and 7.6 million cases of Don Seville.

In 1978, Seville engaged in a promotional campaign designed to increase the public's awareness of rum. It was at this time that a change was taking place in American drinking habits. Drinkers switched from heavier whiskeys to lighter spirits such as rum. By 1990, rum accounted for 9.2 percent of the distilled spirits consumed in the USA compared to 2.1 percent twelve years earlier. It was during this period of time that sales of Don Seville rum increased dramatically.

Questions

_____ 1. The symbol of a seagull, which appears on each bottle of Don Seville rum, is an example of a brand. The brand should be considered part of which element of the marketing mix?

A. product
B. promotion
C. place
D. price
E. both (A) and (B)

_____ 2. The development of the luxury resort by Seville on the island of Antigua is an example of:

A. market development.
B. product development.
C. market penetration.
D. diversification.
E. both (A) and (C)

_____ 3. When Seville introduced Caribe rum to compete in the premium market, it was engaged in:

A. market penetration.
B. market development.
C. product development.
D. diversification.
E. none of the above

_____ 4. The various businesses making up the Seville Organization are known as its:

A. business portfolio.
B. strategic plan.
C. company mission.
D. marketing concept.
E. marketing mix.

_____ 5. Using the Boston Consulting Group approach to portfolio analysis, Don Seville Rum would be considered a(n):

A. star.
B. cash cow.
C. question mark.
D. dog.
E. none of the above

On-Line Data Corporation

The On-Line Data Corporation produces and sells minicomputers. Its highly diversified customers are found in the consumer, governmental, and institutional areas. The firm's marketing department is now organized along functional lines, but management is considering adopting some other organizational format in order to remedy a sales decline it feels is at least partially attributable to its organizational approach.

Questions

1. What types of organizational problems would you expect a firm like On-Line Data to encounter as a result of utilizing a functional approach in its marketing departments.

____

____

____

____

____

2. Briefly evaluate each of the following organizational formats in light of the firm's product/market situation and likely requirements.

A. Geographic Organization

B. Product Management Organization

C. Market Management Organization

D. Product/Market Management Organization

3. On the basis of the analysis above, which organizational format would *you* recommend?

Barth Enterprises

William Barth started Barth Chevrolet in 1974 after having worked as a sales manager for two other dealerships. He had a simple philosophy of meeting his customers personal transportation needs at a fair price. Barth Chevrolet was a success, so much so that he eventually opened dealerships which cover General Motors full range of automobiles and pick-up trucks. Barth opened a Pontiac/Buick/GMC Dealership in 1978 and an Oldsmobile/Cadillac Dealership in 1984. Barth's latest dealership was a Saturn Franchise opened in 1992. Each dealership sells new and used automobiles, vans, pick-up trucks and sport utility vehicles. Lease and rental programs are available for customers who do not wish to purchase vehicles outright.

Also part of the Barth Transportation Network is a Honda Motorcycle and all terrain vehicle (ATV) center opened in 1991. With the exception of the motorcycle shop, now run by Barth's 28 year old son - a motorcycle enthusiast and main impetus for the shop - Barth engaged in careful and extensive research to identify customer needs, wants and demands and their relative satisfaction with existing dealerships. Research in each case, indicated considerable consumer dissatisfaction with existing dealerships. This led Barth to start the Chevrolet and Saturn Dealerships from scratch, but he acquired the other dealerships by buying out the previous owner. Barth pioneered the now common practice of free shuttle service for service customers, a free loaner if the work takes more than one full day, a service department open from 7 a.m. to 9 p.m. on weekdays and to 5 p.m. on Saturdays. Additionally, each dealership has a fully stocked park department for the do-it-yourself and local service stations.

Sales at each dealership have increased steadily despite the periodic downturns in the automotive industry. Barth attributes this success to his philosophy of treating customers fairly and to a pricing strategy of selling vehicle for an average of 10% over invoice. Sales per dealership have averaged 2,000 vehicles per year as opposed to the industry average of 975. Profitability has averaged 18% before taxes. Barth sets realistic quotas for each dealership and then allows his dealership managers considerable flexibility in achieving the goal. A liberal profit sharing plan and autonomous dealership management have resulted in a successful organization controlling 46% of the local market.

The motorcycle franchise, however, is not as successful as the auto dealerships. Although it is marginally profitable, the operation experienced only 2% increase in sales last year, while the market expanded by 12%. The shop currently controls less than 10% of the local market.

Questions

1. Using portfolio analysis, characterize and evaluate each of the following:

   motorcycle/atv dealership

   taken on by urging of son, not really profitable, low growth
   low share - sounds like a dog that should be put to sleep!

   auto dealership

____

____

____

2. Comment on Barth's strategic planning related to the automotive dealerships

____

____

____

____

TESTING TERMS AND CONCEPTS

Part One To test your understanding of the concepts presented in this chapter, write the letter of the most appropriate answer on the line next to the question number. Answers to these questions may be found at the end of this chapter.

_____ 1. Leander Cosmetics is attempting to generate additional sales of its present products by promoting them more aggressively to its present customers. Leander Cosmetics is engaging in:

A. diversification.
B. market penetration.
C. market development.
D. product development.
E. both (A) and (D)

_____ 2. Selecting target markets involves decisions in all but which of the following areas:

A. market positioning.
B. market mix.
C. market segmentation.
D. market targeting.
E. demand measurement and forecasting.

_____ 3. A marketing opportunity must fit the firm's ____________ and ____________.

A. resources and target market
B. market mix and target market
C. resources and market mix
D. resources and objectives
E. objectives and target mix

_____ 4. The collection of businesses and products that make up the company comprise its:

A. business portfolio.
B. business plan.
C. strategic plan.
D. planning portfolio.
E. financial portfolio.

_____ 5. Which of the following is not an element of a firm's marketing mix?

A. place
B. promotion
C. product
D. price
E. people

_____ 6. A strategic business unit (SBU) is one which:

A. has a distinct mission.
B. has its own competition.
C. controls its own resources.
D. can be planned independently of the other businesses.
E. all of the above

_____ 7. The ____________ approach to planning, classifies a firm's SBU's in a matrix which plots market growth rate and relative market share.

A. Boston Consulting Group
B. management by objective
C. General Electric
D. Howard-Seth
E. both (A) and (D)

_____ 8. Industry attractiveness of the General Electric approach to strategic planning is an index made up of all but which one of the following factors?

A. market size
B. relative market share
C. profit margin
D. seasonality
E. industry cost structures

_____ 9. Marketing ____________ is the logic by which the business unit hopes to achieve its marketing objectives

A. mix
B. strategy
C. structure
D. control
E. implementation

_____ 10. A(n) ____________ is an attractive arena for company marketing action in which the particular company would enjoy a competitive advantage.

A. marketing plan
B. threat
C. marketing opportunity
D. objective
E. target market

_____ 11. ____________ ____________ is a system of values and beliefs shared by the people of an organization that constitutes the company's collective identity and meaning.

A. Managerial climate
B. Company culture
C. Human relations
D. Reward procedure
E. Performance appraisal

_____ 12. The Alsace Corporation wants to evaluate the effectiveness of its total marketing program. It is likely to use:

A. annual plan control.
B. sales analysis.
C. expense-to-sales analysis.
D. marketing audit.
E. profitability control.

_____ 13. Barry Hancock, Inc., produces a single product which it sells to different types of markets. Barry Hancock, Inc., should have which type of organization?

A. market management
B. product management
C. geographic management
D. functional
E. none of the above

_____ 14. Which of the following should not be considered a controllable element of a firm's marketing strategy:

A. development of a marketing mix.
B. selection of a target market.
C. an individual consumer that is part of the target market.
D. both (A) and (B)
E. all of the above

_____ 15. High growth, high share businesses or products appear in the Boston consulting group growth-share matrix as:

A. dogs.
B. cash cows.
C. question marks.
D. stars.
E. SBU's.

Part Two To test your understanding of the concepts presented in this chapter, respond to the following questions by writing the letter T or F on the line next to the question number if you believe the statement is true or false, respectively. Answers to these questions may be found at the end of this chapter.

_____ 1. A marketing audit is the process that turns marketing strategies and plans into marketing actions in order to accomplish strategic marketing objectives.

_____ 2. Strategy and implementation are not closely related.

_____ 3. Implementation is difficult and complex -- it is often easier to think up good marketing strategies than to carry them out.

_____ 4. One of the reasons marketing strategies are poorly implemented is that the company's current operations have all been designed to implement previous strategies; therefore, people become resistant to change.

_____ 5. Decision and reward systems include formal and informal operating procedures that guide and standardize such activities as planning, information gathering and distribution, money and manpower budgeting, recruiting and training, performance measurement and control, and personnel evaluation and rewards.

_____ 6. Through the use of a detailed action plan the manager can create a supporting budget that is essentially a projected profit and loss statement.

_____ 7. Company culture is a system of shared values and beliefs that provides a collective identity and meaning for the people in an organization.

_____ 8. A strategic business unit (SBU) is a unit of the company that has a separate mission and objectives and that can be planned independently from other company businesses. As such, an SBU can be a company division, or a product line within a division but an SBU cannot be a single product or brand.

_____ 9. The consumer should be a focal point of business activity but is not considered part of the marketing mix.

_____ 10. Most firms enter a new market by serving many market segments. But if this strategy proves unsuccessful, they gradually drop segments ultimately focusing their efforts on the profitable ones.

_____ 11. A company must choose its competitive strategy based on its industry position and its strengths and weaknesses relative to competitors.

_____ 12. Successful implementation of a marketing plan depends upon, among other things, the appropriate human resources.

_____ 13. Market targeting is arranging for a product to occupy a clear, distinctive and desirable place relative to competing products in the minds of target consumers.

_____ 14. The process of dividing a market into distinct groups of buyers with different needs, characteristics or behavior who might require separate products or marketing mixes is called market positioning.

_____ 15. A firm which has all of its products in the "star" or "cash cow" categories has no need to develop new products.

Answers

Applying Terms and Concepts

Don Seville Rum

1. A
2. D
3. C
4. A
5. A

On-Line Data Corporation

1. The On-Line Data Corporation has probably experienced inadequate planning for specific products and/or markets. Some products/markets may have been stressed to the neglect of others. Functional rivalries may inhibit coordination efforts.

2. A. Geographic Organization. Generally used by firms selling in a national market. However, On-Line Data's product is not strongly affected by geographic factors, and this approach may require a larger sales organization than the firm can support.

   B. Product Management Organization. Best suited to firms producing and selling a variety of products and brands. Typically, such an approach is used to add another layer of management to an existing functional organization in an attempt to overcome its shortcomings.

   C. Market Management Organization. Ideally suited to a firm that sells a line of products to a diverse set of markets. This approach is desirable whenever customers fall into groups with distinct buying patterns or product preferences.

D. Combination (product/market) Management Organization. Large companies that produce many different products flowing into many different geographic and customer markets use some combination of the functional, geographic, product, and market organization forms. This assures that each function, product, and market receives its share of management attention. However, it can also add costly layers of management and reduce organizational flexibility. Still, the benefits of organizational specialization usually outweigh the drawbacks.

Barth Enterprises

1. The motorcycle/atv dealership should be classified as a dog. It is a low growth, low market share business. It is marginally profitable and does not hold much promise to be a great source of cash.

   Barth needs to determine what role the dealership should play in his business portfolio. Divesting himself of it may make sense from a financial standpoint. However, there may be other considerations such as family interests which might lead Barth to allow it to remain.

   The auto dealerships appear to be cash cows. The overall market is not expanding greatly. However, Barth controls a substantial share of the market. The dealerships produce a significant cash flow as indicated by the 18% profit margin. The strategy Barth may decide to build on his market share by investing even further in the industry. This may be achieved by acquiring additional dealerships, marketing program vehicles and/or by consolidating his operations into the now popular auto super store.

2. Barth has adopted the marketing concept where customer interests determine (or at least influence) company plans. His product and service offerings as well as his growth and profitability can be attributed to philosophy or customer sovereignty and mutual gain.

Testing Terms and Concepts

Part One

1. B M
2. B. D. Companies know that they cannot satisfy all consumers in a given market, at least not all consumers in the same way. There are too many different kinds of consumers with too many different kinds of needs. And some companies are in a better position to serve certain segments of the market. Each

company must study the total market and choose the segments it can profitably serve better than its competitors can. This involves four steps: demand measurement and forecasting, market segmentation, market targeting, and market positioning.

3. D M
4. A E
5. E E
6. E E
7. A M
8. B D
9. B M
10. C D A marketing opportunity is an attractive arena for marketing action in which the company could enjoy a competitive advantage. Management should assess each opportunity according to its potential attractiveness and the company's probability of success. The company should pursue only the opportunities that fit its resources and objectives. Companies, however, rarely find ideal opportunities that fit their resources and objectives exactly. Therefore, when evaluating opportunities, management must decide whether the expected returns justify these risks.
11. B D
12. D M
13. A E
14. C E Market strategy planning suggests that a market oriented firm will develop a specific marketing mix to serve a particular segment of the market. Thus both major components of a marketing strategy are controllable by the organization. However, an individual consumer that is part of a target market is not controllable in that the organization cannot force the consumer to buy their product.
15. D M

<u>Part Two</u>

1. F M
2. F M
3. T E
4. T M As a rule, the company's current operations have all been designed to implement past plans and strategies. New strategies requiring new company patterns d habits may be

resisted. And the more different the new strategy from the old, the greater the resistance to implementing it.

5. T D
6. T M
7. T M
8. F M
9. T E
10. F M
11. T M
12. T E
13. F D
14. F D
15. F M No product can be expected to remain in the "star" or "cash cow" category indefinitely. Competition and the evolutionary nature of markets and consumers and other forces in the marketing environment will necessitate the need for new products to replace old products.

CHAPTER 3

THE MARKETING ENVIRONMENT

CHAPTER OVERVIEW

This chapter discusses the environmental forces that affect a company's ability to serve its customers. The microenvironment consists of forces close to the company -- the company itself, its suppliers, marketing intermediaries (channel members), customers, competitors, and publics. The macroenvironment consists of larger societal forces -- the demographic, economic, natural, technological, political, and cultural environments. All companies must adapt to these environments: smart companies anticipate changes and prepare strategies to take advantages of new opportunities, and the most aggressive companies take an environmental management perspective, attempting to influence the forces and factors in their environments.

CHAPTER OBJECTIVES

When you finish this chapter, you should be able to accomplish the following:

1. List and discuss the importance of the elements of the company's microenvironment including the company's marketing intermediaries, customers, competitors and publics.
2. Explain the broad concept of the company's macroenvironment.
3. Outline the key changes occurring in important elements of the company's macroenvironment including shifts in the demographic, economic, technological, political cultural and natural environments.

LECTURE/STUDENT NOTES

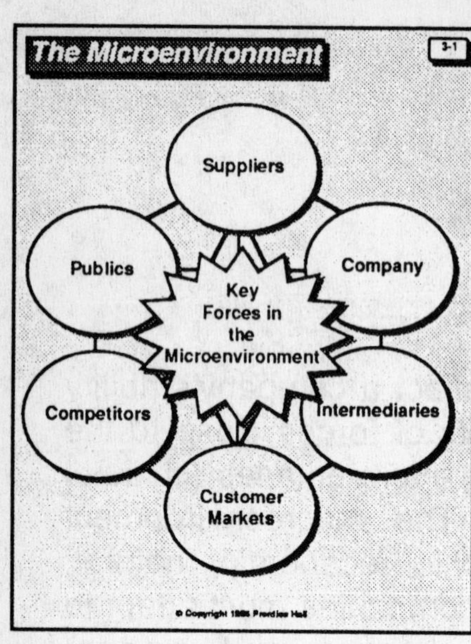

I. The Company's Microenvironment

A. The Company

B. Suppliers

C. Marketing Intermediaries

D. Customers

E. Competitors

F. Publics

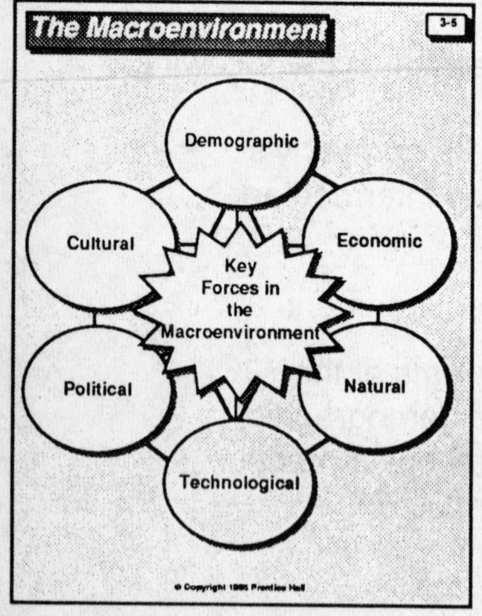

II. The Company's Macroenvironment

A. Demographic Environment

1. Changing Age Structure of the U.S. Population

2. The Changing American Family

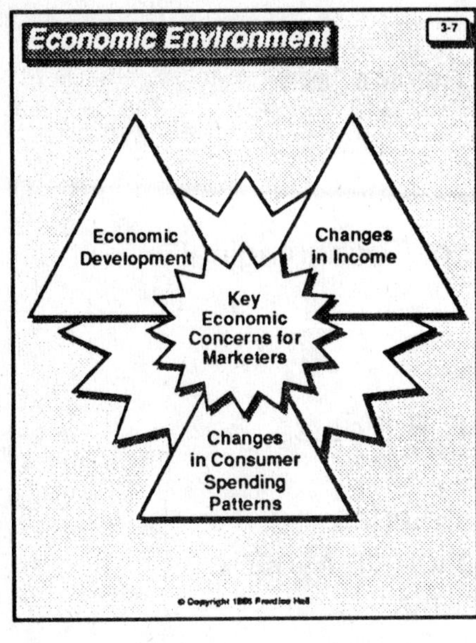

3. Geographic Shifts in Population

4. A Better-Educated and More White-Collar Population

5. Increasing Ethnic and Racial Diversity

B. Economic Environment

1. Changes in Income

2. Changing Consumer Spending Patterns

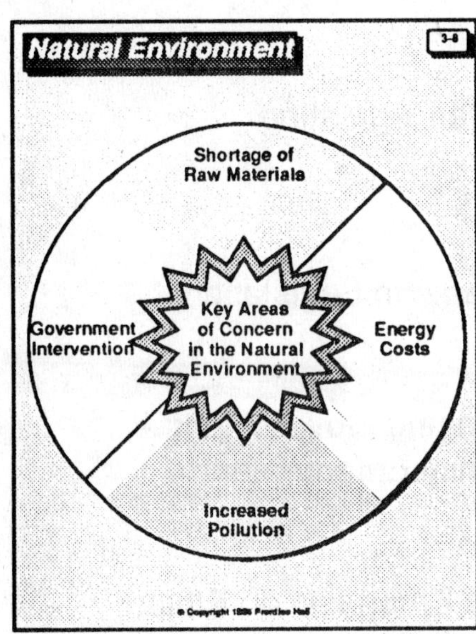

C. Natural Environment

1. Shortages of Raw Materials

2. Increased Cost of Energy

3. Increased Pollution

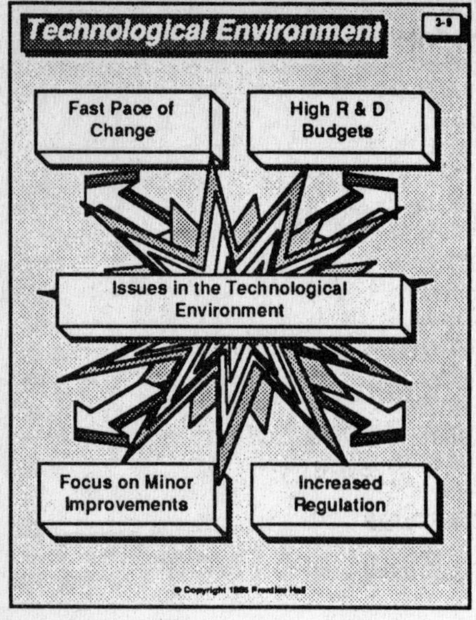

4. Government Intervention in Natural Resource Management

D. Technological Environment

1. Fast pace of Technological Change

2. High R & D Budgets

3. Concentration on Minor Improvements

4. Increased Regulation

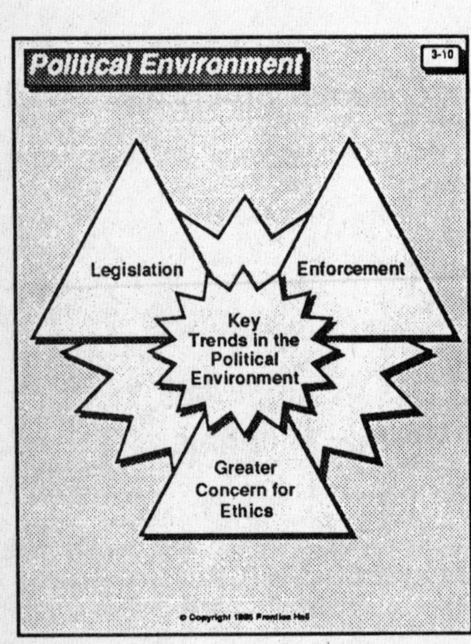

E. Political Environment

1. Legislative Regulating Business

   a. Increasing Legislation

   b. Changing Government Agency Enforcement

2. Increased Emphasis on Ethics and Socially Responsible Actions

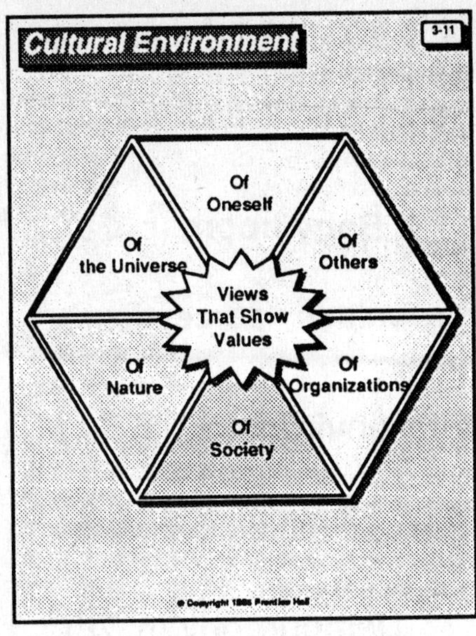

F. Cultural Environment

1. Persistence of Cultural Values

2. Shifts in Secondary Cultural Values

   a. People's Views of Themselves

   b. People's Views of Others

   c. People's Views of Organizations

   d. People's Views of Society

   e. People's Views of Nature

   f. People's Views of the Universe

III. Responding to the Marketing Environment

KEY TERMS

The major increase in the annual birthrate following World War II and lasting until the early 1960's.

Baby boom (p. 78)

Institutions and other forces that affect society's basic values, perceptions, preferences, and behaviors.

Cultural environment (p. 94)

The study of human populations in terms of size, density, location, age, sex, race, occupation, and other statistics.

Demography (p. 78)

Factors that affect consumer buying power and spending patterns.

Economic environment (p. 86)

Differences noted over a century ago by Ernst Engel in how people shift their spending across food, housing, transportation, health care, and other goods and services categories as family income rises.

Engel's laws (p. 87)

A management perspective in which the firm takes aggressive actions to affect the publics and forces in its marketing environment rather than simply watching and reacting to it.

Environmental management perspective (p. 99)

The larger societal forces that affect the whole microenvironment--demographic, economic, natural, technological, political, and cultural forces.

Macroenvironment (p. 75)

The actors and forces outside marketing that affect marketing management's ability to develop and maintain successful transactions with its target customers.

Marketing environment (p. 75)

Firms that help the company to promote, sell, and distribute its goods to final buyers; they include middlemen, physical distribution firms, marketing-service agencies, and financial intermediaries.

Marketing intermediaries (p. 76)

The forces close to the company that affect its ability to serve its customers--the company, market channel firms, customer markets, competitors, and publics.

Microenvironment (p. 75)

Natural resources that are needed as inputs by marketers or that are affected by marketing activities.

Natural environment (p. 88)

Laws, government agencies, and pressure groups that influence and limit various organizations and individuals in a given society.

Political environment (p. 92)

Any group that has an actual or potential interest in or impact on an organization's ability to achieve its objectives.

Public (p. 77)

Forces that create new technologies, creating new product and market opportunities.

Technological environment (p. 90)

APPLYING TERMS AND CONCEPTS

To determine how well you understand the materials in this chapter, read each of the following brief cases and then respond to the questions that follow. Answers are given at the end of this chapter.

Barnes Coal Company

The Barnes Coal Company has been in operation since 1872 and is the second largest producer of anthracite coal within the United States. The majority of its holdings are in northeastern Pennsylvania with major production in the Williamsport, Scranton, Hazelton areas. The bulk of Barnes' production is sold to out-of-state buyers and moves through the Philadelphia and Erie ports. The

Lehigh Valley and Pennsylvania Central Railroads are the prime movers of the coal to these ports of entry.

This year Scott Barnes, President of the Barnes Coal Company, fought passage of a state law which required all mining companies in Pennsylvania to reclaim mined land. All land, according to the bill, must be covered with no less than six inches of topsoil, whether or not the topsoil was evident prior to mining. Enforcement of this law will be by the Pennsylvania Soil and Water Conservation Commission.

Barnes attributed passage of the bill to pressure brought on the state legislators in Harrisburg by the Pennsylvania Beautification Society (PBS). The PBS is a private group interested in promoting tourism and preserving wildlife through the beautification and reforestation of Pennsylvania.

Barnes expects the price of coal to increase by eight percent if the costs associated with compliance are passed on to buyers. Production would likely decrease as buyers shift their purchasing to mines from Ohio, Kentucky, Illinois and West Virginia.

Questions

_____ 1. The Lehigh Valley and Pennsylvania Central Railroads are examples of:

A. financial intermediaries.
B. marketing service agencies.
C. physical distribution firms.
D. suppliers.
E. financial publics.

_____ 2. The law requiring placement of six inches of topsoil over reclaimed land is part of which environment?

A. demographic
B. economic
C. natural
D. political
E. technological

_____ 3. Coal is an example of a(n):

A. infinite resource.
B. renewable resource.
C. nonrenewable resource.
D. inexhaustible resource.
E. none of the above

_____ 4. The Pennsylvania Beautification Society is an example of a:

A. citizen action public.
B. internal public.
C. government public.
D. financial public.
E. general competitor.

_____ 5. Why was this legislation enacted?

A. to protect businesses from themselves
B. to protect consumers from unfair business practices
C. to protect the interests of society from unrestrained business behavior
D. in response to pressure brought on legislature by marketing intermediaries
E. none of the above

<u>The Bank of Calgary</u>

The Bank of Calgary is just one of the lending agencies in the Province of Alberta, Canada, which is faced with a perplexing problem. During the late 1970's and early 1980's the Athabasca Tar Sands, with estimated reserves of 300 billion barrels of crude oil, were being developed. Thousands of new jobs were created in mining, refining, distribution, construction, and support services, with the majority of workers settling in the Edmonton area. Most of these workers scorned apartment living and eagerly sought to buy homes. Many viewed home ownership as an integral part of living, along with marriage, work, and raising a family. Property values skyrocketed as lenders, including the Bank of Calgary, eagerly sought to meet the needs of future homeowners. Mortgage rates stabilized in the 17 to 19 percent range. Prospects for the region remained promising while the tar sands were in production.

Today, however, the economy of Alberta is in a deep slump, in part because of a downturn in the oil and gas industry. Hundreds had their jobs eliminated outright, thousands were placed on indefinite furlough, and many others accepted reduced wages which just covered their absolute necessities.

Economic growth in the area has slowed dramatically, while real estate prices plummeted by over 50 percent in two years. Many homeowners now owe more on their mortgages than they can sell their homes for. So even if they could sell their homes, they wouldn't get enough to pay off their loans.

The problem for the lenders has been compounded by the Scott Realty Company, which has developed a unique plan to assist the beleaguered homeowners. Scott will buy the house from the homeowner for $1 and assume the unpaid mortgage. But Scott Realty never makes any mortgage payments, and leases the house back to the former homeowner for substantially less than the monthly mortgage payment. The former homeowner has a relatively inexpensive place to stay for the approximately nine months it takes the bank to foreclose on the property, while Scott makes easy profit.

The lender can't sue the property owner or Scott Realty because a Depression Era law on the books prevents lenders from suing anyone to recover their losses. Specifically, if Calgary forecloses on a piece of property and in turn sells it for less than the outstanding loan, it can't sue anyone to make up the loss.

Scott Realty sees itself as helping unfortunate property owners who were caught in the escalation of land prices. They reason that the Bank of Calgary is unlikely to suffer much because as a $2 billion financial institution, it can easily absorb the estimated $1.5 million lost to date. And as for the homeowners, they seem to do well; after paying a low rent on their former home, they usually are able to save enough to make a down payment on another home.

Questions

1. The oil extracted from the Athabasca Tar Sands is an example of ____________ resource.
2. The Depression Era law that protects property owners as detailed in this case is part of the ___________ environment.
3. The decrease in the income of the workers mentioned in this case is part of the ___________ environment.
4. The fact that most of the workers in the Edmonton area bought a house indicates that home ownership is a ___________ belief and not easily changed.

Martin Marietta

Martin Marietta - the company that was big in the aerospace and defense industries and which became even bigger after its merger with Lockheed - is also big into aggregate. That's rocks, gravel and sand to the uninitiated. What is one of the nation's largest defense and space contractors doing in the aggregate business? Making money!

The market for aggregate is enormous. The amount used each year equates to approximately nine tons per American citizen. That is 50 pounds of aggregate needed per person per day. And just as the demand for aggregate is likely to increase, so is the price.

Aggregate is used for roads, driveways, concrete foundations and cement blocks. It is used in roofing and gardens. It is a decorative material replacing lawns in desert communities and as walkways and borders around shrubs. It is used in poultry feed and as a scrubbing agent in coal fired power plants. The list of uses of sand, gravel and rock is almost endless.

Make no mistake, aggregate is not rare. In fact, it is found just about everywhere. What makes aggregate increasingly valuable is the lack of government permission to expand existing pits or to open new pits. As existing pits run low on reserves (supply) local state and federal permits to expand become difficult to obtain. Environmentalists, as well as local residents, have blocked hundreds of proposed pits and some are seeking to close existing pits. The blasting vibration, dust, noise, danger and damage to local roads as well as the general unsightliness of the pits make them unpopular.

People don't want gravel pits and mines in their neighborhood. Therefore, it has to be brought in by truck, by rail and even by ship to coastal communities. This adds significantly to the cost. So while the actual cost of the material is quite low at the mine, the delivered cost can be quite high. By one estimate the cost of aggregate doubles for every 30 miles it must be transported by truck.

It is difficult to obtain a permit and those firms that do receive them have virtually a monopoly in the immediate area. One pit in an area may be bad - two are decidedly worse. This plays into the hands of major producers who have the financial resources needed to ensure the years it may take to obtain the needed permits. After several recent acquisitions, Martin Marietta became the nation's second largest aggregate producer just behind Vulcan Materials Co. of Birmingham, Alabama.

Questions

1. Identify the major elements in Martin Marietta's macroenvironment and explain how they might impact the company.

2. Identify the major elements in Martin Marietta's macroenvironment and explain how they might impact the company.

Sources: "Business is Boring: Some Companies Really Dig Aggregate," *Wall Street Journal* March 1, 1995, M. Charles, p. 1.

TESTING TERMS AND CONCEPTS

Part One To test your understanding of the concepts presented in this chapter, write the letter of the most appropriate answer on the line next to the question number. Answers to these questions may be found at the end of this chapter.

_____ 1. Which of the following is not a component of a company's micro-environment?

A. marketing intermediaries
B. customers
C. competitors
D. economic environment
E. publics

_____ 2. Which of the following is an example of a marketing intermediary?

A. competitor
B. public
C. supplier
D. trucking company
E. customer

_____ 3. Organizations that buy goods and services for their production process in order to make profits or achieve other objectives are called ____________ markets.

A. reseller
B. industrial
C. international
D. government
E. consumer

_____ 4. Which of the following is not an example of a firm's financial public?

A. board of directors
B. bank
C. stockholders
D. investment house
E. all of the above

_____ 5. The statistical study of the human population is part of the ____________ environment.

A. cultural
B. social
C. economic
D. demographic
E. technological

_____ 6. Which of the following is not one of the characteristics of the American family?

A. having more children
B. marrying later
C. relatively high divorce rate
D. more working mothers
E. number of nonfamily households is increasing

_____ 7. Which of the following is not one of the major mobility trends taking place in the United States?

A. movement to the sunbelt states
B. movement from the urban to the rural areas
C. movement from the city to the suburbs
D. both (A) and (B)
E. all are major movements

_____ 8. According to Engle's law, as income increases:

A. the percentage spent on food declines.
B. the percentage spent on housing and related operations remains the same.
C. the percentage spent on the remaining categories increases.
D. only (B) and (C)
E. all of the above

_____ 9. Which of the following is not one of the reasons why legislation has been enacted over the years?

A. protection of companies from each other
B. protection of consumers from unfair business practices
C. protection of consumers from unfair legislation
D. protection of the interests of society
E. none of the above

_____ 10. Which of the following statements about the technological environment is true?

A. Most companies are concentrating on making major discoveries rather than minor ones.
B. Much of the research is offensive rather than defensive.
C. The pace of technological change is slowing dramatically.
D. Many companies are concentrating on making minor improvements rather than major discoveries.
E. none of the above

_____ 11. ____________ beliefs and values have a high degree of persistence and are less subject to change.

A. Anthropological
B. Secondary
C. Cultural
D. Subcultural
E. Political

_____ 12. John J. Comer believes that the legal drinking age in Utah should be raised to 21. Comer is expressing a(n) __________ value and belief.

A. core
B. secondary
C. demographic
D. economic
E. social

_____ 13. The Giant Corporation takes a variety of aggressive actions designed to affect the publics and forces in their marketing environment. The firm may be described as taking a(n):

A. passive environmental perspective.
B. reactive environmental perspective.
C. environmentally static perspective.
D. socially active perspective.
E. environmental management perspective.

_____ 14. The Palega Corporation purchases large quantities of pig iron which it processes into cold rolled steel that constitutes its final product. Palega is part of the:

A. reseller market.
B. industrial market.
C. consumer market.
D. producer market.
E. final market.

_____ 15. Groups of people with shared value systems based on common life experiences or situations are called:

A. cultural cliques.
B. minicultures.
C. cultural segments.
D. cultural classes.
E. subcultures.

Part Two To test your understanding of the concepts presented in this chapter, respond to the following questions by writing the letter T or F on the line next to the question number if you believe the statement is true or false, respectively. Answers to these questions may be found at the end of this chapter.

_____ 1. The economic environment is one component of the company's microenvironment.

_____ 2. An advertising agency is an example of a marketing service agency.

_____ 3. Any group that has an actual or potential interest in or impact on an organization's ability to achieve its objective is a competitor.

_____ 4. All elements of a firm's macroenvironment should be considered uncontrollable.

_____ 5. The average age in the United States is increasing because the birth rate is slowing while life expectancy is decreasing.

_____ 6. Approximately one out of five Americans moves each year.

_____ 7. A metropolitan statistical area (MSA) is a separate population classification for a sprawling urban concentration created by the U. S. Bureau of the Census.

_____ 8. A fact about the demographic environment is that the American public is becoming increasingly educated and dominated by white collar workers.

_____ 9. New technology is typically a force for creative destruction, which means that the new technology hurts the old technology.

_____ 10. Demography is by nature discriminatory and should not be used by ethical marketers.

_____ 11. Purchasing power is a function of current income, savings, prices, and credit availability.

_____ 12. Subcultures should be avoided as target markets, as they typically exhibit unique needs.

_____ 13. In recent years, governmental regulation has increasingly focused upon attempts to protect the interests of society against unrestrained business behavior.

_____ 14. A dramatic force shaping the destiny of individuals and nations is technology.

_____ 15. Firms which take an environmental management perspective typically will not press law suits or file complaints with legislators to keep competitors in line.

Answers

Applying Terms and Concepts

Barnes Coal Company

1. C
2. D
3. C
4. A
5. C

The Bank of Calgary

1. finite nonrenewable
2. political
3. economic
4. core

Martin Marietta

1. The Company - Officials, within the Martin Marietta Organization, are enthusiastically pursuing new sources of supply. This commitment, along with an expanding market, should allow the company to pursue its marketing strategy while generating profits.

   Suppliers and Marketing Intermediaries - Martin Marietta must work with their various suppliers of equipment and materials as well as their marketing intermediaries including resellers, physical distribution firms, marketing services agencies and financial intermediaries to ensure a profitable operation. Proper selection of suppliers and marketing intermediaries becomes increasingly important as competition and public concerns increase.

   Customers - The company needs to monitor its customer markets closely. Consumer, business, reseller and government markets all present an opportunity. Martin Marietta must study the markets closely to understand the needs of each market and then decide how best to satisfy them.

   Competitors - The marketing concept states that to be successful, a company must provide greater customer value and satisfaction than its competitors. Thus marketers must do more than simply adapt to the needs of target consumers. They also must gain strategic advantage by positioning their offerings against competitors' offerings against competitors' offerings in the minds of customers.

Publics - There are seven different types of publics that have an actual or potential interest in or impact on an organization's ability to achieve its objectives. Anticipating and reacting to the financial, media, government citizen action, local, general and internal publics becomes increasingly important when there is opposition to the operation of the gravel pits. Strategies need to be developed which address and alleviate concerns thereby allowing the company to more effectively implement its marketing strategy.

2. The Demographic Environment - Given the Geographic shifts in population, Martin Marietta needs to anticipate where growth will take place and work to secure the permits necessary to expand or open the aggregate pits necessary to supply the required materials.

The Natural Environment - Concerns of environmentalists need to be considered for their potential impact on the firm and its ability to serve its customers. Land reclamation and beautification programs are expensive but increasingly important considerations in obtaining needed permits.

The Political Environment - The political environment consists of laws, government agencies and pressure groups that influence and limit organizations and individuals within society. The fact that it may take years to obtain the needed permits and appease the various publics, indicates that Martin Marietta must be cognizant of the various groups and their concerns. They must also be willing to work with the elements of the political environment to promote understanding and ultimately a mutually beneficial relationship.

Testing Terms and Concepts

Part One

1. D E
2. D E
3. B M
4. A E
5. D M

6. A - M The complexion of the American family is changing. People are marrying later and having fewer children. There has also been an increase in the number of working women. And, the number of nonfamily households - single, divorced or widowed - is increasing. (The decrease in family size is resulting from Americans' desire to improve personal living standards, from the increasing desire of women to work outside the home and from improved birth control.)

7. B M

8. E D

9. C - D Legislation affecting businesses has increased steadily over the years. Legislation has been enacted to serve three purposes. The first is to protect companies from each other, the second is to protect consumers from unfair business practices and the third is to protect the interests of society against unrestrained business behavior. This third purpose is important because profitable business activity does not always create a better quality of life. Therefore, regulation has arisen to make certain that firms take responsibility for the social costs of their production or products.

10. D D

11. C M

12. B M

13. E D

14. B M

15. E E

Part Two

1. F E

2. T E

3. F - E A public is any group that has an actual or potential interest in or impact on an organization's ability to achieve its objectives. Every company is surrounded by seven types of publics including financial, media, government, citizen-action, local, general or internal.

4. T M

5. F M

6. T M

7. T M

8. T M

9. T D

10. F - D Demography is the study of human populations in terms of size, density, location, age, sex, race, occupation, and other statistics. The demographic environment is of major interests to marketers because it involves the people who make up markets. And the more a marketer can identify and understand its target market the more they can design and implement strategies to provide customer satisfaction.

11. T E

12. F M

13. T M

14. T E

15. F M

CHAPTER 4

MARKETING RESEARCH AND INFORMATION SYSTEMS

CHAPTER OVERVIEW

Marketing managers need information to make good decisions. This chapter describes the marketing information systems (MIS) that companies use to develop and distribute information to managers. Managers may want information they can't use, and may not realize that helpful information is available. A good MIS provides the information that managers really need. Companies obtain information from internal records, marketing intelligence (information about ongoing events in the marketplace), and marketing research. Research involves defining the problem and setting research objectives, developing a research plan, implementing the plan, and interpreting and presenting the findings. The MIS makes information usable by distributing it to the right person at the right time, aided by recent advances in computers and communications systems.

CHAPTER OBJECTIVES

When you finish this chapter, you should be able to accomplish the following:

1. Explain the concept of the marketing information system emphasizing ways of assessing information needs, the sources used for developing information and ways of distributing information.
2. Outline the marketing research process including defining the problem and research objectives and developing the research plan.
3. Discuss the key issues of planning primary data collection, implementing the research plan and interpreting and reporting the findings.

LECTURE/STUDENT NOTES

I. The Marketing Information System

A. Assessing Information Systems

B. Developing Information

1. Internal Records

2. Marketing Intelligence

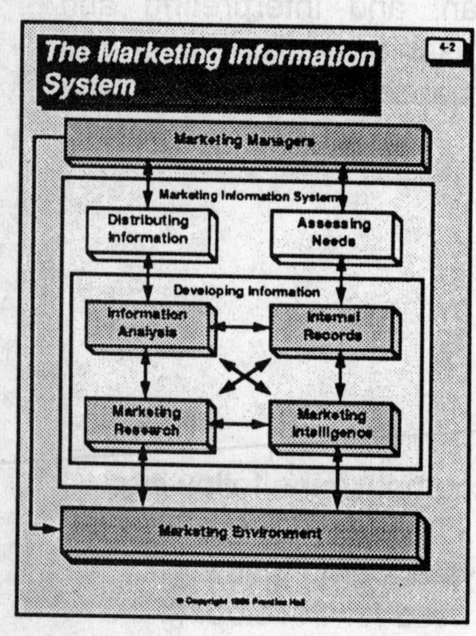

3. Marketing Research

4. Information Analysis

C. Distributing Information

II. The Marketing Research Process

A. Defining the Problem and Research Objectives

B. Developing the Research Plan

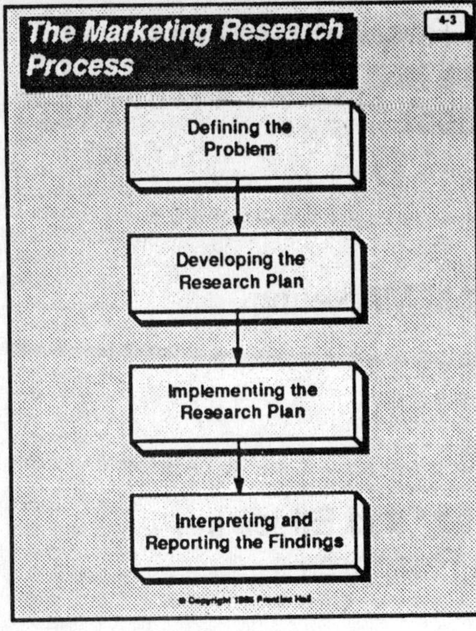

1. Determining Specific Information Needs

2. Gathering Secondary Information

3. Planning Primary Data Collection

   a. Research Approaches

   b. Contact Methods

   c. Sampling Plans

   d. Research Instruments

4. Presenting the Research Plan

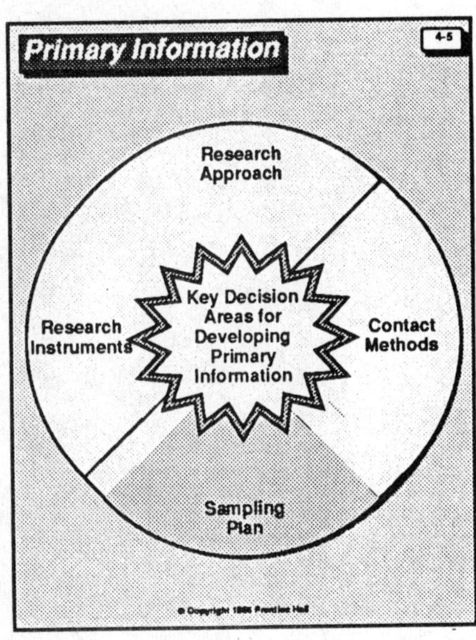

C. Implementing the Research Plan

D. Interpreting and Reporting the Findings

E. Other Marketing Research Considerations

1. Marketing Research in Small Businesses and Nonprofit Organizations

2. International Marketing Research

3. Public Policy and Ethics in Marketing Research

KEY TERMS

Marketing research to test hypotheses about cause-and-effect relationships.

Causal research (p. 123)

Questions that include all the possible answers and allow subjects to make choices among them.

Closed-end questions (p. 132)

Marketing research to better describe marketing problems, situations, or markets, such as the market potential for a product or the demographics and attitudes of consumers.

Descriptive research (p. 121)

The gathering of primary data by selecting matched groups of subjects, giving them different treatments, controlling related factors, and checking for differences in group responses.

Experimental research (p. 127)

Marketing research to gather preliminary information that will help to better define problems and suggest hypotheses.

Exploratory research (p. 121)

Personal interviewing which consists of inviting six to ten people to gather for a few hours with a trained interviewer to talk about a product, service or organization. The interviewer "focuses" the group discussion on important issues.

Focus-group interviewing (p. 130)

Information gathered from sources within the company to evaluate marketing performance and to detect marketing problems and opportunities.

Internal records information (p. 115)

People, equipment, and procedures to gather, sort, analyze, evaluate, and distribute needed, timely, and accurate information to marketing decision makers.

Marketing information system (MIS) (p. 114)

Everyday information about developments in the marketing environment that helps managers prepare and adjust marketing plans.

Marketing intelligence (p. 116)

The function that links the consumer, customer, and public to the marketer through information--information used to identify and define marketing opportunities and problems; to generate, refine, and evaluate marketing actions; to monitor marketing performance; and to improve understanding of the marketing process.

Marketing research (p. 119)

The gathering of primary data by observing relevant people, actions, and situations.

Observational research (p. 126)

Questions that allow respondents to answer in their own words.

Open-end questions (p. 132)

Information collected for the specific purpose at hand.

Primary data (p. 123)

A segment of the population selected for marketing research to represent the population as a whole.

Sample (p. 131)

Information that already exists somewhere, having been collected for another purpose.

Secondary data (p. 123)

Electronic monitoring systems that link consumers' exposure to television advertising and promotion (measured using television meters) with what they buy in stores (measured using store checkout scanners).

Single-source data systems (p. 127)

The gathering of primary data by asking people questions about their knowledge, attitudes, preferences, and buying behavior.

Survey research (p. 127)

APPLYING TERMS AND CONCEPTS

To determine how well you understand the materials in this chapter, read each of the following brief cases and then respond to the questions that follow. Answers are given at the end of this chapter.

Hogan's Shoe Store

Joseph Hogan is the founder of Hogan's Shoe Store located in the business district of Chambersburgh, Pennsylvania. Hogan's has been in business since 1952, and its past success has been attributed to personalized service combined with quality leather footwear offered at reasonable prices. Richard Hogan, the owner's son, assumed control of the store when his father retired two years ago. Richard immediately implemented several changes which included a shift in the store's promotion, favoring radio advertising over newspapers, an increase in the store's hours of operation, a change in the work schedule of store personnel, and an increase in the store's inventory by 10 percent.

Sales at Hogan's have increased an average of 5 percent in each of the past two years, however, net profit has decreased slightly. According to industry data, shoe stores similar to Hogan's had experienced an average increase in sales of 12 percent and an average increase in net profit of 8 percent during the same two-year period.

After casually speaking with the store manager, salesman, and several customers, Hogan concluded that the declining profits could be attributed to the low inventory turnover resulting from the prices charged.

In an effort to increase the store's profitability, Hogan contacted Mary Collins, a distributor for the Hozelton brand of footwear. Although the Hozelton line is constructed of man-made materials; it has a good reputation in the business. Collins assured Hogan that Hozelton quality was comparable to his existing lines and that the retail prices would be lower than that of his merchandise. Collins also stated that Hozelton would be willing to grant advertising allowances to 10 percent of Hogan's advertising budget of $400, whichever was the lesser of the two.

Hogan is seriously considering Collins' proposal, however, he is unsure how his customers will react if he begins to substitute Hozelton for his established line.

Questions

1. List the type of internal reports which might prove useful to Hogan in this situation.

2. List some possible external secondary sources of information which might prove useful to Hogan.

3. Since Hogan is unsure of his exact problem, which type of research (exploratory/causal/descriptive) would be best for him?

4. Do you feel that Hogan needs to collect additional primary data before he makes a decision in this case? Please explain the reasons for your answer.

5. List possible reasons for the decrease in the store's profitability during the past two years.

6. What final suggestions should be made to Hogan regarding his situation?

Margaret Gorman

Margaret Gorman was reading the *Wall Street Journal* when she came upon an article with the headline "TV Networks Turning to Comedies as They Frantically Search for Hits." The article went on to say that fluffy comic programming was being "shipped" up after last season's flings with gumshoes, doctors, lawyers, and oil-drenched soap operas produced one of the most dismal 23 weeks in television history. "All they want now is sitcoms," says a veteran TV writer. The networks were depending on the old, reliable laugh to produce some new hits and reverse the decline in share of viewers during prime time.

Gorman had just formed her own TV company to produce TV programs for the networks and independent stations. After reading this article, Gorman was convinced that this was an excellent opportunity to produce a nonviolent, nonsex adventure series for TV. She believed that something different from standard fare would stand a good chance of getting high ratings. Gorman planed to dramatize important historical events, and at the beginning, middle, and end of each program a group of history professors would discuss causes and effects of the event. To verify her belief that this kind of program would have broad appeal, she had developed a plan for a survey of the university community in which she lived. She wanted to do a good job of research so that she could use the results to help convince network and station executives that the new program would capture the mass market, which she believed was now saturated with comedy; but she did not want violence or sex as an alternative.

Gorman spent a considerable amount of money to secure a computer-generated random sample of telephone numbers of both professors and students -- making sure she had proportionate representation from both groups. She designed a questionnaire (shown below) and hired twenty students to do the telephone interviewing at $2 per completed interview. Each interviewer was given a batch of questionnaires and telephone numbers and told to go home and start at the top of the list of numbers. Calls were to be made between 9 a.m. and 4 p.m. If contact could not be established on the first call, the interviewer was to make up to nine more calls to the same number at different times between 9 a.m. and 5 p.m. in an effort to reach the originally selected respondent. If the respondent could not be reached or refused to cooperate, the interviewer was to move on to the next name on the list and continue in this fashion until twenty questionnaires had been completed.

After two days of interviewing, Gorman was not sure how to evaluate the situation. Mary and Bill, two interviewers, completed twenty calls the first day, but all the others were having difficulty -- they had many refusals, partially completed interviews, not-at-home respondents, busy numbers, changed or not working numbers, and so on. They seemed to be confused, and their questionnaires were often improperly filled out or unusable. Gorman was considering assigning to Mary and Bill, some of the number's given to other interviewers.

Gorman's Questionnaire

1. What is your income? ____________
2. What is your sex? Male _____ Female _____ Bisexual _____
3. What is your age? ______
4. What kind of education do you have? ____________
5. Is your race white or other? W _____ O _____
6. Are you religious? Yes _____ No _____
7. Most people feel that TV is bad and are watching less. Do you agree? Yes _____ No _____
8. Do you watch a lot of TV? Yes _____ No _____ Sometimes _____
9. Do you think we should encourage criminal depravity by showing a lot of violence and sex on TV? Yes _____ No _____
10. Do you agree with most people that most TV programs are not intellectually stimulating? Yes _____ No _____
11. Do you think we can have interesting and intellectually stimulating programs without a lot of violence and sex? Yes _____ No _____
12. What is the least popular television program among your friends?

    ____
13. What's your general opinion of TV programming -- that is, what do you dislike about it, and how can it be improved?

    ____

    ____

    ____

Questions

1. What were the fundamental weaknesses in Gorman's marketing research plan?

2. What should be done to improve Gorman's marketing research plan?

Carlson's Supermarkets

Bud Carlson, owner of a small chain of supermarkets headquartered in Minneapolis, Minnesota, was surveying his company's financial statements when he noticed what he considered disturbing information. Dog and cat food sales dropped an additional 8% on top of last years 11% drop.

Carlson pondered his situation and figured he either needed to get out of pet food sales altogether or to expand his offerings considerably. According to a recent article he read in American Demographics Magazine, supermarkets held a 95% share of the market in the early 1980s; while in the mid '90s, their share of the market was hovering around 10%.

According to the article; three changes in the pet products industry were responsible for the shift. The first involved super premium pet foods which were originally only sold through veterinarians and pet stores. The new foods claimed to offer a healthier alternative to traditional pet food. In time, pet owners concerned about their pet's nutrition and health began to buy the super premium food in increasingly greater quantities.

The second challenge was posed by mass marketers such as Target, Wal-Mart and K Mart. A wide array of pet products along with discount prices on pet food resulting from volume purchasing, attracted buyers in significant numbers. Pet owners slowly shifted their buying behavior from the supermarkets to the mass merchandisers further eroding market share.

The most recent assault has come from pet food superstores. These outlets offers lower prices and a wider variety of pet foods, toys, accessories, clothing and furniture than even the mass merchandisers. And as an added twist, pets are welcome to join their owners as they peruse store offerings

Two weeks later, a disgruntled Carlson began his senior staff meeting by stating "Carlson Supermarkets has experienced another drop in pet food sales and the problem is we are losing sales to those discount stores, and I want to know what we are going to do about it."

Questions

1. If Carlson authorizes a marketing research project to investigate the decline in pet food sales, the article he mentioned as well as the company's financial statements would be considered secondary data and would be reviewed as part of the research plan. What is secondary data and what are the relative advantages and disadvantages of its review as part of a research project?

2. Explain why Carlson was mistaken when he stated "... the problem is we are losing sales to those discount stores ..."

Source: "Reigning Cats and Dogs" *American Demographics,* April 1995, p.10.

TESTING TERMS AND CONCEPTS

Part One To test your understanding of the concepts presented in this chapter, write the letter of the most appropriate answer on the line next to the question number. Answers to these questions may be found at the end of this chapter.

_____ 1. Many marketing managers use internal reports and records to make decisions. Which types of decisions might be made by the marketing managers?

A. planning
B. execution
C. control
D. only (A) and (B)
E. all of the above

_____ 2. Research objectives might be designed to:

A. suggest a hypothesis.
B. describe certain phenomena.
C. test a hypothesis.
D. only (A) an (B)
E. all of the above

_____ 3. ____________ is often identified as the most difficult step in the research process.

A. Data collection
B. Determining the information needs
C. Defining the problem and research objectives
D. Developing the survey instrument
E. Analyzing the findings

_____ 4. ____________ objectives gather primary information that will help to better define the problem and suggest hypothesis.

A. Exploratory
B. Descriptive
C. Causal
D. Casual
E. Formative

_____ 5. Secondary data may be gathered from ____________ sources.

A. internal but not external
B. external but not internal
C. internal as well as external
D. exploratory
E. implicit

____ 6. Which of the following are considered the main advantages of secondary data?

A. available at low cost
B. available quickly
C. completely reliable
D. only (A) and (B)
E. all of the above

____ 7. Primary data might be collected by which of the following ways?

A. observation
B. experimentation
C. survey
D. only (A) and (C)
E. all of the above

____ 8. Which of the following statements is accurate?

A. Observation is best for exploratory research.
B. Experimentation is best suited for descriptive research.
C. Survey work is best suited for casual research.
D. only (A) and (C)
E. all of the above

____ 9. ____________ research is versatile and is the most widely used method for collecting primary data.

A. Observation
B. Experiment
C. Survey
D. Exploratory
E. Formative

____ 10. The most complete, accurate, and expensive information would be gathered in a(n) ____________ survey.

A. observation
B. mail
C. telephone
D. personal interview
E. sample

_____ 11. The segment of the population selected to represent the population as a whole is called a(n):

A. observation set.
B. focus set.
C. sample.
D. population test set.
E. focus group.

_____ 12. A(n) __________ question includes all possible answers and respondents must make a choice among them.

A. open-end
B. closed-end
C. structured
D. unstructured
E. indirect

_____ 13. The phase of the marketing research process that is typically the most expensive and the most subject to error is:

A. development of hypothesis.
B. distributing information.
C. interpreting findings.
D. problem definition.
E. data collection.

_____ 14. All of the following are examples of secondary data sources except:

A. a salesmanager observing how his sales people use their time with customers.
B. an advertising executive getting audience data from A.C. Nielson Company.
C. a brand manager reading an article by a professor about new research on brand loyalty.
D. a marketing researcher calling the U.S. Bureau of Census to determine how many women 20 to 24 years of age live in Buffalo, New York.
E. a marketing manager reviewing the latest copy of the statistical abstract of the United States.

_____ 15. An international marketing researcher may deal with markets that may vary in which of the following:

A. level of economic development.
B. buying patterns.
C. customers and cultures.
D. only (A) and (B)
E. all of the above

Part Two To test your understanding of the concepts presented in this chapter, respond to the following questions by writing the letter T or F on the line next to the question number if you believe the statement is true or false, respectively. Answers to these questions may be found at the end of this chapter.

_____ 1. Marketers typically have more than enough of the right types of information to make decisions.

_____ 2. The proper information should be obtained regardless of the cost.

_____ 3. One major disadvantage of gaining information from internal records is that it is often expensive to obtain.

_____ 4. Experimentation is best suited for testing a hypothesis about some cause-and-effect relationship.

_____ 5. It is possible to gain competitive intelligence from people who do business with competitors.

_____ 6. Given the high cost of recruiting, hiring and training personnel, the most common research activities are a study of employee turnover.

_____ 7. Primary data consist of information collected for the specific purpose at hand.

_____ 8. Primary data may be collected only by mail or personal interview.

_____ 9. Telephone interviewing is the best method of gathering primary data because it is flexible, yields the most reliable information, and results in the lowest cost per contact.

_____ 10. While the wording of questions on a questionnaire is important, the sequencing of questions is not.

_____ 11. A sample is a segment of the population selected to represent the population as a whole.

_____ 12. While closed-end questions are easier to tabulate, open-end questions may be more useful in revealing how people think.

_____ 13. Because international marketing researchers face more and different problems than domestic marketing researchers, they typically use a more complex research process to identify and solve problems.

_____ 14. Personal interviewing is quite flexible and can be used to collect large amounts of information at a low cost per contact.

_____ 15. Many marketing managers use internal records information and reports regularly, especially for making day-to-day planning, implementation and control decisions.

Answers

Applying Terms and Concepts

Hogan's Shoe Store

1. The internal records and reports which might prove useful include: operating and sales expenses, sales reports, inventory records, invoices, accounts receivable, balance sheets, and profit and loss statements.
2. External sources of information which might prove useful include: industry surveys, government publications such as the Census Report and the County and City Data Book, business periodicals, and trade association information.
3. exploratory research
4. Yes -- the primary data he has collected so far is inadequate and unreliable. His sample (several customers, the salesmen, and the store manager) was far too small, and he spoke with these people in a casual, unscientific manner, without any pattern to his questioning.
5. Possible reasons include the following:
change in advertising medium, change in population characteristics, increased competition, increased operating expenses, change in salespeople, product price too high for the current target market, or a downturn in the local economy.

6. Hogan should engage in additional research to identify and define the problem properly. He should set objectives for the research, develop the information sources, and collect and analyze the data before making a decision regarding Collins' offer.

Margaret Gorman

1. There was an inadequate review of secondary data related to the research project.

   The respondents who made up the sample may not be representative of the intended target market. Gorman stated she wanted the programming to have broad appeal; yet her sample was very narrowly defined -- students and professors with telephones who were available between 9 a.m. and 5 p.m.

   The questionnaire was poorly designed. There were too few questions used to gather data on which to draw conclusions and make decisions. The sequencing of the questions was wrong. Some questions were too vague and others were very leading. The questions were biased and would undoubtedly result in answers and opinions that support Gorman's beliefs.

   The interviewers were inadequately trained and supervised. There is the potential for interviewer bias. There was no verification of interviews conducted by Mary and Bill -- their results should be suspect given their high completion rate relative to the other interviewers.

2. Gorman needs to have a better understanding of the situation she faces and therefore needs a better review of the secondary data. This will assist her in defining the "problem" and setting her research objective.

   The sampling plan needs to be carefully analyzed. Gorman needs an appropriate sample unit and sample size. She needs to use an appropriate sampling procedure. There is some question as to whether her current sample plan is appropriate.

   The current questionnaire needs to be discarded and a new one constructed. Questions should be placed in the proper sequence. That is, the demographic and biographic questions should be placed at the end of the questionnaire. A variety of open-end questions seeking the respondent's opinions should be meshed with the closed-end questions. The questions should not be vague or leading. The questionnaire should also be pretested to identify and correct problems which may skew the results.

The interviewers need to be properly trained and monitored as they gather data. This would help to minimize interviewer bias and help ensure the collection of reliable and accurate data.

Gorman may also wish to conduct personal interviews and/or group interviews (focus-group interviews) to complement the telephone interviews. Personal interviewing has several drawbacks, but the advantages may very well offset those disadvantages and yield very significant information.

Carlson's Supermarkets

1. Secondary data consists of information that already exists, having been collected for another purpose. It is typically reviewed in a research project, because it helps the researcher understand better the situation to be studied. Its relative advantages are that it usually can be obtained more quickly and at lower cost than primary data.

   Secondary data can also present problems. The needed information may not exist. Even when data can be found, it might not be very usable. The research must evaluate secondary information carefully to make certain it is relevant (fits research project needs), accurate (reliably collected and reported), current (up to date enough for current decisions), and impartial (objectively collected and reported).

   Secondary data provide a good starting point for research and often help to define problems and research objectives. In most cases, however, the company must also collect primary data.

2. The first step in the marketing research process is often the hardest step. It is defining the problem and research objective. The problem is not that Carlson is losing sales to the mass marketers, rather, the decline in sales is a symptom of the problem. That is, something is causing the decline in sales. The question Carlson needs to ask is "Why are sales declining?" When that question is answered -- perhaps after conducting exploratory research -- Carlson can develop strategies to address the decline.

Testing Terms and Concepts

Part One

1. E E
2. E M

3. C - D Defining the problem and research objectives is often the hardest step in the research process. The manager may know that something is wrong, but not the specific causes. Therefore, the manager must separate the symptoms of the problem from the cause(s) of the problem. When the problem has been carefully defined, the manager and the researcher must set the research objectives.

4. A D
5. C M
6. D M
7. E M
8. A D
9. C D
10. D - M Personal interviewing is quite flexible and can be used to collect large amounts of information. Trained interviewers can hold a respondent's attention for a long time and can explain difficult questions. They can guide interviews, explore issues, and probe as the situation requires. Personal interviews can be used with any type of questionnaire. Interviewers can show subjects actual products, advertisements, or packages and observe reactions and behavior. In many cases, personal interviews can be conducted fairly quickly.

    The main drawbacks of personal interviewing are costs and sampling problems. Personal interviews may cost three to four times as much as telephone interviews. Group interview studies usually use small sample sizes to keep time and costs down, and it may be hard to generalize from the results. Because interviewers have more freedom in personal interviews, there is a greater problem of interviewer bias.

11. C E
12. B M
13. E M
14. A D
15. E D

Part Two

1. F - M Marketers frequently complain that they lack enough information of the right kind or have too much of the wrong kind. Moreover, marketing information is so widely spread throughout the company that it takes great effort to locate even simple facts. Important information often arrives too late to be useful or on-time information is not accurate. Marketing managers need more and better information. Therefore, many companies are not studying their manager's information needs and designing information systems to meet those needs.
2. F M
3. F E
4. T M
5. T E
6. F D
7. T E
8. F M
9. F D
10. F M
11. T E
12. T M
13. F - M International marketing researchers follow the same steps as domestic researchers, from defining the research problem and developing a research plan to interpreting and reporting the results. However, these researchers often face more and different problems. Whereas domestic researchers deal with fairly homogeneous markets within a single country, international researchers deal with markets in many different countries. These different markets often vary dramatically in their levels of economic development, cultures and customs, and buying patterns.
14. F E
15. T E

CHAPTER 5

CONSUMER MARKETS AND CONSUMER BUYER BEHAVIOR

CHAPTER OVERVIEW

The consumer market consists of the individuals and households who buy or acquire goods and services for personal consumption. This chapter discusses basic factors -- cultural, social, personal and psychological that affect how consumers respond to marketing and environmental stimuli. Many of these factors cannot be influenced by marketers, but they are useful for identifying target consumer groups and shaping products and appeals to better serve consumer needs, wants and demands. When making buying decisions people play different roles. These roles must be considered when designing products and preparing promotional campaigns. Buying behavior varies in complexity and effort ranging from variety seeking and habitual buying behavior to dissonance reducing and complex buying behavior. At least in complicated purchases, consumers pass through five stages in the buyer decision process. The stages include need recognition, information search, evaluation of alternatives, purchase decision and postpurchase behavior. The buyer decision process for new products depends on product and consumer characteristics that affect the marketer's product development and marketing program. For companies operating in other countries, understanding and serving the needs of consumers can be especially difficult. Although consumer in different countries may have some things in common, their values, attitudes and behaviors often vary greatly. International marketers must understand such differences and adjust their products and marketing programs accordingly.

CHAPTER OBJECTIVES

When you finish this chapter, you should be able to accomplish the following:

1. Name the elements of the stimulus response model of consumer behavior.

2. Outline the major characteristics affecting consumer behavior and list some of the specific cultural, social, personal and psychological factors that influence consumers.
3. Identify and define the consumer buying roles of initiator, influencer, decider, buyer and user.
4. Illustrate different types of buying decision behavior, including complex, dissonance reducing, habitual, and variety seeking behavior.
5. Explain the buyer decision process and discuss need recognition, information search evaluation of alternatives, the purchaser decision and post purchaser behavior.
6. Express the basics or the buyer decision process for new products and identify stages in the adoption process, individual differences in innovativeness, and the influence of product characteristics on the rate of adoption.

LECTURE/STUDENT NOTES

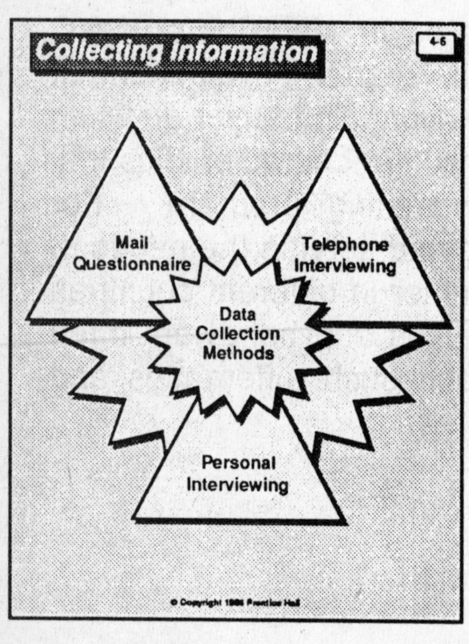

I. Model of Consumer Behavior

II. Characteristics affecting Consumer Behavior

A. Cultural Factors

1. Cultural

2. Subculture

3. Social Class

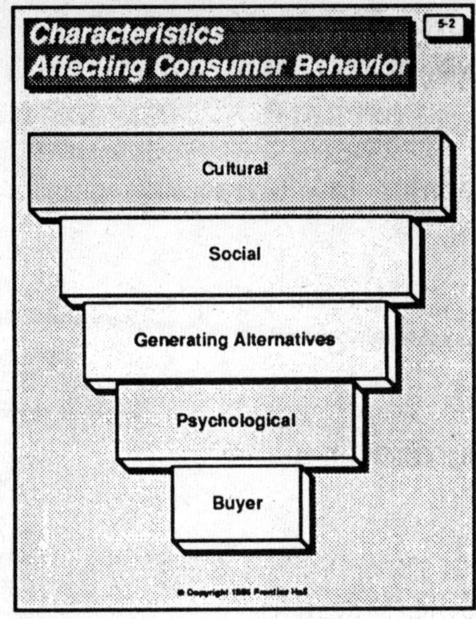

B. Social Factors

1. Groups

2. Family

3. Roles and Status

C. Personal Factors

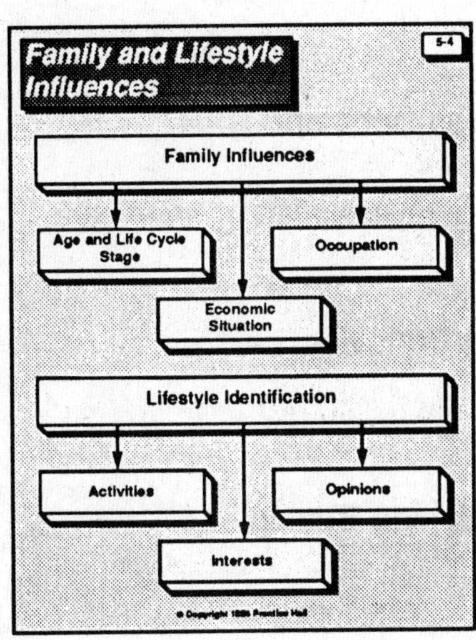

1. Age and Life-Cycle Stage

2. Occupation

3. Economic Situation

4. Lifestyle

5. Personality and Self-Concept

D. Psychological Factors

1. Motivation

a. Freud's Theory of Motivation

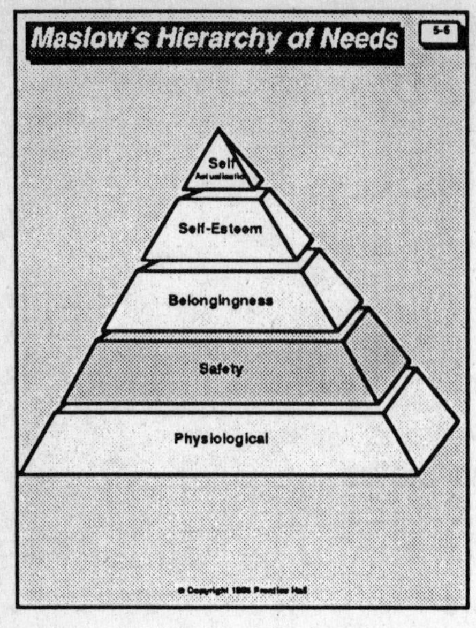

b. Maslow's Theory of Motivation

2. Perception

3. Learning

4. Beliefs and Attitudes

III. Consumer Buying Roles

IV. Types of Buying Decision Behavior

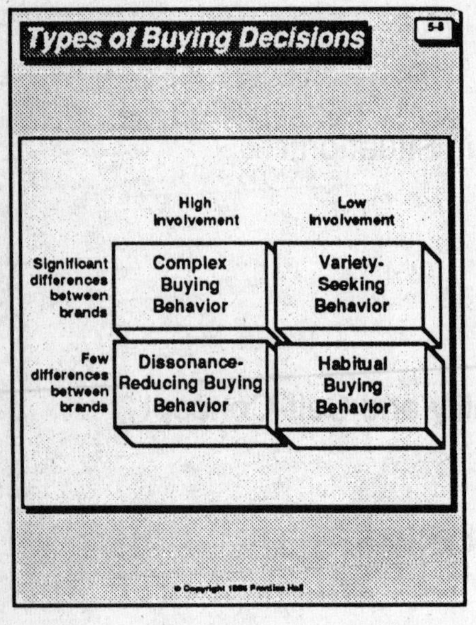

A. Complex Buying Behavior

B. Dissonance-Reducing Buying Behavior

C. Habitual Buying Behavior

D. Variety-Seeking Buying Behavior

V. The Buyer Decision Process

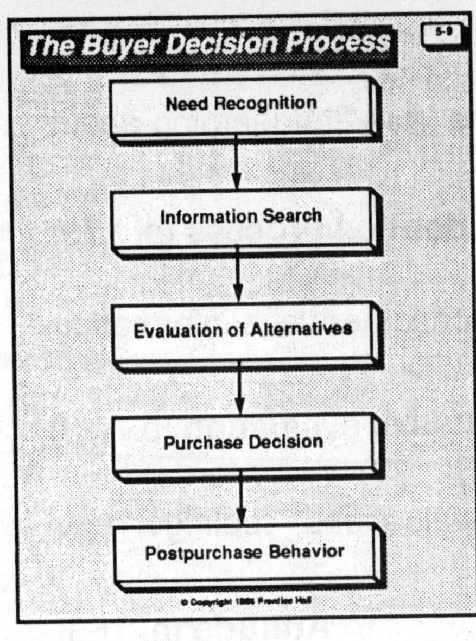

A. Need Recognition

B. Information Search

C. Evaluation of Alternatives

D. Purchase Decision

E. Postpurchase Behavior

VI. The Buyer Decision Process for New Products

Stages in the Adoption Process
5-10
Awareness
Interest
Evaluation
Trial
Adoption

A. Stages in the Adoption Process

B. Individual Differences in Innovativeness

C. Influence of Product Characteristics on Rate of Adoption

KEY TERMS

The mental process through which an individual passes from first learning about an innovation to final adoption.

Adoption process (p. 176)

The stage of the buyer decision process in which the consumer uses information to evaluate alternative brands in the choice set.

Alternative evaluation (p. 173)

A person's consistently favorable or unfavorable evaluations, feelings, and tendencies toward an object or idea.

Attitude (p. 168)

A descriptive thought that a person holds about something.

Belief (p. 166)

The set of beliefs held about a particular brand.

Brand image (p. 173)

Buyer discomfort caused by postpurchase conflict.

Cognitive dissonance (p. 175)

Behavior undertaken when consumers are highly involved in a purchase and perceive significant differences among brands.

Complex buying behaviour (p. 168)

The buying behavior of final consumers--individuals and households who buy goods and services for personal consumption.

Consumer buying behaviour (p. 151)

All the individuals and households who buy or acquire goods and services for personal consumption.

Consumer market (p. 151)

The set of basic values, perceptions, wants, and behaviors learned by a member of society from family and other important institutions.

Culture (p. 152)

Behavior which occurs when consumers are highly involved with an expensive, infrequent or risky purchase, but see little difference among brands.

Dissonance reducing buying behaviour (p. 170)

Two or more people who interact to accomplish individual or mutual goals.

Groups (p. 158)

Buying behavior which occurs under conditions of low consumer involvement and little significant brand differences.

Habitual buying behaviour (p. 170)

The stage of the buyer decision process in which the consumer is aroused to search for more information; the consumer may simply have heightened attention or may go into active information search.

Information search (p. 172)

Changes in an individual's behavior arising from experience.

Learning (p. 166)

A person's pattern of living as expressed in his or her activities, interests, and opinions.

Lifestyle (p. 160)

A need that is sufficiently pressing to direct the person to seek satisfaction of the need.

Motive [or drive] (p. 163)

The first stage of the buyer decision process in which the consumer recognizes a problem or need.

Need recognition (p. 172)

A good, service or idea that is perceived by some potential customers as new.

New product (p. 176)

People within a reference group who, because of special skills, knowledge, personality, or other characteristics, exert influence on others.

Opinion leaders (p. 158)

The process by which people select, organize, and interpret information to form a meaningful picture of the world.

Perception (p. 166)

A person's distinguishing psychological characteristics that lead to relatively consistent and lasting responses to his or her own environment.

Personality (p. 163)

The stage of the buyer decision process in which consumers take further action after purchase based on their satisfaction or dissatisfaction.

Post purchase behaviour (p. 174)

The stage of the buyer decision process in which the consumer actually buys the product.

Purchase decision (p. 174)

The technique of measuring life styles and developing life-style classifications; it involves measuring the major AIO dimensions (activities, interests, opinions).

Psychographics (p. 160)

Relatively permanent and ordered divisions in a society whose members share similar values, interests, and behaviors.

Social classes (p. 156)

A group of people with shared value systems based on common life experiences and situations.

Subculture (p. 153)

Consumer behavior undertaken in situations characterized by low consumer involvement, but significant perceived brand differences.

Variety seeking buying behaviour (p. 171)

APPLYING TERMS AND CONCEPTS

To determine how well you understand the materials in this chapter, read each of the following brief cases and then respond to the questions that follow. Answers are given at the end of this chapter.

The Dawsons

Jeff and Margaret Dawson, after 15 years of marriage and two children, decided this past winter to purchase a power boat. Their income had increased to the point where a $16,000 to $21,000 expenditure was within reason. This boat was a lifelong dream for them. Their only previous experience with boats was a 14-ft Starcraft fishing boat with a 15 hp Mercury outboard motor. Their next purchase was to be in the 20- to 24-ft range with an inboard motor. The prime uses of this boat were to be for water-skiing, fishing, and leisurely motoring on the Finger Lakes of central New York where they lived.

The Dawsons wanted to stay with a Starcraft/Mercury combination if possible. They were disappointed to find, upon attending the Northeast Boat Show at the New York State Fairgrounds in Syracuse, that Starcraft did not produce a boat which suited them. Mercury engines, however, were available in a variety of sizes and price ranges.

Mr. Dawson's reason for wishing to stay with a Mercury engine was his past experience with his outboard motor. In the 14 years he had owned the motor he had had virtually no problems with it. Dawson's fishing friends who owned Johnson and Evinrude motors, however, seemed to experience an abnormally high (compared to Mercury) number of problems, several of which involved major expenditures.

The Dawsons collected literature from exhibitors at the boat show as they viewed a wide variety of boat and motor combinations.

At the boat show, Mercury was introducing a new 210 hp V8 engine. Mercury promoted its new engine as unique because it was the only engine on the market rated at 210 hp, and it introduced V8 cylinder design instead of the more traditional V4 and V6 designs. Dawson was impressed by the information in the literature on this new engine. Fuel consumption, speed, and ease of maintenance were reasonable. Mercury's price, however, was several hundred dollars more than the competition's.

Later, in speaking with his friends about what he had seen at the show, Dawson's friends cautioned him about the potential danger of buying an engine the first year it was produced. They felt it would take a year or two to work the bugs out of the new engine. Although an 8 cylinder engine was common in offshore racing boats, it was still unusual in this horsepower range and motor style for the sport market.

After reviewing the literature from the boat show and visiting several marinas where they spoke with sales representatives and took boats out for a "test drive," the Dawsons decided on a 22-ft craft made by Invader Industries. The boat could be equipped with either a 200 hp Volvo engine or the new 210 hp Mercury. Without hesitation, Dawson ordered the boat with the Mercury. Although they had spent more than they had planned, the Dawsons felt their purchase would be a source of considerable pride and enjoyment.

Questions

_____ 1. Identify the major cultural theme that played a role in the Dawson's decision to purchase a power boat.

A. leisure time
B. health
C. youthfulness
D. informality
E. social

_____ 2. Dawson's fishing friends are an example of a(n) ____________ group.

A. primary
B. secondary
C. aspirational
D. dissociative
E. normal

_____ 3. Which need or needs, according to Maslow's theory of motivation, would be satisfied by Dawson's purchase of the 22-ft Invader power boat?

A. social
B. esteem
C. self-actualization
D. only (A) and (B)
E. all of the above

_____ 4. Which selective process was evident when Dawson remembered information about Mercury motors which supported his attitudes and beliefs?

A. selective attention
B. selective distortion
C. selective retention
D. selective regression
E. selective intention

Caesar Gonzales

Caesar Gonzales played tennis. He had played the game since high school and now he was 50 years old. He still thought he was 25, but after three vigorous sets, he felt like 75. So 50 just about summed, or averaged, it all up. His eyes were slower in focusing and seemed not to pick up the character of opponents' shots as rapidly as they used to. He often probed for volleys, and his ground strokes were not as accurate and powerful as they once were. And he could not cover the court as quickly as he had a mere five years ago.

Caesar had all but resigned himself to his fate when he became aware of a new type of racket -- an oversized, clumsy-looking instrument. He observed a few older players and inept younger players using it on the courts. At first he viewed the object with disdain; then he saw some professional players on TV using the racket. Next Caesar played a tournament match against a fellow he thought he could dispatch with ease and lost, much to his chagrin. The opponent had used an oversized racket.

After pondering these circumstances, Caesar decided to investigate the oversize tennis racket to see what it might have to offer. He had heard of the first large racket, the Prince, but he knew there were other brands and styles. Caesar looked through all the tennis magazines for ads or articles about the rackets; he visited a sporting goods store and examined several different styles and brands of oversized rackets; he talked with tennis instructors and people he saw playing with the racket.

As this point Caesar began to identify various characteristics of each racket style and brand and decided which was most important to him. Some obvious characteristics were size, weight, and price. These he had noted or speculated about from the very first time he saw an oversized racket. After investigating, he knew that other factors were equally or more important: balance, power, control, and ease of handling. Caesar concluded that he ought to try some rackets that met most of his minimum requirements, and he borrowed five from a sporting goods store.

He had decided that to be acceptable, a racket should have a certain minimum level of power, control, and ease of handling. After playing with each racket, Caesar narrowed his choice to two. He had a slight preference for racket A, but it had a price of $235 and Caesar had only $100 to spend. Racket B was not quite as desirable but could be purchased for $99. Caesar decided to buy racket B.

As he stood in the sporting goods store making a decision, one of Caesar's friends passed by and said: "Well, old boy, are you going to buy one of these old man's rackets? I didn't know you were that old." "Just looking. Curious about these things, you know," was Caesar's reply. "Sounds fine. Give me a ride home and we'll talk about it." Caesar walked out with his friend without buying the racket.

Caesar spent the rest of the day and evening ruminating on the purchase of the racket. He could visualize the guffaws and scoffing that he would have to bear when he showed up with the giant racket. Finally he decided that the racket would improve his game more than enough to compensate for any jocularity it might generate. The next day he bought the oversized racket.

Questions

_____ 1. Gonzales progressed through which stages in the buying decision process?

A. need recognition, information search, evaluation of alternatives, purchase decision
B. need recognition, limited problem solving, information search, evaluation of alternatives, purchase decision
C. awareness, interest, evaluation, trial, adoption
D. need recognition, information search, purchase decision dissonance
E. awareness, interest, evaluation, trial, dissonance

_____ 2. If Gonzales did pass through the need recognition stage, at what point was it?

A. when he realized he could not play as well as in the past
B. when he lost the tournament match
C. when he first saw older players using the large racket
D. either or both (A) and (B)
E. none of the above

_____ 3. At what point did awareness of the product occur?

A. when he realized he could not play as well as in the past
B. when he lost the tournament match
C. when he first saw older players using the large racket
D. when he first saw professional players on TV using the racket
E. both (B) and (D)

_____ 4. Gonzales obtained most of his information from:

A. personal sources.
B. public sources.
C. commercial sources.
D. experimental sources.
E. private sources.

_____ 5. At what point in the decision process was Gonzales when he assigned importance weights to product attributes?

A. interest
B. information search
C. trial
D. evaluation of alternatives
E. consideration

_____ 6. The appearance of Gonzales' friend in the store:

A. was an unanticipated situational factor.
B. shifted Caesar's ideas.
C. altered Caesar's importance weights.
D. altered Caesar's beliefs about racket B.
E. none of the above

_____ 7. Gonzales postponed the purchase of the racket because:

A. the attitudes of others and perceived risks.
B. unanticipated situational factors and perceived performance.
C. unconfirmed expectations and situational factors.
D. reduced expectancy values and altered beliefs.
E. cognitive dissonance.

Line-Haul Jeans

Mike Ianari is a Line Haul (long-distance) truck driver for Richards Express, based in North Bergen, New Jersey. Ianari recently saw an advertisement in OVERDRIVE MAGAZINE about a new type of blue jeans called "Line Haul".

"Line Hauls" are made of stretch denim, cut wider in the seat and thighs and have oversized back pockets. The advertisement indicated that unlike tighter fitting designer jeans, Line Hauls at $39.95, were loose fitting, had plenty of stretch, and felt comfortable the first time worn. At 6'4" and 245 pounds Ianari reasoned that these pre-washed, preshrunk jeans would be ideal.

Ianari, remembering the advertisement, was determined to buy a pair of these jeans on his next trip through South Carolina, the state in which STOP 55 Truck Stops, which sold them exclusively, were located. Ianari was even more determined to buy a pair of these jeans after he began noticing that the "Line Haul" label was acquiring quite a following among his fellow drivers. Many truckers are now wearing "Line Haul" caps, T-shirts, vests, and belt buckles featuring the brand's "Tractor with Cab Over" emblem.

Questions

1. Which marketing stimuli can be identified in this case?

 ___

2. Which reference group would Ianari most likely be influenced by to purchase "Line Haul" jeans?

 ___

3. Which need or needs according to Maslow's theory of motivation would be satisfied by Ianari's purchasing of the jeans?

 ___

4. Which selective perceptual process was evident when Ianari remembered that information which supported his attitude and beliefs about "Line Haul" jeans?

 ___

5. After his experience of buying and wearing a pair of "Line Haul" jeans, Ianari has found them to be the most comfortable jeans he has ever worn and refuses to wear any other type of jeans while driving. Which psychological factor most likely accounts for his change in his behavior?

 ___

TESTING TERMS AND CONCEPTS

Part One To test your understanding of the concepts presented in this chapter, write the letter of the most appropriate answer on the line next to the question number. Answers to these questions may be found at the end of this chapter.

_____ 1. Which of the following is not one of the environmental stimuli that may serve to influence buying behavior?

A. economic
B. cultural
C. political
D. promotion
E. all of the above

_____ 2. The values of achievement and success, activity and involvement, efficiency and practicality, progress, individualism, freedom, humanitarianism and youthfulness are examples of ____________ factors.

A. personal
B. cultural
C. social
D. psychological
E. physiological

_____ 3. ____________ are relatively homogeneous and enduring divisions in a society which are hierarchically ordered and whose members share similar values, interests, and behaviors.

A. Subcultures
B. Social classes
C. Cultures
D. Reference groups
E. Roles and status

_____ 4. Social class in the United States is influenced by:

A. occupation.
B. education.
C. income.
D. only (A) and (C)
E. all of the above

_____ 5. Family, friends, neighbors, and co-workers are examples of _____________ groups.

A. primary
B. secondary
C. aspirational
D. dissociative
E. conformity

_____ 6. Robert Moyers, a husband and father of four, decided to purchase a station wagon instead of a sports car. Mr. Moyers' buying behavior was influenced by a(n) _____________ group.

A. orientation
B. aspirational
C. secondary
D. primary
E. opinion

_____ 7. Examples of personal factors that may influence buying behavior include all but which of the following:

A. occupation.
B. life style.
C. personality and self-concept.
D. economic situation.
E. social class.

_____ 8. An individual's economic situation will affect product choice. Which of the following items comprise an individual's economic circumstance?

A. spendable income and borrowing power
B. savings and assets
C. attitude toward spending versus saving
D. only (A) and (B)
E. all of the above

_____ 9. The three AIO dimensions of life style analysis are:

A. activities, ideas, and opinions.
B. activities, interests, and opinions.
C. action, interests, and occupation.
D. action, interests, and opinions.
E. activities, interests, and occupations.

_____ 10. Needs such as recognition, esteem, and belonging are examples of ____________ needs.

A. biogenic
B. psychographic
C. psychological
D. biographic
E. physiogenic

_____ 11. Identify the proper order of needs according to Maslow from the most to the least pressing.

A. physiological, safety, esteem, social, self-actualization
B. safety, physiological, social, esteem, self-actualization
C. safety, physiological, esteem, social, self-actualization
D. safety, physiological, social, self-actualization, esteem
E. physiological, safety, social, esteem, self-actualization

_____ 12. When an individual attempts to fit incoming information into his or her existing mind set, that individual is engaged in which perceptual process?

A. selective retention
B. selective distortion
C. selective attention
D. selective perception
E. selective integration

_____ 13. A drive becomes a motive when it is directed toward a particular:

A. stimulus object.
B. attitude.
C. belief.
D. idea.
E. role.

_____ 14. A need that is sufficiently pressing to direct a person to seek satisfaction of that need is called:

A. motive.
B. desire.
C. want.
D. necessity.
E. obsession.

_____ 15. The Bell Corporation is interested in measuring the life styles of its present and potential customers. The technique Bell will most likely use is:

A. sociometrics.
B. econometrics.
C. psychographics.
D. physiographics.
E. psychometrics.

Part Two To test your understanding of the concepts presented in this chapter, respond to the following questions by writing the letter T or F on the line next to the question number if you believe the statement is true or false, respectively. Answers to these questions may be found at the end of this chapter.

_____ 1. The consumer market consists of all the individuals and households who buy or acquire goods and services for personal consumption.

_____ 2. A company which has adopted the marketing concept may conceivably break an overall market into submarkets and design a marketing mix for each submarket.

_____ 3. The major factors influencing consumer behavior should be considered "controllable" because a marketer has the ability to influence them with the marketing mix.

_____ 4. Economic factors exert the broadest and deepest influences on consumer behavior.

_____ 5. Each culture contains smaller groups or subcultures that provide more specific identification and socialization for members.

_____ 6. Social stratification is exhibited in virtually all human societies.

_____ 7. Primary reference groups tend to be more formal, while secondary reference groups tend to be more informal.

_____ 8. Culture is the basic cause of a person's wants and behavior.

_____ 9. Life cycle refers to the person's pattern of living in the world as expressed in his or her activities, interests, and opinions.

_____ 10. Personality is defined as the distinguishing psychological characteristics that lead to relatively consistent and enduring responses to the environment by an individual.

_____ 11. A person's self-concept relates to the complex mental image the individual has of him or herself.

_____ 12. Reference groups have little or no influence on the buying behavior of group members.

_____ 13. Product and brand images are generally composed of the consumer beliefs about the product.

_____ 14. Generally it is easier to attempt to modify a market offering to make it acceptable to consumer predisposition's than to attempt to change consumer attitudes.

_____ 15. Thomas VanFleet has just joined the United Auto Workers Union. Thomas' union is not considered a secondary group.

Answers

Applying Terms and Concepts

The Dawsons

1. A
2. A
3. E
4. C

Caesar Gonzales

1. A
2. D
3. C
4. C
5. D
6. A
7. A

Line-Haul Jeans

1. Product - The Jeans
   Place - STOP 55 Truck Stops where they are sold
   Price - $39.95
   Promotion - The advertisement in OVERDRIVE MAGAZINE
2. Primary Group
3. Physiological need for comfort and social need for belongingness and the need to identify with his fellow truckers.
4. Selective retention
5. Learning

Testing Terms and Concepts

Part One

1. D E
2. B D
3. B M
4. E - E Social classes are relatively permanent and ordered divisions in a society whose members share similar values, interests and behavior. Social class in the United States is not determined by a single factor such as income but is measured as a combination of factors including attitude, occupation, education, income, and wealth among others.
5. A M
6. D M
7. E D
8. E - M Marketers recognize that when evaluating the financial attractiveness of a market segment they need to consider not only the income of the buyer but also the buyer's savings, credit availability and the willingness to use credit.
9. B M
10. C M
11. E M
12. B E
13. A M
14. A D
15. C D

Part Two

1. T M
2. T D
3. F - D Consumer purchases are strongly influenced by cultural, social, personal, and psychological characteristics. These factors, for the most part, cannot be controlled by the marketer yet they must be taken into account when developing a marketing strategy. In time, it is conceivable, that a marketer may be able to influence, to a limited extent, certain factors such as perception or learning; but generally the factors are considered uncontrollable.
4. F E
5. T M
6. T E
7. F D
8. T D
9. F D
10. T E
11. T M
12. F - D Reference groups serve as direct or indirect points of comparison or reference in the forming of a person's attitudes or behavior. People are often influenced by reference groups to which they do not belong. An aspirational group is one to which the individual wishes to belong.

    Marketers try to identify the reference groups of their target markets. Reference groups influence a person in at least three ways. They expose the person to new behaviors and life styles. They influence the person's attitudes and self-concept because he or she wants to "fit in." And they create pressures to conform that may affect the person's product and brand choices.
13. T M
14. T E
15. F M

CHAPTER 6

BUSINESS MARKETS AND BUSINESS BUYER BEHAVIOUR

CHAPTER OVERVIEW

The business market is much larger than the consumer market. This chapter discusses three main types of organizational markets -- the business, institutional, and government markets -- and describes how they differ from consumer markets. A model of business buyer behavior shows that organizational purchases are complicated by the interpersonal influences operating among the multiple people in the buying center. The largest organizational market is the business market. The chapter describes what buying decisions business buyers make, who participates in the buying process, what influences their decisions, and how the buying decisions are made. The institutional market buys and resells goods produced by others, and the government market consists of federal, state, and local units that acquire goods and services for government purposes. The chapter describes the differences that marketers must take into account between these markets and the business market.

CHAPTER OBJECTIVES

When you finish this chapter, you should be able to accomplish the following:

1. List the characteristics of business markets explaining market structure and demand, the nature of the buying unit and the decision process.
2. Outline the model of business buyer behaviour.
3. Discuss business buyer behavior, types of buying situations, participants in the business buying process and major influences on business buyers.
4. Identify and define the steps of the business buying process.
5. Contrast the differences among business markets institutional markets and government markets.

LECTURE/STUDENT NOTES

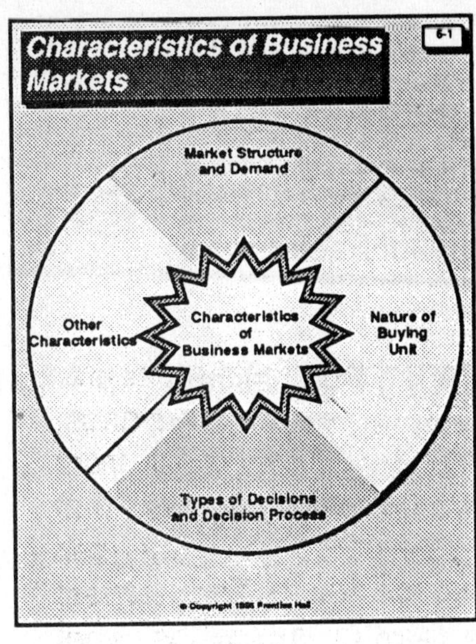

I. Business Markets

A. Characteristics of Business Markets

1. Market Structure and Demand

2. Nature of the Buying Unit

3. Types of Decisions and the Decision Process

4. Other Characteristics of Business Markets

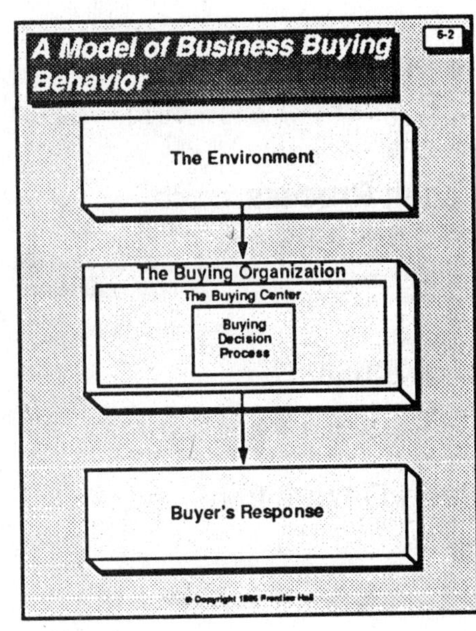

B. A Model of Business Buyer Behavior

II. Business Buyer Behaviour

A. Major Types of Buying Situations

B. Participants in the Business buying Process

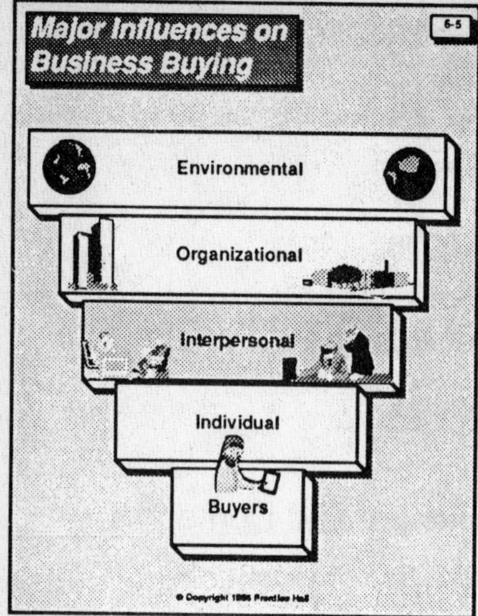

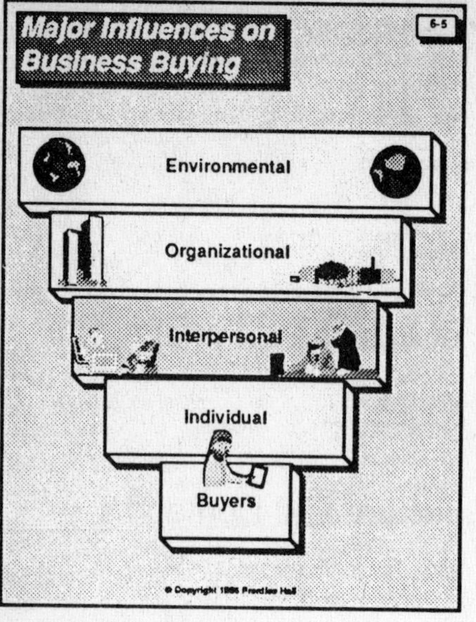

C. Major Influences on Business Buyers

1. Environmental Factors

2. Organizational Factors

a. Upgraded Purchasing

b. Centralized Purchasing

c. Long-term Contracts

d. Purchasing Performance Evaluation

e. Just-in-Time Production Systems

3. Interpersonal Factors

4. Individual Factors

Stages in the Business Buying Process
6-6
Problem Recognition
General Need Description
Product Specification
Supplier Search
Proposal Solicitation
Supplier Selection
Order Routine Specification
Performance Review

D. The Business Buying Process

1. Problem Recognition

2. General Need Description

3. Product Specification

4. Supplier Search

5. Proposal Solicitation

6. Supplier Selection

7. Order-Routine Specification

8. Performance Review

III. Institutional and Government Markets

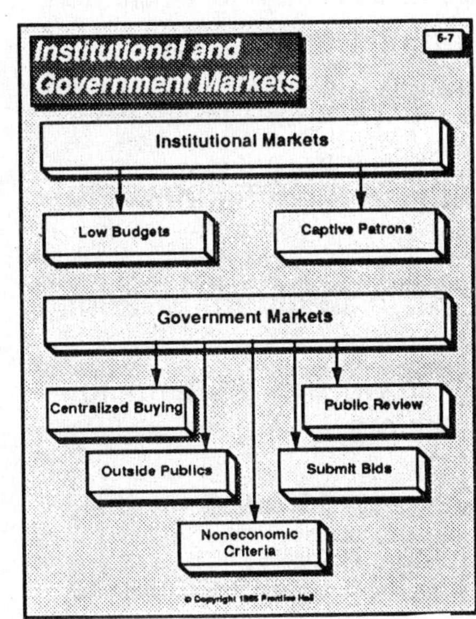

A. Institutional Markets

B. Government Markets

1. Major Influences on Government Buyers

2. Government Buyer Decision Process

KEY TERMS

All the organizations that buy goods and services to use in the production of other products and services or for the purpose of reselling or renting them to others at a profit.

Business market (p. 201)

The decision-making process by which business buyers establish the need for purchased products and services and identify, evaluate, and choose among alternative brands and suppliers.

Business buying process (p. 201)

People in an organization's buying center with formal authority to select the supplier and arrange terms of purchase.

Buyers (p. 208)

All the individuals and units that participate in the business buying-decision process.

Buying centre (p. 208)

People in the organization's buying center who have formal or informal power to select or approve the final suppliers.

Deciders (p. 208)

Business demand that ultimately comes from (derives from) the demand for consumer goods.

Derived demand (p. 201)

People in the organization's buying center who control the flow of information to others.

Gatekeepers (p. 208)

The stage in the business buying process in which the company describes the general characteristics and quantity of a needed item.

General need description (p. 214)

Governmental units--federal, state, and local--that purchase or rent goods and services for carrying out the main functions of government.

Government market (p. 217)

People in an organization's buying center who affect the buying decision; they often help define specifications and also provide information for evaluating alternatives.

Influencers (p. 208)

Schools, hospitals, nursing homes, prisons, and other institutions that provide goods and services to people in their care.

Institutional market (p. 217)

A business buying situation in which the buyer wants to modify product specifications, prices, terms, or suppliers.

Modified rebuy (p. 207)

A business buying situation in which the buyer purchases product or service for the first time.

New Task (p. 207)

The stage of the business buying process in which the buyer writes the final order with the chosen supplier(s), listing the technical specifications, quantity needed, expected time of delivery, return policies, and warranties.

Order routine specification (p. 216)

The stage of the business buying process in which the buyer rates its satisfaction with suppliers, deciding whether to continue, modify, or drop them.

Performance review (p. 217)

The first stage of the business buying process in which someone in the company recognizes a problem or need that can be met by acquiring a good or a service.

Problem recognition (p. 214)

The stage of the business buying process in which the buying organization decides on and specifies the best technical product characteristics for a needed item.

Production specification (p. 214)

The stage of the business buying process in which the buyer invites qualified suppliers to submit proposals.

Proposal solicitation (p. 215)

A business buying situation in which the buyer routinely reorders something without any modification.

Straight rebuy (p. 206)

The stage of the business buying process in which the buyer tries to find the best vendors.

Supplier search (p. 215)

The stage of the business buying process in which the buyer reviews proposals and selects a supplier or supplies.

Supplier selection (p. 216)

Buying a packaged solution to a problem and without all the separate decisions involved.

Systems buying (p. 207)

Members of the organization who will use the product or service; users often initiate the buying proposal and help define product specifications.

Users (p. 208)

An approach to cost reduction in which components are studied carefully to determine if they can be redesigned, standardized, or made by less costly methods of production.

Value analysis (p. 214)

APPLYING TERMS AND CONCEPTS

To determine how well you understand the materials in this chapter, read each of the following brief cases and then respond to the questions that follow. Answers are given at the end of this chapter.

Fort McMurray Community College

Fort McMurray Community College is one of seven community colleges in Alberta. Located in the city of Fort McMurray, it is a two-year school which offers degrees in a variety of programs including business administration, engineering science, mathematics, liberal arts, the natural sciences, and telecommunications. The college also offers certificates in the occupational trades of industrial electricity, welding, automotive mechanics, industrial machining, and drafting.

Carl Palmer, the coordinator of occupational education at the college was faced with the need to acquire two additional vertical milling machines for the industrial machining program in which there had been a substantial increase in enrollment in recent years. After consulting with Vincent Barone, the dean of instruction, the administration decided that the college would apply for a provincial grant, which if received, would allow the college to purchase the machine tools.

Since the college had not purchased such equipment since 1989, an ad hoc committee was formed to gather the appropriate information and write the grant proposal. The committee was composed of Palmer, Michael Whyte, an instructor of industrial machining, and Lisa Klein, the college's assistant business manager. In gathering information the committee met with the department's advisory council, made up of area employers, to learn their opinions as to which makes and models of machine tools were used in their machine shops and which might meet the college's needs. The committee also attended the Northwestern Tool Show held in Seattle, Washington, where members spoke with manufacturers' representatives and also gathered brochures on various pieces of equipment.

The committee learned that a general price increase of 10 percent was expected by most manufacturers on February 1. The committee realized it would not receive final notification of the grant until April 1, but decided that the price increase would not affect the decision to purchase any equipment, even if additional funds had to come from the college.

The committee applied for the grant and also developed the set of specifications for the milling machine that would meet the school's needs. The specification sheets indicated that the firm awarded the contract must supply a machine equal to or better than a Bridgeport series one vertical mill, with the college reserving the right to reject any or all bids. The specification sheets, which also stipulated that the machines must be delivered and set up at the college by August 1, were then distributed to all interested parties that had responded to the invitation to bid notice placed in area newspapers.

Supplier	Manufacturer	Price per Machine (CDN)
Langley Brothers	Jet	$12,995
J and B Industrial Supply	Bridgeport	16,750
Belros Corporation	Enterprise	13,750
Yukon Supply	Bridgeport	16,250
U. T. A.	Savrin	14,950

After careful consideration, the committee rejected the Jet, Enterprise, and Savrin milling machines as not meeting specifications. The committee awarded the bid to Yukon Supply.

Questions

_____ 1. Identify the type of demand faced by Fort McMurray Community College when it decided to place an order for the two milling machines after the price was scheduled to increase.

A. derived demand
B. inelastic demand
C. latent demand
D. full demand
E. elastic demand

_____ 2. Identify the type of demand faced by Fort McMurray Community College when it made a decision to purchase two additional milling machines due to an increase in enrollment in the machine trades program.

A. derived demand
B. inelastic demand
C. latent demand
D. full demand
E. elastic demand

_____ 3. The buying process used by Fort McMurray Community College is an example of ____________ buying.

A. value analysis
B. negotiated contract
C. open bid
D. open-to-buy
E. top-down

4. Identify the type of buying situation faced by Fort McMurray Community College. Provide justification for your answer.

____

____

____

____

____

____

Red Bar Express

Darin Cosentino, executive vice-president of Buffalo Express, recently completed negotiations with the Black Eagle Paper Company of Montreal, Quebec, to be the exclusive transportation company moving Black Eagle newsprint roll paper into the United States.

Buffalo could easily handle the projected annual volume of 50,000 tons with its current fleet of trailers; however, Cosentino believed a special trailer might better haul this high-density, high-weight freight. He authorized Eric Moore, director of operations, to organize a committee to investigate the problem.

Moore's committee posed the problem to representatives of the major trailer manufacturers, including Fruehauf, Intercontinental Truck Body, Great Dane, and Trailmobile. Buffalo has purchased hundreds of trailers from each of these manufacturers in building its fleet of 1,500 trailers, but this was the first time it wanted a manufacturer to modify its product specification to meet the needs of a single shipper.

Each manufacturer supplied a written proposal for the project, with most simply offering their standard trailer with a reinforced frame to handle the weight. Intercontinental, however, sent a sales representative who presented information on a unique trailer design called the Wedge. The Wedge was similar to a standard trailer, with two important differences: first, the front of the trailer was 8 inches lower than the rear; and second, instead of traditional rectangular shape, the sides of the trailer in the front were slightly tapered to form a less blunt front end -- hence the name Wedge.

The trailer was in compliance with Transport Canada regulations, specifying a length of no more than 15 metres or a width exceeding 3 metres. The Wedge with a reinforced frame could easily carry the 20,000-22,000 kg load without difficulty. Additionally, the aerodynamics of the Wedge were projected to decrease fuel consumption by 1 litre per 100 km.

Moore's committee reviewed each manufacturer's proposal regarding trailer design, capacity, price, delivery date, warranty, and construction. After some deliberation, the contract for 25 trailers was awarded to Intercontinental.

Questions

1. The buying decision faced by Buffalo in this case is an example of a ____________ buying situation.

2. The demand for trailers was based on the demand for roll paper, which in turn was based on the consumer demand for newspapers. The demand for trailers and roll paper is an example of ______________ demand.

3. Buffalo's business decision to haul Black Eagle's paper is an example of a(n) ______________ influence on business buying.

4. Moore's buying committee responded more to ____________ (economic/ personal) factors than ____________ (economic/personal) factors in making its decision.

5. ____________ would probably play a dominant role regarding promotion in this case of business buying.

Quality Croutons

Ray Kroc, the founder of McDonald's, as we know it, believed in sharing his good fortune -- not only with his employees, stockholders, and store owners, but also with his suppliers. As McDonald's grew, so too did the company's need for organizations to supply it with food, paper products, and equipment.

It might have been natural for McDonald's to acquire control of their various suppliers to ensure consistency and dependability. As McDonald's expanded horizontally, they could have grown vertically as well. But Ray Kroc did not want it that way. Instead, he chose to use outside suppliers of the needed products and services. McDonald's requires some products to be made to their specifications, but other items they purchase are the same as those available in a local supermarket.

Many of the McDonald's suppliers are internationally known companies such as Tyson, Kraft, Hunt's, Gortons, Coca Cola, Sara Lee, Vlasic, and McCormick. Others are very small operations whose major business -- and in some cases, survival -- is dependent upon McDonald's. One such firm is Quality Croutons, based in Chicago, Illinois. Quality Croutons supplies approximately 80 percent of the croutons used in McDonald's salads.

George Johnson and David Moore were contacted by the Business Development Group of McDonald's to set up the business. McDonald's was interested in having a minority-owned company supply their croutons. Backed by McDonald's, Johnson and Moore had little trouble arranging the needed financing to start the company, even though neither man had any expertise in the banking business. Although McDonald's is still the company's major customer, Quality Croutons has supplied a variety of other firms since their organization in 1986.

Interestingly, many suppliers conduct business with McDonald's on nothing more than a handshake. Suppliers' products are monitored for consistency through periodic inspection, and if the desired quality is lacking, the agreement can be terminated. But if quality is maintained, so is the relationship. The fact that agreements aren't terminated very often is a testament not only to the careful selection of suppliers by McDonald's but also to their genuine desire to have relationships succeed. If, for example, a supplier is experiencing difficulty providing McDonald's with the proper volume of a high-quality product, McDonald's management will work with the supplier to correct the problem rather than simply drop them.

Obviously, the choice of a particular supplier is most critical. Supplier selection involves the senior vice president/chief purchasing officer, the director of purchasing, and other members of management, including representatives from research and development and the business development group. Occasionally, McDonald's chooses suppliers who have sought out a business relationship with them; at other times, McDonald's seeks out existing companies that are in a position to become suppliers. If a suitable existing firm cannot be found, McDonald's will help entrepreneurs establish a business, as they did with Quality Croutons, to provide them with their needed products and services.

Questions

1. Explain the concept of derived demand as it applies to Quality Croutons and McDonald's.

____

____

____

____

____

2. Explain the concept of inelastic demand as it applies to McDonald's buying of croutons.

____

____

____

____

Source: John B. Clark. Marketing Today: Successes, Failures and Turnarounds. 2nd Edition, Prentice Hall, 1991. ABC News Business World Broadcast, 3/12/89.

TESTING TERMS AND CONCEPTS

Part One To test your understanding of the concepts presented in this chapter, write the letter of the most appropriate answer on the line next to the question number. Answers to these questions may be found at the end of this chapter.

_____ 1. In the business buying process, buyer and seller are often much __________ __________ on each other and therefore look to build __________ __________ relationships.

A. more dependent, short-term
B. less dependent, short-term
C. more dependent, long-term
D. less dependent, long-term
E. more dependent, intradependent

_____ 2. Business demand ultimately comes from the demand for consumer goods. This is known as ___________ demand.

A. latent
B. full
C. derived
D. wholesome
E. negative

_____ 3. Business buyers usually face ___________ purchasing decisions than consumers

A. more complex and more formalized
B. more complex but less formalized
C. less complex but more formalized
D. less complex and less formalized
E. none of the above

_____ 4. Margo Lane, purchasing agent for Locker Industries, found that her firm's supply of company letterhead paper was low. She reordered 10,000 sheets from her usual suppler. Lane was engaged in:

A. straight rebuy.
B. modified rebuy.
C. committee buying.
D. new task buying.
E. buying center buying.

_____ 5. The greater the cost and/or risk, the more likely the firm will engage in:

A. straight rebuy.
B. new task buying.
C. modified rebuy.
D. integrated task buying.
E. centralized purchasing.

_____ 6. As compared with consumer purchases, an organizational purchase involves ___________ buyers and more ___________ purchasing.

A. more, emotional
B. more, professional
C. fewer, emotional
D. fewer, professional
E. fewer, systems

_____ 7. ___________ buying occurs when the buyer purchases a packaged solution to the problem and therefore does not have to make all the separate decisions involved.

A. Modified rebuy
B. New task
C. Systems
D. Coordinated
E. Intradependent

_____ 8. ___________ is an approach to cost reduction in which components are carefully studied to determine if they can be redesigned or standardized or made by cheaper methods of production.

A. Value analysis
B. Vendor analysis
C. Seller analysis
D. Problem analysis
E. none of the above

_____ 9. Blanket purchase contracts, as opposed to periodic purchase orders, are becoming increasingly common for:

A. installations.
B. accessory equipment.
C. maintenance repair and operating supplies.
D. consumer goods.
E. none of the above

_____ 10. Business buyers who purchase from suppliers who also buy from them are said to practice:

A. leasing.
B. reciprocity.
C. unfair competition.
D. value analysis.
E. vendor analysis.

_____ 11. Government buying organizations are found at the __________ level.

A. federal
B. provincial
C. local
D. only (A) and (B)
E. all of the above

_____ 12. Of the following, the most complex type of business buying situation is the:

A. modified task.
B. new task.
C. modified rebuy.
D. new rebuy.
E. straight rebuy.

_____ 13. The decision-making unit of a buying organization is called its:

A. buying center.
B. purchasing committee.
C. influencers.
D. deciders.
E. gatekeepers.

_____ 14. The business marketer normally deals with ____________ ____________ buyers than the consumer marketer does.

A. more but smaller
B. fewer but smaller
C. fewer but more geographically dispersed
D. fewer but larger
E. more but larger

_____ 15. When business buyers purchase directly from producers rather than through middlemen, especially for items that are technically complex or expensive, the business buyer is engaged in ____________.

A. reciprocal buying
B. systems buying
C. new tax buying
D. direct purchasing
E. land lease purchasing

Part Two To test your understanding of the concepts presented in this chapter, respond to the following questions by writing the letter T or F on the line next to the question number if you believe the statement is true or false, respectively. Answers to these questions may be found at the end of this chapter.

_____ 1. The buying centre is not a fixed and formally identified unit within a company. Rather, it is a set of buying roles assumed by different people for different purchases.

_____ 2. An influencer is a person who affects the buying decision by helping define specifications and by providing information for evaluating alternatives.

_____ 3. Business buyers are as geographically dispersed as final consumers.

_____ 4. Reciprocity occurs when a buyer selects a supplier who in turn buys from them.

_____ 5. Supplier competition should not be considered an environmental stimulus affecting organizational buyer behaviour.

_____ 6. When a firm is buying something for the first time, it engages in modified rebuying.

_____ 7. A gatekeeper in a buying center is one who controls the flow of money to others in the decision-making process.

_____ 8. Business buyers are becoming less interested in long-term contracts with suppliers.

_____ 9. Recently some large companies have tried to recentralize rather than decentralize purchasing.

_____ 10. Interpersonal factors and group dynamics do not enter into or affect the outcome of the buying procedure.

_____ 11. The buying process begins when someone in the company recognizes a problem or need that can be met by acquiring a specific good or service. Problem recognition can result from internal and/or external stimuli.

_____ 12. One reason many companies that sell to the government have not been more marketing oriented is government spending is determined by elected officials rather than by any marketing effort to develop this market.

_____ 13. A performance review may lead a buyer to continue, modify or drop the buying arrangement.

_____ 14. Research has shown that business buyers always favour the supplier who offered the lowest price, or best product or most service and that personal factors do not influence business buyers.

_____ 15. Many business markets have inelastic demand. That is total demand for many industrial products is not much affected by price changes, especially in the short-run.

Answers

Applying Terms and Concepts

Fort McMurray Community College

1. B
2. A
3. C
4. The administrative and instructional staff of Fort McMurray Community College faced a purchasing decision that involved the gathering of considerable information from a variety of sources. This information included machine manufacturers' distributors, machine specification and capabilities, delivery dates, prices, machine setup, and so on. The buying process was conducted over several months. Also, the college had not purchased such a machine in some years and was unlikely to purchase additional machinery in the near future. Therefore, although this approximated the new-task buying process used by business firms, technically, Fort McMurray Community College used the open bid buying process.

Buffalo Express

1. modified rebuy
2. derived
3. organizational
4. economic, personal
5. Personal selling

Quality Croutons

1. Derived demand means that the demand for the organizational product -- in this case croutons -- comes from the consumer demand for salads with various toppings. In essence if there was no demand for salads in McDonald's Restaurants, there would be no demand for croutons.

2. Total demand for croutons is not much affected by price changes, especially in the short run. A drop in the price of croutons due to lower material costs, improved productivity through automation or improved distribution facilities is not likely to result in McDonald's purchasing much more. McDonald's buys what they need to meet consumer demand. If several suppliers were used and one became a lower cost supplier, McDonald's might shift buying among the suppliers, but total crouton purchases by McDonald's would remain approximately the same.

Testing Terms and Concepts

Part One

1. C M
2. C E
3. A M
4. A E
5. B D
6. B - M As compared with consumer purchases, a business purchase usually involves more buyers and more professional purchasing. Business buying is often done by trained purchasing agents who spend their work lives learning how to buy better. The more complex the purchase, the more likely that several people will participate in the decision-making process. Buying committees made up of technical experts and top management are common in the buying of major goods. Business marketers must have, therefore, well-trained salespeople.
7. C M
8. A M

9. C - D A blanket contract creates a long-term relationship in which the supplier promises to resupply the buyer as needed and at agreed prices for a set time period. The stock is held by the seller and the buyer's computer automatically prints out an order to the seller when stock is needed. Blanket contracting leads to more single-source buying and the buying of more items from that single source. This practice locks the supplier in tighter with the buyer and makes it difficult for other suppliers to break in unless the buyer becomes dissatisfied with prices or service.

10. B D
11. E E
12. B M
13. A M
14. D M
15. D D

Part Two

1. T - D The buying centre includes all members of the organization who play a role in the purchase decision process. This group includes the actual users of the product or service, those who make the buying decision, those who influence the buying decision, those who do the actual buying (purchasing agents), and those who control buying information.

2. T M
3. F E
4. T E
5. F M
6. F M
7. F D
8. F M
9. T - D In companies consisting of many divisions with differing needs, much purchasing is carried out at the division level. Recently, however, some large companies have tried to recentralize purchasing. Headquarters identifies materials purchased by several divisions and buys them centrally. Centralized purchasing gives the company more purchasing clout, which can produce substantial savings. For the business marketer, this development means dealing with fewer, higher-level buyers. Instead of using regional salesforces to sell to a large buyer's separate plants, the seller may use a national account salesforce to service the buyer.

10. F M
11. T M
12. T D
13. T E
14. F D
15. T E

CHAPTER 7

MEASURING AND FORECASTING DEMAND

CHAPTER OVERVIEW

Demand influences and is influenced by an organization's marketing efforts. This chapter describes the methods companies use to measure and forecast market demand. There are many kinds of markets to consider -- potential, available, served, and others. Companies are interested in measuring total market demand and area demand. Companies often use an environmental forecast and an industry forecast to arrive at a company sales forecast. Forecasting methods include surveys of buyer intentions, composites of salesforce opinions, opinions of experts, market tests, time-series analyses, and statistical demand analyses.

CHAPTER OBJECTIVES

When you finish this chapter, you should be able to accomplish the following:

1. Name the different ways of defining the market.
2. Discuss measuring current market demand and contrast the difference between the market-buildup method and the market factor index method.
3. List and explain several ways of forecasting future demand including a survey of buyers intentions composites of salesforce opinions or expert opinions, test marketing, time-series analysis, leading indicators and statistical demand analysis.

LECTURE/STUDENT NOTES

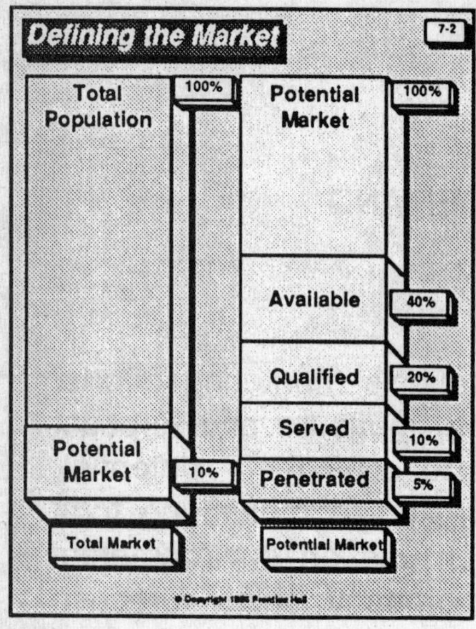

I. Defining the Market

II. Measuring Total Market Demand

A. Estimating total market demand

B. Estimating area market demand

Measuring Current Demand
7-3
Market Demand in the Specified Time Period
Market Potential
Market Forecast
Market Minimum
Planned Expenditure
Industry Marketing Expenditures
Market Demand in the Specified Time Period
Market Potential (prosperity)
Prosperity
Market Potential (recession)
Recession
Industry Marketing Expenditures

1. Market-buildup method

2. Market-factor index method

C. Estimating actual sales and market shares

III. Forecasting Future Demand

A. Survey of buyers' intentions

B. Composite of salesforce opinions

C. Expert opinion

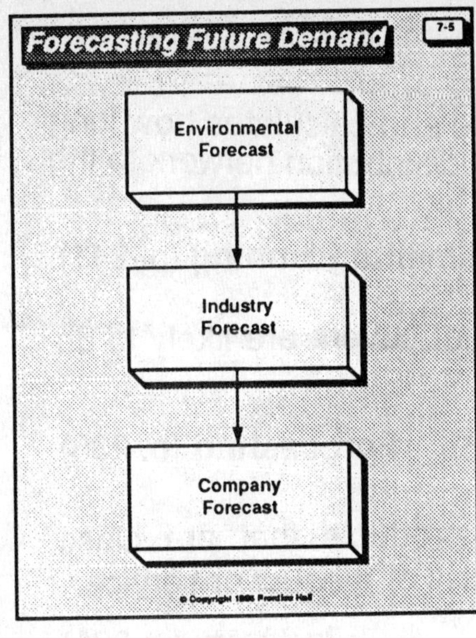

D. Test marketing

E. Time-series analysis

F. Leading indicators

G. Statistical demand analysis

KEY TERMS

A system that starts with a forecast of end-user demand and calculates how long it will take to manufacture and move products through a distribution network to the customer.

Distribution Requirements Planning (p. 241)

The art of estimating future demand by anticipating what buyers are likely to do under a given set of conditions.

Forecasting (p. 236)

A group of firms that offer a product or class of products that are close substitutes for each other. The set of all sellers of a class of product or service.

Industry (p. 231)

Time series that change in the same direction but in advance of company sales.

Leading indicators (p. 241)

The set of all actual and potential buyers of a product or service.

Market (p. 231)

A forecasting method that calls for identifying all the potential buyers in each market and estimating their potential purchases.

Market-buildup factor (p. 234)

A forecasting method that identifies market factors that correlate with market potential and combines them into a weighted index.

Market-factor index method (p. 235)

The upper limit of market demand.

Market potential (p. 232)

The level of total demand for all brands of a given product or service--for example, the total demand for motorcycles.

Primary demand (p. 232)

The demand for a given brand of a product or service.

Selective demand (p. 232)

A set of statistical procedures used to discover the most important real factors affecting sales and their relative influence; the most commonly analyzed factors are prices, income, population, and promotion.

Statistical demand analysis (p. 242)

Breaking down past sales into its trends, cycles, seasons, and erratic components, then recombining these components to produce a sales forecast.

Time-series analysis (p. 241)

The total volume of a product or service that would be bought by a defined consumer group in a defined geographic area in a defined time period in a defined marketing environment under a defined level and mix of industry marketing effort.

Total market demand (p. 232)

APPLYING TERMS AND CONCEPTS

To determine how well you understand the materials in this chapter, read each of the following brief cases and then respond to the questions that follow. Answers are given at the end of this chapter.

Clark Motors

Larry Clark is the president of Clark Motors, a network of six automotive dealerships in New Brunswick. Clark operates Chevrolet dealerships in Moncton, Riverview, and Sackville, a Pontiac/Buick dealership in Fredericton, and Toyota dealerships in Amherst and Oromacto. Each dealership operates in the black, although profits at the Toyota dealerships were limited because new automobiles were in short supply. Prior to 1990, the Toyota dealerships chronically sold out their allotment of automobiles because import quotas limited the availability of vehicles. However, with the increased availability of Toyotas, Clark estimates that he now receives approximately 150 additional Toyotas per dealership, per year.

Clark, while visiting relatives in Sydney, noticed that the community had no Toyota dealership. In fact, the majority of dealerships ignored imports, with the exception of the local Chevrolet dealership, which also sold Subarus. Clark, ever vigilant for an opportunity to make money, also noticed that an attractive building was available for sale or lease on the upper east side of Sydney located near Highway 4. It had formerly housed a Dodge dealership which had gone bankrupt in the sales slump of 1983. Clark reasoned that with minimal effort, the facility could become a Toyota dealership.

Upon returning to his base of operations in Oromacto, Clark contacted Bobby Thompson, Toyota's zone manager, about the possibility of opening a dealership if the need could be justified. Thompson indicated that Toyota would support Clark not only with automobiles, but also with advertising allowances if he (Clark) would open a Toyota dealership in the area. Clark was especially pleased to hear of the advertising allowances because past experience showed that considerable consumer demand was generated by local, as well as, regional advertising.

Clark quickly hired the market research firm of Gauthier and Nault to assess the needs for another dealership in the Sydney area and to determine the residents' interest in purchasing an imported automobile. Two weeks later, Clark also sent two of his dealership managers, three sales managers, and one business manager to the area to assess the attractiveness of the market.

Upon their return he gave them the report generated by the research firm and additional market information supplied by Toyota. He then instructed each manager to develop an estimate of sales potential for a dealership in Sydney.

Two weeks after the managers returned from Sydney, Clark brought them to Oromacto for a meeting. He instructed each manager to offer his/her estimate of sales potential and supporting rationale. Estimates of auto sales ranged from 600 to 900 vehicles per year, averaging 775. After each manager had offered their opinion, Clark instructed them to consider what the others had said. He also said he would reconvene the group in three days, when each manager would be expected to offer a revised sales estimate. During the next meeting, the estimates ranged from 640 to 830 vehicles per year, with an average of 750. Six weeks later, after financing had been arranged, a decision was made to open what eventually became Cindy Toyota (named after Clark's wife), the seventh addition to Clark's Motors.

Questions

_____ 1. Identify the factor that served to reduce Toyota sales prior to 1990.

A. consumer interest
B. access barrier
C. qualified buyers
D. available income
E. qualified available market

2. From the evidence presented in the case, it is clear that Toyota faced a(n) ___________ (expandable/nonexpandable) market.

_____ 3. Identify the approach used by Clark in forecasting the demand for automobiles in Sydney.

A. survey of buyers intentions
B. expert opinion
C. Delphi method
D. composite of salesforce opinions
E. both (B) and (C)

_____ 4. The average estimate of 750 automobiles is an example of:

A. industry sales forecast.
B. economic forecast.
C. company sales forecast.
D. market potential.
E. time-series analysis.

5. Comment on the process used by Clark in arriving at an average sales potential estimate of 750. Include in your comments, why the sales potential range of 600 to 900 with an average of 775 vehicles changed to a range of 640 to 830 vehicles with an average of 750.

____

____

____

____

____

____

____

Xenephon Corporation

The Xenephon Corporation of Saskatchewan has just developed a radical new concept in competition dune buggies. A new suspension system and drive chain provide much better acceleration and stability, while a special alloy frame gives the machine greater strength and lighter weight. Xenephon plans to charge a premium price for its offering.

The company believes that it can obtain immediate distribution in Canada, Mexico, and the U.S. Surveys indicate strong interest in an improved competition machine among residents of all three countries -- because of the popularity of the sport of dune buggy racing. The countries have stringent age and licensing requirements for competition machines.

Questions

1. Keeping in mind that potential buyers for a product or service have four characteristics: interest, income, access and qualifications, define each of the following:

   A. Potential market

   B. Available market

   C. Qualified Available market

   D. Penetrated market

Automobili Lamborghini USA

It has been said, "If you have to ask the price, you can't afford it." While that may have been true in the past, it is probably less so now. Exotic sports cars like the Lamborghini, Vector, Ferrari, Bugatti and McLaren priced to sell at 400 thousand dollars (CDN) or more are not as immune to the economy as they once were. Even the wealthy are becoming more value conscious. True, exotic sports cars are not bought for transportation, they are bought because they fit the lifestyle of the owner. They project a certain image with their seductive design and mesmerizing power.

Very few people will ever see a Lamborghini on the road and only a handful will ever purchase one. In fact, this partly adds to their mystique. But Megatech, the Indonesian investment group who recently purchased Lamborghini from Chrysler wants to change that. Lamborghini only sold 33 cars in the US in 1993, 89 in 1994 and approximately 100 in 1995. Megatech's plans are to eventually sell 1500 to 2000 units per year in the US. These ambitious sales goals will be achieved by a expanding the product line to include a sport utility vehicle in the 100 to 140 thousand dollar range and a sports sedan priced below 280 thousand dollars. Aggressive marketing techniques designed to promote customer awareness are also planned. The activities include advertising in upscale business, travel and lifestyle publications, strategic partnerships with equally upscale products and organizations and allowing auto journalists to test drive a Lamborghini for review in their publications. Lamborghini is also planning appearances at the PPG Indy Car races where prospective buyers can take one out for a test drive and perhaps run a few hot laps on the race track.

A new dealership network and lease program touted in both an advertising and direct mail program will complement other sales efforts.

Questions

1. Explain what is meant by the concept of total market demand as it applies to exotic sports cars.

___

___

___

2. What is the difference between primary demand and selective demand?

____

____

____

3. Explain why the market for Lamborghini automobiles is expandable.

____

____

____

Sources: "Even Lamborghini Must Think Marketing" *Advertising Age*, May 7, 1995, p. 4. "1995 New Cars" *Motor Trend*, October 94, p. 41. *Vector Aeromotive Corporation Annual Report*, 1995.

TESTING TERMS AND CONCEPTS

Part One To test your understanding of the concepts presented in this chapter, write the letter of the most appropriate answer on the line next to the question number. Answers to these questions may be found at the end of this chapter.

_____ 1. A(n) __________ is the set of all actual and potential buyer of a product or service.

A. industry
B. customer
C. consumer
D. market
E. market strategy

_____ 2. Companies commonly use a three stage procedure to arrive at a sales forecast. Which of the following is not one of the three major stages.

A. environmental
B. industry
C. company
D. global
E. neither A nor D

_____ 3. Those individuals who are in the market for something must exhibit which of the following characteristics:

A. interest.
B. income.
C. access.
D. only (A) and (B)
E. all of the above

_____ 4. Statistical demand analysis is a set of statistical procedures used to discover the most important factors affecting sales and their relative influence. Which of the following is not one of the factors most commonly analyzed?

A. prices
B. income
C. population
D. promotion
E. place

_____ 5. The distance between the market minimum and the market potential shows the overall:

A. total market demand.
B. sensitivity of demand.
C. area market demand.
D. market shares.
E. none of the above

_____ 6. An expandable market is one in which:

A. a high level of sales would take place without industry marketing expenditure.
B. the level of primary demand is constant.
C. total market size is affected by the level of industry marketing expenditures.
D. a company's market share is decreasing.
E. none of the above

_____ 7. Two major methods are available for estimating area market demand. The two methods are the _____________ method and the _____________ method.

A. market-build up, bottom-up
B. market-factor index and market-buildup
C. the bottom-up and top-down
D. market-factor index and top-down
E. matrix index and factor-down

_____ 8. The SIC code classifies industries according to which of the following:

A. customer group service.
B. product produced.
C. operation performed.
D. both (B) and (C)
E. all of the above

_____ 9. The demand for a particular brand of a good or service is called __________ demand.

A. primary
B. secondary
C. market
D. expandable
E. selective

_____ 10. Which of the following are reasons why salesforce estimates may need some adjustment in forecasting future demand:

A. they may be naturally pessimistic.
B. they may be naturally optimistic.
C. they may not know the company's marketing plan, which may influence sales.
D. only (B) and (C)
E. all of the above

_____ 11. In time-series analysis, the long-term underlying pattern of growth or decline in sales resulting from basic developments in population, capital formation, and technology is called:

A. slope.
B. cycle.
C. trend.
D. season.
E. erratic events.

_____ 12. The set of statistical procedures designed to discover the most important real factors affecting sales and their relative influence is called:

A. leading indicators.
B. time-series analysis.
C. statistical demand analysis.
D. market test method.
E. none of the above

_____ 13. The __________ method used to estimate area market demand calls for identifying buyers in each market and estimating their potential purchases.

A. market-factor
B. market-buildup
C. Seth-Howard
D. product-market expansion grid
E. market-penetration

_____ 14. The ____________ ____________ demand for a product or service is the total volume that would be bought by a defined consumer group in a defined geographic area in a defined time period in a defined marketing environment under a defined level and mix of industry marketing effort.

A. potential gross
B. penetrated actual
C. qualified legal
D. actual potential
E. total market

_____ 15. The J.B. Training Company forecasts sales by analyzing the cyclical, seasonal trend and erratic components of sales and then recombining these componets to produce a sales forecast. J.B. Training is using the ______________ to forecast sales.

A. Delphi technique
B. market-test method
C. time-series analysis
D. leading indicators
E. customer capture ratio method

Part Two To test your understanding of the concepts presented in this chapter, respond to the following questions by writing the letter T or F on the line next to the question number if you believe the statement is true or false, respectively. Answers to these questions are found at the end of this chapter.

_____ 1. The main characteristic which determines if an individual should be considered a customer is whether the person has sufficient income to purchase the product or service offering.

_____ 2. Before estimating total and area demand, a company will want to know the actual industry sales in its market. Thus, a company must identify its competitors and estimate their sales.

_____ 3. Time series analysis consists of breaking down the original sales into four components -- trend, cycle, environmental and erratic components then recombining these components to produce the sales forecast.

_____ 4. Markets may be expandable or nonexpandable depending upon how they are affected by the level of marketing expenditures.

_____ 5. Area market demand is defined as the total volume that would be bought by a defined consumer group in a defined geographical area in a defined time period in a defined marketing environment under a defined level and mix of industry marketing effort.

_____ 6. Organizations selling in a nonexpandable market can take the market size for granted and concentrate their marketing effort on getting a desired market share (the level of selective demand).

_____ 7. Forecasting is a fairly easy and straight forward process that results in accurate estimates of sales of both consumer and industrial goods.

_____ 8. The market-buildup method of estimating area market demand is used primarily by consumer goods firms.

_____ 9. A four-digit SIC code would yield more specific and detailed information about an industry than a two-digit code.

_____ 10. The buying power index as calculated by Sales and Marketing Magazine is based on three factors, including the area's share of the nation's discretionary income, retail sales, and population.

_____ 11. Time-series analysis and leading indicators are two methods of measuring current market demand.

_____ 12. In time-series analysis, erratic components are by definition unpredictable and should be removed from past data analysis to see the more normal behaviour of sales.

_____ 13. The more stable and predictable customer demand, the more the company needs short-term environmental forecasts and elaborate forecasting procedures for predicting company demand.

_____ 14. A leading indicator changes in the same direction, but in advance of company sales.

_____ 15. The factors most commonly analyzed during a statistical demand analysis are prices, income, population and promotion.

Answers

Applying Terms and Concepts

Clark Motors

1. B (Import Quotas)
2. expandable
3. E
4. C
5. Clark used the expert opinion method to obtain the average sales estimate of 750 vehicles. In particular, he used the Delphi method when he brought the managers in for a second meeting where the managers offered their revised sales estimates. It is probable that the sales range converged during the second meeting because each manager had the opportunity to reflect on the opinions offered by the other managers. In essence, each manager now had a broader base of information on which to base the estimate.

Xenephon Corporation

1. a. Xenephon's potential market consists of those consumers who have expressed a strong interest in their dune buggy.

   b. Xenephon's available market consists of those consumers who live in the company's three-country coverage area, are interested in a high performance dune buggy and are willing to pay Xenephon's price.

c. Xenephon's qualified available market consists of those consumers who have expressed an interest, possess the necessary purchasing power and who can meet the legal requirements for purchase.

d. Xenephon's penetrated market consists of those consumer who have all four characteristics. That is they are interested in the dune buggies, have the income to purchase them, have access to the dealership network and who also meet the age and licensing requirements.

Automobile Lamborghini USA

1. The total market demand for a product or service is the total volume that would be bought by a defined consumer group in a defined geographic area in a defined time period in a defined marketing environment under a defined level and mix of industry marketing effort. Total market demand is not a fixed number but a function of given conditions including elements of the micro and macro environments. As these elements and others such as the level and types of competitive marketing activity change, so too will the level of demand.

2. Primary demand is the total demand for all brands of exotic sports cars while selective demand is the demand for one brand such as the demand for Lamborghinis.

3. Lamborghini has had a fairly steady increase in the sale of automobiles since Megatech purchased the company from Chrysler Corporation in 1994. The increase in selective demand for Lamborghini Automobiles can be attributed at least in part to an increase in marketing expenditures. Therefore, as Lamborghini and the other exotic sports car manufacturers increase their maketing expenditures, the total market demand can be expected to increase. Whether it will increase to the level that would allow Lamborghini to realize its eventual goal of selling 1,500 to 2,000 units a year in the US is debatable and remains to be seen.

Testing Terms and Concepts

Part One

1. D E
2. D D
3. E E
4. E D

5. B D
6. C M
7. B - M Companies face the problem of selecting the best sales territories and allocating their marketing budget optimally among these territories. Therefore, they need to estimate the market potential of different territories. Two major methods are available: the market-buildup method, which is used primarily by industrial goods firms, and the market-factor index method, which is used primarily by consumer goods firms.
8. D D
9. E E
10. E M
11. C D
12. C M
13. B M
14. E M
15. C M

Part Two

1. F M
2. T M
3. F D
4. T E
5. F D
6. T M
7. F - E Forecasting is the art of estimating future demand by anticipating what buyers are likely to do under a given set of conditions. However, very few products or services lend themselves to easy forecasting. Those that do generally involve a product with steady sales or sales growth in a stable competitive situation. But most markets do not have a stable total and company demand, so good forecasting becomes a key factor in company success. Poor forecasting can lead to overly large inventories, costly price markdowns, or lost sales due to being out of stock. The more unstable the demand, the more the company needs accurate forecasts and elaborate forecasting procedures.
8. F M
9. T E
10. F D
11. F M

12. T D
13. F M
14. T E
15. T D

CHAPTER 8

MARKET SEGMENTATION, TARGETING AND POSITIONING FOR COMPETITIVE ADVANTAGE

CHAPTER OVERVIEW

This chapter discusses one of the key concepts in modern marketing strategy: focusing marketing efforts on subsegments of the total market (target marketing), rather than trying to appeal to the entire market with one product (mass or undifferentiated marketing). The first step in target marketing is market segmentation, dividing the total market into submarkets that might merit different products or marketing mixes. Bases for segmenting consumer markets include geographic, demographic, and other variables. Good market segments are measurable, accessible, substantial, and actionable. After identifying these segments, firms must decide whether to go after the mass market, develop separate marketing mixes for several market segments, or focus on one or a few submarkets. Once the targeting strategy has been chosen, the firm must decide how to position its products in consumers' minds, relative to the positions of competing products.

CHAPTER OBJECTIVES

When you finish this chapter, you should be able to accomplish the following:

1. Explain market segmentation and identify several possible bases for segmenting consumer markets, business markets and international markets.
2. List and distinguish among the requirements for effective segmentation, measurability, accessibility, substantiality and actionability.
3. Outline the process of evaluating market segments and suggest some methods for selecting market segments.
4. Illustrate the concept of positioning for competitive advantage by offering specific examples.
5. Discuss choosing and implementing a positioning strategy and contrast positionings based on product, service personnel and image differentiation.

LECTURE/STUDENT NOTES

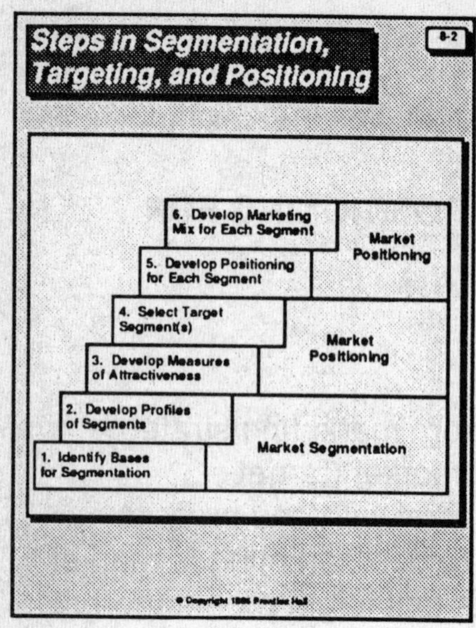

I. Markets

II. Market Segmentation

A. Bases for segmenting consumer markets

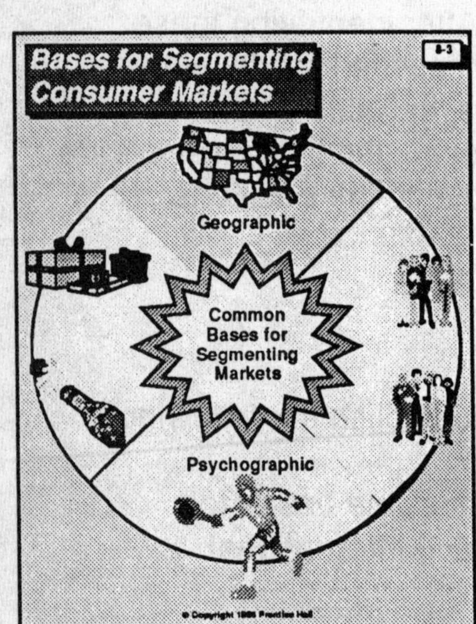

1. Geographic segmentation

2. Demographic segmentation

3. Psychographic segmentation

4. Behavior segmentation

B. Segmenting business markets

C. Segmenting international markets

D. Requirements for effective segmentation

III. Market Targeting

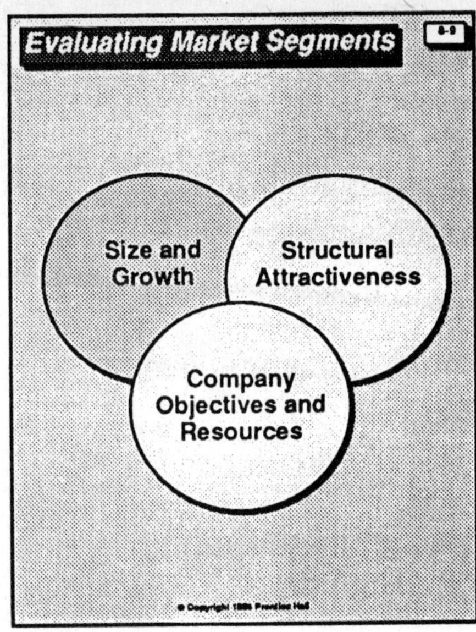

A. Evaluating market segments

1. Segment size and growth

2. Segment structural attractiveness

3. Company objectives and resources

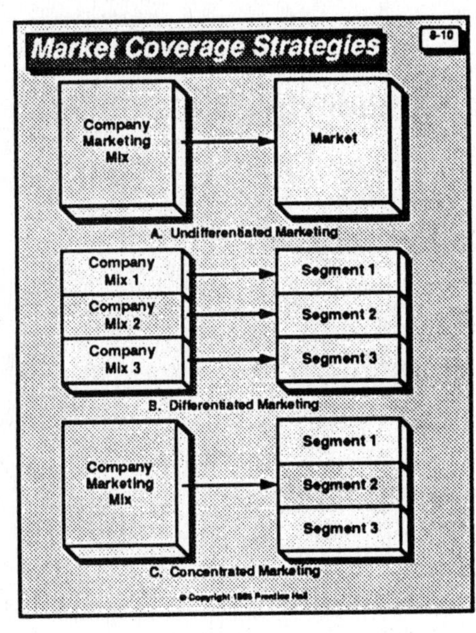

B. Selecting market segments

1. Undifferentiated marketing

2. Differentiated marketing

3. Concentrated marketing

4. Choosing a market coverage strategy

IV. Positioning for Competitive Advantage

A. What is market positioning?

B. Positioning strategies

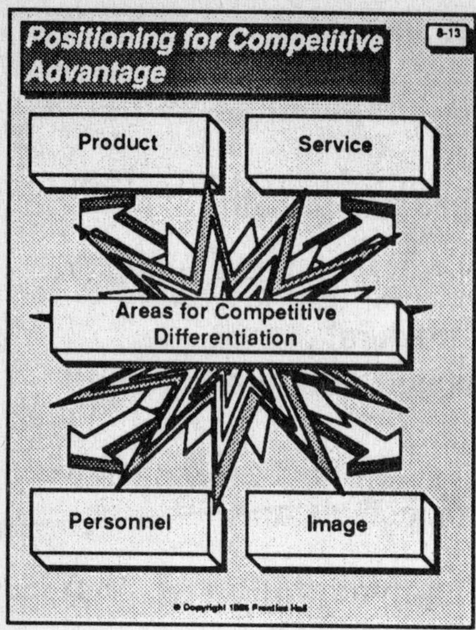

C. Choosing and implementing a positioning strategy

1. Identifying possible competitive advantages

2. Selecting the right competitive advantage

3. Communicating and delivering the chosen position

KEY TERMS

Dividing a market into different age and life-cycle groups.

Age and life-cycle segmentation (p. 255)

Dividing a market into groups based consumer knowledge, attitude, use, or response to a product.

Behavioural segmentation (p. 258)

Dividing the market into groups according to the different benefits that consumers seek from the product.

Benefit segmentation (p. 259)

An advantage over competitors gained by offering consumers greater value, either through lower prices or by providing more benefits that justify higher prices.

Competitive advantage (p. 272)

A market-coverage strategy in which a firm goes after a large share of one or a few submarkets.

Concentrated marketing (p. 269)

Dividing the market into groups based on demographic variables such as age, sex, family size, family life cycle, income, occupation, education, religion, race, and nationality.

Demographic segmentation (p. 255)

A market-coverage strategy in which a firm decides to target several market segments and designs separate offers for each.

Differentiated marketing (p. 268)

Dividing a market into different groups based on sex.

Gender segmentation (p. 256)

Dividing a market into different geographical units such as nations, states, regions, countries, cities or neighborhoods.

Geographic segmentation (p. 254)

Dividing a market into different income groups.

Income segmentation (p. 257)

Forming segments of consumers who have similar needs and buying behavior even though they are located in different countries.

Intermarket segmentation (p. 264)

Formulating competitive positioning for a product and a detailed marketing mix.

Market positioning (p. 251)

Dividing a market into distinct groups of buyers with different needs, characteristics, or behavior who might require separate products or marketing mixes.

Market segmentation (p. 251)

Evaluating each market segment's attractiveness and selecting one or more segments to enter.

Market targeting (p. 251)

A form of target marketing in which companies tailor their marketing programs to the needs and wants of narrowly defined geographic, demographic, psychographic, or behavioral segments.

Micromarketing (p. 251)

Dividing the market into groups according to occasions when buyers get the idea to buy, actually make their purchase, or use the purchased item.

Occasion segmentation (p. 258)

The way the product is defined by consumers on important attributes--the place the product occupies in consumers' minds relative to competing products.

Product position (p. 271)

Dividing a market into different groups based on social class, lifestyle, or personality characteristics.

Psychographic segmentation (p. 257)

A set of buyers sharing common needs or characteristics that the company decides to serve.

Target market (p. 266)

A market-coverage strategy in which a firm decides to ignore market segment differences and go after the whole market with one offer.

Undifferentiated marketing (p. 266)

APPLYING TERMS AND CONCEPTS

To determine how well you understand the materials in this chapter, read each of the following brief cases and then respond to the questions that follow. Answers are given at the end of this chapter.

Crew Toothpaste

Michel Joudrey, a chemist by trade, began mixing his own toothpaste three years ago after being bothered by sensitive teeth and sore gums. He had tried commercially available toothpastes especially formulated for sensitive teeth, but he found that even the most popular pastes -- Sensodyne and Promise -- were of little help. He began to neglect his dental hygiene and in time his teeth also became stained from coffee and tobacco.

As his teeth and gums became increasingly sensitive, Joudrey tried a number of folk remedies. He was surprised to find that aloe, a gel extracted form the Aloe Vera plant, was quite effective in reducing pain during brushing. Looking for a more convenient method of application, Joudrey formulated his own toothpaste by combining aloe with flavoring and most of the other ingredients found in regular toothpaste. Jedra also added a polishing agent to help his toothpaste brighten teeth.

Joudrey passed samples of his paste to friends who had similar dental complaints. Based upon their very favourable responses. Joudrey, at the age of 54, retired from his position at DuPont Research Laboratories to devote his energies to promoting his toothpaste, which we called "Crew."

After desiging an attractive package, Joudrey ordered 400,000 tubes and cartons and hired a company to manufacture and pack the toothpaste. Without benefit of an advertising budget or the blessing of the Canadian Dental Association, Joudrey began to call on wholesalers who serviced drugstore chains and supermarkets. He also called on the health and beauty aid buyers of discount department stores. Distributors at first were hesitant to stock the product, but after reviewing the testimonials Joudrey produced, they agreed to handle Crew if he would advertise it and agree to buy back any unsold tubes.

Crew sells for $3.89 for a 150 ml tube, about twice as much as other "sensitive teeth" toothpastes. Crew is intended for those people who have sensitive teeth, canker sores, fever blisters, or sensitive gums and/or stained teeth.

To almost everyone's amazement, Crew is selling well. Crew is currently stocked in over 700 stores in Ontario and Quebec, including such well-known chains as Shoppers Drug Mart, Pharmasave and Jean Coutu.

Research conducted by Joudrey indicates that most customers prefer Crew over Sensodyne because of Crew's polishing agent, which brightens their teeth without irritation. Customers do admit, however, that they do occasionally buy Sensodyne because of its lower cost.

Although Joudrey had recently begun to make a profit on his investment, he decided to spend the money on advertising. His new campaign will stress Crew's superiority to Sensodyne, the leader of the market.

Questions

_____ 1. Michel Joudrey was practicing which philosophy of marketing?

A. mass marketing
B. product-differentiated marketing
C. selling differentiated marketing
D. target marketing
E. market penetration

_____ 2. The loyalty status of Crew's customers may be used to segment the market. Loyalty status is an example of ____________ segmentation.

A. behavioristic
B. psychographic
C. demographic
D. geographic
E. socialistic

_____ 3. The placement of Crew toothpaste in 700 stores indicates that which requirement for effective segmentation has been met?

A. substantiality
B. measurability
C. accessibility
D. actionability
E. marketability

_____ 4. Which market coverage alternative is Joudrey pursuing?

A. concentrated marketing
B. differentiated marketing
C. undifferentiated marketing
D. mass marketing
E. hybrid marketing

The Colliers

Linda and Miles Collier have decided to bottle and market their own shampoo. They want to distribute this first variety as widely as possible and have therefore, avoided labeling it "natural" or "organic," even though it is. If this brand is successful, they would like to experiment with other formulas for more specialized varieties of shampoos.

Questions

_____ 1. At this stage, Linda and Miles are practicing what kind of marketing?

A. concentrated marketing
B. test marketing
C. differentiated marketing
D. undifferentiated marketing
E. hybrid marketing

_____ 2. Linda maintains that a shopper selects shampoo with one of two possible objectives in mind: one is to get hair very clean and shiny; the other is to condition and protect. If Linda and Miles were to produce and market shampoos according to this distinction, they would have segmented the market on the basis of:

A. age.
B. buyer readiness.
C. benefits.
D. social class.
E. income.

_____ 3. Miles insists that their first step in product differentiation should be to manufacture shampoos for dry, normal, and oily hair types. He maintains that teenagers prefer shampoo for oily hair and thinks that the oily hair segment can even be defined as the 15- to 17-year old age group. If Miles and Linda decide to target a market segment defined in this way, the segment will be useful because it will have all of the following qualities <u>except:</u>

A. measurability.
B. actionability.
C. originality.
D. accessibility.
E. marketability.

_____ 4. Sometimes Linda tells Miles that she would like to work exclusively with herbs and wildflowers and devote their resources to capturing a dominant share of the "natural and organic" market segment. If Linda and Miles were to do this, they would be practicing:

A. concentrated marketing.
B. differentiated marketing.
C. environmental marketing.
D. undifferentiated marketing.
E. hybrid marketing.

Eldin Incorporated

Marjorie Miele, a former vice-president of marketing at General Dynamics of England, was often dismayed at the clutter on her desk. The paperwork was bad enough, she reasoned, but the telephone, calculator, and rolodex file only contributed to the lack of order.

Miele informally researched the problem and found that she was not alone in her thoughts about the need to have a more organized desk. She left General Dynamics to start Eldin Incorporated. After engaging in a formal research project where she studied the office equipment needs of executives, Miele found a definite need for a desk top organizer. Her solution to the problem was the Mark 3 Execusystem.

The Mark 3 Incorporated the more cumbersome office devices into a single unit. The system, which looked much like a desk blotter had a built-in digital clock with alarm and calendar. Other components of the Mark 3 included a radio, calculator, computerized file system, and a telephone with an automatic dialer. The telephone was a "hands-free" model with a "mute" button, ideal for those conference calls where occasional privacy was needed while conferring with other people in the office. The Mark 3 was 60 x 100 cm, weighed 6 kilograms, and was made of black leather with nickel trim.

The profile of potential customers included the following characteristics: college educated, married, male, age 35-49, title of vice president or director, and income over $100,000 a year.

The selling price of the Mark 3 was $685.00 and she calculated her first year break-even point to be 425 units. The potential demand was may times this number as she planned to market the product using mail-order world wide utilizing the Globe and Mail and the Financial Post to advertise. Competition at this level was nonexistent. While many companies produced executive desk products, not one had the features of the Mark 3.

Questions

_____ 1. In the case, Miele determined that the market segment was large enough to be served at a profit. This market met which of the following requirements for effective market segmentation?

A. measurability
B. accessibility
C. substantiality
D. actionability
E. originality

_____ 2. The customer profile developed by Miele is made up of _______ characteristics.

A. geographic
B. demographic
C. psychographic
D. behavioristic
E. socialistic

_____ 3. Which market coverage strategy is Miele pursuing?

A. undifferentiated marketing
B. differentiated marketing
C. concentrated marketing
D. mass marketing
E. hybrid marketing

_____ 4. Miele had designed the Mark 3 to provide those benefits identified and desired by her intended target market. Which basic variable has she used in segmenting this market?

A. geographic
B. demographic
C. psychographic
D. behavioristic
E. socialistic

_____ 5. Which stage of marketing is Eldin Incorporated operating at?

A. mass marketing
B. product differentiated marketing
C. target marketing
D. undifferentiated marketing
E. hybrid marketing

TESTING TERMS AND CONCEPTS

Part One To test your understanding of the concepts presented in this chapter, write the letter of the most appropriate answer on the line next to the question number. Answers to these questions may be found at the end of this chapter.

_____ 1. The process whereby the seller distinguishes between market segments, selects one or more of these segments, and develops products and marketing mixes tailored to each segment is called ____________ marketing.

A. mass
B. target
C. product variety
D. customer-differentiated
E. service

_____ 2. Target marketing calls for three major steps; which of the following is not one of these steps?

A. market positioning
B. market segmentation
C. product segmentation
D. market targeting
E. both (B) and (C)

_____ 3. Which of the following is not one of the typical bases for segmenting consumer markets?

A. geographic
B. socialistic
C. psychographic
D. behaviour
E. both (B) and (C)

_____ 4. Loyalty status is an example of a __________ segmenting dimension.

A. geographic
B. socialistic
C. psychographic
D. behaviour
E. demographic

_____ 5. Many marketers believe that __________ variables are the best starting point for constructing market segments.

A. geographic
B. socialistic
C. psychographic
D. behaviour
E. economic

_____ 6. Benefit segmentation requires determining

A. the major benefits people look for in the product class.
B. the kinds of people who look for each benefit.
C. the major brands that deliver preferred benefits.
D. both (A) and (C)
E. all of the above

_____ 7. __________ is the degree to which effective programs can be designed for attracting and serving the segments.

A. Measurability
B. Accessibility
C. Substantiality
D. Actionability
E. Marketability

_____ 8. A product's market position is determined the way a product is defined by the ____________ on important attributes.

A. customer
B. producer
C. wholesaler
D. retailer
E. reseller

_____ 9. Accessibility, as a requirement for effective segmentation, refers to the degree to which:

A. the segments can be effectively reached and served.
B. which segments are large and profitable enough.
C. an effective program can be formulated for attracting and serving the segments.
D. the size and purchasing power of the segments can be measured.
E. the individuals making up the market segment can be identified and studied.

_____ 10. If a firm decided to ignore market segment differences and to go after the entire market with one market offer, the firm is practicing ____________ marketing.

A. differentiated
B. undifferentiated
C. concentrated
D. target
E. macro

_____ 11. Concentrated marketing:

A. involves higher than normal risks.
B. results in higher than normal costs.
C. involves going after a small share of a large market.
D. both (A) and (C)
E. all of the above

_____ 12. Differentiated marketing:

A. occurs when a firm decides to operate in several segments of the market and designs separate offers to each.
B. may lead to higher sales than undifferentiated marketing.
C. may lead to higher costs than undifferentiated marketing.
D. only (B) and (C)
E. all of the above

_____ 13. When evaluating international market segments, marketers should consider which of the following factors?

A. economic
B. political and legal
C. cultural
D. only (A) and (B)
E. all of the above

_____ 14. Which type of marketing occurs when a company produces two or more products that exhibit different features, styles, sizes, quality and so on, in an effort to offer variety to buyers rather than to appeal to different market segments?

A. mass marketing
B. target marketing
C. product variety marketing
D. economic marketing
E. service marketing

_____ 15. If a firm selects the same segment as the competitors, it should:

A. immediately seek a segment in which there is no competition.
B. expect to lose money.
C. employ an undifferentiated marketing strategy.
D. seek to stress attributes which give it a competitive advantage.
E. both (A) and (C)

Part Two To test your understanding of the concepts presented in this chapter, respond to the following questions by writing the letter T or F on the line next to the question number if you believe the statement is true or false, respectively. Answers to these questions may be found at the end of this chapter.

_____ 1. Mass marketing is designed to offer variety to buyers rather than appealing to different market segments.

_____ 2. Today's companies are moving away from mass marketing and product variety marketing toward target marketing.

_____ 3. Target marketing and market targeting are identical concepts.

_____ 4. Most sellers find it worthwhile to customize their products to satisfy each specific buyer.

_____ 5. Demographic segmentation variables include age, gender, family life cycle, and family life style.

_____ 6. People within the same demographic group can exhibit very different psychographic profiles.

_____ 7. Market segmentation involves dividing a market into distinct groups of buyers who might call for separate products or marketing mixers.

_____ 8. Multivariate demographic segmentation suggests that while a market segment may exhibit many variables, a marketer should concentrate on a single variable for segmentation purposes.

_____ 9. Business markets can be segmented with many of the same variables used in consumer market segmentation.

_____ 10. Undifferentiated marketing strategies are often defended on the grounds of cost effectiveness.

_____ 11. Differentiated marketing creates lower total sales than undifferentiated marketing.

_____ 12. Concentrated marketing occurs when a firm goes after a large share of one or a few submarkets.

_____ 13. There is no single best way for a marketer to segment a market.

_____ 14. When segmenting international markets, marketers can be sure that different countries that are close together often do not vary much in their economic, cultural and political make up.

____ 15. When evaluating different market segments, a firm must look at three factors: segment size and growth, segment structural attractiveness and company objectives and resources.

Answers

Applying Terms and Concepts

Crew Toothpaste

1. D
2. A
3. C
4. A

The Colliers

1. D
2. C
3. C
4. A

Eldin Incorporated

1. C
2. B
3. C
4. D
5. C

Testing Terms and Concepts

Part One

1. B M
2. C E
3. B M
4. D M
5. D D
6. E D
7. D M
8. A - E The products position is the way the product is defined by consumers or important attributes -- the place the product occupies in consumers' minds relative to competing products. Therefore, a product's position is the complex set of perceptions, impressions and feelings that consumers hold for the product as compared with competing products. Marketers do not leave these products' position to chance. Rather, they plan positions that will give their products the greatest advantage in selected target markets and they design marketing mixes to create the planned position.
9. A D
10. B M
11. A M Concentrated marketing is appealing when company resources are limited. Instead of going after a small share of a large market, the firm goes after a large share of one or a few submarkets. Through concentrated marketing, the firm

achieves a strong market position in the segments it serves because of its greater knowledge of segment needs and the special reputation it acquires. And it enjoys many operating economics because of specialization in production distribution and promotion. If the segment is well chosen, the firm can earn a high rate of return on its investment. At the same time, time, concentrated marketing involves higher than normal risks. The particular market segment may turn sour or larger competitors may decide to enter the same segment. For these reasons, many companies prefer to diversify in several market segments.

12. E M
13. E E
14. C D
15. D E

Part Two

1. F E
2. T - M Organizations that sell to consumer and business markets recognize that they cannot appeal to all buyers in those markets -- or at least not to all buyers in the same way. Buyers are too numerous, too widely scattered, and too varied in needs and buying practices. And different companies vary widely in their abilities to serve different segments of the market. Thus, each company has to identify the parts of the market that it can serve best and then develop products and marketing mixes tailored to the specific market segment.
3. F M
4. F E
5. F E
6. T M
7. T M
8. F D
9. T E
10. T M
11. F M
12. T M
13. T E
14. F M
15. T D

CHAPTER 9

DESIGNING PRODUCTS: PRODUCTS, BRANDS, PACKAGING AND SERVICES

CHAPTER OVERVIEW

As the title of this chapter indicates,"product" has many aspects. A product is anything that can be offered to a market, not just tangible objects. Product characteristics lead to several different classification schemes that are useful for marketing strategy development. Brands add value to products and benefit buyers, sellers, and society, but brand decisions and developing good brand names are complex and difficult. Packaging, which is sometimes considered to be a separate element of the marketing mix, both protects and helps to sell the product. Labels identify products, provide information required by law, and perform other functions; companies should pay attention to keeping their labels modern and competitive. Customer service decisions, also part of product strategy, are based on customers' expectations and competitors' service levels. A company must also decide on the length of its product lines and the composition of its product mix.

CHAPTER OBJECTIVES

When you finish this chapter, you should be able to accomplish the following:

1. Define the term product including the core actual and augmented product.
2. Explain product classifications and contrast the differing types of consumer products and industrial products.
3. Outline the range of individual product decisions marketers make discussing the product attributes of quality, features and design.
4. Discuss branding and contrast the differences among line extensions, brand extensions, multibrands and new brands.

5. Illustrate product line and product mix decisions describing stretching and filling the product line length, line modernization, line featuring and line width.

6. List some of the considerations marketers face in making international product decisions, including whether or not to standardize or adapt product and packaging.

LECTURE/STUDENT NOTES

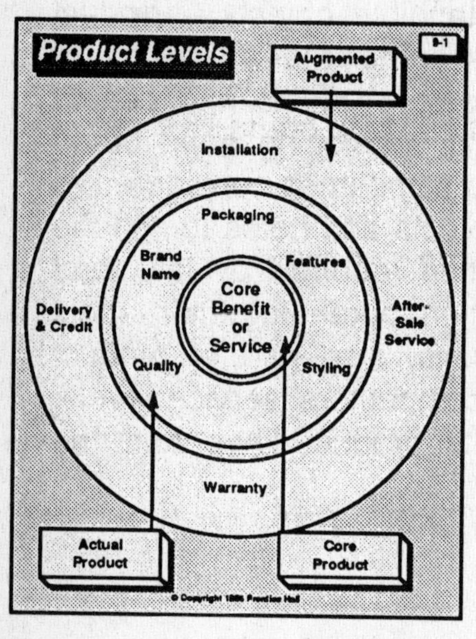

I. What is a product?

II. Product Classifications

A. Consumer Products

B. Industrial products

III. Individual Product Decisions

A. Product attributes

1. Product quality

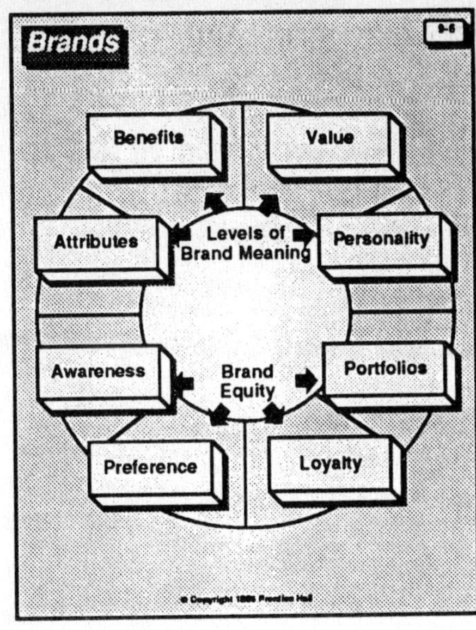

2. Product features

3. Product decision

B. Branding

1. What is a brand?

2. Brand equity

3. To brand or not to brand

Major Brand Decisions

To Brand or Not to Brand
Brand
No Brand

Brand Name Selection
Selection
Protection

Brand Sponsor
Manufacturer's Brand
Private Brand
Licensed Brand

Brand Strategy
New Brands
Line/Brand Extensions
Multibrands

Brand Repositioning
Brand Repositioning
No Brand Repositioning

4. Brand name selection

5. Brand sponsor

6. Brand strategy

7. Brand repositioning

C. Packaging

D. Labeling

IV. Product Line Decisions

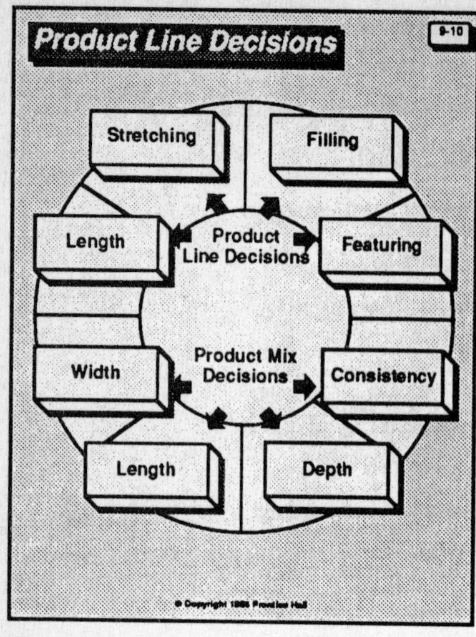

A. Product line length

1. Stretching downward

2. stretching upward

3. stretching both ways

4. filling in the product line

B. Product line modernization

C. Product line featuring

V. Product Mix Decisions

VI. International Product Decisions

KEY TERMS

A product's parts, quality level, features, design, brand name, packaging, and other attributes that combine to deliver core product benefits.

Actual product (p. 291)

Additional consumer services and benefits built around the core and actual products.

Augmented product (p. 291)

A name, term, sign, symbol, or design, or a combination of these intended to identify the goods or services of one seller or group of sellers and differentiate them from those of competitors.

Brand (p. 299)

The value of a brand, based on the extent to which it has high brand loyalty, name awareness, perceived quality, strong brand associations, and other assets such as patents, trademarks, and channel relationships.

Brand equity (p. 300)

Using a successful brand name to launch a new or modified product in a new category.

Brand extension (p. 309)

Industrial products that partly enter the finished product, including installations and accessory equipment.

Capital items (p. 294)

The practice of using the established brand names of two different companies on the same product.

Co-branding (p. 307)

Products bought by final consumers for personal consumption.

Consumer products (p. 292)

Consumer products that the customer usually buys frequently, immediately, and with a minimum of comparison and buying effort.

Convenience goods (p. 292)

The problem-solving services or core benefits that consumers are really buying when they obtain a product.

Core product (p. 290)

Products bought by individuals and organizations for further processing or for use in conducting a business.

Industrial products (p. 293)

Using a successful brand name to introduce additional items in a given product category under the same brand name, such as new flavors, forms, colors, added ingredients, or package sizes.

Line extension (p. 308)

A brand created and owned by the producer of a product or service.

Manufacturer's brand [or national brand] (p. 304)

Industrial goods that enter the manufacturer's product completely, including raw materials and manufactured materials and parts.

Materials and parts (p. 293)

A strategy under which one seller develops two or more brands in the same product category.

Multibranding (p. 310)

The activities of designing and producing the container or wrapper for a product.

Packaging (p. 311)

What the package should be or do for the product.

Packaging concept (p. 312)

A brand created and owned by a reseller of a product or service. Also known as a middleman, distributor or store brand.

Private brand [or store brand] (p. 304)

Anything that can be offered to a market for attention, acquisition, use, or consumption and that might satisfy a want or need. It includes physical objects, services, persons, places, organizations, and ideas.

Product (p. 290)

The process of designing a product's style and function: creating a product that is attractive, easy, safe, and inexpensive to use and service, and simple and economical to produce and distribute.

Product design (p. 298)

A group of products that are closely related because they function in a similar manner, are sold to the same customer groups, are marketed through the same types of outlets, or fall within given price ranges.

Product line (p. 316)

The set of all product lines and items that a particular seller offers for sale to buyers.

Product mix [or product assortment] (p. 319)

The ability of a product to perform its functions. It includes the product's overall durability, reliability, precision, ease of operation and repair, and other valued attributes.

Product quality (p. 295)

Services that augment actual products.

Product-support services (p. 315)

Any activity or benefit that one party can offer to another party that is essentially intangible and does not result in the ownership of anything.

Services (p. 290)

Consumer goods that the customer, in the process of selection and purchase, characteristically compares on such basis as suitability, quality, price and style.

Shopping product (p. 293)

Payments demanded by retailers from producers before they will accept new products and find "slots" for them on the shelves.

Slotting fees (p. 304)

Consumer products with unique characteristics or brand identification for which a significant group or buyer is willing to make a special purchase effort.

Specialty product (p. 293)

Industrial products that do not enter the finished product at all.

Supplies and services (p. 294)

Consumer products that the consumer either does not know about or knows about but does not normally think of buying.

Unsought products (p. 293)

APPLYING TERMS AND CONCEPTS

To determine how well you understand the materials in this chapter, read each of the following brief cases and then respond to the questions that follow. Answers are found at the end of this chapter.

Ajax Supermarkets

Several Ajax supermarkets have been located in upper-class neighbourhoods throughout the Toronto area for over 35 years. Ajax enjoys an excellent reputation for a wide range of high-quality, high-priced, difficult-to-find food items, and it caters almost exclusively to the upper-income market segment. The number of supermarkets in the Toronto area has been increasing steadily, and Ajax has experienced a slowing in its growth trend. Dollar sales are up significantly, but unit volume is only slightly ahead of last year in most of the Ajax locations in established neighbourhoods, and profit margins have been squeezed.

Management is considering a number of alternatives as possible remedies. One of these is the establishment of the Ajax brand name on several product lines. Ajax has carried only the highest-quality national brands in the past, and there is some question in the minds of two members of the management committee about whether the use of a private label would be appropriate in Ajax's prestige stores. Another possibility under review is the addition of generic lines. During the last meeting of the management committee it was pointed out that the lower prices of generics have a strong appeal to consumers during inflationary times. The attraction is even stronger during recessions when there is high unemployment. Furthermore, profit margins on the generics could be expected to be about the same as the current average, with only slightly reduced quality that would be barely detectable by consumers.

Questions

_____ 1. The alternatives being considered deal with:

A. brand repositioning.
B. product line stretching.
C. the depth of the product line.
D. brand extension decisions.
E. both (A) and (C)

_____ 2. If the generic labels are added, this would be a(n):

A. augmentation of the core product.
B. blanket family name.
C. downward stretch in the product line.
D. widening of the product line.
E. none of the above

_____ 3. The decision to add or not to add generics concerns not only quality considerations, but also considerations regarding the:

A. core product offered by Ajax.
B. consistency of the product line.
C. products that must be deleted to make room for the new line.
D. classification of the generic line.
E. breadth of the product line.

_____ 4. What is the proper decision for Ajax regarding the addition of generic products?

A. Add them -- this will broaden its market.
B. Adding generics is a line-filling decision that will not broaden the market but will create an opportunity to sell more to the existing market.
C. Generics should increase sales, but will not add much to profit margins.
D. The addition of generics is a bad idea because it may damage the company's prestige reputation.
E. none of the above

_____ 5. The addition of a private brand with the Ajax label would:

A. damage the quality image Ajax has built over many years.
B. offer the company an opportunity to capitalize on its reputation and widen profit margins.
C. only reduce profit margins even further.
D. attract another market segment.
E. both (A) and (C)

Irish Shoes

James O'Donovan is president of Irish Shoes, a Kelowna, BC distributor of specialty athletic shoes. Three years ago O'Donovan was a centre for the University of British Columbia Thunderbirds. He spent two seasons at that position until serious foot and ankle injuries ended his career. It seems that the constant running, jumping, and dead stops placed excessive pressure on his back, legs, and feet. This ultimately resulted in permanent damage which surgery could not correct.

In discussing his problems with Dr. H. N. Woofe, a prominent Canadian podiatrist, O'Donovan learned that the type of difficulty he suffered was quite common, although usually not so severe, in the athletic community. Collegiate tennis, basketball, and football players, in addition to track and field athletes, were very susceptible to the problem. Dr. Woofe also mentioned that amateur joggers were also coming to her complaining of foot and leg problems.

With Dr. Woofe and her two partners providing technical advice and financial backing, O'Donovan developed a unique athletic shoe. The sole of the shoe contains a polyurethane pad, partially filled with mineral oil. There is sufficient resilience within the pad to prevent it from bursting on impact from the foot as the wearer runs and jumps. The pads essentially act as shock absorbers, significantly reducing impact and so pressure on the legs, feet, and back.

O'Donovan called his creation the Irish Shoe. To further distinguish it from the inevitable competitors, he designed a symbol of an eagle in flight, and had it made as a blue rubber implant into the sole of the shoe.

The shoe sells for $140, about the price of other quality shoes; its acceptance has been phenomenal. In only six months, O'Donovan has nearly sold out his initial factory runs of 5,000 pairs. He has since placed another order for 2,000 pairs from his manufacturer in Italy. Irish shoes are distributed throughout Canada -- although on a very limited basis in all provinces -- by independent shoe stores. Store managers indicate that it is not unusual for shoe store patrons to drive over 160 kilometres to a store which stocks the shoes and to ask for them by name.

Although the shoe was originally intended for athletes, distributors have noted that approximately 60 percent of sales have been to nonathletes. In fact, senior citizens are the most avid fans of the shoe. This has O'Donovan and the podiatrists working on designs for shoes more appropriate for work settings and leisure activities.

Questions

_____ 1. The comfort provided by the Irish Shoe is an example of a _____________ product.

A. core
B. augmented
C. tangible
D. intangible
E. actual

_____ 2. The shoe itself is an example of a(n) _____________.

A. nondurable good
B. durable good
C. service
D. intangible
E. convenience

_____ 3. The fact that customers drive many kilometres to a store which carries the shoe and ask for it by name indicates that this shoe has achieved _____________ goods status for those customers.

A. convenience
B. homogeneous shopping
C. heterogeneous shopping
D. specialty
E. unsought

_____ 4. The Blue Eagle implant, which has come to symbolize Irish Shoes, is an example of:

A. brand.
B. brand name.
C. brand mark.
D. trademark.
E. both (A) and (C)

_____ 5. Irish Shoes is an example of a _____________ brand.

A. manufacturer
B. private
C. national
D. dealer brand
E. both (B) and (D)

<u>Martha Hamel</u>

Martha Hamel was in her third year of high school when her father lost his job. His employer was closing the carpet manufacturing plant in Windsor, where he worked as a weaver. Martha's father, George, had spent 29 years working at the plant and at the age of 53, was out looking for another job. His employer had moved south to Mexico with its cheaper labour and more favourable tax structure. George was offered an opportunity to move south with his employer, but family concerns made that option unworkable. George decided he would make the best of his situation but without much of a formal education, and manufacturing plants either closing or downsizing, his prospects were not promising.

Martha never forgot the effect the plant closing had on her father. This once proud and fiercely independent man was suddenly racked by self doubt. His sense of self worth was shaken and his ability to provide for his family uncertain. George shielded his family from most of the problem but the strain was evident. George ultimately did land a position with another firm, but Martha decided she would do what she could to take control over her life. So if she were ever faced with a situation like her father's, she would have greater flexibility than he had had. Control for Martha meant a university education. Eight years later, Martha had earned a B. Comm (Accounting) from Laurier, an MBA in Marketing from Queen's and a Chartered Accountants designation.

Questions

1. When Martha chose to pursue an education, she ultimately realized the product she was buying existed on three levels. Explain how a university degree exists on each of the following levels.

   a. core product: ____

   ____

   ____

   ____

b. actual product: ______________________________

____

____

____

____

c. augmented product: ______________________________

____

____

____

____

2. Discuss the implications of your answer to the final question, for university administratrators.

____

____

____

____

____

TESTING TERMS AND CONCEPTS

Part One To test your understanding of the concepts presented in this chapter, write the letter of the most appropriate answer on the line next to the question number. Answers to these questions are found at the end of this chapter.

_____ 1. A product may be a(n):

A. physical object.
B. idea.
C. place.
D. only (A) and (B)
E. all of the above

_____ 2. A product may be thought about on three levels. Which of the following is not one of those levels?

A. augmented
B. core
C. fragmented
D. actual
E. both (A) and (C)

_____ 3. Product mix ____________ refers to how many different product lines the company carries.

A. consistency
B. depth
C. length
D. width
E. lining

_____ 4. Goods that the consumer, in the process of selection and purchase, characteristically compares on such bases as suitability, quality, price, and style are called ____________ goods.

A. shopping
B. specialty
C. unsought
D. convenience
E. emergency

_____ 5. David Martin is an avid beer drinker. The only type of beer he drinks, however, is Molson beer. Molson beer, for David, should be considered a(n) ____________ good.

A. shopping
B. specialty
C. unsought
D. convenience
E. emergency

_____ 6. The classification system for industrial goods is based upon:

A. how they enter the production process.
B. their relative cost.
C. how they are purchased.
D. both (A) and (B)
E. all of the above

_____ 7. Goods that enter the manufacturer's product completely are called ____________.

A. capital items
B. supplies and services
C. materials and parts
D. accessory equipment
E. expense items

_____ 8. A manufacturers' brand is also known as a ____________ brand.

A. national
B. dealer
C. private
D. distributor
E. trade

_____ 9. A good package may:

A. protect the product.
B. promote the product.
C. raise total distribution costs.
D. lower total distribution costs.
E. all of the above

_____ 10. Brand repositioning may require changing:

A. the product.
B. the image of the product.
C. consumer perceptions of the product.
D. only (B) and (C)
E. all of the above.

_____ 11. A brand-____________ strategy is any effort to use a successful brand name to launch new or modified products.

A. modification
B. extension
C. commercialization
D. augmentation
E. repositioning

_____ 12. Brand quality is one of the marketer's major positioning tools. Quality, therefore, should be measured in terms of __________ perceptions.

A. manufacturer's
B. consumer's
C. dealer's
D. competitor's
E. legislator's

_____ 13. At the very least, a label should __________ the product or brand.

A. describe
B. grade
C. identify
D. promote
E. protect

_____ 14. A product-__________ is a group of products that are closely related because they function in a similar manner, are sold to the same customer groups, are marketed through the same type of outlets or fall within given price ranges.

A. group
B. market
C. lead
D. line
E. stretch

_____ 15. While many people would suggest that branding benefits society as a whole; which of the following is not necessarily one of the benefits of branding?

A. Branding leads to higher and more consistent product quality.
B. Branding increases innovation by giving producers an incentive to look for new features that can be protected against imitating competitors.
C. Branding results in more product variety and choice for consumers.
D. Branding creates status consciousness and increases the prices of goods and services.
E. Branding increases shopper efficiency because it provides more information about products and where to buy them.

Part Two To test your understanding of the concepts presented in this chapter, respond to the following questions by writing the letter T or F on the line next to the question number if you believe the statement is true or false, respectively. Answers to these questions are found at the end of this chapter.

_____ 1. Marketers should attempt to sell the benefits of a product and not just its features.

_____ 2. The core product is the most fundamental level and answers the question, "What is the customer really buying?"

_____ 3. The classification system for consumer goods is based on how the good is to be used by the customer.

_____ 4. The distinction between a consumer good and an industrial good is based on the purpose for which the product is purchased.

_____ 5. Supplies and services are industrial goods that do not become part of the final product.

_____ 6. The intent of "generics" is to bring down the cost of the product for the consumer by saving on packaging and advertising.

_____ 7. Brands serve to decrease shopper efficiency because they are too numerous.

_____ 8. Product augmentation is wasteful -- it leads to higher prices without increasing consumer satisfaction.

_____ 9. A disadvantage of private brands is that they often result in a lower profit margin than manufacturer brands.

_____ 10. A brand extension strategy is any effort to use a successful brand name to launch product modifications or new products.

_____ 11. A desirable quality of a brand name is that it should be distinctive.

_____ 12. Product line stretching occurs when a company lengthens its product beyond its current range.

_____ 13. A slotting fee is a payment demanded by retailers from producers before they will accept new products and find "slots" (room) for them on the shelves.

_____ 14. The downward stretch of a product line does not carry the risk that new low-end items may damage the reputation and/or sales of higher-end items.

_____ 15. International marketers must first figure out what products to introduce in which countries, and then they must decide how much to standardize or adopt their products for world markets.

Answers

Applying Terms and Concepts

Ajax Supermarkets

1. B
2. C
3. A
4. D
5. B

Irish Shoes

1. A
2. B
3. D
4. E
5. E

Martha Hamel

1. a. The core product identifies what the customer is really buying. In this situation Martha is acquiring the means to control her professional life. Her education will give her the flexibility to pursue a variety of opportunities as she wishes. Her degrees will provide significant earning potential and personal as well as professional satisfaction. Martha's education also provided her with specific technical skills which have enhanced her critical thinking, problem solving and decision making and communication skills. Her conceptual and human skills were also more developed as a result of her education. Martha might say the prestige associated with her graduation from the various colleges is also part of the core product.

b. The actual product would be the degrees earned from each university. The university name and reputation and level of degree would further identify her accomplishment.

c. The augmented product would be the variety of services and activities provided by the colleges and universities which enhanced her educational experience. These might have included counseling, financial aid, library, computer facilities, housing, placement, clubs and organizations, social and cultural events (concerts, speakers and sporting events). These services and activities add quality, texture and variety and are designed to enrich the educational experience.

2. University administrators must realize they are selling a product, just as their competition is doing. When students choose to attend a particular school, they are really buying a total product. The more administrators understand what students really need, want, and demand, the more they will be able to offer these prospective students and distinguish themselves from the competition.

Testing Terms and Concepts

Part One

1. E E
2. C E
3. D M
4. A M
5. B - M Specialty goods are consumer goods with unique characteristics or brand identifications for which a significant group of buyers is willing to make a special purchase effort. Buyers normally do not compare specialty goods. Also, they typically will not accept any substitute for the product they are interested in purchasing.
6. D M
7. C E
8. A E
9. E M
10. E M
11. B D
12. B M

13. C E
14. D D
15. D D

<u>Part Two</u>

1. T E
2. T E
3. F - M Consumer goods are those bought by final consumers for personal consumption. Consumer goods include convenience, shopping, specialty and unsought goods. This classification is based on consumer shopping habits -- that is how the consumer actually shops for and buys the product.
4. T E
5. T M
6. T E
7. F M
8. F - D A product is more than a simple set of tangible features. In fact, some products (a haircut or a doctor's exam) have no tangible features at all. Consumers tend to see products as complex bundles of benefits that satisfy their needs. When developing products, marketers must first identify the <u>core</u> consumer needs that the product will satisfy. They must then design the <u>actual</u> product and find ways to <u>augment</u> it in order to create the bundle of benefits that will best satisfy consumers.
9. F M
10. T M
11. T E
12. T M
13. T D
14. F D
15. T M

CHAPTER 10

DESIGNING PRODUCTS: NEW PRODUCT DEVELOPMENT AND PRODUCT LIFE-CYCLE STRATEGIES

CHAPTER OVERVIEW

Few products last forever, and companies must continually develop new products to replace aging ones. This first part of this chapter describes an eight-step procedure for developing new products: idea generation, development, business analysis, product development, test marketing, and commercialization. The second part describes typical marketing strategies at each product life cycle stage that follows product development: introduction, growth, maturity, and decline.

CHAPTER OBJECTIVES

When you finish this chapter, you should be able to accomplish the following:

1. Identify the challenge companies face in creating a new product development strategy.
2. List different sources for idea generation and discuss how an idea moves ahead through idea screening, concept development and concept testing.
3. Outline how a potential product advances from a concept to a product through market strategy development, business analysis and product development.
4. Explain the purpose of test marketing and distinguish among standard, controlled and simulated test markets.
5. Evaluate the product life cycle theory, detailing the extent to which you accept the sequence of the introduction, growth, maturity and decline stages.

LECTURE/STUDENT NOTES

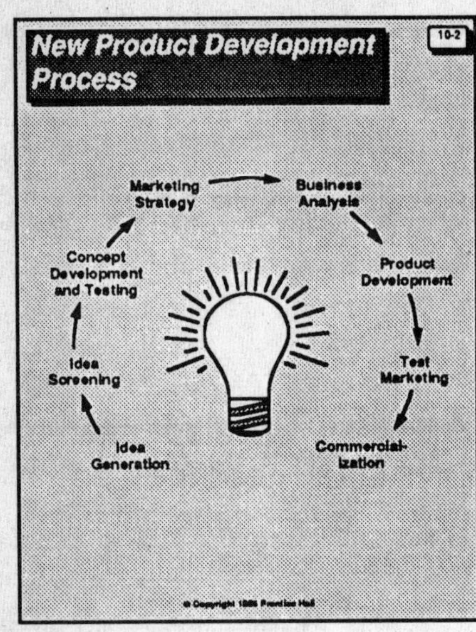

I. New-Product Development Strategy

A. New Product Success and Failure

B. The New Product Dilemma

II. The New-Product Development Process

A. Idea Generation

1. Internal Sources

2. Customers

3. Competitors

4. Distributors, Suppliers, and Others

B. Idea Screening

C. Concept Development and Testing

1. Concept Development

2. Concept Testing

D. Marketing Strategy Development

E. Business Analysis

F. Product Development

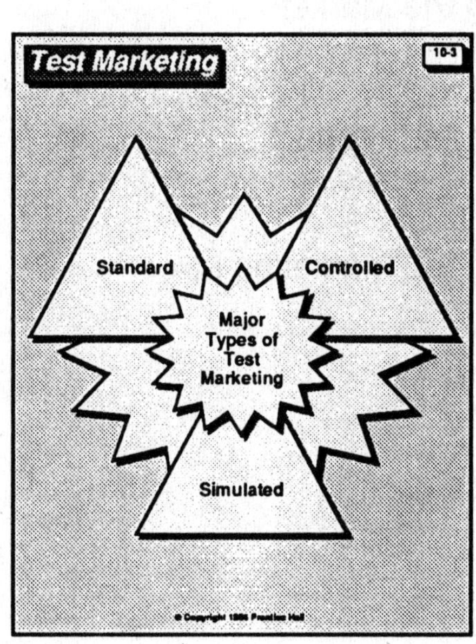

G. Test Marketing

1. Standard Test Markets

2. Controlled Test Markets

3. Simulated Test Markets

4. Test marketing Business Products

H. Commercialization

I. Speeding Up New-Product Development

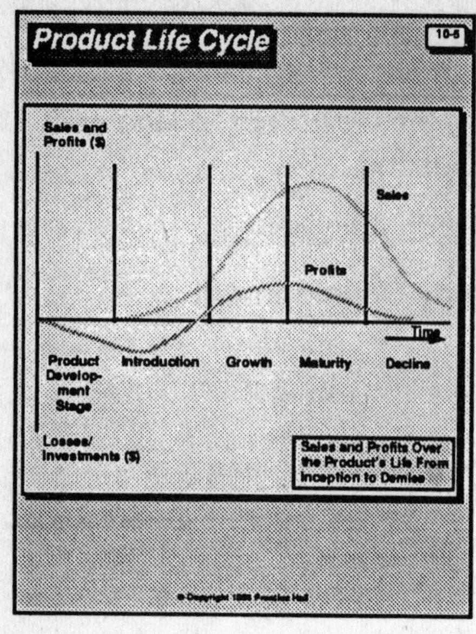

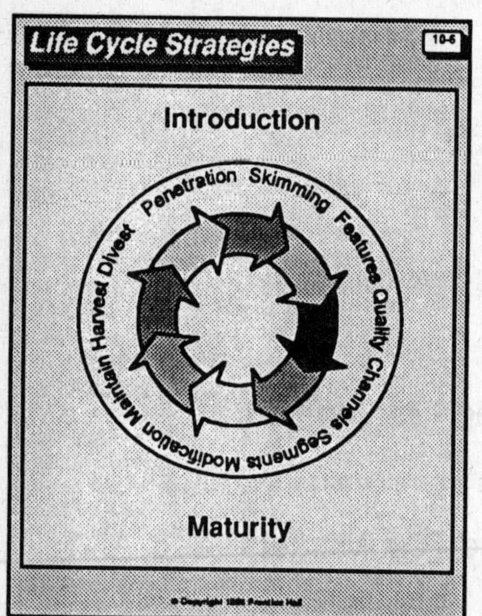

III. Product Life-Cycle Strategies

A. Introduction Stage

B. Growth Stage

C. Maturity Stage

1. Modifying the Market

2. Modifying the Product

3. Modifying the Marketing Mix

D. Decline Stage

KEY TERMS

A review of the sales, costs, and profit projections for a new product to find out whether these factors satisfy the company's objectives.

Business analysis (p. 341)

Introducing a new product into the market.

Commercialization (p. 344)

Testing new product concepts with a group of target consumers to find out if the concepts have strong consumer appeal.

Concept testing (p. 339)

The product life-cycle stage at which a product's sales decline.

Decline stage (p. 353)

Fashions that enter quickly, are adopted with great zeal, peak early, and decline very fast.

Fad (p. 349)

A currently accepted or popular style in a given field.

Fashion (p. 348)

The product life cycle stage at which a product's sales start climbing quickly.

Growth stage (p. 350)

The systematic search for new-product ideas.

Idea generation (p. 336)

Screening new product ideas in order to spot good ideas and drop poor ones as soon as possible.

Idea screening (p. 337)

The product life-cycle stage when the new product is first distributed and made available for purchase.

Introduction stage (p. 349)

Designing an initial marketing strategy for a new product based on the product concept.

Marketing strategy development (p. 340)

The stage in the product life cycle where sales growth slows or levels off.

Maturity stage (p. 350)

The development of original products, product improvements, product modifications, and new brands through the firm's own R & D efforts.

New-product development (p. 333)

The idea that consumers will favor products that offer the most quality, performance and features and that the organization should therefore devote its energy to making continuous product improvements. A detailed version of the new-product idea stated in meaningful consumer terms.

Product concept (p. 338)

A strategy for company growth by offering modified or new products to current market segments. Developing the product concept into a physical product in order to assure that the product idea can be turned into a workable product.

Product development (p. 341)

The course of a product's sales and profits over its lifetime. It involves five distinct stages: product development, introduction, growth, maturity, and decline.

Product life cycle (PLC) (p. 348)

A new-product development approach in which one company department works individually to complete its stage of the process before passing the new product along to the next department and stage.

Sequential product development (p. 346)

An approach to developing new products in which various company departments work closely together, overlapping the steps in the product-development process to save time and increase effectiveness.

Simultaneous product development (p. 348)

A basic and distinctive mode of expression.

Style (p. 348)

The stage of new-product development where the product and marketing program are tested in more realistic market settings.

Test marketing (p. 342)

APPLYING TERMS AND CONCEPTS

To determine how well you understand the materials in this chapter, read each of the following brief cases and then respond to the questions that follow. Answers are at the end of the chapter.

Scented Disc Player

The House of Butler, a perfume maker and subsidiary of the William Schwab Corporation, is selling a device it calls "The Newest Horizon in Home Entertainment." The device is called the Scented Disc Player.

The player, which costs about $25, is a box about the size of a portable radio (30 cm wide, 35 cm long, and 8 cm high). The discs are scented pads nearly identical in size to a 45 RPM record. When slipped into the player, a scent is given off as the disc is heated. Each "play" lasts about two minutes, but the aroma from the play may linger for as long as an hour.

The company currently offers 50 scents, including Spring Garden, Ocean Mist, Spruce, Locker Room, and Arousal. Butler believes that virtually any scent can be reproduced and plans to introduce many more as the market builds. A long-play disc can give up to 100 plays and cost approximately $7, while a short-play disc costs $2, but gives only 15 plays. Butler has been working on the device for three years. It acquired the rights to the player from an inventor who wishes to remain anonymous.

After significant development work in the laboratory, the device was introduced on a trial basis in June 1994 in three markets. Information gathered from these markets in Winnipeg, St. John's and Sudbury, which led Butler to decide on the final selling price, promotional campaign, and distribution strategy. Information from these markets also led to development of the long-play disc.

The company is limiting distribution of the player to 300 stores this fall so it won't be treated as a fad. It is now in national distribution and is currently being sold in such stores as Eaton's and The Bay. Sales at this point are relatively low and profits are negligible as Butler builds its distribution system and heavily promotes the device. Competition currently is nonexistent and Butler expects to turn a profit in the upcoming Christmas selling season.

Questions

_____ 1. The idea for the Scented Disc Player came from:

A. internal source.
B. customers.
C. competition.
D. suppliers.
E. another source.

_____ 2. The Scented Disc Player is currently in the ____________ stage of its life cycle.

A. introduction
B. growth
C. maturity
D. decline
E. market modification

_____ 3. The Scented Disc Player is an example of a product ____________. (class or form)

_____ 4. The introduction of the long-playing disc is an example of:

A. product modification.
B. market modification.
C. commercialization.
D. concept development.
E. test marketing.

_____ 5. The introduction of the Scented Disc Player in the Idaho, Louisiana, and Georgia markets is an example of:

A. commercialization.
B. business analysis.
C. product development.
D. market testing.
E. market penetration.

Lunenberg Yacht

Howard Nelson, a sailing enthusiast and crew member on the Defiant Racing Yacht, recently completed work on what he calls "A New Concept in Racing." His new AC-4 is a one-person, 15-foot fiberglass sailboat that is a one-fourth, scale version of the traditional racing yachts that compete in the Americas' Cup races.

His craft, which is suitable for sailors of all ages and levels of experience, is the result of four years of design and test work by his company, Lunenberg Yacht, located in Lunenberg, NS. The boat features a semi-horizontal cockpit which allows the sailor to steer via a foot lever, leaving hands free to work the sail control lines, which are conveniently placed in front of the helmsman. Another unique feature of the AC-4 is that Boom swing is not a problem on this lightweight boat (250 kg plus 160 kg of removable ballast), as only the sailor's head is above deck.

Nelson pooled ideas from amateur and experienced sailors as well as from dealer/distributors and design engineers before arriving at the final version of the AC-4. After significant testing in the laboratory and in the field for stability, safety, ease of handling, and positioning of the rigging, Nelson produced and sold a limited number of boats this summer at Hancock's Marina in Halifax, Nova Scotia, to gauge customer and dealer reaction.

Based on the success of the Hancock Marina experience, he plans to introduce the boat to marina dealers at the Montreal Boat Show in March. He has also determined that with a selling price of $4,800 on a cost of $3,900, his break-even point will be 200 boats, assuming his current fixed and variable costs do not change appreciably. Sales projections, however, are for a minimum of 250 boats in the coming year. Nelson has further determined that if demand begins to exceed his productive capability of 300 boats per year, the price of the AC-4 will be raised to $5,400.

Questions

_____ 1. The testing of the AC-4 in the laboratory and field for stability, safety, ease of handling and positioning of rigging is an example of ____________ testing.

A. functional
B. consumer
C. market
D. concept
E. viability

_____ 2. When Nelson decided to introduce the AC-4 to marina owners at the Montreal Boat Show in March, he decided on the _____________ step in the new product development process.

A. market test
B. commercialization
C. product development
D. market strategy
E. market development

_____ 3. Lunenberg Yacht was engaged in _____________ when the AC-4 was sold on a limited basis at Hancock's Marina in Halifax, Nova Scotia, the summer before introduction at the Montreal Boat Show.

A. concept testing
B. product development
C. consumer testing
D. market testing
E. idea screening

_____ 4. The review of estimated sales, costs, break-even, and profit projections are part of the _____________ stage of the new product development process.

A. market strategy development
B. market analysis
C. concept analysis
D. business analysis
E. commercialization

_____ 5. The AC-4 is currently in the _____________ stage of its life cycle.

A. market modification
B. growth
C. introduction
D. product modification
E. marketing-mix modification

Oat Bran

Everyone seems to be selling it, and we've all heard it over and over again that oat bran can lower cholesterol levels. But a study detailed in the *New England*

Journal of Medicine says it's not necessarily so. This prompts the question: Is oat bran good for your health or not?

Judging by the number of new oat bran cereals introduced in the last few years, cereal manufacturers suggest the answer is yes. Kellogg, with approximately 40 percent of the ready-to-eat cereal market, recently introduced Heartwise, Common Sense Oatbran, S. W. Graham, Nut and Honey, Crunch Biscuits, Oatbake, and Golden Crunch Mueslix for health-conscious consumers. General Mills, holding a 27 percent share of the market, has introduced Benefit; Ralston Purina with 5 percent of the market, has put out Oatbran Options; Nabisco, with 6 percent of the market, has introduced Wholesome and Harty, a hot breakfast cereal; and Quaker Oats Company, with 8 percent of the market, has brought out a new ready-to-eat version of its Quaker Oatbran. (It should be noted that Heartwise and Benefit also contain an exotic grain called psyllium, which like oat bran, is being hailed as a cholesterol reducer, and that S. W. Graham is made from whole-wheat flour, both ingredients are aimed at health-conscious consumers.)

Consider the impact the oat bran mania has had on one cereal alone. General Mills' Cheerios is now the most popular cereal in the United States, having replaced Kellogg's Frosted Flakes. Cheerios gained a startling 3.1 percentage points in market share (from 6.2 to 9.9 percent in just 12 -- with each percentage point worth $66 million in revenues. General Mills has benefited enormously from the oat bran craze -- more so than Kellogg, because while 20 percent of Kellogg's cereals are made with oats, 40 percent of General Mills cereals are.

Oat bran was a manufacturer's dream come true. Consumers loved it -- not for the taste, but because research suggested you could eat it and reduce your cholesterol level and the chance you would get heart disease. Cereal makers loved it for the profits to be made, and farmers loved it because it increased the demand for their grain. The demand for oat bran increased by 800 percent in 1988 alone, and the growth has been sustained. In 1989, sales of all oat bran products totaled over $1 billion. It seems that high-fiber food is the hottest craze to hit supermarket shelves in years.

There is now some evidence that rice bran and corn bran also have cholesterol-reducing properties. Although this evidence is preliminary and far from conclusive, it might stimulate the market for these grains as well.

But what of the oat bran study reported in the *New England Journal of Medicine*, which concluded that "Oat-bran has little cholesterol-lowering effect and that high-fiber and low-fiber dietary grain supplements reduce serum cholesterol levels about equally, probably because they replace dietary fats." Dr. Timothy Johnson of *ABC News* makes these points: (1) A low-fat diet is extremely important in lowering cholesterol, and the extent to which oat bran contributes to this is debatable; (2) despite the criticism raised by the *New England Journal of Medicine* study of some of the hype about oat bran, it is a nutritious food worth eating in moderation; (3) the benefit of grain fiber, both soluble and insoluble, on the gastrointestinal tract is considerable -- perhaps decreasing the risk of several ailments, including colon cancer.

So the answer to the question posed appears to be: If consumers substitute oat and oat bran products for cheese and eggs and other foods that are high in cholesterol, they will succeed in lowering their cholesterol level -- but through the substitution effect rather than through any independent cholesterol-lowering benefit from oat bran.

Questions

1. What typically happens during the market maturity stage of the product life cycle?

____

____

____

____

____

2. Explain how cereal manufacturers could modify the market, the product or the marketing mix to stimulate sales during the market maturity stage of the product life cycle.

   a. The market: ______________________________

   ____

   ____

   ____

   ____

   b. The product: ______________________________

   ____

   ____

c. The marketing mix: ____________________________

3. If oat bran is found to have no unique ability to lower cholesterol levels, what is likely to happen to those products whose main attribute is oat bran?

Sources: "Big G Is Growing Fat on Oat Cuisine," *Business Week*, September 18, 1989, p. 29; "Kellogg Pours It On," *Advertising Age,* August 28, 1989, pp. 1, 52; "Cereal Makers Roll More Oats," *Advertising Age*, March 6, 1989, p. 34; "Comparison of the Effects of Oat Bran and Low-Fiber Wheat on Serum Lipoprotein Levels and Blood Pressure," *The New England Journal of Medicine*, January 18, 1990, pp. 147-152; "Kellogg Pours Out More New Cereals," *Advertising Age*, July 25, 1988, pp. 2, 66; and "The Next Wave of High Fiber Grains," *U.S. News & World Report*, May 22, 1989, p. 73 and "Does Oat Bran Work?", *ABC News, Nightline Broadcast,* January 17, 1990.

TESTING TERMS AND CONCEPTS

Part One To test your understanding of the concepts presented in this chapter, write the letter of the most appropriate answer on the line next to the question number. Answers to these questions are at the end of this chapter.

_____ 1. Which of the following is typically not considered a reason why new products fail?

A. The idea for the product is good, but the market has been underestimated.
B. A product has been incorrectly positioned in a market.
C. Top management pushes through a favorite idea in spite of negative market research findings.
D. Unexpected competition is encountered.
E. All of the above.

_____ 2. The greatest number of new product ideas come from:

A. customers.
B. company internal sources.
C. competitors.
D. company external sources (distributors and suppliers).
E. investors and patent attorneys.

_____ 3. Simulated test marketing:

A. takes longer to complete than standard test marketing.
B. are much more expensive than controlled test marketing.
C. does not allow competitors to get a look at the companies new product.
D. is best used at trade shows.
E. does not allow management to project national sales.

_____ 4. A product concept is:

A. an idea for a product that the company can see itself offering to the market.
B. the particular picture consumers acquire of an actual or potential product.
C. a detailed version of the idea expressed in meaningful terms.
D. all of the above
E. none of the above

_____ 5. In launching a new product, a company must make several decisions. Which of the following is not a decision it makes during commercialization?

A. when (timing)
B. where (geographic strategy)
C. to whom (target market prospects)
D. what (product form)
E. how (introductory marketing strategy)

_____ 6. A product life cycle can describe a:

A. product class.
B. product form.
C. brand.
D. only (A) and (B)
E. all of the above

_____ 7. Identify the proper order of a typical life cycle:

A. introduction, growth, maturity, decline.
B. introduction, maturity, growth, decline.
C. introduction, decline, maturity, growth.
D. decline, introduction, growth, maturity.
E. introduction, maturity, decline, disposal.

_____ 8. Product ____________ is a period of rapid market acceptance and increasing profits.

A. development
B. introduction
C. growth
D. maturity
E. decline

_____ 9. In using a ____________ modification strategy during the maturity stage of the product life cycle, the company is attempting to increase consumption of the current product.

A. market
B. product
C. market mix
D. quality improvement
E. competition

_____ 10. A ____________ is a currently accepted or popular style in a given field whose sales curve is similar to that of a typical product.

A. fashion
B. style
C. fad
D. product form
E. product class

_____ 11. During the maturity stage of the life cycle, profits are ____________ while sales are ____________.

A. growing
B. declining, holding steady
C. growing, slowing
D. declining, slowing or declining
E. holding steady, growing

_____ 12. The number of competitors is typically greatest during the __________ stage of the product life cycle.

A. introduction
B. growth
C. maturity
D. decline
E. market modification

_____ 13. A strategy of quality improvement which aims at increasing product performance is an aspect of ____________ modification.

A. feature
B. style
C. price
D. market
E. product

_____ 14. Under the ____________ product development approach to new product development, one company department works individually to complete its stage of the process before passing the new product along to the next department and stage.

A. internal
B. interdepartmental
C. simultaneous
D. intradepartmental
E. sequential

____ 15. The purpose of the idea screening stage of the new product development process is:

A. to identify good ideas.
B. to generate as many ideas as possible.
C. to drop poor ideas.
D. both (A) and (C)
E. all of the above

Part Two To test your understanding of the concepts presented in this chapter, respond to the following questions by writing the letter T or F on the line next to the question number if you believe the statement is true or false, respectively. Answers to these questions are at the end of this chapter.

____ 1. One way in which a company can obtain new products is through acquisition--that is, buying a company, a patent, or a license to produce someone else's product.

____ 2. Research has found that the new product failure rate for consumer goods exceeds the failure rate of industrial products.

____ 3. Successful new product development may be even more difficult in the future because of growing social and governmental constraints.

____ 4. Distributors and suppliers are typically not regarded as a valuable source of new product ideas.

____ 5. Marketing strategy is both a cause and result of the product life cycle.

____ 6. Harvesting a declining product refers to gradually reducing market support in order to increase short run profits.

____ 7. The Simms Corporation has greatly improved the safety of its electric hedge trimmers. This action would be an example of the strategy of feature improvement.

_____ 8. Market testing is the stage when the product and marketing program are introduced into more realistic market settings.

_____ 9. Product classes have a shorter life cycle than product forms.

_____ 10. During the growth stage of the product life cycle sales and profits peak and begin to decline due to the growing numbers of competitors.

_____ 11. During the introduction stage of the product life cycle, profits are negative or low because of low sales and heavy distribution and promotion expenses.

_____ 12. Once a product has begun its life cycle, typically a firm can do little to extend it.

_____ 13. Functional tests are conducted under laboratory and field conditions to make sure the product performs safely and effectively.

_____ 14. When a product has reached the decline phase of its life cycle, it should be automatically dropped.

_____ 15. Top management should carefully define and communicate its new product development strategy to company personnel after the new product development process has begun so as not to prejudice the process and stifle creativity.

Answers

Applying Terms and Concepts

Scented Disc Player

1. E
2. A
3. Form
4. A
5. D

Lunenberg Yacht

1. A
2. B
3. D
4. D
5. C

Oat Bran

1. During the market maturity stage of the product life cycle, sales typically slow down because many producers are selling the product. Overcapacity leads to greater competition. Competitors begin marking down prices and increasing their advertising and sales promotions. They may also increase their research and development budgets to find better versions of the product. Usually, these steps lead to a drop in profits, and some of the weaker competitors withdraw.

2. a. Through market modification, the manufacturer tries to increase the consumption of the product by looking for new users and market segments. The firm would also look for ways to increase usage among current customers, or it might reposition the brand to appeal to a larger or faster-growing market segment -- in this case, health-conscious consumers.

   b. Using product modification, the manufacturer could increase the amount of oat bran in its cereals to attract new users and more usage.

   c. Marketing-mix modification means the manufacturer would try to improve sales by changing one or more marketing-mix elements. Prices could be cut to attract new users and competitors' customers. A new advertising campaign highlighting changes in the product and/or new research could be launched. Aggressive sales promotion -- trade deals, coupons, gifts, and contests -- could be used. The company could also seek new distribution channels, such as mass merchandisers, to move the product.

3. If oat bran is found to have no unique ability to lower cholesterol levels, what is likely to happen to those products whose main attribute is oat bran? It is likely that certain brands of cereal will quickly move through the growth and maturity stages of the product life cycle to the sales decline stage. Sales and profits will continue to decline; competition will be reduced as some firms pull their product from the market; and the minimal amounts will be spent to promote the product, which will remain essentially unchanged. The strategic focus will be on improving productivity in view of a low cash flow. Eventually, many of the brands of cereal could be pulled from the market.

Testing Terms and Concepts

Part One

1. A E
2. B E
3. C M
4. C - M Ideas which survive the idea screening stage of the new product development process must be developed into product concepts. It is important, however, to distinguish between a product idea, a product concept and a product image. A product idea is an idea for a possible product that the company can see itself offering to the market. A product concept is a detailed version of the idea stated in meaningful consumer terms. A product image is the way consumers perceive an actual or a potential product.
5. D M
6. E E
7. A E
8. C E
9. A D
10. A - M The product life cycle concept can be applied to styles, fashions and fads. A style is a distinctive mode of expression which once invented may last for generations coming in and out of vogue. A fashion is a currently accepted or popular style in a given field. Fashions tend to grow slowly, remain popular for a while, then decline slowly. Thus one fashion gives way to another. Fads, on the other hand, are fashion that enter quickly, are adopted with great zeal, peak early and decline very fast. Fads tend to last only a short time and attract a very limited following.
11. D M
12. C M
13. E D
14. E D
15. D E

Part Two

1. T E
2. F E
3. T M
4. F E

5. T - M The current position of a product in its life cycle suggests the best marketing strategies to develop and implement. The resulting strategies, then affect product performance in later stages of the life cycle. Thus, marketing strategy becomes both a cause and an effect of the product life cycle.

6. T E
7. T D
8. T M
9. F D
10. F M
11. T E
12. F - M Competition and the changing nature of the market will force the marketer to engage in market modification, product modification or marketing mix modification. Effective manipulation of the marketing mix elements can significantly extend the product's life cycle.

13. T D
14. F M
15. F D

CHAPTER 11

PRICING PRODUCTS: PRICING CONSIDERATIONS AND APPROACHES

CHAPTER OVERVIEW

This chapter discusses factors to consider in setting prices, along with general approaches to pricing. Marketers must consider internal factors (objectives, marketing mix strategies, costs, and organizational considerations) and external factors (the nature of the market, demand, competition, and other environmental factors) in making pricing decisions. Product costs set the floor on prices, and consumer perceptions set the ceiling. These factors lead to cost-based pricing approaches and consumer-based pricing in which the prices that competitors charge, or that a company thinks competitors might charge, have a large influence on the company's prices.

CHAPTER OBJECTIVES

When you finish this chapter, you should be able to accomplish the following:

1. Outline the factors affecting pricing decisions, especially marketing objectives, marketing mix strategy, costs and organizational considerations.
2. Identify and define external factors affecting pricing decisions, including the effects of market and demand, competitors' costs, prices and offers, and other external factors.
3. Contrast the differences in general pricing approaches and be able to distinguish among cost plus and target profit pricing, value based pricing and going rate and sealed bid pricing.

LECTURE/STUDENT NOTES

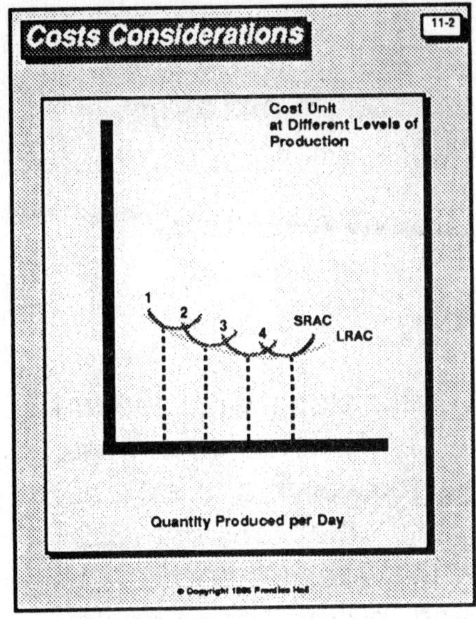

I. Factors to Consider When Setting Prices

A. Internal factors affecting pricing decisions

1. Marketing objectives

2. Marketing mix strategy

3. Costs

4. Organizational consideration

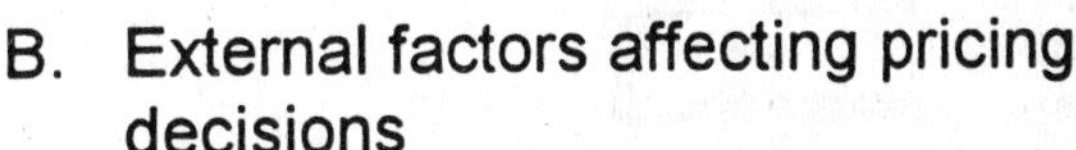

B. External factors affecting pricing decisions

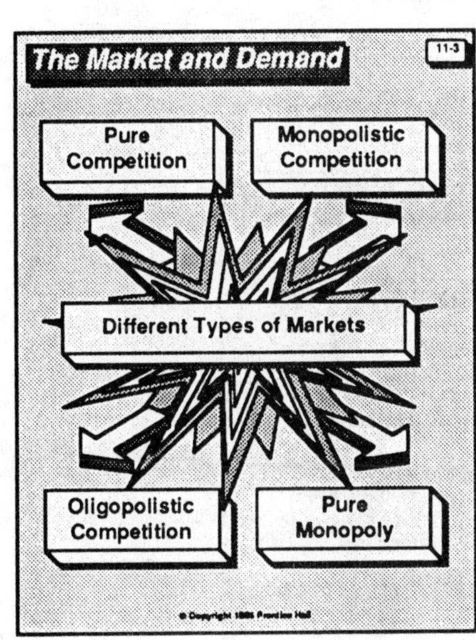

1. The market and demand

2. Competitors' costs, prices and offers

3. Other external factors

II. General Pricing Approaches

A. Cost based pricing

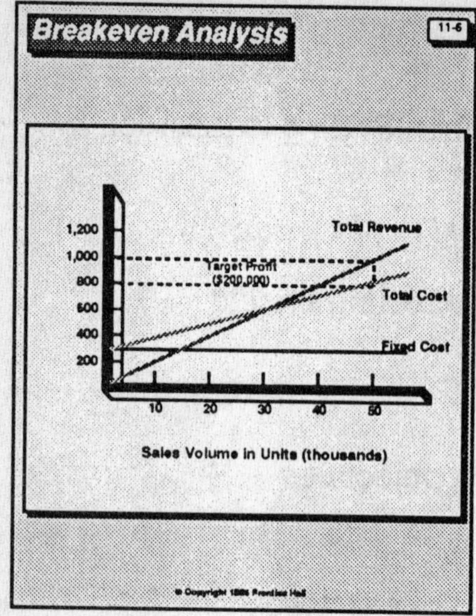

1. Cost-plus pricing

2. Breakeven analysis and target profit pricing

B. Value based pricing

C. Competition based pricing

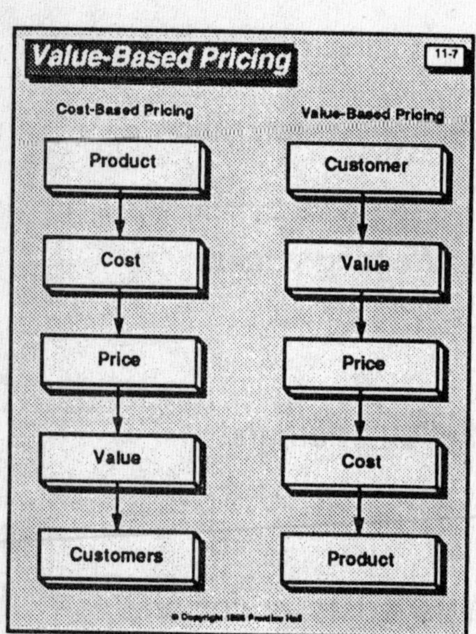

1. Going rate pricing

2. Sealed-bid pricing

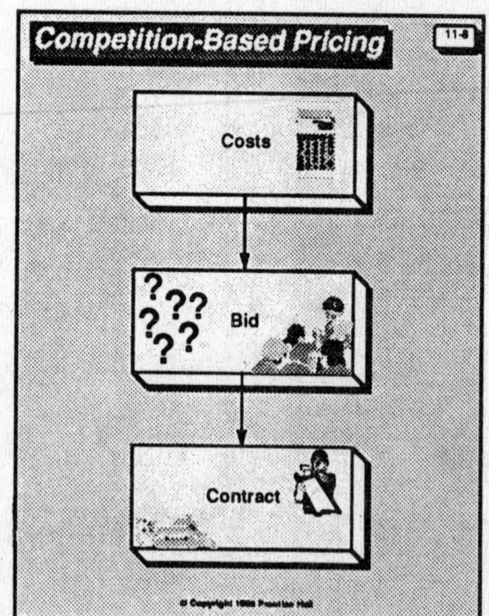

KEY TERMS

Setting price to break even on the costs of making and marketing a product, or to make a target profit.

Breakeven pricing (target profit pricing) (p. 377)

Adding a standard markup to the cost of the product.

Cost-plus pricing (p. 376)

A curve that shows the number of units the market will buy in a given time period, at different prices that might be charged.

Demand curve (p. 373)

The drop in the average per-unit production cost that comes with accumulated production experience.

Experience curve [learning curve] (p. 368)

Costs that do not vary with production or sales level.

Fixed costs (p. 366)

Setting price based largely on following competitors' prices rather than on company costs or demand.

Going-rate pricing (p. 379)

A market in which many buyers and sellers trade over a range of prices rather than a single market price.

Monopolistic competition (p. 369)

A market in which there are a few sellers who are highly sensitive to each other's pricing and marketing strategies.

Oligopolistic competition (p. 370)

The amount of money charged for a product or service, or the sum of the values that consumers exchange for the benefits of having or using the product or service.

Price (p. 363)

A measure of the sensitivity of demand to changes in price.

Price elasticity (p. 373)

A market in which many buyers and sellers trade in a uniform commodity--no single buyer or seller has much effect on the going market price.

Pure competition (p. 369)

A market in which there is a single seller--it may be a government monopoly, a private regulated monopoly, or a private nonregulated monopoly.

Pure monopoly (p. 370)

Setting price based on how the firm thinks competitors will price rather than on its own costs or demand--used when a company bids for jobs.

Sealed-bid pricing (p. 379)

The sum of the fixed and variable costs for any given level of production.

Total costs (p. 367)

Setting price based on buyer's perceptions of value rather than seller's cost.

Value based pricing (p. 377)

Costs that vary directly with the level of production.

Variable costs (p. 366)

APPLYING TERMS AND CONCEPTS

To determine how well you understand the materials in this chapter, read each of the following brief cases and then respond to the questions that follow. Answers are at the end of this chapter.

Scott Refining Company

The Scott Refining Company had been producing gasoline from the same refinery in Leduc, Alberta for over fifteen years, but the outlook over the near term was grim and something had to be done soon. The members of the executive committee of Scott were involved in a heated discussion about price policy.

During the past four months, the gasoline industry had been engaged in a price war in the provinces of Alberta, Saskatchewan, and Manitoba. Prices had declined to the point where refiners were breaking even -- at best. Industry prices had gone down by over 9 percent, but gasoline sales volume had gone up only 4 percent.

The Sunpower Oil Company, one of Scott's competitors, had experienced sales gains of over 10 percent, but this extra litreage was the result of luring away competitors' dealers by offering even lower prices than those offered to established Sunpower dealers. Scott experienced a 4.8 percent gain in gasoline sales, while prices had declined 8 percent as a result of the price war. Part of Scott's price decline had been offset by lower average production costs as the plant moved from 87 percent to 96 percent of rated capacity. The competition's costs, however, had either remained stable or increased because all were operating at near rated capacity prior to the price war.

Clifford Cole, one member of Scott's executive committee, suggested getting together with some of the competitors to see if they couldn't reach some kind of agreement to stop this cut-throat competition and set prices at a reasonable level. Linda Klein, another member, said she thought the company ought to set a resale (retail) price for its own dealers and refuse to sell to them if they cut prices below this level. Several other solutions were offered, but after several hours the meeting was adjourned without any decision.

Questions

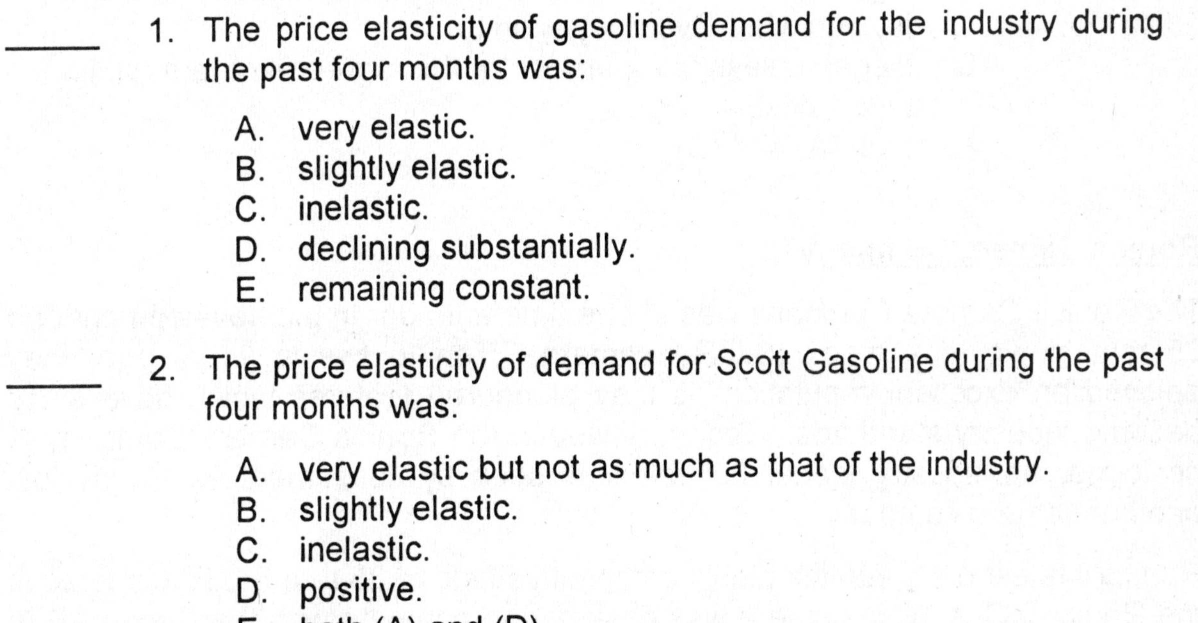

_____ 1. The price elasticity of gasoline demand for the industry during the past four months was:

A. very elastic.
B. slightly elastic.
C. inelastic.
D. declining substantially.
E. remaining constant.

_____ 2. The price elasticity of demand for Scott Gasoline during the past four months was:

A. very elastic but not as much as that of the industry.
B. slightly elastic.
C. inelastic.
D. positive.
E. both (A) and (D)

_____ 3. The decline in Scott's production costs was probably a result of:

A. lower variable costs.
B. the experience curve.
C. lower total costs.
D. spreading fixed costs offer greater volume.
E. higher variable costs.

_____ 4. Regarding the pricing practices of Sunpower Oil Company:

A. Scott should consider doing the same thing.
B. Scott should not meet Sunpower prices if Sunpower offers a lower price to a Scott dealer because matching competitors' prices is illegal.
C. it is probably illegal unless Sunpower can show lower costs in serving the dealers who get lower prices.
D. it is probably legal because sellers can lower their prices to whomever they wish.
E. both (A) and (D)

_____ 5. The suggestion that several competitors get together to set a "reasonable" price is:

A. probably illegal per se.
B. probably an acceptable practice as long as no small competitors are injured.
C. legal because firms can raise prices whenever they want to, with whomever they wish to.
D. illegal unless all parties to the agreement are selling below cost.
E. both (A) and (C)

Ronica Camera Company

The Ronica Camera Company was at one time a leader in the development of a 35 mm single lens reflex (S.L.R.) camera. Ten to twelve years ago, they enjoyed an excellent reputation as they pioneered features which have since become industry standards. Today, however, the Ronica Camera Company is no longer an industry leader but rather is seen by consumers as simply just another camera company.

Ronica's latest entry into the highly competitive field of 35 mm S.L.R. cameras is the Ronica XG-2. This camera was designed to compete with the Canon AE-6, Rollei SL 35-C, Yashica FR-2, and Vivitar XV-4.

The XG-2 features a shutter speed of 4 to 1/1,000 seconds with automatic aperture and shutter control, ASA range from 12-1,600 split range view-finder, microprism, automatic film loading, and hot shoe provision for flash attachment. (These features, however, are common to most 35 mm S.L.R.'s).

The suggested retail selling price for the XG-2 is $480. However, like its competitors' prices, the discount price is only about 75 percent of the suggested retail price. Ronica did not discount its prices in the past, but has now found this to be a necessity as consumers became increasingly price sensitive. Also, like its competitors, the XG-2 is not sold through discount department stores where consumers display little brand loyalty. Ronica has used the standard industry markup of 25 percent of cost in calculating its suggested retail price. The discounted selling price, however, just covers the costs associated with producing and selling the XG-2.

Ray Walsh, Ronica's president, is concerned about the long-term viability of the company. He was especially disturbed to hear that the Japanese and Germans are both expected to introduce new, lightweight (less than 400 grams) cameras with electronic circuitry designed to provide an even greater range of features. The selling price of these new cameras is expected to be comparable to the discounted price of existing S.L.R.'s.

Questions

1. Which type of market situation is the Ronica Camera Company facing?

   ____

2. The pricing objective for the Ronica XG-2 is probably

   ____

3. The fact that Ronica Camera Company is using an industry standard markup gives indication that the company is using __________ pricing.

4. Identify the type of demand curve that the Ronica Camera Company is facing, as well as the factors which have led you to this conclusion.

   ____

   ____

   ____

   ____

   ____

Perfume

It seems $20 or so a mililitre isn't too high a price to pay to feel good about yourself -- or so the marketers of perfumes hope.

There are over 700 different brands of perfume on the market, with new brands introduced each year. Celebrities such as Cher, Sophia Loren, Jane Seymour, Elizabeth Taylor, and Linda Evans are spokespersons for brands they hope women will enjoy. Even designers and high-profile stores have been getting in on the act.

Marketers hope that when a consumer buys a perfume, she will adopt it as her own. The right perfume can help a woman feel feminine and attractive, independent and confident, special and with a more positive outlook. So is $20/ml too much to spend to feel good about yourself? Many consumers believe the benefits are well worth the price.

But consumers might be surprised to learn that the cost of producing many perfumes is actually quite low. The ingredients might cost $1, with a similar amount going for the bottle and package. The sales representative might receive an additional $1, with the balance of the sales price split between the retailer and the producer of the brand.

The makers of Obsession spent $17 million to launch their perfume, while it cost an estimated $10 million to promote Poison. The high profile of glamorous celebrities and organizations such as Giorgio's helps promote an image of prestige. The high price enhances the image.

Questions

1. Explain the nature of the demand curve for a prestige product as it applies to more expensive perfumes.

___

___

___

___

___

2. Assuming perfume marketers are in monopolistic competition, discuss the relative freedom they have in pricing.

___

3. Discuss the elasticity of demand facing marketers of more expensive perfumes.

4. What factors are likely to influence the price elasticity of demand for perfume?

Sources: "France's BIC Bets U.S. Consumers Will Go for Perfume on the Cheap," *The Wall Street Journal,* January 12, 1989, p. B 4; "$22 Million Campaign Urges: Spritz Your BIC," *Advertising Age*, February 20, 1989, pp. 3-69; "Will $4 Perfume Do the Trick for BIC?", *Business Week*, June 20, 1988, pp. 89-92; "BIC Begins Campaign for New Perfume Line," *The New York Times*, March 20, 1989, p. 9; and "Of Flicks and Flickers," *Financial World*, January 10, 1989, pp. 60-61. "BIC Markets Perfume," *ABC News Business World Broadcast*, March 5, 1989.

TESTING TERMS AND CONCEPTS

Part One To test your understanding of the concepts presented in this chapter, write the letter of the most appropriate answer on the line next to the question number. Answers to these questions are found at the end of this chapter.

_____ 1. Historically ____________ has operated as the major determinant of a buyer choice.

A. product
B. place
C. price
D. promotion
E. packaging

_____ 2. Which of the following is not one of the external factors affecting price decisions?

A. Nature of the market and demand
B. Costs
C. Economy
D. Competition
E. Resellers

_____ 3. An industry characterized by many buyers and sellers trading in a homogeneous commodity where no single buyer or seller has much influence on the going market price operates in:

A. pure competition.
B. monopolistic competition.
C. monopoly.
D. oligopoly.
E. regulated monopoly.

_____ 4. If demand is elastic rather than inelastic and the firm is interested in increasing total revenue, the firm should:

A. not change the price.
B. decrease production.
C. raise the price.
D. lower the price.
E. decrease promotional efforts.

_____ 5. In nonregulated monopolies, companies are:

A. free to price at what the market will take and most frequently do.
B. sometimes constrained in making pricing decisions due to fear of government regulation.
C. willing to charge very high prices, since they are not afraid of competition.
D. always charging the highest possible price.
E. both (A) and (C)

_____ 6. Demand sets a(n):

A. floor to the price that a company can charge for its product.
B. larger return on investment for a company's product.
C. ceiling to the price that a company can charge for its product.
D. average price that the company can charge for its product.
E. both (A) and (B)

_____ 7. In perceived value pricing:

A. a high price set by the seller is used to appeal to several different market segments.
B. nonprice marketing mix variables are used to build up demand.
C. a low price is set by the seller to offset reduced application of other marketing mix variables.
D. a low price set by the seller is used to impart perceived value.
E. both (C) and (D)

_____ 8. Which of the following is not one of the reasons offered why the cost plus approach to pricing is still popular?

A. It simplifies pricing.
B. If all firms use this method, their prices tend to be similar and price competition is minimized.
C. Many people feel that the approach is fairer to both buyers and sellers.
D. The approach considers both demand and competition.
E. none of the above

_____ 9. When a company faces intense competition or changing consumer wants and at the same time suffers from over capacity, it is most likely to adopt a ____________ in its pricing strategy.

A. survival objective
B. current profit maximization objective
C. market share leadership objective
D. product quality leadership objective
E. long-term profit maximization objective

_____ 10. Demand curves:

A. show the relationship between price and quantity demanded.
B. are typically downward sloping.
C. always indicate that the higher the price, the greater demand will be.
D. only (A) and (B)
E. all of the above

_____ 11. Steven Goss found that when he raised his price, the quantity purchased by consumers dropped slightly, but overall he made more money. Goss is facing a(n):

A. inelastic demand curve.
B. elastic demand curve.
C. upward sloping demand.
D. unitary elasticity.
E. less competitive environment.

_____ 12. Which pricing method is being used when a firm competes for business and bases its price on expectations of how competitors will price rather than In relation to its own costs or demand?

A. Cost-plus pricing
B. Value based pricing
C. Sealed bid pricing
D. Psychological pricing
E. Demand oriented pricing

_____ 13. In a normal demand curve, demand and price are:

A. equal.
B. inversely related.
C. independent of one another.
D. maintaining a constant relationship.
E. used to calculate profit.

_____ 14. Realistic Gel Corporation competes in a market characterized by many buyers and sellers who trade over a range of prices rather than a single price. (The range of prices occurs because sellers can differentiate their offer to buyers.) Realistic is engaged in __________ competition.

A. monopolistic
B. pure
C. oligopolistic
D. interdependent
E. market directed

_____ 15. Which of the following statements about the price elasticity of demand is true?

A. Buyers are less price sensitive when the product they are buying is unique.
B. Buyers are less sensitive when the product is high in quality, prestige or exclusiveness.
C. Buyers are less price sensitive when substitute products are hard to find or when they cannot easily compare the quality of substitutes.
D. only (A) and (B)
E. all of the above

Part Two To test your understanding of the concepts presented in this chapter, respond to the following questions by writing the letter T or F on the line next to the question number if you believe the statement is true or false, respectively. Answers to these questions are found at the end of this chapter.

_____ 1. Price is the only element of the marketing mix which produces revenue; the other elements represent costs.

_____ 2. Companies set survival as the major objective if plagued with over capacity, intense competition and/or changing consumer wants.

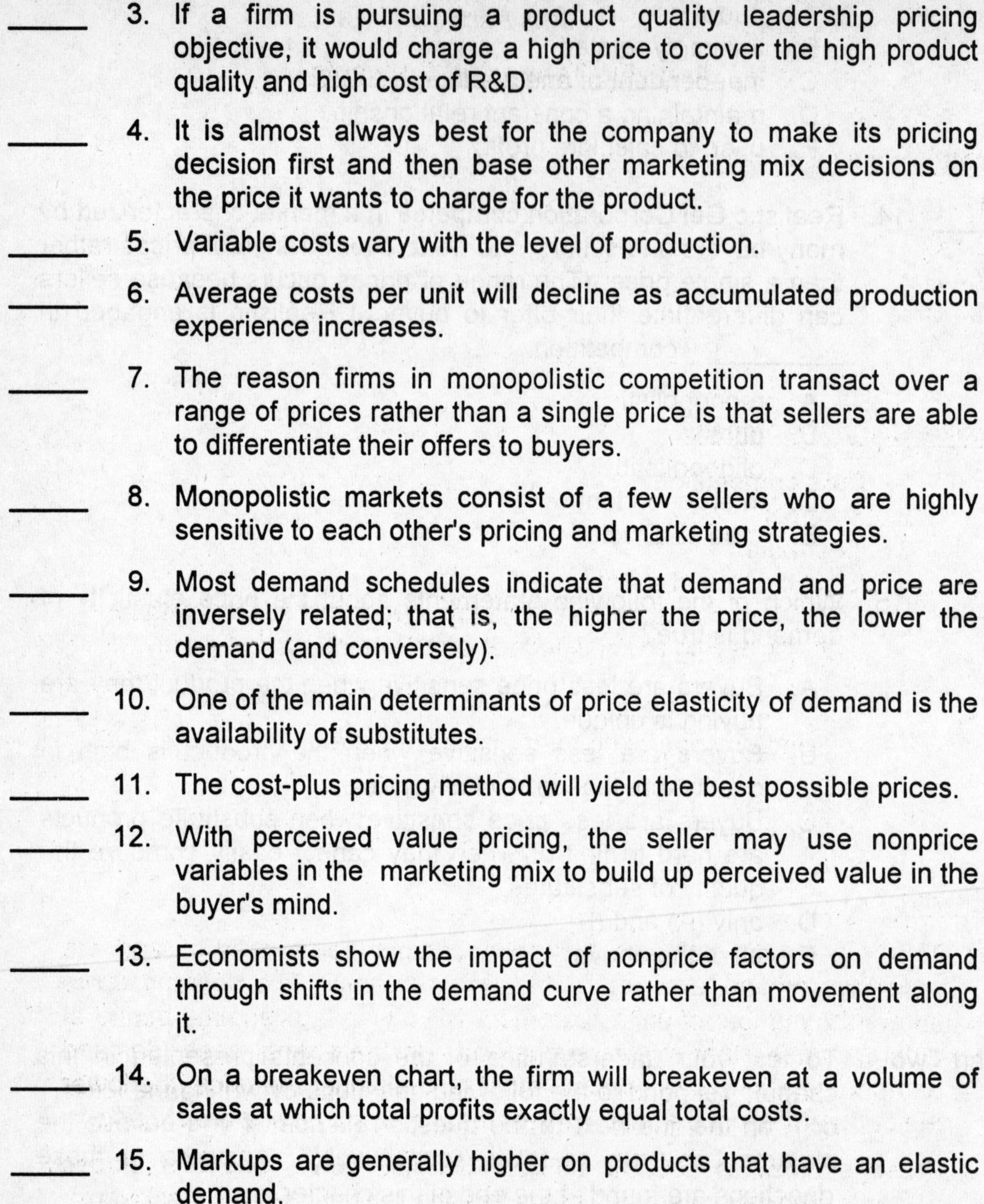

_____ 3. If a firm is pursuing a product quality leadership pricing objective, it would charge a high price to cover the high product quality and high cost of R&D.

_____ 4. It is almost always best for the company to make its pricing decision first and then base other marketing mix decisions on the price it wants to charge for the product.

_____ 5. Variable costs vary with the level of production.

_____ 6. Average costs per unit will decline as accumulated production experience increases.

_____ 7. The reason firms in monopolistic competition transact over a range of prices rather than a single price is that sellers are able to differentiate their offers to buyers.

_____ 8. Monopolistic markets consist of a few sellers who are highly sensitive to each other's pricing and marketing strategies.

_____ 9. Most demand schedules indicate that demand and price are inversely related; that is, the higher the price, the lower the demand (and conversely).

_____ 10. One of the main determinants of price elasticity of demand is the availability of substitutes.

_____ 11. The cost-plus pricing method will yield the best possible prices.

_____ 12. With perceived value pricing, the seller may use nonprice variables in the marketing mix to build up perceived value in the buyer's mind.

_____ 13. Economists show the impact of nonprice factors on demand through shifts in the demand curve rather than movement along it.

_____ 14. On a breakeven chart, the firm will breakeven at a volume of sales at which total profits exactly equal total costs.

_____ 15. Markups are generally higher on products that have an elastic demand.

Answers

Applying Terms and Concepts

Scott Refining Company

1. C
2. C
3. D
4. C
5. A

Ronica Camera Company

1. Pure competition
2. Survival
3. Cost-plus
4. Elastic demand curve
   - Industry characterized by many buyers and sellers, with no seller having much influence on the going market price.
   - Customers see the products as being homogeneous.
   - Company operating at/or about breakeven.
   - Customers do not exhibit brand loyalty.
   - Customers are price sensitive.

Perfume

1. The relationship between the price charged for a product and the resulting demand level yields the demand curve. The demand curve shows the number of units customers will buy in a given time period at different prices that might be charged. In the normal case, demand and price are inversely related -- that is, the higher the price, the lower the demand. Most demand curves, therefore, are downward sloping.

   Prestige products have a different demand curve, one that slopes upwards and backward (it resembles the letter *C* written backward). This demand curve suggests that the quantity demanded will actually increase if the price is raised -- up to a point. However, if consumers perceive the price as being too high, demand will begin to drop.

   For perfumes perceived as prestige products, a high price actually enhances their image and sales.

2. Under monopolistic competition, the market consists of many buyers and sellers who trade over a range of prices rather than a single market price. A range of prices is possible because sellers can differentiate their offers to buyers; either the physical product can be varied in quality, features, or style, or the accompanying services can be varied. Because buyers see differences in sellers' products, they will pay different prices.

   Sellers try to develop differentiated offers for different customer segments and, in addition to price, freely use branding, advertising, and personal selling to set their offers apart. Because there are many competitors, each firm is less affected by competitors' marketing strategies.

3. Price elasticity is related to the change in demand and total revenue resulting from a given change in price.

   If demand is inelastic and the perfume marketer raises the price, demand may drop slightly, but total revenue will either remain the same or increase because although fewer units will be sold, the higher price per unit will preserve or enhance total revenue.

   If demand is elastic and the perfume marketer raises the price, demand will drop dramatically, resulting in a decrease in total revenue. The increased price per unit will not be sufficiently great to offset the decrease in the number of units sold.

   If demand is elastic rather than inelastic, sellers will consider lowering their price. A lower price will produce more total revenue. This makes sense as long as the extra costs of producing and selling more of the product do not exceed the extra revenue.

4. Buyers are less price-sensitive when the product they are buying is unique or when it is high in quality, prestige, or exclusiveness. They are also less price-sensitive when substitute products are hard to find or when they cannot easily compare the quality of substitutes. Finally, buyers are less price-sensitive when the total expenditure for a product is low relative to their income or when the cost is shared by another party. All of these factors are true of perfumes.

Testing Terms and Concepts

Part One

1. C E
2. B E

3. A M
4. D - D When demand is elastic there is an inverse relationship between price and total revenue. Therefore, if demand is elastic rather than inelastic, sellers will generally consider lowering their price. A lower price, in theory, will produce more total revenue. This practice makes sense as long as the extra costs of producing and selling more do not exceed the extra revenue.
5. B D
6. C M
7. B D
8. D M
9. A M
10. D - E The demand curve shows the number of units the market will buy in a given time period at different prices that might be charged. In the normal case, demand and price are inversely related; that is, the higher the price, the lower the demand. Thus the demand curve, for a normal good, is downward sloping. But for prestige goods, however, the demand curve sometimes slopes upward. This means that a price increase may actually result in an increase in demand. In this case the higher price may lead the consumer to believe the product is better or otherwise more desirable. If, however, the company charges too high a price, demand may drop.
11. A M
12. C M
13. B E
14. A M
15. E D

Part Two

1. T E
2. T E
3. T E
4. F M
5. T E
6. T M
7. T E
8. F M
9. T E

10. T - E Buyers are less price sensitive when the product is unique or when it is high in quality, prestige or exclusiveness. They are also less price sensitive when substitute products are hard to find or when they cannot easily compare the quality of substitutes. Finally, buyers are less price sensitive when the total expenditure for a product is low relative to their income or when the cost is shared by another party.

11. F - D Cost-plus pricing is the simplest pricing method in that it involves adding a standard markup to the cost of the product. This approach, however, ignores current demand and competition and, therefore, will not likely lead to the best price. Still, markup pricing remains popular for many reasons. First, sellers are more certain about costs than about demand. By tying the price to cost, sellers simplify pricing -- they do not have to make frequent adjustments as demand changes. Second, when all firms in the industry use this pricing method, prices tend to be similar and price competition is thus minimized. Third, many people feel that cost-plus pricing is fairer to both buyers and sellers. Sellers earn a fair return on their investment but do not take advantage of buyers when buyers' demand becomes great.

12. T M
13. T D
14. F M
15. F D

CHAPTER 12

PRICING PRODUCTS: PRICING STRATEGIES

CHAPTER OVERVIEW

Pricing is a dynamic process, not a static one. This chapter discusses pricing strategies for innovative and imitative new products, strategies for pricing the different parts of the product mix, strategies for adjusting prices for different customers and conditions, and strategies for changing prices and responding to competitors' price changes.

CHAPTER OBJECTIVES

When you finish this chapter, you should be able to accomplish the following:

1. Identify the new product pricing strategies of market skimming and market penetration.
2. List and define the product mix pricing strategies: product line, optional product, captive product, by-product and product bundle pricing.
3. Define the major price adjustment strategies of discount and allowance pricing, segmented, psychological and promotional pricing and value, geographical and international pricing.
4. Discuss the key issues related to price changes including initiating price cuts and price increases, buyer and competitor reactions to price changes and responding to price changes.

LECTURE/STUDENT NOTES

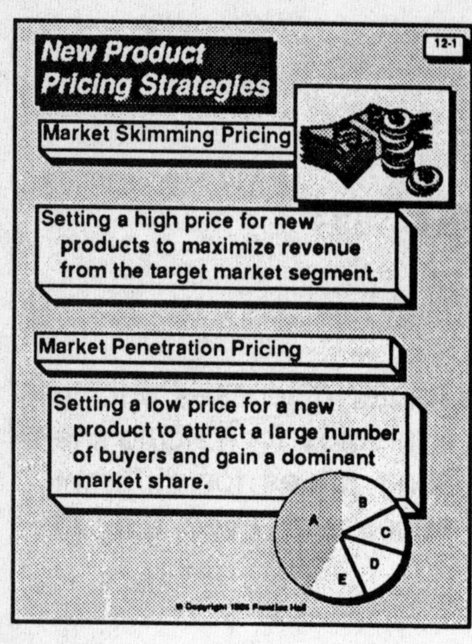

I. New-Product Pricing Strategies

A. Market-Skimming Pricing

B. Market-Penetration Pricing

II. Product-Mix Pricing Strategies

A. Product Line Pricing

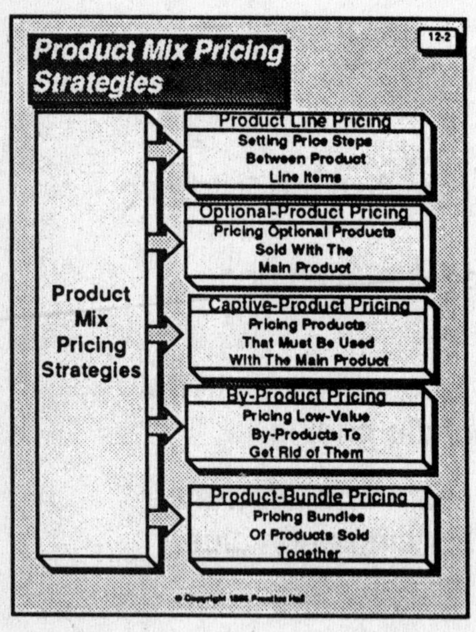

B. Optional-Product Pricing

C. Captive-Product Pricing

D. By-Product Pricing

E. Product-Bundle Pricing

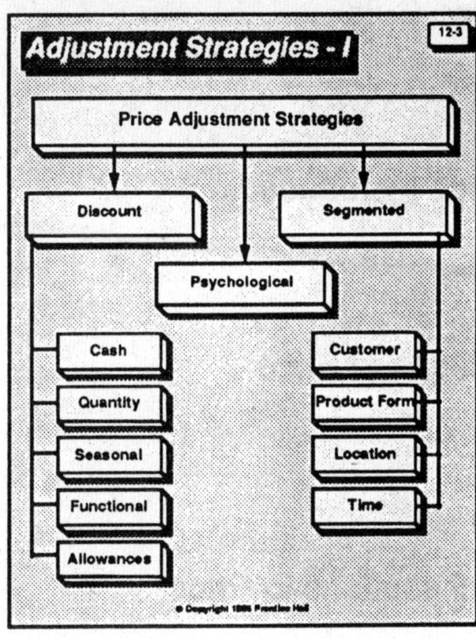

III. Price-Adjustment Strategies

A. Discount and Allowance Pricing

B. Segmented Pricing

C. Psychological Pricing

D. Promotional Pricing

E. Value Pricing

F. Geographical Pricing

G. International Pricing

IV. Price Changes

A. Initiating Price Changes

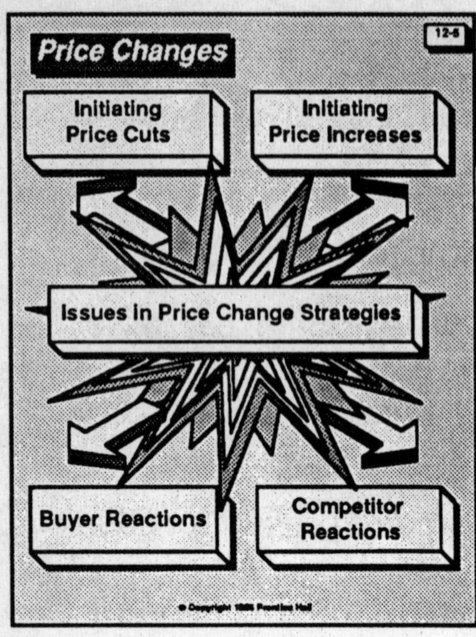

1. Initiating Price Cuts

2. Initiating Price Increases

3. Buyer Reactions to Price Changes

4. Competitor Reactions to Price Changes

B. Responding to Price Changes

KEY TERMS

Promotional money paid by manufacturers to retailers in return for an agreement to feature the manufacturer's products in some way.

Allowance (p. 394)

A geographic pricing strategy in which the seller designates some city as a basing point and charges all customers the freight cost from that city to the customer location, regardless of the city from which the goods are actually shipped.

Basing-point pricing (p. 399)

Setting a price for by-products in order to make the main product's price more competitive.

By-product pricing (p. 392)

Setting a price for products that must be used along with a main product, such as blades for a razor and film for a camera.

Captive-product pricing (p. 392)

A price reduction to buyers who pay their bills promptly.

Cash discount (p. 393)

A geographic pricing strategy in which goods are placed free on board a carrier, and the customer pays the freight from the factory to the destination.

FOB-origin pricing (p. 397)

A geographic pricing strategy in which the company absorbs all or part of the actual freight charges in order to get the business.

Freight-absorption pricing (p. 400)

A price reduction offered by the seller to trade channel members who perform certain functions such as selling, storing, and recordkeeping.

Functional discount (p. 394)

Setting a low price for a new product in order to attract a large number of buyers and a large market share.

Market-penetration pricing (p. 390)

Setting a high price for a new product to skim maximum revenues layer by layer from the segments willing to pay the high price; the company makes fewer but more profitable sales.

Market-skimming pricing (p. 390)

The pricing of optional or accessory products along with a main product.

Optional-product pricing (p. 392)

Combining several products and offering the bundle at a reduced price.

Product-bundle pricing (p. 393)

Setting the price steps between various products in a product line based on cost differences between the products, customer evaluations of different features, and competitors' prices.

Product-line pricing (p. 391)

Temporarily pricing products below the list price, and sometimes even below cost, to increase short-run sales.

Promotional pricing (p. 396)

A pricing approach that considers the psychology of prices and not simply the economics; the price is used to say something about the product.

Psychological pricing (p. 395)

A price reduction to buyers who buy large volumes.

Quantity discount (p. 394)

Prices that buyers carry in their minds and refer to when they look at a given product.

Reference prices (p. 396)

A price reduction to buyers who buy merchandise or services out of season.

Seasonal discount (p. 394)

Selling a product or service at two or more prices, even though the difference in prices is not based on differences in cost.

Segmented pricing (p. 394)

A geographic pricing strategy in which the company charges the same price plus freight to all customers, regardless of their location.

Uniform delivered pricing (p. 397)

Offering just the right combination of quality and good service at a fair price.

Value pricing (p. 397)

A geographic pricing strategy in which the company sets up two or more zones--all customers within a zone pay the same total price; the more distant the zone, the higher the price.

Zone pricing (p. 398)

APPLYING TERMS AND CONCEPTS

To determine how well you understand the materials in this chapter, read each of the following brief cases and then respond to the questions that follow. Answers are at the end of this chapter.

Jaffe Computer Company

Clark Jaffe began the Jaffe Computer Company in 1988 in order to produce a portable computer, packing it with useful programs and selling it at a reasonable price. The result was the Jaffe I, a 24-pound machine with a 5 inch diagonal screen and a selling price of less than $2,000.

The machine was designed for the business-person who needed processing at remote locations such as construction sites. The Jaffe I with 512K and high-resolution color/graphics was also designed to serve as a terminal for large computers made by DATADEC. The Jaffe I became the first practical lap-top computer.

The pricing strategy for the Jaffe I was to introduce the machine at $1,895 and when sales dropped off, to gradually lower the price. The machines were produced in Ottawa, Ontario, but sold throughout the United States and Canada; Jaffe charges a common freight cost to each customer regardless of location. Distribution is through independent electronics shops and computer stores.

Sales to date have been outstanding, each retail location averaging 10 computer sales per month. In an effort to further increase company sales and profits, Jaffe instituted a new policy whereby any retailer taking delivery of more than 12 machines per month would receive a 5 percent discount on all machines delivered that month. The discount would be passed along to the customers or used to increase store profits.

Jaffe also instituted two additional changes in the company pricing policy. First, any customer who purchased a Jaffe Special Use Program (beyond those included in the purchase price) would receive $25 back from the Jaffe Computer Company. Second, certain nonprofit agencies, such as schools, were to receive a $200 reduction in the retail price for purchasing the computer. Jaffe would reimburse the retailer upon verification of the customer's purchase and nonprofit status.

Questions

_____ 1. The Jaffe Computer Company appears to be using which pricing policy regarding the Jaffe I?

A. market skimming
B. penetration pricing
C. predatory pricing
D. zone pricing
E. integrated pricing

_____ 2. Which geographical pricing policy is this company using regarding freight charges?

A. FOB origin
B. uniform delivered
C. zone pricing
D. basing-point pricing
E. both (A) and (B)

_____ 3. When Jaffe authorized a change in company policy to grant a discount of 5 percent to all retailers taking delivery of more than 12 computers per month, he was offering a ___________ discount.

A. cash
B. functional
C. seasonal
D. quantity
E. trade

_____ 4. When Jaffe modified the base price of the Jaffe I for nonprofit agencies, he was engaging in ___________.

A. market penetration.
B. promotional pricing.
C. segmented pricing.
D. geographic pricing.
E. both (A) and (C)

_____ 5. The $25 cash refund offer is an example of:

A. discriminatory pricing.
B. cash rebate.
C. promotional pricing.
D. by-product pricing.
E. both (B) and (C)

Axton Corporation

The Axton Corporation has just completed preparation for the introduction of a unique new product. The firm had worked for years before achieving its breakthrough to find a way to convert some of the "waste" materials generated by the production of its existing line of products into a profitable market offering. The product Axton has developed appears to be a dream come true. Not only can it be produced from waste materials, but Axton has developed a series of accessories that can be added to the basic item in order to customize the offering to the tastes of individual customers. Just prior to introduction, Axton management was notified that its new offering had been granted patent protection.

Questions

1. With regard to its introductory pricing strategy, Axton can employ ___________-___________ pricing if it wishes to derive maximum immediate advantage from its unique, patent-protected product.

2. Should Axton decide to adopt an introductory strategy that is designed to maximize market share while slowing competitive entry, it will employ ___________ ___________.

3. The fact that Axton's new product can be produced from the "waste" material of current products allows the firm to utilize ___________ pricing.

4. Axton's ability to customize its basic offering by offering a wide range of accessories will enable the firm to employ ____________ pricing.

5. The use of products that have formerly been wasted to produce a new product that is expected to be highly profitable should enable Axton to stimulate the sales and profitability of its existing products through lower prices. Such an action would be a form of ____________ ____________.

Maislin Power

Maislin Power produces diesel engines at its manufacturing plant in Montreal, Quebec. Although the basic engine can be modified to perform a variety of functions, it is most often used as the power plant in locomotives, tugboats and ocean going ships. It can also be used as a power generator to supply electricity.

The base price for its most popular engine -- the AL1 -- is $190,000 and is typically sold F.O.B. origin. Other geographical pricing schemes are used depending upon the pricing strategies of the competition. Maislin has two major competitors in this market including White Motor in Toronto, Ontario and Connors Diesel in Saskatoon, Saskatchewan.

Recently two customers have inquired as to the delivered cost of an AL1 from Maislin. One potential customer, St. Albert Medical Centre (AMC), is interested in purchasing an engine to serve as a back-up generator should the centre lose electrical power. The other potential customer is Marsden Construction, located in Halifax, Nova Scotia. Marsden was recently awarded a contract by Java National Oil to construct an off-shore drilling platform. The engine would serve as the primary source of electrical power aboard the rig.

Relevant transportation costs for the AL1 from Montreal to St. Albert are $500, from Montreal to Toronto $1,000, from Montreal to Halifax $2,000, from Toronto to St. Albert $1,500, from Toronto to Halifax, $4,000 and from Saskatoon to Halifax, $5,000.

Maislin realizes it must be flexible in its pricing to remain competitive. Customers view Maislin, White and Connors engines as roughly equal in capability, dependability, and serviceability. None of the three has a price advantage.

1. What would the transportation charge be to the St. Albert Medical Centre if Maislin sold an AL1 Engine with the following terms:

a. F.O.B. base point Toronto ______________________

b. F.O.B. Origin ______________________

c. Freight absorption (F.O.B. destination) ______________________

2. What would the transportation charges be to Marsden Construction if Maislin sold an AL1 engine with the following terms:

   a. F.O.B. base point Toronto ______________________

   b. F.O.B. Origin ______________________

   c. Freight absorption (F.O.B. destination) ______________________

3. If Maislin sold an AL1 engine to both St. Albert Medical Centre and Marsden Construction terms F.O.B. base point Toronto, what would the net transportation charge be to Maislin? Explain your answer.

____

____

____

____

____

TESTING TERMS AND CONCEPTS

Part One To test your understanding of the concepts presented in this chapter, write the letter of the most appropriate answer on the line next to the question number. Answers to these questions are at the end of this chapter.

____ 1. Which of the following is not one of the conditions favourable to a market penetration pricing policy?

A. The market is price sensitive, and a low price leads to market growth.
B. Production costs per unit increase as the level of production increases.
C. Distribution costs decrease as sales increase.
D. A low price discourages actual and potential competition.
E. none of the above

_____ 2. A market skimming pricing policy:

A. starts with a high price which is gradually lowered.
B. starts with a high price and keeps it high.
C. starts with a low price and gradually raises it.
D. starts with a low price and keeps it low.
E. both (A) and (B)

_____ 3. The additional charge for bucket seats over a bench seat in an automobile is an example of:

A. product line pricing.
B. optional product pricing.
C. captive product pricing.
D. by-product pricing.
E. dual product.

_____ 4. By-product pricing may:

A. increase the final price of the main product.
B. decrease the final price of the main product.
C. have no effect on the final price of the main product.
D. either (A) or (B)
E. none of the above

_____ 5. Robin Sloan received an invoice with the following terms of payment: 10/20, N/30. These terms mean that:

A. 10 percent of the bill must be paid on the 20th of the month and the net is due in 30 days.
B. 20 percent of the bill must be paid on the 10th of the month and the net is due in 30 days.
C. payment is due within 30 days but the buyer can deduct 10 percent of anything paid within 20 days.
D. both (A) and (C)
E. none of the above

_____ 6. When McCormiks Restaurant store offers a 15 percent discount on all purchases to individuals 55 years of age or older, McCormiks is practicing:

A. segmented pricing.
B. promotional pricing.
C. psychological pricing.
D. product mix pricing.
E. psychographic pricing.

_____ 7. Kandy Industries sells its products FOB origin. In this case:

A. each customer pays for its own freight costs.
B. the seller pays for the freight costs.
C. each customer pays an average freight cost.
D. the seller becomes a high-cost firm to distant customers.
E. both (A) and (D)

_____ 8. Under which of the following does the seller agree to pay all of the freight cost for a customer?

A. zone pricing
B. Freight absorption pricing
C. FOB origin pricing
D. basing-point pricing
E. both (A) and(D)

_____ 9. The Lapham Company will sell up to 500 units of its product for $15 each, but charges only $13 per unit if the buyer purchases more than 500 units at one time. Lapham is offering:

A. functional discounts.
B. seasonal discounts.
C. quantity discounts.
D. cash discounts.
E. trade discounts.

_____ 10. Under which circumstances should a firm attempt to initiate a price cut?

A. excess capacity
B. excess sales
C. excess profits
D. excess market share
E. excess variable costs

_____ 11. Which of the following is <u>not</u> necessary for price segmentation to work:

A. The cost of segmenting the market should not exceed the extra revenue obtained from price discrimination.
B. The various segments of the market must show identical intensities of demand.
C. Competitors should not be able to undersell the firm in the segment being charged the higher price.
D. Members of the segment paying the higher price should not be able to turn around and resell the product to the segment paying the high price.
E. none of the above

_____ 12. A price increase may carry which of the following meanings to the buyer?

A. The item is an unusually good value.
B. The item is "hot" (in demand) and may be unobtainable unless purchased soon.
C. The seller is charging what the traffic will bear.
D. only (A) and (B)
E. all of the above

_____ 13. Cash discounts are offered to buyers in an effort to

A. improve the sellers liquidity.
B. reduce bad debts.
C. reduce credit collection costs.
D. only (A) and (B)
E. all of the above

_____ 14. L.C.'s Wholesale Club charges its customers low prices to attract high sales volume. The high volume results in lower costs which in turn allows L.C. to keep prices low. L.C. appears to be practicing ______________________________ pricing.

A. market penetration
B. competition based
C. market oriented
D. market skimming
E. cost oriented

_____ 15. The IFSO Corporation sells to all buyers at the same factory price. The firm loads the goods on a common carrier for the customer who pays actual freight costs to his destination and assumes title as soon as the goods are loaded. IFSO uses:

A. basing point pricing.
B. uniform delivered pricing.
C. zone pricing.
D. FOB origin pricing.
E. postage stamp pricing.

Part Two To test your understanding of the concepts presented in this chapter, respond to the following questions by writing the letter T or F on the line next to the question number if you believe the statement is true or false, respectively. Answers to these questions are found at the end of this chapter.

_____ 1. Market skimming as a pricing strategy may make sense if the high price supports the image of a superior product.

_____ 2. Market penetration starts out with a high price which is gradually lowered until the market is fully penetrated.

_____ 3. A firm that is practicing captive product pricing may charge a low price on the main product but set a high markup on the supplies.

_____ 4. Manufacturers must offer the same functional discounts within each trade channel if they perform identical services.

_____ 5. Seasonal discounts may be granted to buyers because they allow sellers to maintain steadier production throughout the year.

_____ 6. Promotional allowances are payments or price reductions to reward dealers for participating in advertising and sales support programs.

_____ 7. The offering of a few products as loss leaders (items sold below cost) to attract customers to the store in the hope that they will buy other products at normal markups is considered illegal.

_____ 8. Advocates of FOB origin pricing feel that this is a fair way to allocate freight charges because each customer pays its own freight cost.

_____ 9. Uniform delivered pricing occurs when all customers within a given zone or region pay the same total price.

_____ 10. Price bundling can promote the sale of products that customers might not otherwise buy, but the combined price must be low enough to get them to buy the bundle.

_____ 11. Psychological pricing considers the impact of consumer perceptions as well as traditional economic influences.

_____ 12. Segmented pricing is illegal unless price differences can be justified on the basis of actual cost savings.

_____ 13. A company should set a single price for a product and keep it constant as it moves through its life cycle.

_____ 14. With promotional pricing, companies will temporarily price their products below list price and sometimes even below cost.

_____ 15. With product-form segmented pricing, different versions of the product are priced differently according to differences in their costs.

Answers

Applying Terms and Concepts

Jaffe Computer Company

1. A
2. B
3. D
4. C
5. E

Axton Corporation

1. market-skimming
2. market-penetration
3. by-product
4. optional product
5. product line

Maislin Power

1. a. $1,500
   b. $ 500
   c. - 0 -
2. a. $4,000
   b. $5,000
   c. - 0 -
3. Zero

When Maislin sold to Marsden, they actually incurred $5,000 in transportation costs, but only billed Marsden $4,000. Yet, when they sold to St. Albert Medical Centre, they actually incurred only $500 in Transportation costs (since the engine was shipped directly to St. Albert) but collected $1,500. In both cases, transportation was charged as if the engine came from Toronto rather than from Montreal. Maislin made $1,000 on a phantom freight charge in the sale to St. Albert Medical Centre but it was cancelled out when they absorbed $1,000 of the freight charge on the sale to Marsden Construction.

Testing Terms and Concepts

Part One

1. B D
2. A E
3. B M
4. D - E In the production of certain products, by-products may be produced as well. If the by-product has no value and/or is costly to store or dispose of, this will have an effect of raising the price of the main product. On the other hand if the product has some value, the marketer should accept a price that more than covers the cost of storage or disposal. This practice will have an effect of reducing the main products price thereby making it more competitive.
5. C M
6. A E
7. E M
8. B M
9. C E
10. A M
11. B D
12. E D
13. E M
14. A M
15. D D

Part Two

1. T E
2. F E
3. T M
4. T E
5. T M
6. T E

7. F D
8. T D
9. T M
10. T M
11. T M
12. F - D Companies will often adjust their basic prices to allow for differences in customers, location, products or time. With segmented pricing, therefore, the company sells a product or service at two or more prices, even though the difference in prices is not based on differences in costs.

For segmented pricing to be an effective strategy for the company, certain conditions must exist. The market must be segmentable and the segments must show different degrees of demand. Members of the segment paying the lower price should not be able to turn around and resell the product to the segment paying the higher price. Competitors should not be able to undersell the firm in the segment being charged the higher price. Nor should the costs of segmenting and watching the market exceed the extra revenue obtained from the price difference. The practice should not lead to customer resentment and ill will. Finally, the segmented pricing must be legal.

13. F M
14. T M
15. F D

CHAPTER 13

PLACING PRODUCTS: DISTRIBUTION CHANNELS AND LOGISTICS MANAGEMENT

CHAPTER OVERVIEW

Distribution channels help move products from producers to ultimate customers. Intermediaries are used because they can perform important functions more efficiently than producers. Channels have traditionally been made up of firms acting in their own interests, but vertical marketing systems are developing that are in the interest of the total channel. In designing channels, manufacturers consider consumer service needs, set objectives in light of various constraints, identify channel alternatives, and evaluate them. Physical distribution involves the actual movement of goods to customers. Physical distribution is a cost of doing business but it is also a tool for creating demand. With careful planning and coordination of distribution, companies can work to create market satisfaction at a reasonable cost.

CHAPTER OBJECTIVES

When you finish this chapter, you should be able to accomplish the following

1. Describe the nature of distribution channels and explain why marketing intermediaries are used.
2. Discuss channel behaviour and organization explaining corporate, contractual and administered vertical marketing systems, horizontal and hybrid marketing systems.
3. Outline the basic elements of channel design decisions by analyzing consumer service needs and setting channel objectives and constraints.
4. Identify major channel alternatives, the types and number of marketing intermediaries and the responsibilities of channel members, and the ways of evaluating major alternatives.

5. Illustrate the channel management decisions of selecting, motivating, and evaluating channel members.

6. Explain the importance and goals of physical distribution and logistics management and identify the major logistics functions of order processing, warehousing, inventory and transportation.

LECTURE/STUDENT NOTES

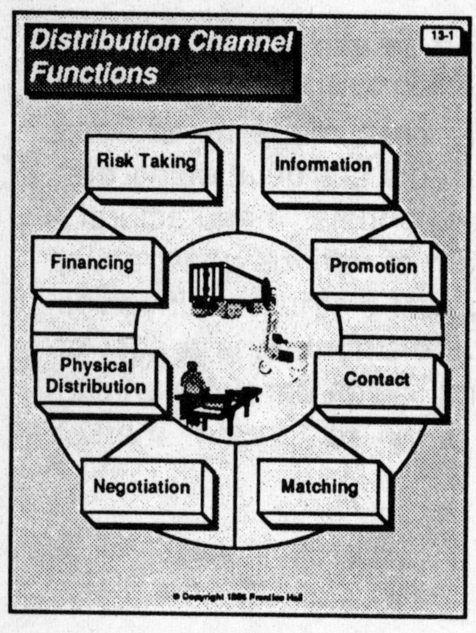

I. The Nature of Distribution Channels

A. Why are marketing intermediaries used?

B. Distribution channel functions

C. Number of channel levels

D. Channels in the service sector

II. Channel Behavior and Organization

A. Channel behavior

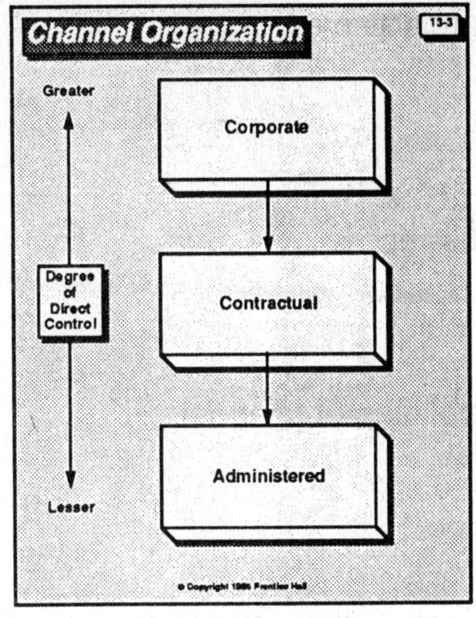

B. Vertical marketing systems

1. Corporate VMS

2. Contractual VMS

3. Administered VMS

C. Horizontal marketing systems

D. Hybrid marketing systems

III. Channel Design Decisions

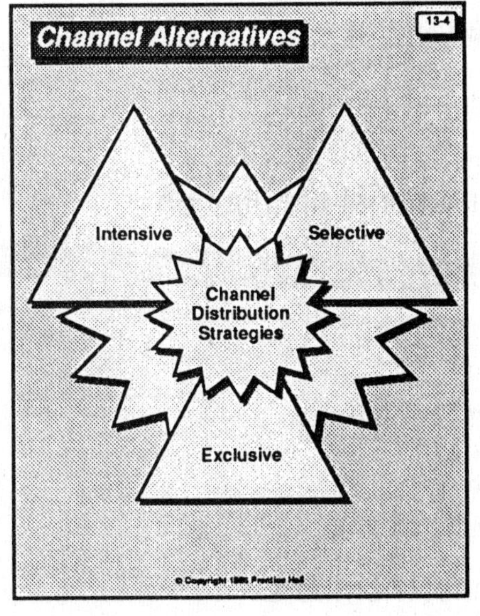

A. Analyzing consumer service needs

B. Setting the channel objectives and constraints

C. Identifying major alternatives

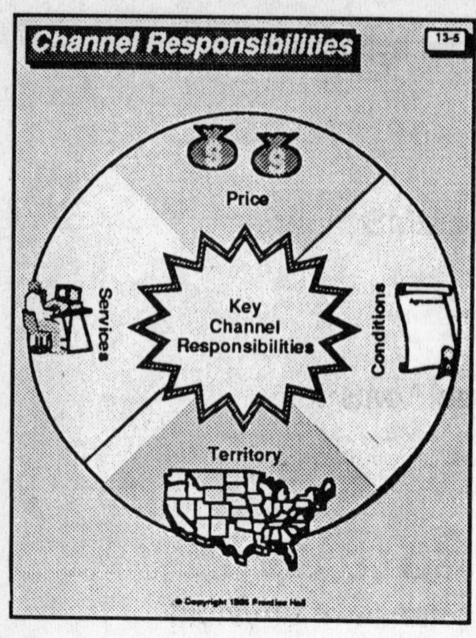

1. Types of middlemen
2. Number of marketing intermediaries
3. Responsibilities of channel members

D. Evaluating the major alternatives

1. Economic criteria
2. Control criteria
3. Adaptive criteria

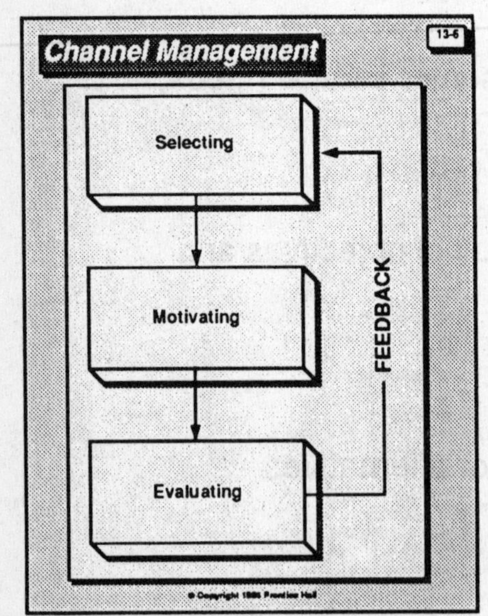

E. Designing international distribution channels

IV. Channel Management Decisions

A. Selecting channel members

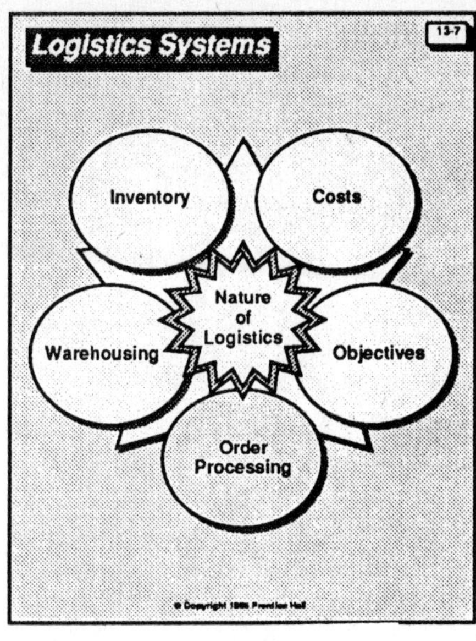

B. Motivating channel members

C. Evaluating channel members

V. Physical Distribution and Logistics Management

A. Nature and importance of physical distribution and marketing logistics

B. Goals of the logistics system

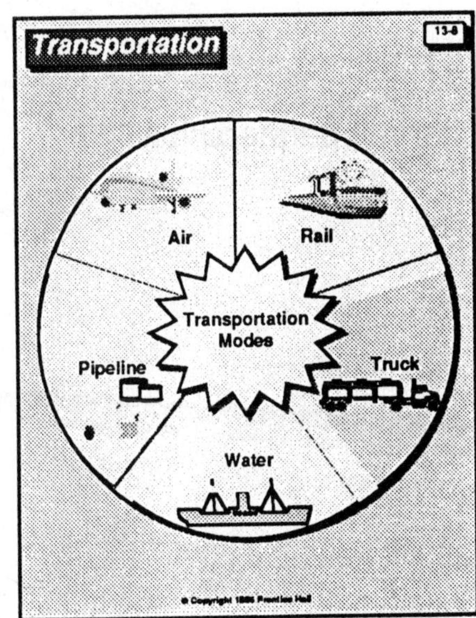

C. Major logistics functions

1. Order processing

2. Warehousing

3. Inventory

4. Transportation

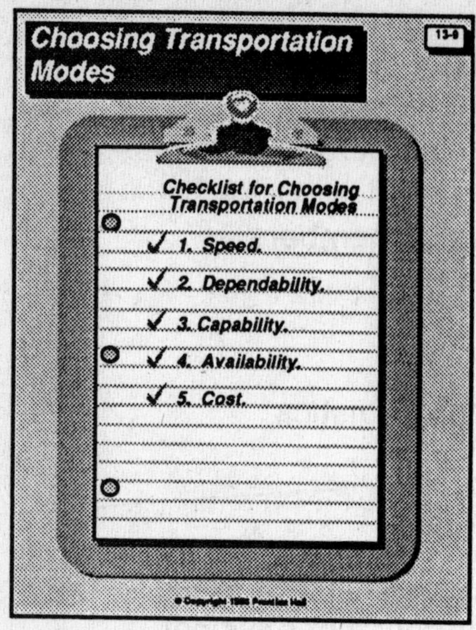

a. rail

b. truck

c. water

d. pipeline

e. air

D. Integrated logistics management

1. Cross-functional teamwork inside the company

2. Building channel partnerships

KEY TERMS

A vertical marketing system that coordinates successive stages of production and distribution, not through common ownership or contractual ties but through the size and power of one of the parties.

Administered VMS (p. 425)

Disagreement among marketing channel members on goals and roles -- who should do what and for what rewards.

Channel conflict (p. 421)

Each layer of marketing intermediaries that performs some work in bringing the product and its ownership closer to the final buyer.

Channel level (p. 417)

Putting the goods in boxes or trailers that are easy to transfer between two transportation modes. They are used in "intermodal" systems commonly referred to as piggyback, fishyback, trainship, and airtruck.

Containerization (p. 443)

A vertical marketing system in which independent firms at different levels of production and distribution join together through contracts to obtain more economies or sales impact than they could achieve alone.

Contractual VMS (p. 424)

A channel consisting of one or more independent producers, wholesalers, and retailers, each a separate business seeking to maximize its own profits even at the expense of profits for the system as a whole.

Conventional distribution channel (p. 422)

A vertical marketing system that combines successive stages of production and distribution under single ownership--channel leadership is established through common ownership.

Corporate VMS (p. 423)

A marketing channel that has no intermediary levels.

Direct-marketing channel (p. 417)

A large and highly automated warehouse designed to receive goods from various plants and suppliers, take orders, fill them efficiently, and deliver goods to customers as quickly as possible.

Distribution centre (p. 440)

A set of interdependent organizations involved in the process of making a product or service available for use or consumption by the consumer or industrial user.

Distribution channel (marketing channel) (p. 416)

Giving a limited number of dealers the exclusive right to distribute the company's products in their territories.

Exclusive distribution (p. 431)

A contractual vertical marketing system in which a channel member, called a franchiser, links several stages in the production-distribution process.

Franchise organization (p. 424)

An agreement in which producers of a strong brand sometimes sell to dealers only if the dealers will take some or all of the rest of the line.

Full-line forcing (p. 436)

A channel arrangement in which two or more companies at one level join together to follow a new marketing opportunity.

Horizontal marketing systems (p. 425)

Multichannel marketing occurring when a single firm sets up two or more marketing chanels to reach one or more customer segments.

Hybrid marketing channels (p. 426)

A marketing channel containing at least one intermediary level.

Indirect marketing channel (p. 417)

The concept which recognizes that providing better customer service and trimming distribution costs requires team work, both inside the company and among all the marketing channel organizations.

Integrated logistics management (p. 443)

Stocking the product in as many outlets as possible.

Intensive distribution (p. 431)

A trade promotion practice whereby manufacturers pay a fee to retrailers to receive preferential treatment for their products.

Over-and-above allowance (p. 420)

The tasks involved in planning, implementing, and controlling the physical flow of materials and final goods from points of origin to points of use to meet customer requirements at a profit. Also known as market logistics.

Physical distribution [or marketing logistics] (p. 437)

Contractual vertical marketing systems in which retailers organize a new, jointly owned business to carry on wholesaling and possibly production.

Retailer cooperatives (p. 424)

The use of more than one but less than all of the intermediaries who are willing to carry the company's product.

Selective distribution (p. 431)

A distribution channel structure in which producers, wholesalers, and retailers act as a unified system--one channel member owns the others, has contracts with them, or has so much power that they all cooperate.

Vertical marketing system (VMS) (p. 422)

Contractual vertical marketing systems in which wholesalers organize voluntary chains of independent retailers to help them compete with large corporate chain organizations.

Wholesaler-sponsored voluntary chains (p. 424)

APPLYING TERMS AND CONCEPTS

To determine how well you understand the materials in this chapter, read each of the following brief cases and then respond to the questions that follow. Answers are given at the end of this chapter.

Ramer Gourmet Popcorn Shop

Cynthia Ramer opened her first Gourmet Popcorn Shop in November 1979, at the Riverside Mall in Victoria, BC. In addition to her fresh-popped popcorn, she sold a full range of popcorn merchandise, including unpopped corn, flavoured oils and salts, and various styles of corn poppers. She has since abandoned most of the popcorn merchandise and now concentrates on selling her flavoured popcorn and a small selection of flavoured salts.

Ramer's organization had grown by 1983 to include eight outlets in the Victoria and Richmond areas. Four shops were located in shopping malls, two in large hotel complexes, and two in office complexes, each location averaging $200,000 in sales per year.

In a bold venture, Ramer allowed her system of preparing and flavouring popcorn to become a franchise operation. She sold distribution rights to an independent group. The franchise contract set very strict requirements on nearly all facets of the operation, including pricing. Ramer also forced C. R. Purchasing to act as the wholesaler servicing the franchise locations.

After two years, Ramer Gourmet Popcorn Shops were a huge success, with over 30 franchise locations in operation in BC, in addition to their own eight shops. It seemed as if they were everywhere people were likely to congregate -- hotels, subways, airports, and hospitals, in addition to shopping malls and office complexes. Ramer was beginning to experience some difficulty with her suppliers of popcorn and thought that if the operation continued to grow, she would consider moving into the farm business to assure a steady supply of popcorn. Ramer had no concern about the long-term viability of her organization. A report released in January by the Morden Manitoba-based Popcorn Institute indicated the popcorn consumption was expected to exceed 15 billion litres annually, up from the 10 billion litres consumed in 1988. Besides, her gourment popcorn was so chic, it was sometimes purchased as a gift or used as hors d'oeuvre's at parties.

Last month, Ramer began hearing complaints that several of the franchise locations were lowering their prices and/or selling new flavours of popcorn, even though this was clearly in violation of the franchise agreement.

Questions

_____ 1. The marketing strategy of Ramer Gourmet Popcorn Shops is to have ____________ distribution.

A. intensive
B. selective
C. exclusive
D. market
E. blanket

_____ 2. The type of channel system currently used in marketing Ramer Gourmet Popcorn is:

A. conventional marketing system.
B. corporate vertical marketing system.
C. contractual vertical marketing system.
D. both (B) and (C)
E. none of the above.

_____ 3. What is occurring when several of the individual popcorn shop owners begin lowering their prices in violation of the franchise agreement?

A. channel cooperation
B. channel discommunication
C. horizontal channel conflict
D. vertical channel conflict
E. channel interdependence

_____ 4. Ramer Gourmet Popcorn is currently sold through a ____________-level channel system.

A. zero
B. one
C. two
D. direct
E. sub

Fast Eddie

Fast Eddie is a former race car driver who retired from racing to manufacture equipment specifically designed for the dirt track driver. His twenty years of racing on clay ovals in Manitoba, Saskatchewan, Alberta and BC, as well as his engineering degree from General Motors Institute of Technology (GMIT), provided him with the background necessary to produce some of the finest automotive equipment to be found. His 30,000 square feet plant, located in Gimli, Manitoba, produces conventional carburetors as well as fuel injection systems, turbochargers, a complete line of intake manifolds, high-temperature titanium exhaust valves, and camshafts.

Fast Eddie sells his products directly to independent retailers located throughout the Prairies. He sells to only one retailer in a given area. Rather than suggesting a retail selling price, he allows the retailers to promote and sell his parts as they see fit. Fast Eddie has no formal contract with each retailer. This arrangement works to his advantage and his disadvantage. While he reserves the right to pull his parts from any store at any time, he has very little control over the retailers. Many of them carry a number of lines that directly compete with Fast Eddie parts.

Each retailer is small and sometimes located in a small town. Since inventory in each store is limited, Fast Eddie needs to have his goods delivered quickly and efficiently. It is not unusual for a customer to buy a substitute rather than wait for delivery of another brand.

Questions

_____ 1. Fast Eddie automotive parts are sold utilizing a(n) ____________ distribution strategy.

A. intensive
B. exclusive
C. selective
D. market
E. blanket

_____ 2. The type of channel system currently used in distributing Fast Eddie automotive parts is a:

A. conventional marketing system.
B. corporate vertical marketing system.
C. contractual vertical marketing system.
D. two-level system.
E. zero-level system.

_____ 3. If Fast Eddie opened his own retail outlets to sell his automotive parts, he would be establishing a(n) ____________ marketing system.

A. horizontal
B. conventional
C. corporate
D. contractual
E. interdependent

_____ 4. Fast Eddie automotive products are currently sold through a ____________-level channel system.

A. zero
B. one
C. two
D. three
E. sub

_____ 5. If Fast Eddie, in addition to selling to retailers, also sold his automotive parts directly to companies that build race cars, Fast Eddie would be:

A. operating a multichannel marketing system.
B. operating a hybrid marketing system
C. engaged in direct marketing.
D. all of the above
E. none of the above

6. Which mode of transportation do you believe Fast Eddie should use to transport his goods to his customers, and why?

____

____

____

____

Pro Image

The marketing of professional and university team sportswear and novelty items is a $3 billion-a-year industry. Since 1985, approximately 300 sports fan shops have opened. Most are independent operations, but franchisers are an increasingly important part of the retailing scene. Pro Image wasn't the first franchiser of the one-stop sports fan shop, but they are battling to lead the pack. In the franchise field, Pro Image competes with such firms as SpectAthlete, Sports Fantasy, Fan Fair, and Sports Arena Ltd.

Fan shops seems to sell just about anything from T-shirts, sweatshirts, sweaters, and caps to coffee mugs, key chains, pennants, bedspreads, and football helmet telephones. While many items are licensed from teams and emblazoned with team logos, most shops also sell authentic merchandise like team jackets and jerseys.

Pro Image was founded in 1985 by Chad and Kevin Olson. Three years later they controlled over 130 stores, with an additional 100 franchised. Each franchise store costs roughly $100,000, approximately $16,000 for the franchise fee and the rest for inventory and store improvements.

Since Pro Image recognizes the importance of a good location, it requires franchisees to locate in high-traffic regional malls. Pro Image assists franchisees in site selection, lease negotiation, and advertising. Store owners must create an upscale image with glass store fronts and wood-slat wall displays. Pro Image requires new owners to attend a four-day training session. They also sponsor an annual convention. Other assistance includes a business hotline and a computerized inventory and sales system. As an added service, they stock hard-to-get items in a 4,500-square-foot warehouse, making them more readily available to franchisees.

Pro Image recognizes that consumers want to wear what their sports heroes wear on the field. Therefore, they stock authentic merchandise that comes directly from the same manufacturers that supply leagues and teams. But authentic merchandise carries a relatively high price. Replica merchandise is available for the more price-conscious. Though it's very similar to the authentic merchandise, it's not exactly the same product worn by the pro players.

The main customer base for Pro Image is men between 18 and 40, although women are becoming increasingly important customers. They purchase the product for themselves, their spouses, or their children.

Competition for the sports fan market is intense. Pro Image must battle not only other franchise operations but also independents, department stores, general retailers, and athletic stores that sell similar merchandise. The latter three constitute the major competition for Pro Image since they control approximately 90 percent of the total licensed merchandise market.

Retailers and their customers aren't the only ones benefiting from the boom in sportswear and novelty item merchandising. Consider NFL Properties, the licensing arm of the National Football League. Since 1980, NFL Properties has seen its souvenir revenues increase by nearly 400 percent to approximately $1.5 billion US. The licensing division of NFL Properties oversees the authorization and sale of more than 700 items.

Team owners love NFL Properties. In the past decade, with two player strikes, relatively stagnant television income, and escalating player salaries, team owners have come to appreciate the approximately $1.5 million US they receive each year from Properties' activities.

Also benefiting are a variety of charities. Each year NFL Properties raises and distributes nearly $700,000 US to deserving organizations.

Questions

1. Explain why an organization such as NFL Properties might choose to have independent retailers, franchise operations, department stores, mass merchandisers, and athletic stores sell NFL-authorized merchandise to consumers rather than sell the merchandise directly to consumers through their own chain of retail outlets.

2. Discuss the nature of the vertical marketing system employed by Pro Image.

3. Suppose you are interested in opening a sports fan shop. What do you see as the advantages and disadvantages of becoming part of a franchise operation?

Sources: "NFL Properties' Values Booming," *The Sporting News*, October 30, 1989, p. 64; "Franchising Jockeying for Position," *Venture*, September 1988, pp. 76-80; and "Unlicensed Comic Books Have NFL in Poor Humor," *Advertising Age*, December 19, 1988, p. 36; "Pro-Image," *ABC News Business World Broadcast*, October 2, 1988.

TESTING TERMS AND CONCEPTS

Part One To test your understanding of the concepts presented in this chapter, write the letter of the most appropriate answer on the line next to the question number. Answers to these questions are found at the end of this chapter.

_____ 1. Physical distribution as a marketing channel function involves:

A. the development and dissemination of persuasive communications about the offer.
B. the searching out and communicating with prospective buyers.
C. the assumption of risks in connection with carrying out the channel work.
D. the transporting and storing of the goods.
E. acquiring and using funds to cover the costs of channel work.

_____ 2. The institutions that make up a marketing channel are connected by several types of flow. The ____________ flow describes directed flows of influence from one party to other parties in the system.

A. information
B. promotion
C. payment
D. title
E. physical

_____ 3. A vertical marketing system (VMS) consists of the producer(s), wholesaler(s), and retailer(s) acting as a unified system. A(n) ____________ vertical marketing system consists of independent firms at different levels of production and distribution who join together to obtain greater economies of scale or sales impact than they could achieve alone.

A. corporate
B. contractual
C. administered
D. conventional
E. horizontal

_____ 4. In a direct-length marketing channel:

A. the manufacturer sells directly to the consumers.
B. a wholesaler must be present.
C. a retailer or wholesaler is between the producer and consumer.
D. either (B) or (C)
E. none of the above

_____ 5. Stephanie Champagne is a farmer who sells her produce directly to a supermarket chain which in turn sells it to customers. This is an example of ____________ ____________ marketing channel system.

A. zero-length
B. one-level
C. two-level
D. direct-level
E. sub-level

_____ 6. Demox is a small company that produces only scientific laboratory beakers. These beakers are an insignificant purchase for laboratories, since they are relatively inexpensive and are only a small part of a large supply of needed laboratory equipment. Which of the following would be the greatest obstacle to Demox's selling its beakers independently by itself?

A. lack of mass distribution economics
B. a heterogeneous product assortment
C. reduced contacts
D. selective distribution
E. either (B) or (D)

_____ 7. Christine Robert, a fashion designer and producer of women's fashions, sells her fashions through her own chain of boutiques (retail outlets). Christine Robert, as the producer and retailer is an example of:

A. franchise organization.
B. corporate VMS.
C. administered VMS.
D. contractual VMS.
E. conventional VMS.

_____ 8. Iron City Mineral Water is bottled in Hamilton, Ontario, and is sold throughout Ontario by independent beverage wholesalers. Each wholesaler attempts to have Iron City sold in as many grocery stores and restaurants as possible. The strategy for distributing Iron City is ____________ distribution.

A. selective
B. intensive
C. exclusive
D. interdependent
E. reciprocal

_____ 9. Which of the following is not one of the major criteria used to evaluate major channel alternatives?

A. economic criteria
B. promotion criteria
C. adaptive criteria
D. control criteria
E. both (B) and (C)

_____ 10. When the Hotchkiss Wholesale Company was offered advertising allowances, premiums, and sales contests by their supplier, the supplier was attempting to motivate Hotchkiss in using the ____________ approach.

A. carrot-and-stick
B. partnership
C. distribution programming
D. intensive distribution
E. exclusive distribution

_____ 11. ____________ occurs when a single firm sets up two or more marketing channels to reach one or more customer segments.

A. Symbolic marketing
B. Horizontal marketing
C. Multimarketing
D. Megamarketing
E. VMS marketing

_____ 12. The difference between storage warehouses and distribution warehouses is that:

A. the latter are for already-ordered goods, while the former are not.
B. the former store goods for moderate to long periods of time, while the latter move goods out as quickly as possible.
C. the former serve storage functions for manufacturers, while the latter do not.
D. the former are used by producers, while the latter are used by retailers.
E. the former are used for perishable goods, while the latter are not.

_____ 13. ____________ consists of putting the goods into boxes or trailers that are easy to transfer between two transportation modes.

A. Parking
B. Packaging
C. Crating
D. Containerization
E. Storage

_____ 14. Which of the following is not one of the key functions performed by members or marketing channels?

A. production
B. contact
C. promotion
D. financing
E. risk taking

_____ 15. ____________ involved planning, implementing and controlling the physical flow of materials and final goods from points of origin to points of use to meet the needs of customers at a profit.

A. Production resources planning
B. Physical distribution
C. Integrated marketing
D. Vertical marketing
E. Multichannel marketing

Part Two To test your understanding of the concepts presented in this chapter, respond to the following questions by writing the letter T or F on the line next to the question number if you believe the statement is true or false, respectively. Answers to these questions are at the end of this chapter.

_____ 1. Place decisions are relatively difficult to change because they involve relatively long-term commitments to other firms.

_____ 2. A distribution channel is the set of firms and/or individuals that take title, or assist in transferring title to the particular good or service as it moves from the producer to the consumer.

_____ 3. A one-level channel of distribution is also called a direct marketing channel.

_____ 4. From a producer's point of view, the problem of control decreases as the number of channel levels increases.

_____ 5. The physical flow between the institutions making up a marketing channel describes the movement of physical products from raw materials to final customers.

_____ 6. The main quality of a vertical marketing system (VMS) which differentiates it from a conventional marketing system is that the channel members act as a unified system.

_____ 7. Hybrid (multichannel distribution) occurs when a company uses more than one channel system to reach customers.

_____ 8. Selective distribution occurs when the product is stocked in as many outlets as possible.

_____ 9. Intermediaries play an important role in matching supply and demand.

_____ 10. A typical physical distribution objective involves getting the right goods to the right places at the right time for the least cost.

_____ 11. Trucks are the nation's largest (in total tonne kilometres) transportation carrier.

_____ 12. Water is ideally suited for shipping low-value, low-bulk freight.

_____ 13. A properly designed physical distribution system will achieve the dual goals of maximizing customer service and minimizing distribution costs.

_____ 14. The storage function is primarily concerned with achieving a match between production and consumption cycles.

_____ 15. A major reason producers give some of the selling jobs to intermediaries is the greater efficiency intermediaries offer in making goods available to target markets.

Answers

Applying Terms and Concepts

Ramer Gourmet Popcorn Shop

1. A
2. D
3. C
4. C

Fast Eddie

1. B
2. A
3. C
4. B
5. D
6. Trucks -- Fast Eddie's customers are scattered in many locations. He needs a fast, frequent dependable, and flexible delivery system. Trucks will provide these needed services.

Pro Image

1. NFL Properties might choose to use a variety of retailers to reach target markets for several reasons, but two are especially important. First, NFL Properties may lack the financial resources to carry out direct marketing activities. Second, direct marketing activities would require NFL Properties to become an intermediary, which would not only mean that they would have to develop expertise in retailing and wholesaling activities, but might also mean they would have to carry products from other organizations to sell along with their own merchandise lest their own assortment be viewed as too narrow by target customers.

   The usefulness of intermediaries largely boils down to their greater efficiency in making goods and services available to target markets. Through their contacts, experience, specialization, and scale of operation, intermediaries usually offer the firm more than it can achieve on its own.

2. A conventional distribution channel consists of one or more independent producers, wholesalers, and retailers. Each is a separate business seeking to maximize its own profits, even at the expense of profits for the system as a whole. No channel member has much control over the other members, and there are no formal means of assigning roles and resolving channel conflict. By contrast, a vertical marketing system (VMS) consists of producers, wholesalers, and retailers acting as a unified system. One channel member either owns the others, has contracts with them, or wields so much power that all must cooperate. The vertical marketing system may be dominated by the producer, the wholesaler, or the retailer. VMS's came into being to control channel behavior and manage channel conflict. They achieve economies through size, bargaining power, and elimination of duplicated services.

   Pro Image is a contractual vertical marketing system. Specifically, it's a service firm-sponsored retailer franchise organization wherein Pro Image licenses a system of retailers to bring selected products to customers.

3. The advantages of associating with a franchise organization such as Pro Image include company assistance with site selection, lease negotiation, advertising, financing, purchasing and inventory control systems, and training; networking through newsletters, meetings, and conventions; and a proven store design and layout and pricing strategy. There is also a greater likelihood of increased sales and profitability from associating with a franchise operation because of the name recognition.

Testing Terms and Concepts

Part One

1. D M
2. B D
3. B D
4. A E
5. B E
6. A D
7. B M
8. B M
9. B M When evaluating channel alternatives, the producer must consider economic control and adoptive criteria. Evaluating economic criteria involves comparing the likely profitability of

different channel alternatives. This involves estimating the sales that each channel would produce and costs of selling different volumes through each channel. The company must also consider control issues. Using middlemen usually means giving them some control over the marketing of the product, and some middlemen take more control than others. Other things being equal, the company prefers to keep as much control as possible. Finally, the company must apply adaptive criteria. Channels often involve long-term commitments to other firms, making it hard to adapt the channel to the changing marketing environment. The company wants to keep the channel as flexible as possible.

10. A M

11. C - E In the past, many companies used a single channel to sell a single market or market segment. Today, with the proliferation of customer segments and channel possibilities, more and more companies have adopted multichannel distribution. Thus, multimarketing occurs when a single firm sets up two or more marketing channels to reach one or more customer segments while the multimarketer gains sales with each new channel, they also risk offending existing channels. Existing channels can cry "unfair competition" and threaten to drop the multimarketer unless it limits the competition or repays them in some way, perhaps by offering them exclusive models or special allowances.

12. B D

13. D E

14. A M

15. B D

Part Two

1. T E

2. T E

3. F E

4. F M

5. T D

6. T - M A conventional distribution channel consists of one or more independent producers, wholesalers, and retailers. Each is a separate business seeking to maximize its own profits, even at the expense of profits for the same system as a whole. No independent producers, wholesalers, and retailers. Each is a separate business seeking to maximize its own profits, even

at the expense of profits for the same system as a whole. No channel member has much control over the other members, and there are no formal means for assigning roles and resolving channel conflict.

A vertical marketing system (VMS) by contrast, consists of producers, wholesalers, and retailers acting as a unified system. Either one channel member owns the others, has contracts with them, or wields so much power that they all cooperate. The vertical marketing system can be dominated by the producer, wholesaler, or retailer. VMSs came into being to control channel behaviour and manage channel conflict. They achieve economies through size, bargaining power, and elimination of duplicated services.

7. T E
8. F E
9. T - E From the economic system's point of view, the role of intermediaries is to transform the assortment of products made by producers into the assortments wanted by consumers. Producers make narrow assortments of products in large quantities. But consumers want broad assortments of products in small quantities of many producers and break them down into smaller quantities and broader assortments wanted by consumers. Thus, intermediaries play an important role in matching supply and demand.
10. T M
11. F M
12. F E
13. F - D Many companies state their objective as getting the right goods to the right places at the right time for the least cost. Unfortunately, no physical distribution system can both maximize customer service and minimize distribution costs. Maximum customer service implies large inventories, the best transportation, and many warehouses--all of which raise distribution costs. In contrast, minimum distribution costs imply cheap transportation, low inventories, and few warehouses.
14. T M
15. T D

CHAPTER 14

PLACING PRODUCTS: RETAILING AND WHOLESALING

CHAPTER OVERVIEW

This chapter describes the many different types of retailers and wholesalers, and the marketing decisions that they make. Retailers sell to consumers for their personal, nonbusiness use. The characteristics of store retailers vary along several dimensions: amount of service, product line length and breadth, prices, control of outlets, and type of store cluster. Nonstore retailing involves direct marketing through a variety of media, direct (door-to-door) selling, and automatic vending. Wholesalers sell products for resale or for business use, and include merchant wholesalers who take title to the goods they sell, brokers and agents who do not, and manufacturers' sales branches and offices that are sales outlets for the producer. Retailers and wholesalers both make marketing decisions and their price, promotion, and place strategies. The future of both retailing and wholesaling will see increased innovation and efficiency as sellers seek better ways to serve customers.

CHAPTER OBJECTIVES

When you finish this chapter, you should be able to accomplish the following:

1. Discuss traditional store retailing and contrast the different ways to segment store by amount of service provided, breadth and depth of product line, relative price levels, control of outlets and type of store cluster.
2. Identify and define the types of nonstore retailing including direct marketing, direct selling and automatic vending.
3. Outline the key retailer marketing decisions target market and positioning product, price, promotion and place.

4. Contrast the differences among types of wholesalers including full service and limited service merchant wholesalers, brokers and agents and manufacturers' sales branches.
5. Explain the wholesaler marketing decisions of target market and positioning and marketing mix decisions and describe trends in wholesaling.

LECTURE/STUDENT NOTES

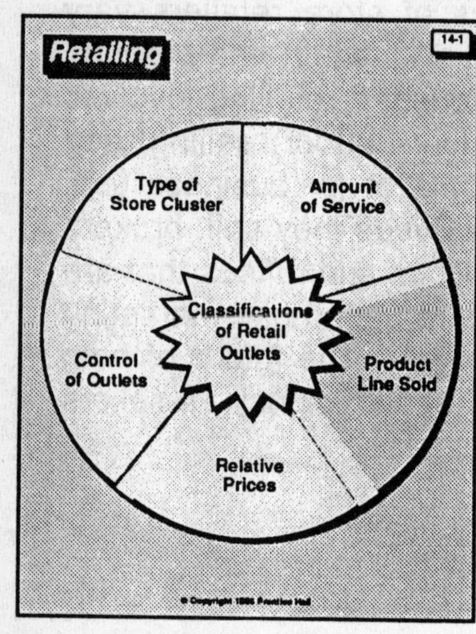

I. Retailing

II. Store Retailing

A. Amount of service

B. Product line

1. Specialty store

2. Department store

3. Supermarket

4. Convenience store

5. Superstore, combination store, and hypermarket

6. Service business

C. Relative prices

1. Discount store

2. Off-price retailers

3. Catalog showroom

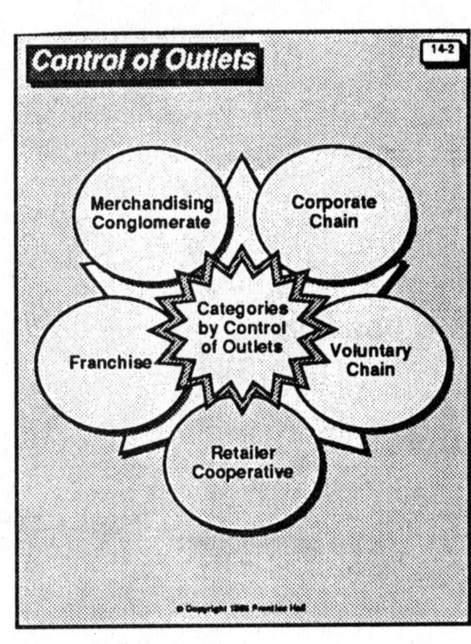

D. Control of outlets

1. Corporate chain

2. Voluntary chain and retailer cooperative

3. Franchise organization

4. Merchandising conglomerate

E. Type of store cluster

1. Central business district

2. Shopping centre

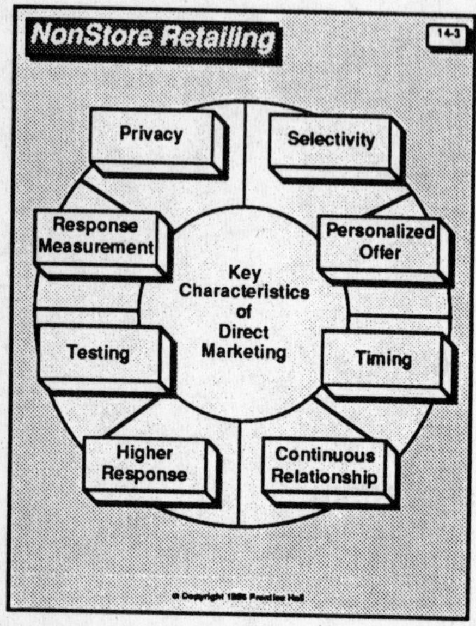

III. Nonstore Retailing

A. Direct marketing

B. Direct selling

C. Automatic vending

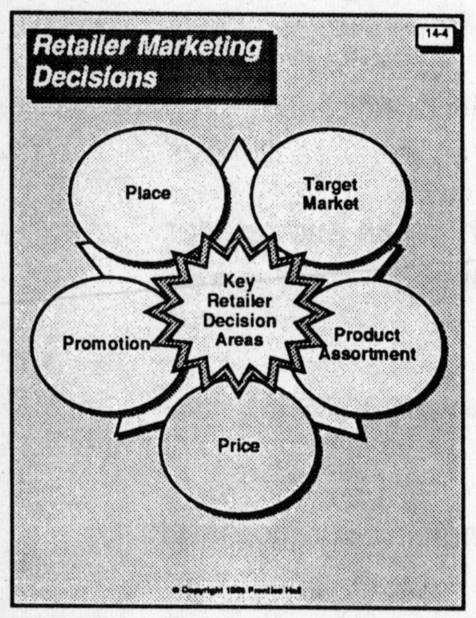

IV. Retailer Marketing Decisions

A. Target market and positioning decision

B. Product assortment and services decision

C. Price decision

D. Promotion decision

E. Place decision

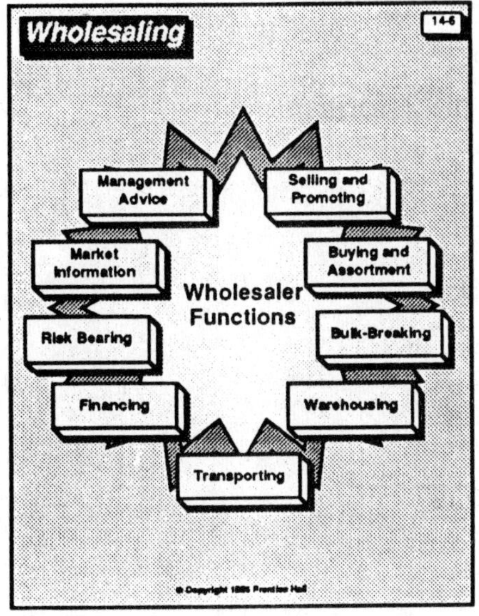

V. The Future of Retailing

VI. Wholesaling

VII. Types of Wholesaling

A. Merchant wholesalers

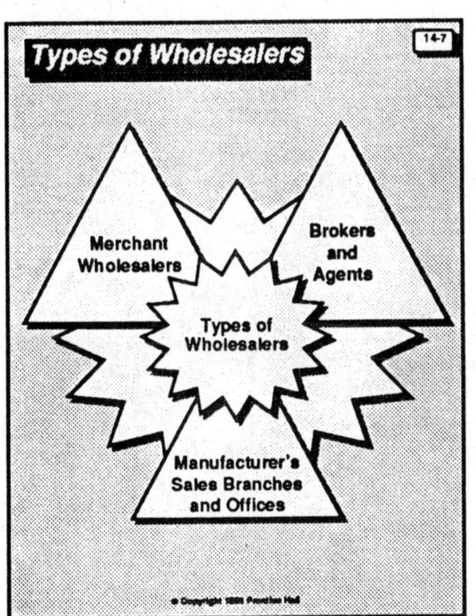

1. Full-service wholesalers

2. Limited-service wholesalers

B. Brokers and agents

C. Manufacturers' sales branches and offices

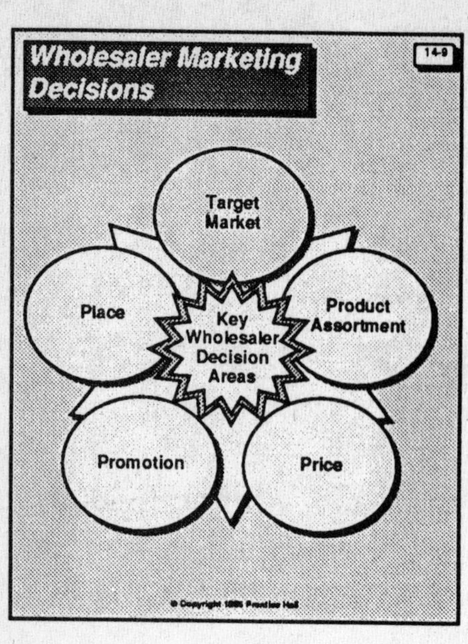

VIII. Wholesaler Marketing Decisions

A. Target market and position decision

B. Marketing mix decisions

IX. Trends in Wholesaling

KEY TERMS

A wholesaler who represents buyers or sellers on a more permanent basis, performs only a few functions, and does not take title to goods.

Agent (p. 476)

Selling through vending machines.

Automatic vending (p. 467)

A wholesaler who does not take title to goods and whose whole function is to bring buyers and sellers together and assist in negotiations.

Broker (p. 476)

A retail operation that sells a wide selection of high markup, fast moving brand name goods at discount prices.

Catalogue showroom (p. 462)

Two or more outlets that are commonly owned and controlled, have central buying and merchandising, and sell similar lines of merchandise.

Chain stores (p. 462)

A small store, located near a residential area, open long hours seven days a week, and carrying a limited line of high-turnover convenience goods.

Convenience store (p. 458)

A retail organization that carries a wide variety of product lines--typically clothing, home furnishings, and household goods; each line is operated as a separate department managed by specialist buyers or merchandisers.

Department store (p. 456)

Marketing through various advertising media that interact directly with consumers, generally calling for the consumer to make a direct response.

Direct marketing (p. 464)

A retail institution that sells standard merchandise at lower prices by accepting lower margins and selling at higher volume.

Discount store (p. 460)

Selling door to door, office to office, or at home-sales parties.

Door-to-door retailing (p. 465)

Off-price retailing operations that are owned and operated by manufacturers and that normally carry the manufacturer's surplus, discontinued, or irregular goods.

Factory outlets (p. 460)

A contractual association between a manufacturer, wholesaler, or service organization (a franchiser) and independent businesspeople (franchisees) who buy the right to own and operate one or more units in the franchise system.

Franchise (p. 462)

Huge stores that combine supermarket, discount, and warehouse retailing; in addition to food, they carry furniture, appliances, clothing, and many other products.

Hypermarkets (p. 459)

Off-price retailers that are either owned and run by entrepreneurs or are divisions of larger retail corporations.

Independent off-price retailers (p. 461)

Wholesaling by sellers or buyers themselves rather than through independent wholesalers.

Manufacturers' sales branches and offices (p. 477)

Independently owned businesses that take title to the merchandise they handle.

Merchant wholesalers (p. 474)

Retailers that buy at less than regular wholesale prices and sell at less than retail. They include factory outlets, independents, and warehouse clubs.

Off-price retailers (p. 460)

Businesses whose sales come primarily from retailing.

Retailers (p. 454)

All activities involved in selling goods or services directly to final consumers for their personal, nonbusiness use.

Retailing (p. 454)

A group of retail businesses planned, developed, owned, and managed as a unit.

Shopping centre (p. 463)

A retail store that carries a narrow product line with a deep assortment.

Specialty store (p. 455)

Large, low-cost, low-margin, high-volume, self-service stores that carry a wide variety of food, laundry, and household products.

Supermarkets (p. 457)

A store almost twice the size of a regular supermarket that carries a large assortment of routinely purchased food and nonfood items and offers services such as dry cleaning, post offices, photo finishing, check cashing, bill paying, lunch counters, car care, and pet care.

Superstore (p. 459)

Off-price retailer that sells a limited selection of brand-name grocery items, appliances, clothing, and a hodgepodge of other goods at deep discounts to members who pay annual membership fees.

Warehouse club (or wholesale club) (p. 461)

A concept of retailing that states that new types of retailers usually begin as low-margin, low-price, low-status operations but later evolve into higher-priced, higher-service operations, eventually becoming like the conventional retailers they replaced.

Wheel of retailing concept (p. 473)

A firm engaged primarily in wholesaling activity.

Wholesaler (p. 473)

All activities involved in selling goods and services to those buying for resale or business use.

Wholesaling (p. 473)

APPLYING TERMS AND CONCEPTS

To determine how well you understand the materials in this chapter, read each of the following brief cases and then respond to the questions that follow. Answers are given at the end of this chapter.

Chan's

Cindy Chan is presently assembling the resources necessary to launch "Chan's," a retail chain designed to meet the clothing need of the professional woman. Her intended customer is twenty-five to forty years old and willing to pay more to acquire the proper look.

Chan is planning to open three outlets in Vancouver. Each outlet will have approximately 5,000 square feet of selling space and feature suits, as well as coordinated separates for the working woman. Casual and sports wear will be limited. However, higher quality professional attire will be offered in a wide range of styles, fabrics, sizes, in patterns and solids. Clothing accessories will include hats, scarves, belts, and stockings, with a small selection of handbags.

Chan, a former vice president of purchasing for S. Altman Department Stores in Calgary, will function as the buyer while Joan Wilder will be responsible for sales and operations. Each store will have a manager with two assistants and two to four sales associates (depending upon sales and volume). Each sales associate is expected to offer honest and objective opinions regarding the clothing and accessories that are "right" for the customer. Each sales associate must have prior personal sales experience and demonstrated the ability to provide personalized attention to a client. The sales associates are to be from the same approximate age bracket as the intended target market.

As an extra service, Chan has hired a fashion consultant to service the three stores. She will be available by appointment to meet the fashion needs of individual customers.

Questions

1. Chan's should be classified as a ____________ (single/limited) line retailer.

2. Chan's main merchandise assortment is best described as _________ (narrow/wide) and ____________ (shallow/deep).

3. Where should Chan locate her three stores and why?

   ____

   ____

   ____

   ____

   ____

4. Which type of services do you believe Chan's should offer its customers?

   ____

   ____

   ____

   ____

5. Chan's should be classified as a ___________ (self/limited/full) service retailer.

Freed Slack Company

Samuel Freed began the Freed Slack Company in Winnipeg, in December 1981. Over the years his company has served the needs of approximately nine million mail order customers, over half as repeat customers.

Freed's current offering consists of men's double-knit dress slacks available in blue tweed, navy, brown, gray, tan, and green, in waist sizes 30" to 44" and inseam sizes from 28" to 35". The slacks are sold at $11.55 per pair with a minimum order of two pairs. They feature Quatral polyester, Tanalon nonsnag zippers, Bana-roll anti-roll waistline, and reinforced belt loops accommodating belts up to one and a half inches. Freed slacks are sold with a moneyback guarantee; however, returns average less than two percent. Postage of $4.85 per shipment is paid by the customer.

Freed has indicated that the current production run will last approximately two years before it is changed. In the past Freed has featured casual slacks, sportswear, dress shirts, and work clothes. It is his practice to feature a type of menswear for a period of time, allowing him to concentrate his buying, manufacturing, and selling efforts on a limited product line, thereby reducing costs of operation.

Freed's literature boasts that his product's quality is comparable to that of slacks costing two or three times as much. A recent article in Canadian Consumer magazine agreed with this claim. Freed will quote the magazine in promoting his next dress slack offering.

Prospective customers receive a flyer which describes the products and includes a small sample of material. Also included for their convenience is a postcard order blank, postage paid by the company. Freed acquires mailing lists of possible customers from the Addresser Company, a mailing list brokerage house in Moncton, New Brunswick.

Questions

_____ 1. The Freed Slack Company should be classified as a(n) _________ service retailer.

A. self
B. limited
C. full
D. augmented
E. customer

_____ 2. The textbook would classify the Freed Slack Company on the basis of:

A. type of store cluster.
B. control of outlets.
C. relative price.
D. nonstore retailing
E. store retailing.

_____ 3. Freed's merchandise assortment is best described as _________ and __________.

A. wide, deep
B. wide, shallow
C. narrow, deep
D. narrow, shallow
E. wide, extensive

_____ 4. Which type of nonstore retailing is Freed involved in:

A. telemarketing.
B. direct mail marketing.
C. electronic shopping.
D. catalog marketing.
E. integrated marketing.

5. Comment on the pricing policy of the Freed Slack Company.

____

____

____

____

____

____

____

____

Noisebreakers

The volume of noise in our daily lives is considerable and increasing steadily. Vehicle exhaust systems, power transformers, dishwashers, ventilation systems, vacuum cleaners, heavy equipment and machinery are just a few of the things that continually assault our senses. Too much noise cannot only cause hearing loss but also distraction and anxiety -- both of which can affect one's disposition and productivity. While most people simply live with the offending sounds, some have found them to be a debilitating force.

David Martin, an engineer and physicist by training, has developed what he believes is a product whose time has come -- a personalized noise abatement system he calls the noise breaker. The Noisebreaker operates by having a microphone pick up incoming sounds and then electronically producing an opposite sound. The mirror image of the sound is broadcast back through a speaker system built into the device. As the competing sounds collide, they partially cancel each other out. While the noise is not eliminated entirely, the Noisebreaker substantially reduces the volume of the offending sounds. While noise abatement systems have long been available and primarily used in the broadcasting and recording industries, this is the first such product aimed at the consumer market.

Martin's initial product looks remarkably like a personal stereo with headphones. It is small enough to be clipped to a belt and worn while one is jogging, driving or simply sitting back relaxing. The Noisebreaker reduces background noise, which in turn reduces distraction and anxiety.

Martin expects the Noisebreaker to retail for $149. Future applications in the industrial and commercial markets will be forthcoming. Martin envisions attaching the device directly to the offending object. He is hoping a commercial version of the Noisebreaker will do for noise pollution what recycling and legislation have done for environmental pollution.

Questions

1. What are the relative advantages of selling the Noisebreaker through each of the following:

   A. Specialty store ______________________________

   ____

   ____

   ____

   ____

   ____

   B. Discount store ______________________________

   ____

   ____

   ____

   ____

   ____

C. Direct marketing ____

____

____

____

____

____

TESTING TERMS AND CONCEPTS

Part One — To test your understanding of the concepts presented in this chapter, write the letter of the most appropriate answer on the line next to the question number. Answers to these questions are at the end of this chapter.

_____ 1. Which of the following statements about retailing is not true?

A. Retailing involves selling to final consumers.
B. Retailing is a major industry.
C. Manufacturers and wholesalers cannot make retail sales.
D. Retail sales may be done by person, mail, telephone, or vending machines.
E. none of the above

_____ 2. A retailing operation that depends on location and long hours to attract customers for its limited line of frequently purchased products is called a:

A. specialty store.
B. department store.
C. superstore.
D. convenience store.
E. supermarket.

_____ 3. Department stores:

A. typically carry several product lines.
B. operate separate departments managed by specialist buyers of merchandise.
C. have not experienced a decline in market share or profitability.
D. both (A) and (B)
E. all of the above

_____ 4. Which of the following types of retailing operations combines supermarket, discount, and warehouse retailing principles?

A. hypermarket
B. discount operation
C. self-service store
D. superstore
E. both (B) and (C)

_____ 5, _________ is a concept of retailing which states that many new types of retailing forms began as low-margin, low-price, low-status operations.

A. Mass merchandising
B. Off-pricing
C. Wheel of retailing
D. Scrambled merchandising
E. Hypermarketing

_____ 6. _________ includes all activities involved in selling goods and services to those buying for resale or business use.

A. Wholesaling
B. Retailing
C. Mass merchandising
D. Market strategy planning
E. Organizational marketing

_____ 7. Which of the following is not one of the major "product" variable decisions to be made by a retailer?

A. product assortment decision
B. target market decision
C. services mix decision
D. store atmosphere decision
E. both (B) and (D)

_____ 8. The widest variety of wholesaling services is provided by:

A. agents.
B. brokers.
C. full-service wholesalers.
D. rack jobbers.
E. commission merchants.

_____ 9. According to many "experts," the key to retailing success is:

A. location.
B. price.
C. promotion.
D. large selection of merchandise.
E. packaging.

_____ 10. Wholesalers differ from retailers by:

A. paying less attention to promotion, atmosphere, and location than retailers.
B. having transactions which are larger than those of retailers.
C. having different legal regulations than retailers.
D. all of the above
E. none of the above

_____ 11. Merchant wholesalers:

A. own the goods they sell.
B. may be subclassified into two groups, full-service and limited-service wholesalers.
C. as a group sell more than agents and brokers.
D. both (A) and (B)
E. all of the above

_____ 12. Agents and brokers:

A. take title to the goods they sell.
B. earn a commission on the sales they generate.
C. perform a wide variety of functions for their customers.
D. both (A) and (C)
E. all of the above

_____ 13. All of the following wholesaling trends are expected to continue in the future except:

A. smaller, more specialized companies.
B. increased use of computerized and automated systems.
C. continued blurring of distinctions between large and small wholesalers.
D. increased services to retailers.
E. large wholesalers going global.

_____ 14. Which of the following trends have contributed to the growth of direct marketing:

A. the rise of the time poor society
B. consumers' desire for personalized attention
C. the development of toll-free telephone numbers and the increased use of credit cards.
D. rising interest in bringing a product to market on your own.
E. all of the above

_____ 15. The BETA Corporation views itself as a manufacturing specialist. The firm has no interest or expertise in selling but does require aggressive representation of the full line throughout its market area. BETA is most likely to use:

A. selling agents.
B. manufacturer's agents.
C. commission merchants.
D. purchasing agents.
E. integrated direct marketing.

Part Two To test your understanding of the concepts presented in this chapter, respond to the following questions by writing the letter T or F on the line next to the question number if you believe the statement is true or false, respectively. Answers to these questions are found at the end of this chapter.

_____ 1. Retailing includes all activities involved in selling goods and services directly to final consumers for the purpose of resale.

_____ 2. Helpful salespeople would more likely be found in limited-service retail stores than in full-service retail stores.

_____ 3. A specialty store carries a narrow product line with a deep assortment within that line.

_____ 4. One tactic of a department store waging a "comeback war" is to offer every day low pricing to meet the discount threat.

_____ 5. Supermarkets are large, low-cost, high-margin, high volume, self-service stores.

_____ 6. A discount store sells standard merchandise at lower prices by accepting lower profit margins and selling higher volume.

_____ 7. A factory outlet store is properly classified as an off-price retailer.

_____ 8. A franchisee is the independent businessperson who buys the right to own and operate one or more units in the franchise system.

_____ 9. Low markups are set on some items that can work as loss leaders or traffic builders in the hope that customers will buy additional items with higher markups once they are in the store.

_____ 10. Many retailing innovations are explained by the wheel-of-retailing concept.

_____ 11. Merchant wholesalers are independently owned businesses that do not own (take title to) the goods they sell.

_____ 12. Wholesalers typically locate in low rent, low tax areas and put little money into their physical setting and offices.

_____ 13. The list of services performed by wholesalers is limited to selling and promoting, buying and assortment building, bulk breaking, warehousing transportation and financing.

_____ 14. Direct marketing's growing use in consumer marketing is largely a response to the "demassification" of mass markets, which has resulted in an ever-greater number of fragmented market segments with highly individualized needs and wants.

_____ 15. Wholesalers are prohibited by law from selling to final consumers.

Answers

Applying Terms and Concepts

Chan's

1. limited line
2. narrow and deep
3. Cindy Chan should probably locate in regional and community shopping centres to facilitate comparison shopping with the other speciality and department stores.
4. Possible services include:
   * free alterations
   * evening and weekend hours
   * gift certificates
   * lay-away and credit programs
   * store sponsored fashion show
   * garment bags with selected purchases
   * merchandise return policy
   * coupons for free dry-cleaning with selected purchases.
5. full service

Freed Slack Company

1. A
2. D
3. C
4. B
5. The Freed Slack Company can charge a relatively low price for its products because of long production runs, volume purchase of materials, specialization of labor, low overhead, and few services offered. The low price encourages customers to buy and try the product and for the low price customers probably do not expect expertly tailored clothing.

Noisebreaker

1. A A specialty store carries a narrow product line with a deep assortment within that line. Electronic enthusiasts, who shop in such stores as Radio Shack, are inclined to seek out and purchase

electronic wizardry. These innovators are willing to pay a higher price as the product comes on the market. Knowledgeable salespeople serve as a resource for their technically minded customers.

B. A discount store sells standard merchandise at lower prices by accepting lower margins and selling higher volume. The Noisebreaker would get considerable exposure in discount stores but would be sold at a reduced price. The purchaser would be those consumers making up the early and late majority who buy items with minimal support from sales personnel.

C. Direct marketing uses various advertising media to interact directly with consumers, generally calling for the consumer to make a direct response. Mass advertising typically reaches an unspecified number of people, most of whom are not in the market for a product or will not buy it until some future date. Direct-advertising vehicles are used to obtain immediate orders directly from targeted consumers. Although direct marketing initially consisted mostly of direct mail and mail-order catalogs, it has taken on several additional forms in recent years, including telemarketing, direct radio and television marketing, and online computer shopping.

   Direct marketing has boomed in recent years. All kinds of organizations use direct marketing: manufacturers, retailers, services companies, catalog merchants, and nonprofit organizations, to name a few. Its growing use in consumer marketing is largely a response to the "demassification" of mass markets, which has resulted in an ever-greater number of fragmented market segments with highly individualized needs and wants. Direct marketing allows sellers to focus efficiently on these minimarkets with offers that better match specific consumer needs.

   Thus direct marketing can lead to greater selectivity and messages that can be personalized and customized. This may translate to improved sales and productivity.

Testing Terms and Concepts

Part One

1. C M
2. D E

3. D M
4. A E
5. C M
6. A E
7. B M
8. C - E Full-service wholesalers typically supply the greatest array of services for their suppliers and customers. Their services include selling and promoting, buying and assortment building, bulk-breaking, warehousing, transportation, financing, risk bearing, market information, management services and advice.
9. A D
10. D D
11. E M
12. B M
13. A D
14. E D
15. A D

Part Two

1. F E
2. F E
3. T E
4. T M
5. F E
6. T E
7. T E
8. T E
9. T M
10. T - M According to the wheel of retailing concept, many new types of retailing forms begin as low-margin, low-price, low-status operations. They challenge established retailers that have become "fat" over the years by letting their costs and margins increase. The new retailers' success leads them to upgrade their facilities and offer more services. In turn, their costs increase, forcing them to increase their prices. Eventually, the new retailers become like the conventional retailers they replaced. The cycle begins again when still newer types of retailers evolve with lower costs and prices.
11. F M
12. T E
13. F M

14. T - D Direct marketing has boomed in recent years. All kinds of organizations use direct marketing: manufacturers, retailers, service companies, catalogue merchants, and nonprofit organizations, to name a few. Its growing use in consumer marketing is largely a response to the "demassification" of mass markets, which has resulted in an ever-greater number of fragmented market segments with highly individualized needs and wants. Direct marketing allows sellers to focus efficiently on these minimarkets with offers that better match specific consumer needs.

Other trends have also fueled the growth of direct marketing. The increasing number of two income families decreased the time households have to shop. The higher costs of driving, traffic congestion and parking headaches, the shortage of retail sales help, and longer lines at checkout counters all have promoted in-home shopping. The development of toll-free telephone numbers and the increased use of credit cards have helped describe new clothes, toys, and other products that their growing baby will need. Direct marketing can also be timed to reach prospects at just the right moment. Moreover, because it reaches more interested prospects at the best times, direct-marketing materials receive higher readership and response. Direct marketing also permits easy testing of specific messages and media. And because results are direct and immediate, direct marketing lends itself more readily to response measurement. Finally, direct marketing provides privacy -- the direct marketer's offer and strategy are not visible to competitors. Despite its many advantages to both consumers and marketers, direct marketing has also generated controversy in recent years. Critics claim that overly-aggressive or unethical direct marketing practices can irritate or harm consumers. Marketers should be aware of the major ethical and public policy issues surrounding direct marketing.

15. F D

CHAPTER 15

PROMOTING PRODUCTS: MARKETING COMMUNICATION STRATEGY

CHAPTER OVERVIEW

Communicating with its various publics is an important part of a company's marketing efforts. This chapter discusses the four major tools in the company's communication mix: advertising, sales promotion, public relations, and personal selling. Companies can develop more effective communications when they understand the elements of the communication process: senders, receivers, messages, media, encoding, decoding, responses, and feedback. Determining how much to spend on promotion is difficult to do well, and many companies use methods that are flawed. Allocating the promotion budget to the different communication tools is based on the type of product and market, the use of push versus pull strategies, buyer readiness stages, and product life cycle considerations. Companies are paying more attention to the need to coordinate all the promotional tools for maximum impact. This is especially important given the changing nature of marketing communications. The communications environment has changed giving growth to direct marketing in the forms of direct mail and catalog marketing, telemarketing television marketing and online shopping. Marketers also recognize they need to engage in more socially responsible communication while minimizing customer irritation, unfairness, deception and fraud, and invasion of privacy.

CHAPTER OBJECTIVES

When you finish this chapter, you should be able to accomplish the following:

1. Define the initial steps in developing effective communication starting with identifying a target audience and determining the response sought.
2. Describe issues in implementing communications beginning with choosing a message, choosing media, selecting a message source and collecting feedback.

3. Determine the ways of setting a total promotional budget, affordable, percentage of sales, competitive parity and objective and task methods.
4. Explain the nature of each promotion tool--advertising, personal selling, sales promotion and public relations--and the factors in setting the promotion mix, type of product and market, push vs. pull strategies, buyer readiness states and product life cycle stage.
5. Discuss the changing communications environment emphasizing the growth of direct marketing, integrated marketing communications and issues in producing socially responsible marketing communication.

LECTURE/STUDENT NOTES

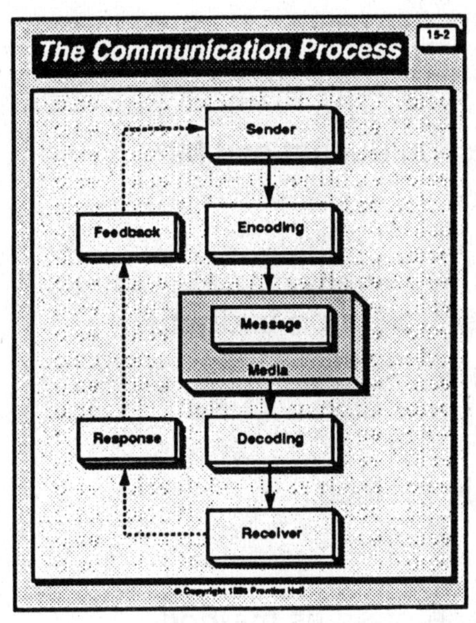

I. Steps in Developing Effective Communication

A. Identifying the target audience

B. Determining the response sought

C. Choosing a message

1. message content

2. message structure

3. message format

D. Choosing a media

1. Personal communication channels

2. Nonpersonal communication channels

E. Selecting the message source

F. Collecting feedback

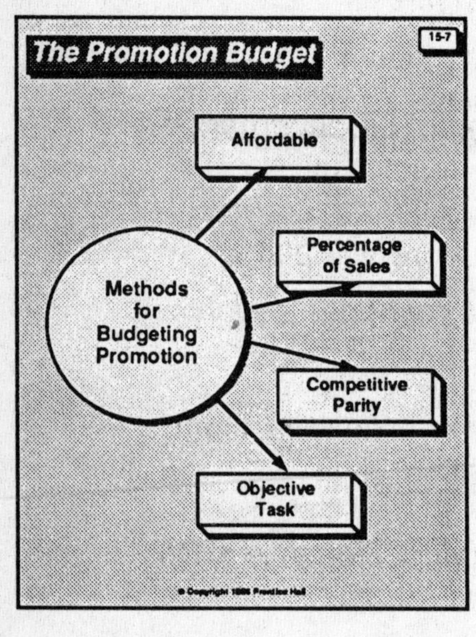

II. Setting the Total Promotion Budget and Mix

A. Setting the total promotion budget

1. Affordable method

2. Percentage-of-sales method

3. Competitive-parity method

4. Objective-and-task method

B. Setting the promotion mix

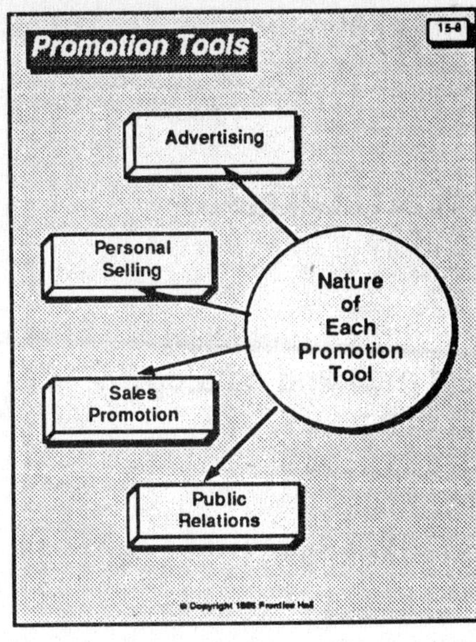

1. The nature of each promotion tool

   a. advertising

   b. personal selling

   c. sales promotion

   d. public relations

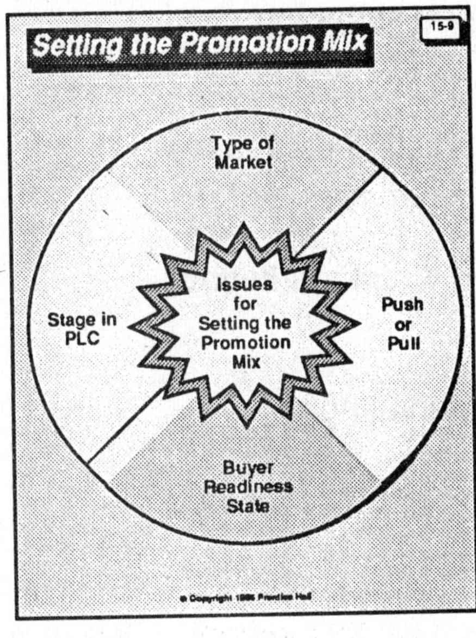

2. Factors in setting the promotion mix

   a. type of product/market

   b. push versus pull strategy

   c. buyer readiness stage

   d. product life-cycle state

III. The Changing Face of Marketing Communications

A. The changing communications environment

B. Growth of direct marketing

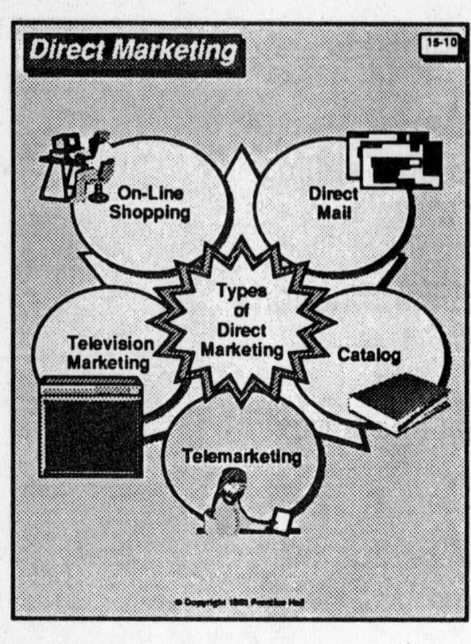

1. Forms of direct marketing communication

   a. direct mail and catalog marketing

   b. telemarketing

   c. television marketing

   d. online shopping

2. Direct-marketing databases

3. Integrated direct marketing

IV. Socially Responsible Marketing Communication

A. Advertising

B. Personal selling

C. Direct mailing

1. Irritation, unfairness, deception and fraud

2. Invasion of privacy

KEY TERMS

Any paid form of nonpersonal presentation and promotion of ideas, goods, or services by an identified sponsor.

Advertising (p. 491)

Setting the promotion budget at the level management thinks the company can afford.

Affordable method (p. 500)

The stages consumers normally pass through on their way to purchase, including awareness, knowledge, liking, preference, conviction, and purchase.

Buyer-readiness states (p. 493)

Direct marketing through catalogs that are mailed to a select list of customers or made available in stores.

Catalogue marketing (p. 507)

Setting the promotion budget to match competitors' outlays.

Competitive-parity method (p. 501)

Marketing through various advertising media that interact directly with consumers, generally calling for the consumer to make a direct response.

Direct marketing (p. 507)

Direct marketing through single mailings that include letters, ads, samples, fold outs, and other "salespeople on wings" sent to prospects on mailing lists.

Direct mail marketing (p. 507)

Message appeals that attempts to stir up negative or positive emotions that will motivate purchases; examples include fear, guilt, shame, love, humor, pride and joy appeals.

Emotional appeal (p. 496)

Direct marketing campaigns that use multiple vehicles and multiple stages to improve response rates and profits.

Integrated direct marketing (p. 511)

The concept under which a company carefully integrates and coordinates its many communication channels to deliver a clear consistent and compelling message about the organization and its products.

Integrated marketing communication (p. 512)

An organized set of data about individual customers or prospects that can be used to generate and qualify customer leads, sell products and services and maintain customer relationships.

Marketing database (p. 510)

Advertising messages directed to the audience's sense of what is "right" or "proper."

Moral appeal (p. 496)

Media that carry messages without personal contact or feedback, including media, atmospheres, and events.

Non-personal communication channels (p. 498)

Developing the promotion budget by (1) defining specific objectives, (2) determining the tasks that must be performed to achieve these objectives, and (3) estimating the costs of performing these tasks; the sum of these costs is the proposed promotion budget.

Objective-and-task method (p. 501)

Shopping through interactive on-line computer services, two-way systems that link consumers with sellers electronically.

On-line shopping (p. 509)

Setting the promotion budget at a certain percentage of current or forecasted sales or as a percentage of the sales price.

Percentage-of-sales method (p. 501)

Channels through which two or more people communicate directly with each other, including face to face, person to audience, over the telephone, or through the mail.

Personal communication channels (p. 497)

Personal presentation by the firm's sales force for the purpose of making sales and building customer relationships.

Personal selling (p. 491)

The specific mix of advertising, personal selling, sales promotion, and public relations tools that the company uses to pursue its advertising and marketing objectives.

Promotion mix (p. 491)

Building good relations with the company's various publics by obtaining favorable publicity, building up a good "corporate image," and handling or heading off unfavorable rumors, stories, and events. Major PR tools include press relations, product publicity, corporate communications, lobbying and counseling.

Public relations (p. 492)

A promotion strategy that calls for spending a lot on advertising and consumer promotion to build up consumer demand; if successful, consumers will ask their retailers for the product, the retailers will ask the wholesalers, and the wholesalers will ask the producers.

Pull strategy (p. 504)

A promotion strategy that calls for using the salesforce and trade promotion to push the product through channels; the producer promotes the product to wholesalers, the wholesalers promote to retailers, and the retailers promote to consumers.

Push strategy (p. 504)

Message appeals that relate to the audience's self interest and show that the product will produce the claimed benefit; examples include appeals of product quality, economy, value or performance.

Rational appeal (p. 496)

Short-term incentives to encourage purchase or sales of a product or service.

Sales promotion (p. 491)

Using the telephone to sell directly to consumers.

Telemarketing (p. 508)

Direct marketing via television using direct response advertising or home shopping channels.

Television marketing (p. 509)

Personal communication about a product between target buyers and neighbors, friends, family members, and associates.

Word-of-mouth influence (p. 497)

APPLYING TERMS AND CONCEPTS

To determine how well you understand the materials in this chapter, read each of the following brief cases and then respond to the questions that follow. Answers are at the end of this chapter.

Shock Cola

Larry Clark, a successful bottler of soft drinks, quietly introduced a cola last year which is taking the industry by storm. Shock, short for "The Shock Treatment," defies the trend of reducing the sugar and caffeine in colas. Clark maintains that soft drinks were meant to be a treat--not a health food. And what a treat Shock is. It contains 6.0 milligrams of caffeine per ounce--twice what Coke and Pepsi offer and the maximum allowed by the Food and Drug Administration. And it is made with the highest quality beet and cane sugar, not the cheaper corn sweetener found in off-brand soft drinks. Clark has found that the combination of caffeine and sugar can give people a buzz unlike that of any other colas on the market.

Shock at $2.29 per six-pack and $1.19 for the two-litre bottle, is less expensive than name-brand colas. In fact, Clark views Shock as a premium cola at a popular price. And the public seems to agree. Last year Clark shipped only 60,000 cases of Shock; current sales projections are for 450,000. Interestingly, he spends very little on advertising as earnings are reinvested to improve bottling capacity and the distribution system. Any money left is then spent on newspaper advertising. Included in each ad is a coupon good for $.25 off the retail price of a six-pack or two-liter bottle.

Clark doesn't advertise very much because Shock's virtues are mostly spread by its aficionados. The messages, especially among younger drinkers include "It's cheap and it's legal," and "Get the treatment." Clark only smiles when he hears one of these lines.

Questions

_____ 1. Clark sets the promotional budget for Shock Cola using the _____________ method.

A. affordable
B. percentage-of-sales
C. competitive-parity
D. objective and task
E. none of the above

_____ 2. The coupon included in the newspaper advertisement is an example of a(n) _____________.

A. advertisement
B. personal selling
C. publicity
D. sales promotion
E. public relations

3. Clark is using the coupon as a ____________ (pushing, pulling) promotional strategy.

_____ 4. Clark's belief that Shock is an inexpensive treat suggests that a promotional campaign should stress a(n) _____________ and _____________ appeal.

A. emotional and rational
B. emotional and moral
C. rational and moral
D. sociological and psychological
E. emotional and moral

_____ 5. The word of mouth advertising used by the cola's fans, is an example of a(n) ____________ communication channel.

A. personal
B. nonpersonal
C. suprapersonal
D. superpersonal
E. extrapersonal

Angela Brown

Angela Brown had been interested in purchasing a portable radio/cassette player/recorder for some time. She was confused, however, by the wide variety of portables on the market. Prices ranged from $129 for a basic portable to $349 for the most elaborate models. Many possessed features she would probably not use, but she was unsure which features were the most desirable.

Brown's friend, Anna Henry, had purchased a Toshiba SR 100 portable while she was attending McGill University. When Henry returned home over the semester break, she shared her experience with her friend.

Henry said that she believed the best features included: automatic reverse, automatic replay, music selection system, AM filter, battery condition metre, sleep switch, 3-way power mode. She indicated that her Toshiba did not have all these features, but that an Aiwa CZ101 did and it cost $180.

Brown went to her library and found that the December issue of Canadian Consumer Product Reports magazine had an article which rated portable radio-cassette player/recorders. The article indicated that the Aiwa CZ101 was an excellent value because it possessed features not found on more expensive models. The article also indicated that the Aiwa possessed minimal flutter and excellent sensitivity and tone quality.

Questions

_____ 1. The article in Canadian Consumer Product Reports magazine indicating that the Aiwa CZ101 was an excellent value for the money could be promoted by Aiwa as a(n) _____________ reason for buying the CZ 101.

A. rational
B. moral
C. emotional
D. none of the above
E. all of the above

_____ 2. When Henry told her friend about the attributes of the Aiwa CZ101, this was an example of a(n) _____________ channel.

A. personal
B. nonpersonal
C. moral
D. emotional
E. social

_____ 3. The article in the magazine about the portable radio/cassette player/recorder is an example of:

A. sales promotion.
B. publicity.
C. advertising.
D. personal selling.
E. corporate communications.

_____ 4. The product review by Canadian Consumer Product Reports, magazine which is a nonprofit publication and which accepts no advertising, is a credible source because of its:

A. expertise.
B. trustworthiness.
C. likability.
D. clientele.
E. both (A) and (B)

Bagelicious

According to the AIDA concept, effective advertisements must get the *A*ttention, hold the *I*nterest, arouse consumer *D*esire and result in *A*ction. The specific action is the purchase of the advertised product or service. This is difficult to accomplish when consumers are bombarded with over 1,500 advertisements per day. To accomplish this action marketers must use promotional methods that make them stand out.

Arron Kaura is an articling student and part owner of Cafe Asante in Winnipeg. One day Arron noticed that unlike the neighbouring cities of Regina and Minneapolis, Winnipeg did not have a restaurant specializing in bagels. Arron saw this as a tremendous opportunity because of the increasing consumption of bagels by North Americans. Health conscious consumers were turning to bagels as a quick, healthy and nutritious substitute for doughnuts and bread products. Arron, therefore, decided to create Bagelicious, Winnipeg's first restaurant specializing in bagels. The menu at Bagelicious consisted of 12 different types of bagels ranging from plain to one made from a combination of flax and bran. Bagels could be purchased to takeout or eat-in. Arron planned to offer a wide selection of cream cheese spreads for use with the bagels and a selection of deli sandwiches made with the bagels.

To reach the largest possible market, Arron planned a phased roll-out of his concept. His first step was to build a restaurant in the southern section of Winnipeg close to the site of the new Jewish Congress Centre. This restaurant would have an oversized kitchen commissary area that would be fully utilized in the next phase. Phase Two called for Arron to introduce kiosks and food carts in the downtown area, the Universities of Winnipeg and Manitoba and at Winnipeg's most popular tourist destination, The Forks. Arron wanted six satellite locations in operation by the end of his second month of operation. A competitive analysis revealed there were currently no direct competitors, but that the Great Canadian Bagel was close to leasing space in Winnipeg. This analysis also revealed the existence of several small indirect competitors. None of these is a threat to Bagelicious due to their small size and out of the way locations.

Arron needed to find a way to stand out from the competition. He decided the best way to do this was through a promotional campaign targeted to health conscious consumers. He built his plan around the name Bagelicious and the fact it contained information about the product and its taste. Arron also decided to team up with the local "adult contemporary" radio station, for a series of promotions. This included becoming the lunch sponsor for the station's "Office of the Day" and sponsoring a series of remote broadcasts by the hosts of the drive-in program. Finally, Arron decided to team up with a community group to display his social responsibility.

Questions

1. Describe how Arron's plan uses the AIDA model to get consumers to buy his products.

____

____

____

____

____

____

2. Arron decides that sales might improve if he had a spokesperson for his product. Describe the factors that make a spokesperson or source credible. Arron decides to hire former Winnipegger and current CNN anchor Lyndon Soles as his spokesperson. Does Mr. Soles meet the criteria described earlier?

____

____

____

____

____

____

Sources: This case prepared by Robert Warren and is based on the business plan for "Bagelicious". Other sources for this case include personal interviews with Arron Kaura and Daren Cosentino.

TESTING TERMS AND CONCEPTS

Part One To test your understanding of the concepts presented in this chapter, write the letter of the most appropriate answer on the line next to the question number. Answers to these questions may be found at the end of this chapter.

_____ 1. The process of putting a thought into symbolic form is:

A. encoding.
B. decoding.
C. feedback.
D. noise.
E. media.

_____ 2. The occurrence of unplanned static or distortion during the communication process is termed:

A. decoding
B. noise
C. encoding
D. feedback
E. multivariate distortion

_____ 3. Which of the following is not one of the six buyer readiness states?

A. awareness
B. knowledge
C. understanding
D. liking
E. conviction

_____ 4. In developing an effective message, communicators may use the AIDA model. AIDA stands for:

A. attention, information, desire, action.
B. attention, interest, desire, activity.
C. arousal, interest, decision, action.
D. arousal, information, desire, action.
E. attention, interest, desire, action.

_____ 5. Promotional campaigns which are directed to the audience's sense of what is right and proper are ____________ appeals.

A. emotional
B. economic
C. rational
D. moral
E. psychological

_____ 6. In the ____________ process, communication first flows from television, magazines and other mass media to opinion leaders and then from there to less active segments of the population.

A. atmospheric communication
B. rational communication
C. conditional communication
D. two-step-flow of communication
E. Seth-Howard Research

_____ 7. ___________ are designed environments that create or reinforce the buyer's leanings toward purchase or consumption of the product.

A. Events
B. Atmospheres
C. Mass media
D. Selective media
E. Two-step flow of communication

_____ 8. Which of the following is not one of the major factors affecting the credibility of the sender?

A. expertise
B. trustworthiness
C. humor
D. likability
E. both (A) and (D)

_____ 9. GERI Ltd. sets its promotional budget to match its rivals' expenditures. GERI uses the ___________ method.

A. affordable
B. percentage-of-sales
C. competitive-parity
D. objective-and-task
E. percentage-of-profit

_____ 10. The Cromer Manufacturing Company has mounted an aggressive rebate program to boost sales. Cromer is employing:

A. sales promotion.
B. advertising.
C. personal selling.
D. publicity.
E. public communications.

_____ 11. A ___________ strategy calls for spending a lot of money on advertising and consumer promotion to build up consumer demand. If effective, consumers will ask their retailers for the product, the retailers will ask the wholesalers for the product, and the wholesalers will ask the producers for the product.

A. push
B. hard-sell
C. soft-sell
D. pull
E. market build-up

_____ 12. In the introduction stage of the product life cycle of a consumer good:

A. personal selling is emphasized over advertising.
B. advertising and publicity are cost effective in producing high awareness.
C. sales promotion is nonexistent.
D. publicity is nonexistent.
E. advertising and public relations loses effectiveness rapidly.

_____ 13. The most logical method of setting a promotion budget is the ____________ method, whereby the company sets its promotion budget on what it wants to accomplish with promotion.

A. economic viability
B. percentage of sales
C. competitive parity
D. affordable
E. objective and task

_____ 14. Marketing communicators must make all but which of the following decisions?

A. identify the target audience
B. determine the response sought
C. choose a message
D. choose the media through which to send the message
E. determine the product to produce

_____ 15. ____________ influence carriers great weight in influencing purchasing decisions for products that are expensive, risky or highly visible.

A. Sales promotion
B. Public relations
C. Personal
D. Corporate
E. Legislative

Part Two To test your understanding of the concepts presented in this chapter, respond to the following questions by writing the letter T or F on the line next to the question number if you believe the statement is true or false, respectively. Answers to these questions are at the end of this chapter.

_____ 1. Advertising is any paid form of personal presentation and promotion of ideas, goods, or services by an identified sponsor.

_____ 2. The sender in the communication process is also called the source.

_____ 3. Feedback is the part of the receiver's response that the receiver communicates back to the sender.

_____ 4. The six-buyer-readiness states include awareness, knowledge, liking, preference, conviction and desire.

_____ 5. Moral appeals attempt to stir up some negative or positive emotion which will motivate a purchase.

_____ 6. Message structure decisions include deciding whether to draw a conclusion or leave it to the audience, whether to present a one-sided or two-sided argument, and whether to present the strongest arguments first or last.

_____ 7. The credibility of the source does not affect the degree to which consumers believe what is being said.

_____ 8. An argument in favor of the competitive-parity method of setting a promotional budget is that the budget is set by the availability of funds rather than opportunities.

_____ 9. Advertising is an efficient way to reach large numbers of geographically dispersed buyers at a low cost per exposure (contact).

_____ 10. Personal selling is the company's most expensive cost per contact tool.

_____ 11. Consumer goods companies normally devote more of their funds to sales promotion and personal selling and less to advertising and public relations.

_____ 12. All personal communication channels are directly controlled by the sender of the message.

_____ 13. In putting the message together, the marketing communicator must solve three problems: what to say (message content), how to say it logically (message structure) and how to say it symbolically (message format).

_____ 14. A push strategy calls for spending a lot of money on advertising and consumer promotion to build up consumer demand.

_____ 15. Integrated direct marketing involves using multiple-vehicle, multiple-stage promotional campaigns.

Answers

Applying Terms and Concepts

Shock Cola

1. A
2. D
3. pulling
4. A
5. A

Angela Brown

1. A
2. A
3. B
4. E

Bagelicious

1. *Attention:* By teaming with the local "adult contemporary" station, Arron will reach a large number of consumers in his target group. More importantly, by taking part in the station's promotions he will gain the attention of this group.

   Interest: Hearing the Bagelicious name and a description of its unique product offerings will attract the interest of consumers.

   Desire: Wanting to take part in a popular trend, eating bagels, and visit a new restaurant will raise consumers' desire.

   Action: Once in the restaurant people will want to buy a bagel or bagel sandwich.

2. An effective spokesperson should have the following characteristics:

Expertise: The source is seen as having experience in the area.

Trustworthiness: This refers to how objective and honest consumers think the source is.

Likability: The audience wants a source they consider attractive in terms of being open, humourous and natural.

Mr. Soles would have problems in the expertise area because the audience would see him as news anchor and not a bagel expert. His position and reputation as a fair and honest person makes him a trustworthy source. Mr. Soles is very likable because people in Winnipeg remember him as a good-natured, friendly person.

Testing Terms and Concepts

Part One

1. A E
2. B E
3. C M
4. E M
5. D M
6. D - D Nonpersonal communication effects buyers directly. In addition, using mass media often affects buyers indirectly by causing more personal communication. Mass communications affect attitudes and behavior through a two-step-flow-of-communication process. In this process, communications first flow from television, magazines, and other mass media to opinion leaders and then from these to the less active sections of the population. This two-step flow process means the effect of mass media is not as direct, powerful, and automatic as once supposed. Rather, opinion leaders step between the mass media and their audiences. Opinion leaders are more exposed to mass media, and they carry messages to people who are less exposed to media.
7. B M
8. C M
9. C E
10. A E
11. D M
12. B D
13. E M
14. E D
15. C D

Part Two

1. F E
2. T E
3. T E
4. F M
5. F E
6. T D
7. F M
8. F D
9. T M
10. T E

11. F M

12. F - M Some personal communication channels are directly controlled by the communicator. For example, company salespeople contact buyers in the target market. But other personal communications about the product may reach buyers through channels not directly controlled by the company. These might include independent experts making statements to target buyers--consumer advocates, consumer buying guides, and others. Or they might be neighbors, friends, family members, and associates talking to target buyers. This last channel, known as word-of-mouth influence, has considerable effect in many product areas.

13. T M

14. F D

15. T E

CHAPTER 16

PROMOTING PRODUCTS: ADVERTISING, SALES PROMOTION, AND PUBLIC RELATIONS

CHAPTER OVERVIEW

Three major tools for promoting products to mass markets are advertising, sales promotion, and public relations. Advertising is the nonpersonal presentation and promotion of ideas, goods, or services by an identified sponsor. Sales promotion uses short-term incentives to stimulate action by consumers, channel members, and salesforces. Sales promotion is growing at a faster pace than advertising, and more is spent on it than on advertising by many consumer goods companies. Public relations is a cost-effective and credible way of building good relations with the company's various publics, but it has tended to be underutilized by marketers. This chapter describes the major tools available for each of these types of promotion, and discusses the decisions made in planning, implementing, and evaluating advertising, sales promotion, and public relations campaigns.

CHAPTER OBJECTIVES

When you finish this chapter, you should be able to accomplish the following:

1. Describe the major decisions in advertising including setting objectives, and budget, creating the advertising message, selecting advertising media, and choosing media types, vehicles and timing and evaluating advertising.
2. Discuss the growth and purpose of sales promotion, setting objectives and selecting consumer--promotion, trade promotion and business--promotion tools.
3. Outline the major public relations tools and decisions.

I. Advertising

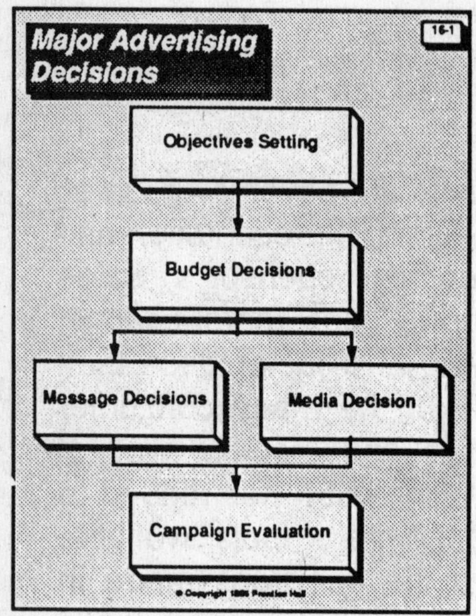

II. Major Decisions in Advertising

A. Setting objectives

B. Setting the advertising budget

C. Advertising strategy

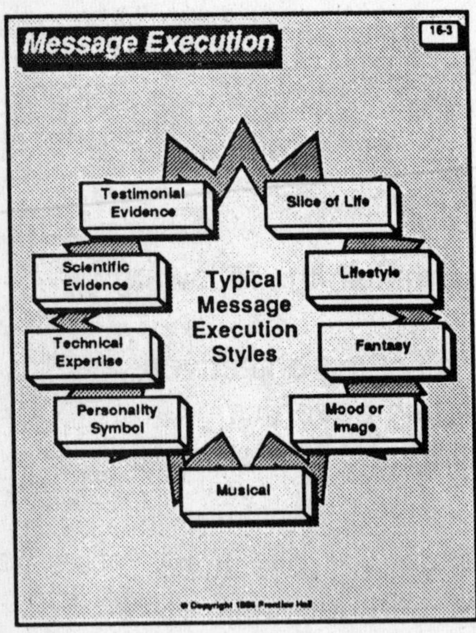

1. Creating the advertising message

   a. the changing message environment

   b. message strategy

   c. message execution

2. Selecting advertising media

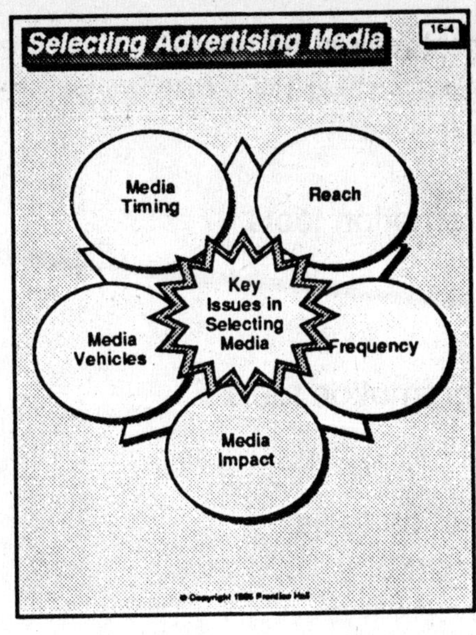

a. deciding on reach, frequency, and impact

b. choosing among major media types

c. selecting specific media vehicles

d. deciding on media timing

D. Advertising evaluation

1. Measuring the communication effect

2. Measuring the sales effect

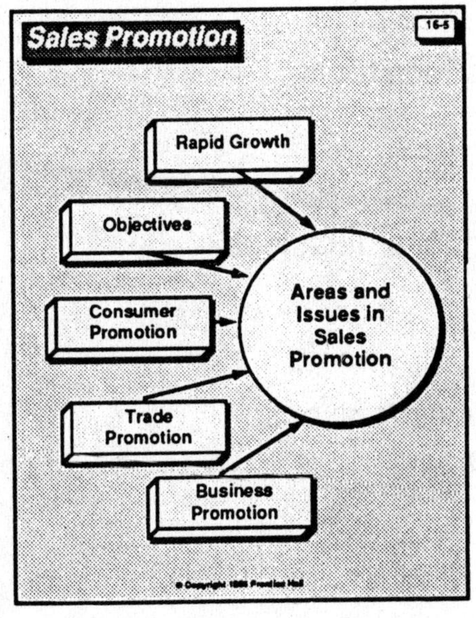

E. International advertising decisions

III. Sales Promotion

A. Rapid growth of sales promotion

B. Purpose of sales promotion

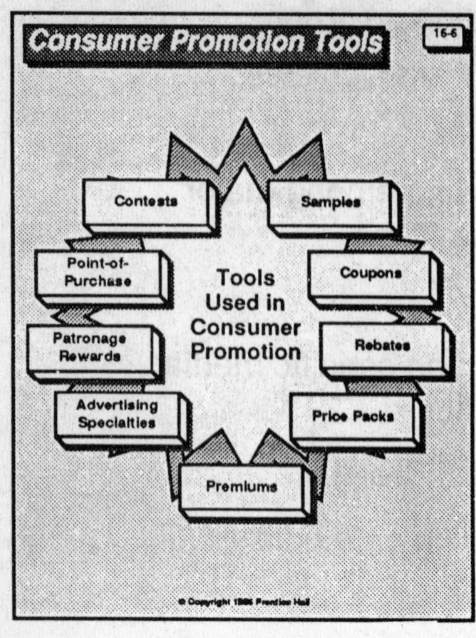

C. Setting sales-promotion objectives

D. Selecting sales-promotion tools

1. Consumer-promotion tools

2. Trade-promotion tools

3. Business-promotion tools

E. Developing the sales-promotion program

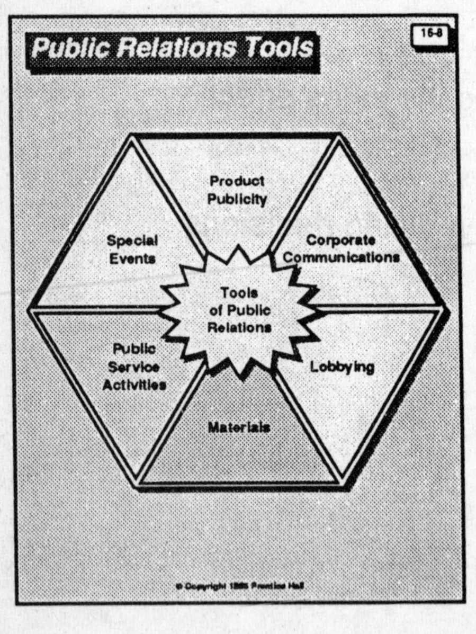

IV. Public Relations

A. Major public relations tools

B. Major public relations decisions

1. Setting public relations objectives

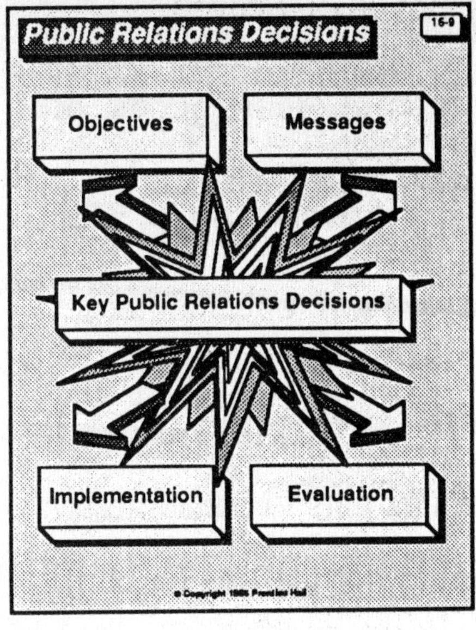

2. Choosing public relations messages and vehicles

3. Implementing the public relations plan

4. Evaluating public relations results

KEY TERMS

Any paid form of nonpersonal presentation and promotion of ideas, goods, or services by an identified sponsor.

Advertising (p. 545)

A specific communication task to be accomplished with a specific target audience during a specific period of time.

Advertising objective (p. 547)

Useful articles imprinted with an advertiser's name, given as gifts to consumers.

Advertising specialties (p. 565)

Promotional money paid by manufacturers to retailers in return for an agreement to feature the manufacturer's products in some way.

Allowance (p. 567)

Offers to refund part of the purchase price of a product to consumers who send a "proof of purchase" to the manufacturer.

Cash refund offers (rebates) (p. 564)

Advertising that compares one brand directly or indirectly to one or more other brands.

Comparison advertising (p. 548)

Sales promotion designed to stimulate consumer purchasing, including samples, coupons, rebates, prices-off, premiums, patronage rewards, displays, and contests and sweepstakes.

Consumer promotion (p. 561)

Promotional events that give consumers the chance to win something--such as cash, trips, or goods--by luck or through extra effort.

Contests, sweepstakes, games (p. 566)

Certificates that give buyers a saving when they purchase a product.

Coupons (p. 564)

A straight reduction in price on purchases during a stated period of time.

Discount (p. 567)

The number of times the average person in the target market is exposed to an advertising message during a given period.

Frequency (p. 555)

Advertising used to inform consumers about a new product or feature and to build primary demand.

Informative advertising (p. 548)

The qualitative value of an exposure through a given medium.

Media impact (p. 555)

Specific media within each general media type, such as specific magazines, television shows, or radio programs.

Media vehicles (p. 556)

Cash or other awards for the regular use of a certain company's products or services.

Patronage rewards (p. 566)

Advertising used to build selective demand for a brand by persuading consumers that it offers the best quality for their money.

Persuasive advertising (p. 548)

Displays and demonstrations that take place at the point of purchase or sale.

Point-of-purchase promotions (POP) (p. 566)

Goods offered either free or at low cost as an incentive to buy a product.

Premiums (p. 565)

Reduced prices that are marked by the producer directly on the label or package.

Price packs (cents-off deals) (p. 565)

Building good relations with the company's various publics by obtaining favourable publicity, building up a good "corporate image," and handling or heading off unfavourable rumours, stories, and events. Major PR tools include press relations, product publicity, corporate communications, lobbying, and counselling.

Public relations (p. 569)

Activities to promote a company or its products by planting news about it in media not paid for by the sponsor.

Publicity (p. 569)

The percentage of people in the target market exposed to an ad campaign during a given period.

Reach (p. 555)

Advertising used to keep consumers thinking about a product.

Reminder advertising (p. 549)

Short-term incentives to encourage purchase or sales of a product or service.

Sales promotion (p. 561)

Sales promotion designed to motivate the salesforce and make salesforce selling efforts more effective, including bonuses, contests, and sales rallies.

Sales-force promotion (p. 561)

Offers of a trial amount of a product to consumers.

Samples (p. 564)

Sales promotion designed to gain reseller support and to improve reseller selling efforts, including discounts, allowances, free goods, cooperative advertising, push money, and conventions and trade shows.

Trade promotion (p. 561)

APPLYING TERMS AND CONCEPTS

To determine how well you understand the materials in this chapter, read each of the following brief cases and then respond to the questions that follow. Answers are given at the end of this chapter.

Barone Wine

Mario Barone opened his new winery in the Tuscany district of Italy with pageantry rivaling that of the opening ceremonies of the modern Olympic Games. Tuscan standard bearers hurled their flags into the air as the music of Nanini, Vivaldi, and Goldoni, Italy's renowned composers, was performed by the symphony orchestra of Milan. White doves were released to announce arrival of the Cardinal of Siena, who bestowed his blessing on the winery and vineyards. Italian dignitaries looked on as a parade marched through town. Fireworks lit the evening sky, with Barone's winery, housed in a medieval castle, looming in the background.

The event last November, which was covered by media representatives from 12 countries writing for 32 different publications, signaled a major undertaking for Barone. The $100 million winery was built in the heart of Arezzo, Tuscany's most respected wine district. The winery, surrounded by 7,000 hectares of prime grape-growing land, was capable of producing 5.0 million litres of wine annually.

Barone had made his fortune by importing table wines such as Lambrusco and Sangria and bottling them under a variety of now popular brand names. Barone wines, based in Toronto, had sales last year of $260 million.

The opening of the Arezzo Winery was a bold move not only because it would mark the first time Barone produced its own wines, but also because the winery would be Barone's entry into the high-quality premium wine market.

Barone hoped to break into the fast-growing market for fine wines now dominated by Californian and French vintners. A recent article in Vintner, the prestigious newsletter from the union of international oenologists, indicated that the worldwide market for premium wines had been growing by 15 percent annually, compared to only a 2.6 percent growth in the table wine market.

Barone's promotional campaign will be designed to build selective demand for the wine. One of the company's promotions is a magazine advertisement that shows an apparently wealthy couple leaning against a Rolls-Royce Silver Shadow on which has been placed a bottle of Barone's wine. (Starch Readership scores indicated the advertisement to be extremely effective.) This particular advertisement will be run in three consecutive issues of Macleans, Canadian Business, Saturday Night and Psychology Today magazines.

Questions

_____ 1. The winery's magazine promotion campaign would fall under which class of advertising objectives?

A. persuasive
B. comparison
C. information
D. reinforcement
E. remind

_____ 2. Which style of message execution is used by the magazine ad?

A. slice-of-life
B. life style
C. personality symbol
D. testimonial
E. fantasy

_____ 3. The communication-effect research on the magazine advertisement (Starch Readership scores) is an example of:

A. a consumer panel.
B. direct ratings.
C. testimonial evidence.
D. a recognition test.
E. technical expertise.

_____ 4. Scheduling the magazine advertisement in three consecutive issues is an example of ____________ (continuity/pulsing).

5. Which major promotional tool was Barone using to announce the opening of his winery?

A. advertisement
B. personal selling
C. public relations
D. sales promotion
E. trade promotion

Tyco Car Wax

The Tyco Car Wax Company is planning to sponsor a sales promotion activity from October 1 to December 31 of this year. Tyco is allowing any resident of

Canada who is 18 years of age with a valid driver's license to enter the activity. Each individual must complete an entry form and send it to Tyco's headquarters in Goose Bay, Labrador. No purchase is necessary, and each person may enter as many times as he or she wishes.

Tyco is providing retailers with signs and cardboard displays to call attention to the promotion. Each display will contain a packet of entry forms which individuals may tear off, complete, and send to Tyco headquarters.

The prizes for this activity include:

	# of Prizes	Prize
First Prize	1	a vehicle of the winner's choice, value not to exceed $25,000
Second Prize	10	free gasoline for one year, value per prize not to exceed $1,000
Third Prize	1,000	Tyco Car Wax t-shirt, value per prize $5
Fourth Prize	2,000	can of Tyco Car Wax, value per prize $1.50

In addition to the prizes listed above, each entrant receives a certificate entitling the bearer to a certain savings on the purchase of any Tyco car care product.

Each winner is responsible for the GST and any provincial sales tax. The activity is void where prohibited and all entries must be postmarked by December 31 of this year. Winners will be selected by the independent certified public accounting firm of Hartley and Sanger, whose decisions are final. Tyco car wax employees and their immediate families are restricted from participating in this activity.

Questions

_____ 1. This Tyco Car Wax sales promotion activity is best described as a:

A. contest.
B. sweepstakes.
C. game.
D. sales contest.
E. trade promotion.

_____ 2. The main tool of the Tyco sales promotion activity is for __________ (consumer/trade) promotion.

_____ 3. When Tyco prepared cardboard signs and displays for use in stores to call attention to the sales promotion activity, Tyco was using:

A. trade promotion.
B. advertising allowances.
C. point-of-purchase displays.
D. premiums.
E. advertising specialties.

_____ 4. When Tyco sent each individual who participated in the sales promotion activity a certificate entitling the bearer to a stated saving on the next purchase of any Tyco car care product. Tyco was distributing:

A. samples.
B. coupons.
C. price packs.
D. premiums.
E. advertising specialty.

_____ 5. When Tyco decided that the first, second, third, and fourth prizes would not exceed $25,000, $10,000, $5,000, and $3,000, respectively, Tyco was deciding on:

A. conditions of participation.
B. distribution vehicle for promotion.
C. size of the incentive.
D. timing of promotion.
E. reach, frequency and impact.

Skin So Soft

Is Skin So Soft a bath oil or an insect repellent? Avon, the makers of Skin So Soft (SSS), insists it is a bath oil. But while the company appreciates the revenue from sales to sports enthusiasts, pet owners, outdoorsmen, and even the military, Avon knows that those customers are purchasing Skin so Soft for a reason other than to smell nice. Some people believe that the product, when mixed with equal parts of water and applied to the skin, is an effective insect repellent.

Avon officials claim to be baffled why mosquitoes, fleas, and other bugs don't like their product. Scientists say there is no ingredient in SSS that should make it act like a repellent, but speculate that the fragrance, a proven people pleaser is offensive to the keen sense of smell of some insects. SSS clearly doesn't ward off all bugs, and some research suggests that it is effective on only one strain of mosquito. The research also suggests that its effectiveness is short-lived. But that hasn't slowed the sales of SSS. Even pet owners are getting in on the act. According to one study, the flea count on dogs can be cut by one-third in just two days after a sponge bath with a mixture of SSS and water, and fleas seem to stay off longer than when regular flea dips are used alone. An added benefit is that the mixture leaves the dog's coat shinier and more pleasant-smelling. Unfortunately, the treatment doesn't work for cats; it seems their skin is too sensitive for the chemicals in the mixture. Horses, however, benefit from the treatment.

Avon is prohibited by law from touting SSS as an insect repellent. But advertisements such as "Millions of People Know the Secret of Skin So Soft, Do You?" are beginning to bug Avon's competitors, the makers of traditional insect repellents. They believe that Avon should register the product with the EPA and subject it to the safety and effectiveness testing required by law. Avon professes innocence and maintains any benefits from secondary usage are spread by word of mouth among its devotees.

Recent findings that some traditional insect repellents contain chemicals suspected of being hazardous to health have enhanced the sales of Skin So Soft, currently in the tens of millions of dollars -- prompting one to wonder if SSS should really be translated as Sweet Smell of Success.

Questions

1. Explain how Avon could use each of the following consumer promotion tools to increase the short term sales of Skin-So-Soft and to help build long-term market share.

   A. Sample ____

   B. Coupons ______________________________________

C. Cash refund offers

D. Price packs

E. Advertising specialties

F. Patronage rewards

G. Point of purchase

H. Contests, sweepstakes, and games

2. Avon is prohibited by law from advertising Skin-So-Soft as an insect repellent, so word of its effectiveness as a repellent is primarily spread by devotees. What are the relative advantages and disadvantages of this word-of-mouth advertising.

Sources: "Offbeat Bite-Fighter for Flea High Season," *Self*, May 1988, p. 36: "A Rumor That Keeps Buzzing," *Time,* September 5, 1988, p. 53; and "Deet Is Still the Buzz Word," *Boston Globe,* July 12, 1989, p. 25; "Avon's Skin So Soft." *ABC News Business World Broadcast*, September 3, 1989.

TESTING TERMS AND CONCEPTS

Part One To test your understanding of the concepts presented in this chapter, write the letter of the most appropriate answer on the line next to the question number. Answers to these questions are at the end of this chapter.

_____ 1. Which of the following is not a mass-promotion tool?

A. advertising
B. personal selling
C. sells promotion
D. public relations
E. both (B) and (D)

_____ 2. Which of the following is not an advertising objective to inform?

A. telling the market about a new product
B. suggesting new uses for a product
C. explaining how the product works
D. correcting false impressions
E. building brand preference

_____ 3. Typical advertising objectives include all but which of the following?

A. to inform
B. to persuade
C. to remind
D. to design
E. none of the above

_____ 4. A related form of persuasive advertising is _____________ advertising.

A. reinforcement
B. comparison
C. reminder
D. informative
E. relative

_____ 5. Dan Roots has a product in the introduction stage of the life cycle, where his objective is to build primary demand. Which advertising objective should Roots be pursuing?

A. persuade
B. inform
C. design
D. remind
E. desire

_____ 6. Measuring the communication effect reveals whether an ad is communicating well. This process is called:

A. ad continuity.
B. ad pulsing.
C. copy testing.
D. measuring the sales effect.
E. sales evaluation.

_____ 7. Milestones Percussion, Inc., displayed photographs of its drum sets being used on elaborate stages, surrounded by bright lights and a cheering audience. This message, execution style is referred to as:

A. lifestyles.
B. fantasy.
C. mood or image.
D. musical.
E. technical expertise.

_____ 8. Message execution refers to:

A. style, tone, words, and format.
B. style, design, image, and format.
C. design, tone, words, and format.
D. design, image, words, and format.
E. style, tone, image, and format.

_____ 9. Sales promotion may take which of the following forms?

A. consumer promotion
B. trade promotion
C. salesforce promotion
D. only (A) and (C)
E. all of the above

_____ 10. In an effort to determine the effectiveness of a sales promotion program a company may use ____________ to learn how many individuals recall the program.

A. experiments
B. games
C. consumer surveys
D. contests
E. sweepstakes

_____ 11. A company which is dealing with legislators and government officials to promote or defeat legislation and regulations is involved in?

A. lobbying
B. counseling
C. corporate communications
D. product publicity
E. patronage

_____ 12. The best measure of publicity effectiveness is a(n) ___________ report.

A. awareness
B. exposures
C. awareness/knowledge/attitude
D. sales and profit impact
E. frequency and reach

_____ 13. ___________ are the most effective, but most expensive, way to introduce a new product.

A. Samples
B. Coupons
C. Cash refunds
D. Price packs
E. Premiums

_____ 14. ___________ refers to the qualitative value of a message exposure through a given medium.

A. Reach
B. Tone
C. Frequency
D. Impact
E. Style

_____ 15. Many analysts believe that ___________ activities do not build long-term consumer preference and loyalty as does ___________.

A. sales promotion, public relations
B. advertising, personal selling
C. public relations, sales promotion
D. sales promotion, personal selling
E. sales promotion, advertising

Part Two To test your understanding of the concepts presented in this chapter, respond to the following questions by writing the letter T or F on the line next to the question number if you believe the statement is true or false, respectively. Answers to these questions are found at the end of this chapter.

_____ 1. Advertising consists of personal forms of communication conducted through paid sponsorship.

_____ 2. Persuasive advertising becomes important when a company's objective is to build selective demand.

_____ 3. Some reminder advertising has become comparison advertising which compares one brand directly or indirectly with one or more other brands.

_____ 4. Messages should be rated exclusively for their believability.

_____ 5. The message execution style which shows one or more persons using the product in a normal setting is referred to as a slice-of-life.

_____ 6. Sales promotion activities are not designed to be customer franchise building.

_____ 7. Reach is a measure of how many times the average person in the target market is exposed to the message.

_____ 8. Ad continuity refers to scheduling exposures unevenly within a given period of time.

_____ 9. Sales promotion objectives are derived from basic marketing communication objectives, which are derived from more basic marketing objectives developed for the product.

_____ 10. Push money is a form of trade promotion.

_____ 11. Lobbying is an activity of public relations.

_____ 12. If the number of stories is insufficient, a publicist may well decide to create news.

_____ 13. Advertising media do not vary appreciably in availability, cost and quality from country to country.

_____ 14. The most basic issue international advertisers face concerns the degree to which global advertising should be adapted to the unique characteristics of various country markets.

_____ 15. Many sellers think of sales promotion as a tool for breaking down brand loyalty and advertising as a tool for building up brand loyalty.

Answers

Applying Terms and Concepts

Barone Wines

1. A
2. B
3. D
4. continuity
5. C

Tyco Car Wash

1. B
2. consumer
3. C
4. B
5. C

Skin So Soft

1. a. *Samples:* Samplers are offers of a trial amount of a product. A small container of Skin-So-Soft could be included free of charge along with each Avon order delivered to a customer.

   b. *Coupons:* Coupons are certificates that give buyers a savings when they purchase specified products. A coupon for a specified savings off the regular price of Skin-So-Soft could be included in each Avon catalog or distributed by the Avon salesperson when servicing customers.

   c. *Cash refund offers:* Rebates are price reductions given after the purchase rather than at the time of sale. Avon could allow the consumer to receive a portion of the retail price back, after the consumer sends a "proof-of-purchase" to them.

   d. *Price packs*: Price packs offer consumers savings off the regular price of a product, Skin So Soft could be sold as a single item at a reduced price, or it could be bundled with another product and sold at a price below that which both would cost if sold separately.

   e. *Advertising specialties:* Advertising specialties are useful items imprinted with an advertiser's name that are given as gifts to consumers. Avon could imprint the company or product name on pens, T-shirts, caps, coffee mugs, key rings, and so on.

f. *Patronage awards:* Patronage rewards are cash or other rewards for the regular use of a certain company's products or services. Avon could keep track of the volume of purchases per customer and allow customers who reach a certain level to receive a container of Skin So Soft (or other product) at no cost.

g. *Point of purchase:* Point-of-purchase promotions include displays and demonstrations at the point of purchase or sale. The Avon sales representative could use Skin So Soft during an in-home demonstration of Avon products.

h. *Contests, sweepstakes, and games:* A contest calls for consumers to submit an entry that will be judged by a panel charged with selecting the best entries. Avon could have contestants supply a new phrase utilizing the letters SSS. Sweepstakes call for consumers to submit their names for a drawing. A game presents consumers with something every time they buy that may or may not help them to win a prize. Avon could distribute letters of the company name with their other products, offering as a prize to whoever gets all the letters to spell Avon a container of Skin So Soft. (Avon would probably choose one letter for minimal distribution to cut down on the total number of winners.)

2. Personal communication channels involve two or more persons communicating directly with one another. They might communicate face-to-face, person-to-person, over the telephone, or through the mail. Personal communication channels are effective because they individualize presentation and feedback.

   There are three types of personal communication channels: advocate channels, consisting of company salespeople contacting buyers in the marketplace; expert channels, consisting of independent persons with expertise making claims to target buyers; and social channels, consisting of neighbors, friends, family members, and associates talking to target buyers. This last channel, known as word-of-mouth influence, is the most persuasive in many product areas.

   Word-of-mouth has the advantage of being more believable in that acquaintances have nothing to gain financially from the advice they are giving to potential buyers. Most of the time, they are simply trying to provide assistance.

   The disadvantages of word-of-mouth are that it may be inaccurate and biased. The product's supporters may be well-intentioned but ill-informed, and therefore impart poor information.

Personal influence is especially important when the product is expensive, risky, purchased infrequently, or has significant social status. But even with a product as "simple" as Skin So Soft, personal influence can greatly impact sales.

Testing Terms and Concepts

Part One

1. B E
2. E M
3. D E
4. B M
5. B M
6. C - D Copy testing involves measuring whether an ad is communicating well. This process can be carried out before or after an ad is printed or broadcast. There are three methods of advertising pretesting including direct rating, portfolio testing and laboratory testing. There are two popular methods of post-testing ads. They are recall tests and recognition tests.
7. C M
8. A D
9. E M
10. C E
11. A E
12. C - D The easiest measure of publicity effectiveness is the number of exposures in the media. Public relations people give the clients "clipping books" showing all the media that carried news about products and summaries.

    However, this exposure measure is not very satisfying. It does not tell how many people actually read or heard the message, nor what they thought afterward. In addition, since the media overlap in readership and viewership, it does not give information on the net audience reached. A better measure is the change in product awareness, knowledge and attitude resulting from the publicity campaign. Assessing this change requires measuring the before and after levels of these measures.
13. A M
14. D M
15. E D

Part Two

1. F M
2. T M
3. F E
4. F E
5. T D
6. F - D In general, sales promotions should be consumer franchise building--they should promote the product's positioning and include a selling message along with the deal. Ideally, the objective is to build long-run consumer demand rather than to prompt temporary brand switching. If properly designed, every sales-promotion tool has consumer franchise building potential
7. F M
8. F M
9. T M
10. T E
11. T E
12. T M
13. F E
14. T - M International advertisers face many complexities not encountered by domestic advertisers. The most basic issue concerns the degree to which global advertising should be adapted to the unique characteristics of various country markets. Some large advertisers have attempted to support their global brands with highly standardized worldwide advertising. Standardization produces many benefits--lower advertising costs, greater coordination of global advertising efforts, and a more consistent worldwide company or product image. However, standardization also has drawbacks. Most importantly, it ignores the fact that country markets differ greatly in their cultures, demographics, and economic conditions. Thus, most international advertisers think globally but act locally. They develop global advertising strategies that bring efficiency and consistency to their worldwide advertising efforts. Then they adapt their advertising programs to make them more responsive to consumer needs and expectations within local markets.
15. T D

CHAPTER 17

PROMOTING PRODUCTS: PERSONAL SELLING AND SALES MANAGEMENT

CHAPTER OVERVIEW

"Everyone lives by selling something." The high cost of personal selling in a company's promotion mix calls for an effective process of sales management, consisting of several steps: setting salesforce objectives; designing salesforce strategy, structure, size and compensation; and recruiting, selecting, training, supervising, and evaluating salespeople. The focus of personal selling is on being a customer-oriented, active order-getter. Training helps salespeople master the seven steps of the selling process: prospecting and qualifying, the preapproach, the approach, presentation and demonstration, handling objections, closing the sale, and the follow-up.

CHAPTER OBJECTIVES

When you finish this chapter, you should be able to accomplish the following:

1. Explain the roll and nature of personal selling and the role of the sales force.
2. Describe the basics of managing the salesforce and tell how to set salesforce strategy, how to pick a structure--territorial, product customer or complex--and how to ensure that salesforce size is appropriate.
3. Identify the key issues in recruiting, selecting, training, and compensating salespeople.
4. Discuss supervising salespeople, including directing motivating and evaluating performance.
5. Apply the principles of personal selling process, and outline the steps in the selling process--qualifying, preapproach and approach, presentation and demonstration, handling objectives, closing and follow-up.

LECTURE/STUDENT NOTES

I. The Role of Personal Selling

A. The nature of personal selling

B. The role of the salesforce

II. Managing the Salesforce

A. Designing salesforce strategy and structure

1. Salesforce Structure

a. Territorial salesforce structure

b. product salesforce structure

c. customer salesforce structure

d. complex salesforce structures

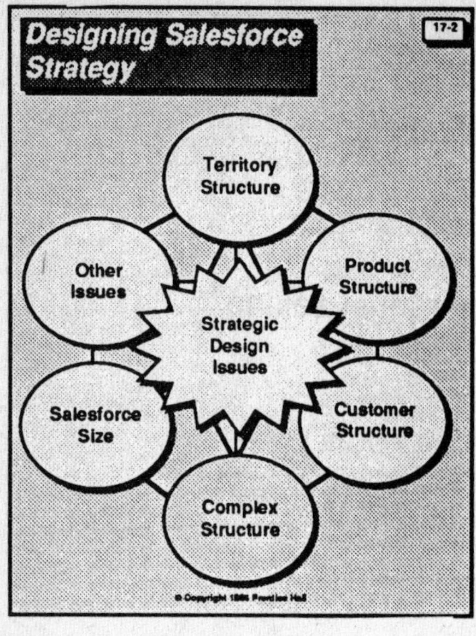

2. Salesforce size

3. Other salesforce strategy and structure issues

   a. outside and inside salesforces

   b. team selling

B. Recruiting and selecting salespeople

1. What makes a good salesperson

2. Recruiting procedures

3. Selecting salespeople

C. Training salespeople

D. Compensating salespeople

E. Supervising salespeople

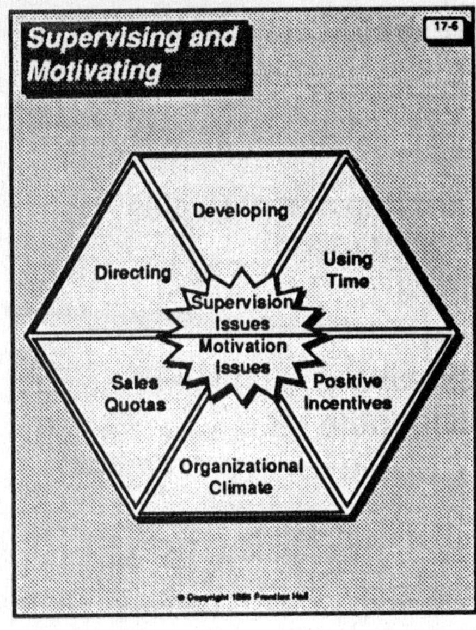

1. Directing salespeople

   a. developing customer targets and call norms

   b. using sales time efficiently

2. Motivating salespeople

   a. organizational climate

   b. sales quotas

   c. positive incentives

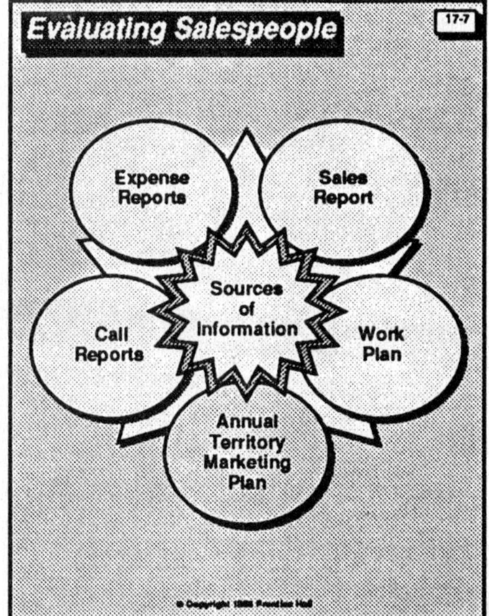

F. Evaluating salespeople

1. Sources of information

2. Formal evaluation of performance

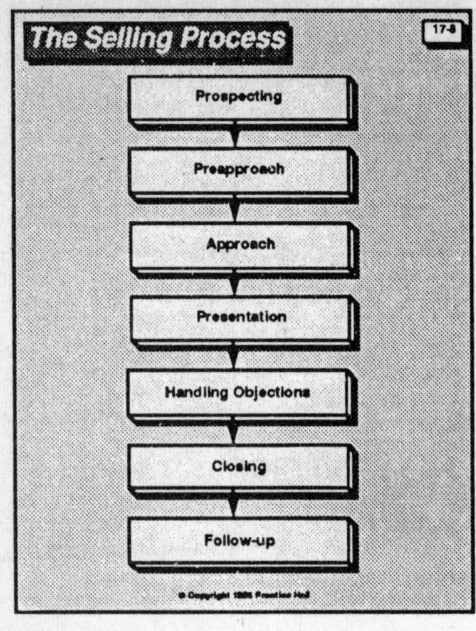

a. comparing salespeople's performance

b. comparing current sales with past sales

c. qualitative evaluation of salespeople

III. Principles of Personal Selling

A. The Personal selling process

B. Composite of sales force opinions

1. Prospecting and Qualifying

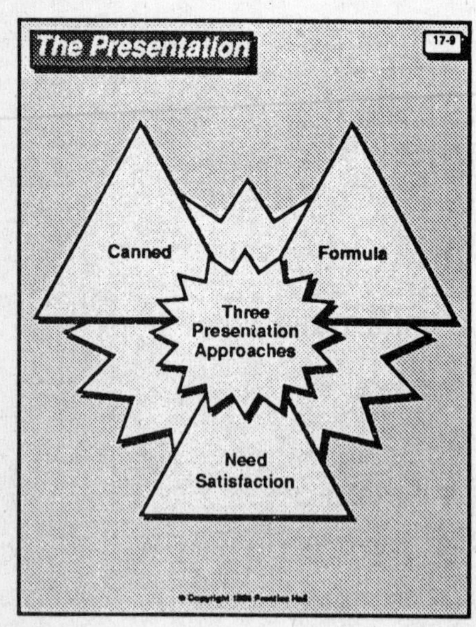

2. Preapproach

3. Approach

4. Presentation and Demonstration

5. Handling Objections

6. Closing

7. Follow-Up

C. Relationship marketing

KEY TERMS

The step in the selling process in which the salesperson meets and greets the buyer to get the relationship off to a good start.

Approach (p. 600)

The step in the selling process in which the salesperson asks the customer for an order.

Closing (p. 601)

A salesforce organization in which salespeople specialize in selling only to certain customers or industries.

Customer sales-force structure (p. 586)

The last step in the selling process in which the salesperson follows up after the sale to ensure customer satisfaction and repeat business.

Follow-up (p. 601)

The step in the selling process in which the salesperson seeks out, clarifies, and overcomes customer objections to buying.

Handling objections (p. 601)

Salespeople who conduct business from their offices via telephone or visits from prospective buyers.

Inside sales-force (p. 587)

Outside salespeople who travel to call on customers.

Outside sales-force (p. 587)

The step in the selling process in which the salesperson learns as much as possible about a prospective customer before making a sales call.

Preapproach (p. 600)

The step in the selling process in which the salesperson tells the product "story" to the buyer, showing how the product will make or save money for the buyer's company.

Presentation (p. 600)

A salesforce organization in which salespeople specialize in selling only a portion of the company's product or lines.

Product sales-force structure (p. 586)

The step in the selling process in which the salesperson identifies qualified potential customers.

Prospecting (p. 599)

The process of creating, maintaining and enhancing strong, value laden relationships with customers and other stakeholders.

Relationship marketing (p. 601)

The analysis, planning, implementation, and control of salesforce activities. It includes setting salesforce objectives; designing salesforce strategy; and recruiting, selecting, training, supervising, and evaluating the firm's salespeople.

Sales-force management (p. 585)

An individual acting for a company by performing one or more of the following activities: prospecting, communicating, servicing, and information gathering.

Salespersons (p. 583)

Standards set for salespeople, stating the amount they should sell and how sales should be divided among the company's products.

Sales quotas (p. 596)

The steps that the salesperson follows when selling, which include prospecting and qualifying, preapproach, presentation and demonstration, handling objections, closing, and follow-up.

Selling process (p. 599)

Using teams of people from sales, marketing, engineering, finance, technical support, and even upper management to service large complex accounts.

Team selling (p. 588)

Using the telephone to sell directly to consumers.

Telemarketing (p. 587)

A salesforce organization that assigns each salesperson to an exclusive geographic territory in which that salesperson carries the company's full line.

Territorial sales-force structure (p. 595)

An approach to setting salesforce size, whereby the company groups accounts into different size classes and then determines how many salespeople are needed to call on them the desired number of times.

Workload approach (p. 587)

APPLYING TERMS AND CONCEPTS

To determine how well you understand the materials in this chapter, read each of the following brief cases and then respond to the questions that follow. Answers are given at the end of this chapter.

Hemphill Industries

Guy Bovi was a May graduate of St. Paul's College in Quebec City, who accepted a position with Hemphill Industries of Vancouver. Bovi was hired as a sales representative and would be assigned, after training, to the Pacific region of BC, Washington and Oregon, currently staffed by Elana Watt who was retiring in six months.

Hemphill Industries manufactures and distributes industrial machine tools (lathes and milling machines) under the Hemphill brand name throughout the United States and Canada. Its products are handled by sales representatives employed by Hemphill Industries, with each representative concentrating on a given geographic location.

When Bovi was hired, he was told that in the coming year he was expected to increase sales to existing Hemphill customers by 15 percent and sales to new customers in the region by 5 percent. For his efforts, he would earn a base salary of $21,000 plus a commission of 2 percent on all sales exceeding $500,000. The $500,000 figure was considered modest and would be increased in subsequent years, as several of the computerized machine tools manufactured by Hemphill had a selling price in excess of $80,000. In addition to this salary, Bovi would have use of a company vehicle and an expense account to a limit of $300 per month.

Bovi would report to the district sales manager, Claude Caron, who would also supervise his training program. The training program consisted of twelve weeks of in-house training, followed by several months of field training with an

The in-house training was designed to familiarize the sales representative with company policies and procedures. Approximately six weeks of the training was devoted to machine setup and operation. The balance of the program included training the representative to identify customer needs and then propose solutions to the problems utilizing Hemphill machine tools.

Hemphill sales representatives were responsible for making their own contact with customers and concentrating on speaking with a single purchasing agent or buying committee. It was stressed that sales representatives are expected to answer all questions posed by the customer.

Questions

_____ 1. When Bovi was assigned to the Pacific region to be the exclusive sales representative of Hamphill Machine Tools in that area, Mephill appeared to use which sales-force structure?

A. territorial-structured
B. product-structured
C. customer-structured
D. market-structured
E. matrix-structured

_____ 2. When Bovi was told to increase sales to existing customers by 15 percent and sales to new customers by 5 percent, he was in essence being given:

A. a salesforce strategy.
B. a salesforce structure.
C. an objective.
D. an annual call schedule.
E. workload analysis.

_____ 3. Guy Bovi, as a sales representative, will probably find that the ____________ approach to selling will be most effective.

A. supporting sales
B. order taker
C. sales oriented
D. customer problem solving
E. product-oriented

_____ 4. Hemphill's strategy of speaking to an individual purchasing agent or buying committee is an example of which sales approach strategy?

A. sales representative to buyer
B. sales representative to buyer group
C. conference selling
D. seminar selling
E. both (A) and (B)

_____ 5. As a seller of expensive machine tools, Bovi is faced with a position requiring:

A. little product knowledge.
B. little customer knowledge.
C. very creative selling.
D. routine order taking.
E. routine problem solving skills.

<u>**Nonverbal Communication**</u>

In recent years marketers have begun to pay close attention to the role of nonverbal factors in the communication process. Communication is a complex process composed of many elements with signals, both verbal and nonverbal, continually flowing back and forth between the communicators. Studies have indicated that such wordless signals as the vocal element (tone, pitch, volume, resonance), the facial element (expression, eye contact), the proximity element (physical distance between communicators), the kinetic element (body and limb movements), the physical element (grooming, dress), and general deportment all play a role in the communication process. Nonverbal clues may actually alter what the receiver has "heard." Receivers tend to search out such cues to determine the "real" message.

Questions

1. Explain the significance of such findings for a salesperson.

____

____

____

_____ 2. Nonverbal skills would be <u>most</u> useful to salespeople in which of the following sales positions?

A. inside order takers
B. outside order takers
C. sales engineers
D. creative sales
E. detailers

_____ 3. The adept use of nonverbal communication would be evidence of which of the following traits of a successful salesperson?

A. empathy
B. ego drive
C. aggressiveness
D. deceptiveness
E. perseverance

_____ 4. A salesperson who believes in the usefulness of nonverbal behavior would be most likely to use which of the following types of sales presentations?

A. canned approach
B. formulated approach
C. need-dissatisfaction approach
D. AIDA approach
E. none of the above

Goodwin Publishing Co.

Nikki Lawson was sales manager for Goodwin Publishing Company, a small firm located in Charlottetown, PEI. Goodwin specializes in business texts used at both the undergraduate and graduate levels. Cathy Goodwin, founder of the company, focused on business texts because she had been a professor of marketing at Mount Allison College. Goodwin was dissatisfied with the quality of available books so she wrote her own, Marketing in Canada. The text sold well -- so well in fact that she left teaching to devote herself to the publishing business. Goodwin's book is still in print, now co-authored by two of Goodwin's colleagues at Mount Allison. Goodwin controls 23 other titles, several of which are industry standards selling in excess of 20,000 copies per year. Sales for the company totaled $14 million last year and returned a respectable profit.

There had been considerable consolidation in the publishing business the last few years. The industry is now dominated by a few firms. Individual company names still appear as publishers but most are now subsidiaries of some conglomerate. Goodwin is still one of the few true independents and she wanted to stay that way.

Goodwin decided the company needed to increase profits. The profits would be used to increase the stockholder dividend and to begin buying back company stock. There was little indication of stockholder discontent and Goodwin wanted that to continue. And what better way than to increase the value of their holdings and their dividends. Sales projections were flat so the only way to increase profits was to reduce costs.

Goodwin had always treated her employees well. Her 20 sales representatives enjoyed privileges that were the envy of the industry. The sales staff was paid a straight salary and enjoyed generous fringe benefits including a company car and a liberal expense account. Goodwin thought that perhaps the company was too generous. Goodwin asked Carlson to review several aspects of the sales department operation. Company records indicated that approximately 10,200 sales calls to college faculty were made last year, with each sales representative averaging 17 visitations per week, over a 30-week academic year. Carlson was also asked to review the compensation program and general role of the sales force.

Questions

1. Using workload analysis, calculate how many sales representatives could be terminated, if Goodwin instructed Carlson to increase the average number of sales calls per representative from 17 to 19 per week holding the total number of calls constant.

2. Discuss the relative merits of each of the following compensation programs for a sales representative:

A. Straight salary ______________________________

____

____

____

B. Straight commission ______________________________

____

____

____

C. Salary plus bonus ______________________________

____

____

____

D. Salary plus commission ______________________________

____

____

____

3. Discuss the general role of the salesforce and the link they provide between the company and its customers.

____

____

____

____

____

____

____

____

____

____

TESTING TERMS AND CONCEPTS

Part One To test your understanding of the concepts presented in this chapter, write the letter of the most appropriate answer on the line next to the question number. Answers to these questions are found at the end of this chapter.

_____ 1. Which of the following tasks involves the identification and cultivation of new customers?

A. prospecting
B. communications
C. selling
D. information gathering
E. presentation and demonstration

_____ 2. Which of the following involves the most creative form of selling?

A. order taking
B. technical specialist
C. selling intangible products
D. selling tangible products
E. detailing

_____ 3. When a sales representative brings resource people from the company to meet with one or more buyers to discuss problems and mutual opportunities, the firm is engaged in __________ selling.

A. sales representative to buyer group
B. conference
C. seminar
D. sales team to buyer group
E. group

_____ 4. Many companies determine the size of the salesforce by using:

A. industry averages.
B. the buildup approach.
C. the workload approach.
D. the customer-contact approach.
E. relationship marketing approach.

_____ 5. Which of the following elements in a compensation package provide the greatest amount of incentive for sales representative?

A. salary
B. fringe benefits
C. expense allowances
D. commissions
E. use of company vehicle

_____ 6. Which of the following has not been identified as a desirable trait of a sales representative?

A. sympathy
B. enthusiasm
C. self-confidence
D. initiative
E. product knowledge

_____ 7. Which of the following statements about sales training is not true?

A. Sales training can be a major expenditure for a company.
B. Sales training has become more important in recent years.
C. Sales training is needed only by new recruits.
D. The growth in technically complex products has extended the length of sales training programs.
E. both (A) and (C)

_____ 8. A sales representative attempts to learn as much as possible about the prospective company and its buyers during the _____________ step(s) of selling.

A. approach
B. preapproach
C. prospecting and qualifying
D. presentation and demonstration
E. closing

_____ 9. The customer oriented approach to selling which trains salespeople in customer problem solving, is most consistent with the ____________ concept.

A. production
B. product
C. selling
D. marketing
E. societal-marketing

_____ 10. ____________ describes the feeling that the sales representatives get regarding their opportunities, value, and rewards for good performance.

A. Organizational climate
B. Sales quota
C. Competitive climate
D. Positive incentives
E. Corporate culture

_____ 11. Which of the following is not considered to be one of the positive motivators a company may use to stimulate the salesforce?

A. sales meetings
B. sales contests
C. awards
D. variable sales quotas
E. both (A) and (B)

_____ 12. A good sales representative attempts to reduce a buyer's cognitive dissonance during the ____________ step of selling.

A. presentation and demonstration
B. handling objections
C. closing
D. follow-up
E. prospecting

_____ 13. __________ is the analysis, planning, implementation and control of salesforce activities.

A. Salesmanship
B. Salesforce management
C. Sales promotion
D. Personal selling
E. Human resource management

_____ 14. Once a company has decided on the desired selling approach, it can use either a(n) __________ or a(n) __________ salesforce to accomplish company objectives.

A. indirect, commission
B. direct, field
C. field, inside
D. indirect, inside
E. direct, contractual

_____ 15. When a sales manager establishes a schedule with the desired number of sales calls per period for current and prospective accounts, the sales manager is:

A. developing a call list.
B. establishing a client list.
C. developing customer targets and call norms.
D. developing a contact schedule.
E. establishing workforce size and compensation.

Part Two To test your understanding of the concepts presented in this chapter, respond to the following questions by writing the letter T or F on the line next to the question number if you believe the statement is true or false, respectively. Answers to these questions may be found at the end of this chapter.

_____ 1. Salespeople have been found to be unnecessary for nonprofit organizations.

_____ 2. Prospecting requires sales representatives to communicate information skillfully to potential customers about a company's products and services.

_____ 3. Sales assistants are inside salespeople who provide clerical backup for the outside salespeople.

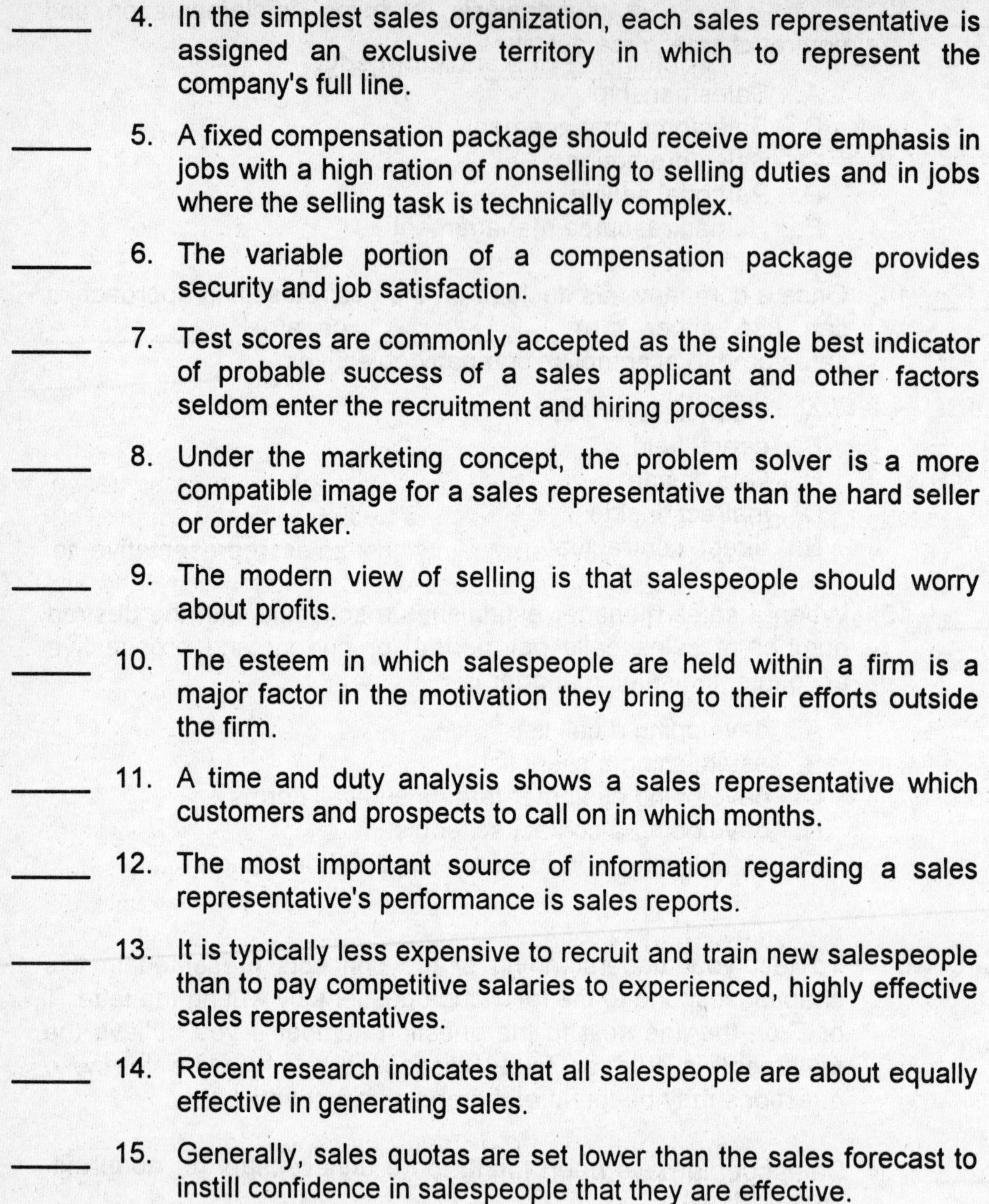

_____ 4. In the simplest sales organization, each sales representative is assigned an exclusive territory in which to represent the company's full line.

_____ 5. A fixed compensation package should receive more emphasis in jobs with a high ration of nonselling to selling duties and in jobs where the selling task is technically complex.

_____ 6. The variable portion of a compensation package provides security and job satisfaction.

_____ 7. Test scores are commonly accepted as the single best indicator of probable success of a sales applicant and other factors seldom enter the recruitment and hiring process.

_____ 8. Under the marketing concept, the problem solver is a more compatible image for a sales representative than the hard seller or order taker.

_____ 9. The modern view of selling is that salespeople should worry about profits.

_____ 10. The esteem in which salespeople are held within a firm is a major factor in the motivation they bring to their efforts outside the firm.

_____ 11. A time and duty analysis shows a sales representative which customers and prospects to call on in which months.

_____ 12. The most important source of information regarding a sales representative's performance is sales reports.

_____ 13. It is typically less expensive to recruit and train new salespeople than to pay competitive salaries to experienced, highly effective sales representatives.

_____ 14. Recent research indicates that all salespeople are about equally effective in generating sales.

_____ 15. Generally, sales quotas are set lower than the sales forecast to instill confidence in salespeople that they are effective.

Answers

Applying Terms and Concepts

Hemphill Industries

1. A
2. C
3. D
4. E
5. C

Nonverbal Communication

1. The salesperson must communicate effectively to sell effectively. Insights into nonverbal communication can assist a sales representative in better preparing the sales presentation to be more effective in dealing with a client. These insights also allow the sales representative to better understand the customer's responses and attitudes and can help the salesperson frame, tailor, and adjust the sales presentation.
2. D
3. A
4. D

Goodwin Publishing Company

1. Carlson currently supervises 20 sales representatives who average 17 visitations per week. Given Goodwin's directive, the number of sales representatives could be reduced by 2. The calculations are as follows: 10,200 calls divided by 30 weeks equals 340 calls per week. 340 divided by 19 calls per sales representative equals (approximately) 18 sales representatives.

   A relatively modest increase in the required number of sales calls per week per sales representative, reduced the sales force by 2.

2. a. *Straight salary* provides maximum security for the sales representative. Their earnings are guaranteed regardless of sales. There may be minimal incentive for the sales representative to make additional calls to generate additional sales.

b. *Straight commission* provides maximum incentive for the sales representative since their earnings are based on how much they sell. While there is relatively little security for the sales representative; the company only pays a commission when sales are generated.

c. *Salary plus bonus* provides some security for the sales representative but also provides an incentive. The incentive is based on the bonus to be received after other goals and objectives have been met. The bonus may be paid based on such goals and objectives as an increase in sales, increase in profitability, reduction of costs, increase in new accounts, or sales of certain products.

d. *Salary plus commission* provides some security for the sales representatives but also provides an incentive. The incentive is based on the commission earned from the generation of sales.

3. In many cases, salespeople serve both masters--the seller and the buyer. First, they represent the company to the customers. They find and develop new customers and communicate information about the company's products and services. They sell products by approaching customers, presenting their products, answering objections, negotiating prices and terms, and closing sales. In addition, salespeople provide services to customers, carry out market research and intelligence work, and fill out sales call reports.

   At the same time, salespeople represent customers to the company, acting inside the firm as a "champion" of customers' interests. Salespeople relay customer concerns about company products and actions back to those who can handle them. They learn about customer needs, and work with others in the company to develop greater customer value. Thus, the salesperson often acts as an "account manager" who manages the relationship between the seller and buyer.

   As companies move toward a stronger market orientation, their sales forces are becoming more market focused and customer oriented. The old view was that salespeople should worry about sales and the company should worry about profit. However, the current view holds that salespeople should be concerned with more than just producing sales--they also must know how to produce customer satisfaction and company profit. They should be able to look at sales data, measure market potential, gather market intelligence, and develop marketing strategies and plans. They should know how to orchestrate the firm's efforts toward delivering customer value and satisfaction. A market-oriented rather than a sales-oriented sales force will be more effective in the long run. Beyond winning new customers and making sales, it will help the company to create long-term, profitable relationships with customers.

Testing Terms and Concepts

Part One

1. A E
2. C M
3. B E
4. C E
5. D E
6. A M
7. C D
8. B M
9. D - D The customer-oriented approach--the one most often used in today's professional selling--trains salespeople in customer problem solving. The salesperson learns how to identify customer needs and find solutions. This approach assumes that customer needs provide sales opportunities, that customers appreciate good suggestions, and that they will be loyal to salespeople who have their long-term interests at heart. In one survey, purchasing agents described these qualities as the ones they most disliked in salespeople: pushy, arrogant, unreliable, too talkative, fails to ask about needs. The qualities they valued most included reliability and credibility, integrity, innovativeness in solving problems, and product knowledge. Thus, the problem solver salesperson, fits better with the marketing concept than with the production, product or selling concepts.
10. A M
11. D M

12. D - D The last step in the selling process--follow-up--is necessary if the salesperson wants to ensure customer satisfaction and repeat business. Right after closing, the salesperson should complete any details on delivery time, purchase terms, and other matters. The salesperson should schedule a follow-up call when the initial order is received to make sure there is proper installation, instruction, and servicing. This visit would reveal any problems, assure the buyer of the salesperson's interest, and reduce any buyer concerns that might have arisen since the sale.

13. B E
14. E D
15. C D

<u>Part Two</u>

1. F E
2. F M
3. T E
4. T E
5. T D
6. F M
7. F M
8. T M
9. F - E The old view is that salespeople should worry about sales and the company should worry about profit. However, a newer view holds that salespeople should be concerned with more than just producing sales--they must also know how to produce customer satisfaction and company profit. They should know how to look at sales data, measure market potential, gather market intelligence, and develop marketing strategies and plans. Salespeople need marketing-analysis skills, especially at higher levels of sales management. A market-oriented rather than a sales-oriented salesforce will be more effective in the long run.
10. T M
11. F M
12. T E
13. F D
14. F M
15. F D

CHAPTER 18

BUILDING CUSTOMER RELATIONSHIPS THROUGH SATISFACTION, VALUE AND QUALITY

CHAPTER OVERVIEW

This chapter describes in detail how companies can go about winning customers and out performing competitors. The answer lies in the marketing concept--in doing a better job of meeting and satisfying customer needs. Companies need to define customer value and satisfaction and then deliver these better than the competition. Marketers must understand the key to retaining customers is to engage in relationship marketing which involves creating, maintaining and enhancing relationships with customers and other interested parties. Increasingly, marketing is moving away from a marketing mix focus to a relationship focus--from a focus on individual transactions toward a focus on building value laden relationships and marketing networks. Customer satisfaction and company profitability are closely linked to product and service quality. Higher levels of quality result in greater customer satisfaction, which at the same time supports higher prices and often lower costs. Therefore total quality marketing, with both an internal and external focus is becoming increasingly important in today's competitive marketplace.

CHAPTER OBJECTIVES

When you finish this chapter, you should be able to accomplish the following:

1. Define customer value and customer satisfaction.
2. Explain how companies deliver value and satisfaction through a value chain and a value delivery system.
3. Discuss attracting new users and retaining customers by developing relationship marketing.
4. Clarify the concept of total quality marketing defining quality and discussing the importance of building profitable relationships with customers.

LECTURE/STUDENT NOTES

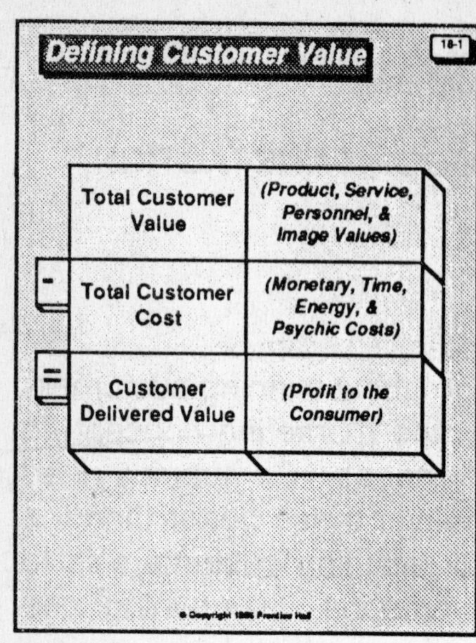

I. Defining Customer Value and Satisfaction

A. Customer value

B. Customer satisfaction

II. Delivering Customer Value and Satisfaction

Value Chain
18-3
Support Activities
Firm Infrastructure
Human Resource Management
Technology Development
Procurement
Inbound Logistics
Operations
Outbound Logistics
Marketing and Sales
Service
Primary Activities

A. Value chain

B. Value delivery system

III. Retaining Customers

A. The cost of lost customers

B. The need for customer retention

C. The key: customer relationship marketing

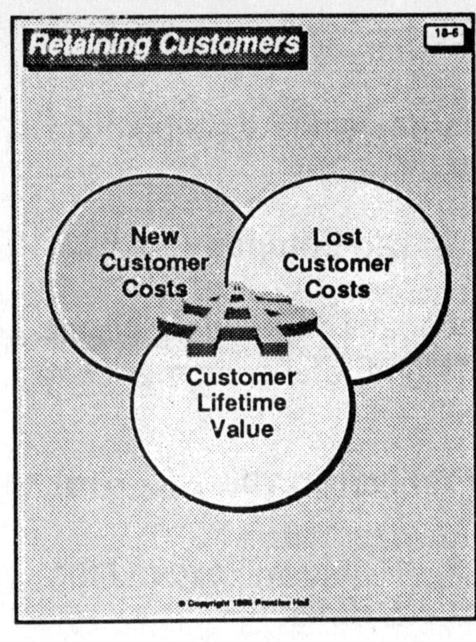

1. Financial benefits

2. Social benefits

3. Structural ties

D. The Ultimate test: Customer profitability

IV. Implementing Total Quality Marketing

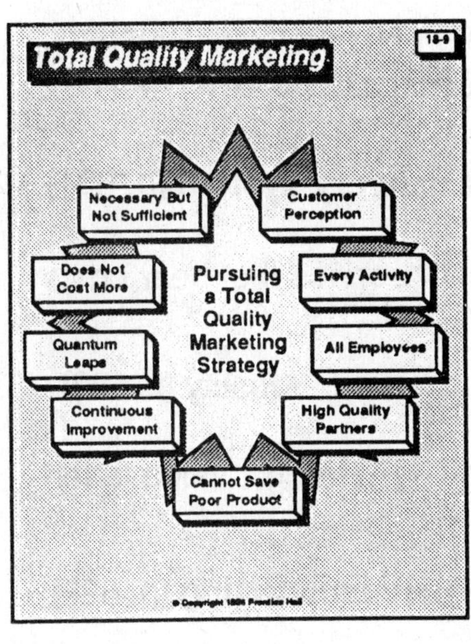

A. Total quality management

B. Marketing's role in total quality

KEY TERMS

A company that focuses on customer developments in designing its marketing strategies and on delivering superior value to its target customers.

Customer-centred company (p. 613)

The consumers' assessment of the product's overall capacity to satisfy his or her needs. The difference between total customer value and total customer cost of a marketing offer--"profit" to the customer.

Customer delivered value (p. 615)

The amount by which revenues from a given customer over time will exceed the company's costs of attracting, selling, and servicing that customer.

Customer lifetime value (p. 628)

The system made up of the value chains of the company and its suppliers, distributors, and ultimately customers who work together to deliver value to customers.

Customer value delivery system (p. 621)

The totality of features and characteristics of a product or service that bear on its ability to satisfy stated or implied needs.

Quality (p. 629)

The process of creating, maintaining, and enhancing strong, value-laden relationships with customers and other stakeholders.

Relationship marketing (p. 623)

The total of all monetary, time, energy and psychic costs associated with a marketing offer.

Total customer cost (p. 615)

The total of all of the product, services, personnel, and image values that a buyer receives from a marketing offer.

Total customer value (p. 615)

A major tool for identifying ways to create more customer value.

Value chain (p. 619)

APPLYING TERMS AND CONCEPTS

To determine how well you understand the materials in this chapter, read each of the following brief cases and then respond to the questions that follow. Answers are at the end of this chapter.

Eastern Townships University

Eastern Townships University is a midsized institution located in Quebec. Eastern offers baccalaureate degree programs in a variety of areas including anthropology, art, biology, business administration, chemistry, computer science, economics, education, English, French, history, linguistics, mathematics, music, philosophy, sociology, and theatre. The university also offers graduate degree programs in art, biology, economics, education, linguistics, mathematics, and philosophy. Eastern is a widely respected institution but one whose enrollment has declined slightly over the last few years. The university is also faced with increasing costs and declining financial support from the province. In a recent session, the provincial legislature ruled that Eastern may raise its tuition and fees, as needed, to offset its declining support.

Michelle Romuld, President of the University, is concerned about these trends and recognizes the need to more effectively market the university. In support of this concept, President Romuld has created the position of Vice President for Enrollment, Marketing and Development. Reporting to the Vice President will be the Dean of Student Services as well as the Directors of Admissions, Financial Aid, Publications and Communication, Alumni Affairs and Placement.

Dr. Romuld recognizes the importance of these various areas as they impact enrollment, retention and student satisfaction. In the coming years, she wishes them to work in a more coordinated and synergistic fashion. President Romuld has scheduled a meeting for next week and the new vice president will be on the agenda to discuss enrollment, retention and student satisfaction at Eastern Townships University.

Questions

1. How might a prospective student use the concept of customer delivered value when making a decision to attend Eastern Townships University?

2. How can Eastern Townships University use the concept of customer delivered value to attract new students, and/or improve the retention rate of current students?

Saturn Corporation

On October 25, 1990, the first Saturn automobiles were made available for sale to the general public. In eight short years, Saturn went from an idea to reality. In part, what makes this accomplishment so remarkable is that Saturn is a revolutionary new automobile constructed and sold in a revolutionary new way.

To combat the growing presence of Japanese automobiles, to breathe new life into General Motors--the parent of Saturn Corporation--and to bring the Saturn to market; new relationships had to be forged. New relationships between General Motors and the United Auto Workers, between engineers and designers and production personnel, between (potential) buyers and marketing personnel, and between the company and its suppliers, dealers and the community of Spring Hill, Tennessee--where the Saturn is built. There was a spirit of cooperation and shared commitment and of renewal.

The results of these new relationships have been astounding, with the company, its people, and its products winning a stunning array of awards. Trade groups, publishers, professional associations and government agencies have bestowed recognition on Saturn for its efforts to recruit women and minorities, for excellence in communications and community relations, for preservation of the environment, for innovative marketing techniques, for innovative engineering and product design, and for commitment to customer sovereignty.

Customers, when surveyed by J. D. Power and Associates, consistently rank Saturn Automobiles as having fewer problems and higher quality and higher overall customer satisfaction than many other brands including such prestigious nameplates as Lincoln, Mercedes-Benz, Volvo and BMW. The surveys suggest that Saturn has set standards for product quality that others must strive to match if they wish to compete.

Questions

1. What has Saturn Corporation done that suggests a deviation from classic marketing theory?

____

____

____

____

____

____

____

2. Explain how Saturn Corporation appears to be practicing relationship marketing.

____

3. Discuss how Saturn Corporation appears to have adopted the concept of total quality management.

Chiropractic Care

Dr. Carole Babiak graduated two years ago from the London College of Chiropractic in London, Ontario. Dr. Babiak would eventually open her own office, but upon graduation, she needed two things -- an income to support herself and to begin paying off her $80,000 in school loans, and experience. Experience, not in how to provide appropriate chiropractic and patient care, but experience in how to run a business and have a successful practice.

Upon graduation, Dr. Babiak accepted a position as associate in Cranberry Chiropractic, a practice owned by Dr. Tim Darrow, located in Sudbury, Ontario. Dr. Babiak's salary was a modest $40,000 per year and her primary task was performing spinal adjustments. Dr. Babiak averaged seven adjustments per hour. At seven patients an hour, there was hardly enough time to review the patient's file and perform the adjustment before the receptionist was calling to say the next patient had arrived. Dr. Babiak was dismayed there was no time to get to know the patient. No time to discuss patient care, preventative measures, exercise or nutrition. At $40 per session, Dr. Babiak thought the patient deserved better. She thought she deserved better as well. She hadn't spent the equivalent of nine years in college to work for a task master who's only apparent interest was in making money. "Where was the concern for the patient?" Dr. Babiak decided when she opened her own practice; she would run her office with the patient in mind first and foremost.

Two years of Dr. Darrow were enough. After arranging the needed financing, Dr. Babiak's own practice in Sudbury would open in July.

Questions

1. When Dr. Babiak opens her own chiropractic office, she intends to engage in customer relationship marketing. What is the intent of customer relationship marketing?

____

____

____

____

____

____

____

____

2. Explain the five different levels of relationship that can be formed between the patient and the chiropractor.

   A. Basic ____

   ____

   ____

   ____

B. Reactive ____________________

____

____

____

C. Accountable ____________________

____

____

____

D. Proactive ____________________

____

____

____

E. Partnership ____________________

____

____

____

TESTING TERMS AND CONCEPTS

Part One To test your understanding of the concepts presented in this chapter, write the letter of the most appropriate answer on the line next to the question number. Answers to these questions are found at the end of this chapter.

____ 1. To succeed in today's fiercely competitive marketplace, companies will have to move from a ____________ philosophy to a ____________ philosophy.

A. product and selling, customer and marketing
B. production and product, selling
C. profit oriented, sales oriented
D. marketing, selling
E. customer oriented, company and supplier oriented

_____ 2. Securing and retaining customers will be most effectively done in companies in which all departments and employees have teamed up to form a competitively superior ____________ system.

A. customer value delivery
B. production
C. conventional distribution
D. marketing information
E. communications/promotion

_____ 3. Customers typically buy from the firm they believe offers the highest customer delivered value which is the difference between total customer ____________ and total customer ____________.

A. cost, service
B. service, value
C. cost, profitability
D. service, profitability
E. value, cost

_____ 4. Customer satisfaction with a purchase depends upon the products performance relative to a buyer's ____________.

A. past purchases
B. decision making process
C. expectations
D. negotiating skills
E. costs

_____ 5. Highly satisfied customers produce several benefits for the company. Which of the following is not one of these benefits?

A. They are less price sensitive.
B. They remain customers for a shorter period of time.
C. They buy additional products as the company introduces related products or improvements.
D. They talk favourably about the company and its products.
E. Both (A) and (C)

_____ 6. Customer service centered companies must deliver superior value to their target customers. This means they must be adept in building __________, not just building __________ and they must be skillful in __________ engineering and not just __________ engineering.

A. products, delivery systems, sales, product
B. market, delivery systems, profit, product
C. distribution systems, products, profit, product
D. products, distribution systems, market, product
E. customers, products, market, product

_____ 7. Every firm consists of a collection of activities performed to design, produce, market, deliver and support the firm's products. Together, these activities constitute a(n) __________, which is a major tool for identifying ways to create additional customer value.

A. customer link
B. distribution system
C. integration system
D. value chain
E. production system

_____ 8. Which of the following is not one of the core business processes identified in the textbook?

A. product development process
B. inventory management process
C. order-to-payment process
D. customer service process
E. information management process

_____ 9. Today, more companies are "Partnering" with other members of the supply chain to improve the performance of the __________ system.

A. product delivery
B. customer value delivery
C. service delivery
D. production
E. distribution

_____ 10. Classic marketing theory and practice placed emphasis on creating __________ rather than __________.

A. products, sales
B. sales, profitability
C. transactions, relationship
D. products, profitability
E. sales, products

_____ 11. ___________ marketing involves creating, maintaining, and enhancing strong relationships with customers and other stakeholders.

A. Product-oriented
B. Production-oriented
C. Sales-oriented
D. Relationship
E. Distribution system oriented

_____ 12. Which of the following is not one of the value-building marketing tools used to develop stronger customer bonding and satisfaction?

A. financial benefits
B. social benefits
C. structural ties
D. cross market purchasing
E. both (B) and (D)

_____ 13. The American Society for Quality Control defines quality as the totality of features and characteristics of a product or service that bear on its ability to satisfy stated or implied needs. This is a ___________ centred definition of quality.

A. customer
B. product
C. profit
D. supplier
E. service

_____ 14. ___________ quality refers to freedom from defects and the consistency with which a product delivers a specified level of performance.

A. Performance
B. Conformance
C. Product
D. Service
E. Value chain

_____ 15. The process of creating, maintaining and enhancing strong value-laden relationships with customers and other stakeholders is known as ____________ marketing.

A. value delivery
B. product-centered
C. relationship
D. conformance
E. performance

Part Two To test your understanding of the concepts presented in this chapter, respond to the following questions by writing the letter T or F on the line next to the question number if you believe the statement is true or false, respectively. Answers to these questions are at the end of this chapter.

_____ 1. A key to winning customers and outperforming competitors lies in adoption of the marketing concept--in doing a better job of meeting and satisfying customer needs.

_____ 2. In a seller's market, if sellers fail to deliver acceptable product and service quality, they will quickly lose customers to competitors.

_____ 3. Total quality marketing implies that marketers spend time and effort not only to improve external marketing, but also to improve internal marketing.

_____ 4. Customers are value-maximizers, that is they choose the marketing offer which gives them the most value within the bounds of search costs and limited knowledge, mobility and income.

_____ 5. In a seller's market a price can never be set which will exceed total customer value.

_____ 6. Delivered value should be viewed as "profit to the customer."

_____ 7. Buyers operate under various constraints and sometimes make choices that give more weight to their personal benefit than to company benefit.

_____ 8. Although the customer-centered firm seeks to deliver high customer satisfaction relative to competitors, it does not attempt to maximize customer satisfaction.

_____ 9. Under the chain value concept, the firm's success depends not only on how well each department performs its work, but also on how well the activities of various departments are coordinated.

_____ 10. As companies struggle to become more competitive, they are less inclined to cooperate with their suppliers and distributors.

_____ 11. A contemporary view of marketing is that it should be responsible only for formulating a promotion-oriented marketing mix.

_____ 12. Offensive marketing typically costs more than defensive marketing because it takes a great deal of effort to coax satisfied customers away from competitors.

_____ 13. Classic marketing theory and practice centres on the art of retaining existing customers rather than attracting new customers.

_____ 14. Ultimately, marketing is the art of attracting and keeping profitable customers.

_____ 15. Customer satisfaction and company profitability are not closely linked to product and service quality.

Answers

Applying Terms and Concepts

Eastern Townships University

1. Generally, a prospective student will choose to attend the university which they believe offers the highest delivered value. To evaluate competing universities, the student will consider the differences between two factors. The first would be the values associated with a university including its product (courses of study and degrees offered), services (financial aid, counseling, health, placement, housing, etc.), personnel (reputation, quality, and helpfulness of instructional and support staff), and image, next, the prospective student will consider the total cost associated with attending a particular university. Included in the analysis of costs will be monetary costs such as tuition, fees, housing and transportation as well as nonmonetary costs such as time, energy and any physical costs.

2. Eastern Townships University should consider conducting a customer value assessment as well as an image assessment. These assessments will provide information about how the various publics (prospective students, current students, parents, alumni employers, high school guidance counselors, community colleges, transfer counselors, among others) view Eastern Townships University. University personnel could then evaluate the information and develop strategies to increase customer value. This would be accomplished by emphasizing identified strengths while minimizing the impact of perceived weaknesses. The University could also develop strategies to reduce both monetary and nonmonetary costs. Depending upon the information gained from the assessment studies, the university might develop any number of strategies including developing new courses or programs of study, reducing class size, improving scheduling, opening a branch campus, streamlining the registration process, developing internships, scheduling a greater number and wider variety of social activities, and developing creative tuition payment plans to name just a few. The exact strategies developed should be those that serve to increase customer value.

<u>Saturn Corporation</u>

1. Classic marketing theory and practice has traditionally centred on the art of attracting new customers and creating transactions while discussion was focused on presale and sale activity. Saturn on the other hand, appears to be focused not only on attracting new customers, but retaining them as well. They are relationship oriented and engage in considerable postsale activity. Saturn is interested in developing and maintaining long-term, mutually beneficial relationships with their customers.

2. Relationship marketing involves creating, maintaining, and enhancing strong relationships with customers and other stakeholders. Increasingly, marketing is moving away from a marketing mix focus to a relationship focus--from a focus on individual transactions and toward a focus on building value-laden relationships and marketing networks. Relationship marketing is more long-term oriented. The goal is to deliver long-term value to customers and the measure of success is long-term customer satisfaction. Relationship marketing requires that all of the company's departments work together with marketing as a team to serve the customer. It involves building relationships at many levels--economic, social, technical, and legal--resulting in high customer loyalty. And as the case indicated, Saturn

has established new relationships with its employees, suppliers, dealers, and customers which have resulted in extremely high levels of customer satisfaction.

3. The American Society for Quality Control defines quality as the totality of features and characteristics of a product or service that bear on its ability to satisfy stated or implied needs. This is clearly a customer-centered definition of quality. It suggests that a company has delivered quality whenever its product and service meet or exceed customers needs, requirements, and expectations. A company that satisfies most of its customers' needs most of the time is a quality company. And given the high levels of customer satisfaction, as demonstrated by the J. D. Power and Associate Surveys, it appears that Saturn has embraced the concept of total quality management.

Chiropractic Care

1. Relationship marketing involves creating, maintaining, and enhancing strong relationships with customers and other stakeholders. Increasingly, marketing is moving away from a focus on individual transactions and toward a focus on building value-laden relationships and value delivery networks. Relationship marketing is oriented more toward the long term. The goal is to deliver long-term value to customers, and the measure of success is long-term customer satisfaction. Relationship marketing requires that all of the company's departments work together with marketing as a team to serve the customer. It involves building relationships at many levels--economic, social, technical, and legal--resulting in high customer loyalty.

2. a. *Basic* - The doctor performs the spinal adjustment and does not follow-up the office visit in any way.

   b. *Reactive* - The doctor performs the spinal adjustment and encourages the patient to call whenever he or she has any questions or problems.

   c. *Accountable* - The doctor or others in the practice phones the patient a short time after the office visit to determine how the patient is responding to the treatment. The doctor may also solicit any suggested improvements or enhancements to the care (massage therapy, exercise consultation, referral, x-rays, etc.) and any specific disappointments. This information helps the practice to continuously improve its patient care.

d. *Proactive* - The doctor occasionally telephones the patient with suggestions for improved health care and/or to inform them of new services offered.

e. *Partnership* - The doctor works continuously with the patients and others to discover ways to deliver better value. This may include informational brochures, seminars at schools, hospitals, athletic clubs, and area companies, public service demonstrations, patient newsletter, in office health care lectures, developing relationships with pharmacists, attorneys and allied health professionals, more convenient office hours, improved billing procedures new services such as massage therapy and advice on exercise, diet and nutrition and so on.

Testing Terms and Concepts

Part One

1. A D
2. A M
3. E D
4. C - M Customer satisfaction with a purchase depends upon the product's performance relative to a buyer's expectations. A customer might experience various degrees of satisfaction. If the product's performance falls short of expectations, the customer is dissatisfied. If performance matches expectations, the customer is satisfied. If performance exceeds expectations, the customer is highly satisfied or delighted.
5. B D
6. E D
7. D M
8. E D
9. B M
10. C M
11. D E
12. D M
13. A E
14. B E
15. C E

Part Two

1. T E

2. F E
3. T M
4. T M
5. F E
6. T M
7. T M
8. T - D Although the customer-centred firm seeks to deliver high customer satisfaction relative to competitors, it does not attempt to maximize customer satisfaction. A company can always increase customer satisfaction by lowering its price or increasing its services, but this may result in lower profits. In addition to customers, the company has many stakeholders, including employees, dealers, suppliers, and stockholders. Spending more to increase customer satisfaction might divert funds from increasing the satisfaction of these other "partners." Thus, the purpose of marketing is to generate customer value profitably. Ultimately, the company must deliver a high level of customer satisfaction while at the same time delivering at least acceptable levels of satisfaction to the firm's other stakeholders. This requires a very delicate balance: The marketer must continue to generate more customer value and satisfaction but not "give away the house."
9. T D
10. F M
11. F E
12. T D
13. F M
14. T E
15. F E

CHAPTER 19

CREATING COMPETITIVE ADVANTAGE: COMPETITOR ANALYSIS AND COMPETITIVE MARKETING STRATEGIES

CHAPTER OVERVIEW

Companies must pay attention to their competitors as well as to their customers. Companies may define and identify their competitors from an industry point of view or from a broader market point of view. Competing firms' objectives, strategies, strengths and weaknesses, and reaction patterns, must all be identified. The company must decide which competitors to attack and to avoid--competitors who are strong or weak, close or distant, well-behaved or disruptive. The competitive intelligence system collects, analyzes, and distributes competitive information to relevant decision makers. Companies follow different competitive strategies depending on whether they are market leaders, challengers, followers, or nichers. A variety of attacking and defensive strategies can be identified from principles of military warfare. Whatever strategies can be identified from the principles of military warfare. Whatever strategies are followed, companies should be market-centred--oriented toward both customers and competitors--rather than simply competitor-centred or customer-centred.

CHAPTER OBJECTIVES

When you finish this chapter, you should be able to accomplish the following:

1. Discuss competitor analysis, emphasizing determining competitors objectives and strategies, strengths and weaknesses, and reactions--and assess whether to attack or avoid particular competitors.
2. Explain the fundamentals of competitive strategies based on competitive positions in the market for market-leaders, market-challengers, market-followers, and market-nichers.
3. Illustrate the need for balancing customer and competitor orientations, and contrast the differences among competitor- centred, customer-centred, and market-centred orientations.

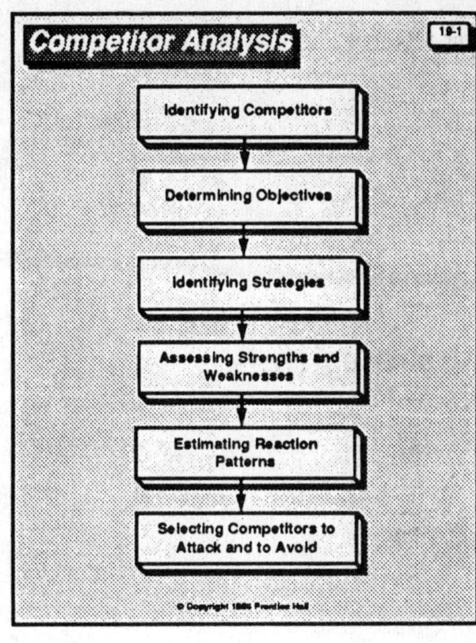

I. Competitor Analysis

A. Identifying the Company's Competitors

B. Determining Competitors' Objectives

C. Identifying Competitors' Strategies

D. Assessing Competitors' Strengths and Weaknesses

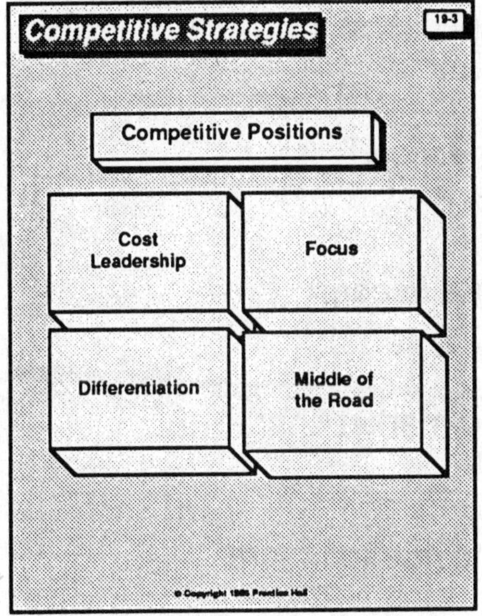

E. Estimating Competitors' Reactions

F. Selecting Competitors to Attack and Avoid

1. Strong or weak competitors

2. Close or distant competitors

3. "Well-behaved" or "disruptive" competitors

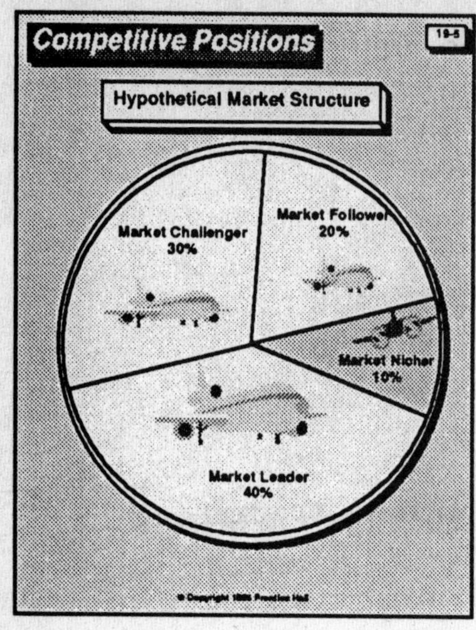

G. Designing a competitive intelligence system

II. Competitive Strategies

A. Basic competitive strategies

B. Competitive positions

C. Market-leader strategies

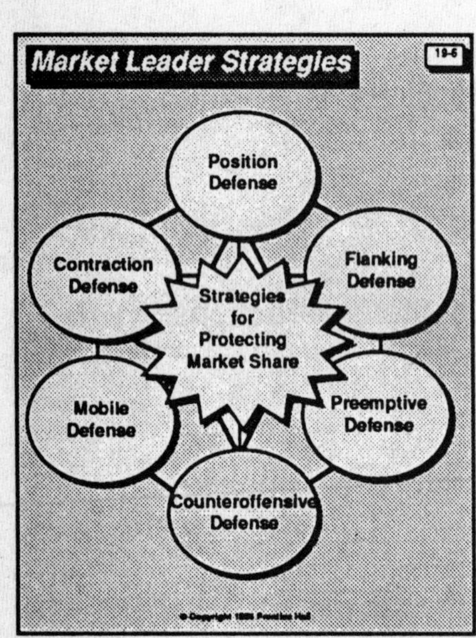

1. Expanding the total market

a. New users

b. New uses

c. More usage

2. Protecting market share

3. Expanding market share

D. Market-challenger strategies

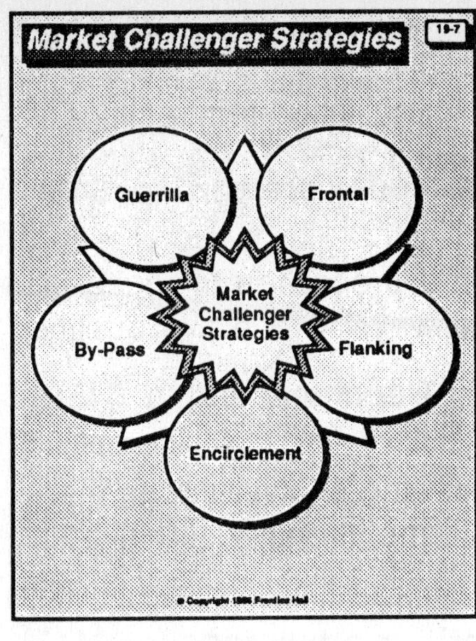

1. Defining the strategic objective and the competitor

2. Choosing an attack strategy

E. Market-follower strategies

F. Market-nicher strategies

III. Balancing Customer and Competitor Orientations

KEY TERMS

A method whereby firms can link their long-term strategy to their short-term actions.

Balanced score card (p. 645)

The process of comparing the company's products and processes to those of competitors or leading firms in other industries to find ways to improve quality and performance.

Benchmarking (p. 645)

An advantage over competitors gained by offering consumers lower prices than competitors for similar products or by providing more benefits that justify higher prices.

Competitive advantage (p. 641)

Strategies that strongly position the company against competitors and that give the company the strongest possible strategic advantage.

Competitive marketing strategies (p. 641)

The process of identifying key competitors; assessing their objectives, strengths and weaknesses, strategies, and reaction patterns; and selecting which competitors to attack or avoid.

Competitor analysis (p. 641)

A company whose moves are mainly based on competitors' actions and reactions; it spends most of its time tracking competitors' moves and market shares and trying to find strategies to counter them.

Competitor-centred company (p. 662)

A company that focuses on customer developments in designing its marketing strategies and on delivering superior value to its target customers.

Customer-centred company (p. 662)

Analysis conducted to determine what benefits target customers value and how they rate the relative value of various competitors' offers.

Customer value analysis (p. 647)

A company that pays balanced attention to both customers and competitors in designing its marketing strategies.

Market-centred company (p. 662)

A runner-up firm in an industry that is fighting hard to increase its market share.

Market challenger (p. 652)

A runner-up firm in an industry that wants to hold its share without rocking the boat.

Market follower (p. 652)

The firm in an industry with the largest market share; it usually leads other firms in price changes, new product introductions, distribution coverage, and promotion spending.

Market leader (p. 652)

A firm in an industry that serves small segments that the other firms overlook or ignore.

Market nicher (p. 652)

A group of firms in an industry following the same or a similar strategy in a given target market.

Strategic group (p. 644)

APPLYING TERMS AND CONCEPTS

To determine how well you understand the materials in this chapter, read each of the following brief cases and then respond to the questions that follow. Answers are at the end of this chapter.

MBA Cologne

William Lovell, a Vancouver-based entrepreneur, was proud of the MBA he earned at Simon Fraser University. He was also proud of his accomplishments to date and comfortable with his dreams of successes yet to come. Lovell had learned to set goals and pursue them in quiet dignity. He learned to respect others, and to be a man of his word. Lovell recognized that while he did not always agree with the actions of others, he knew that such diversity often provided strength for an organization. He also learned the arts of diplomacy and compromise and of strength through knowledge and perseverance.

Lovell had made his mark in the trucking industry and slowly branched out to other fields. His latest venture was distribution of a men's cologne called MBA.

MBA is imported by Lovell from Michaels' of Milan, Ltd., an Italian based cosmetic manufacturer.

Lovell reasoned that if a man aspired to a position of authority and responsibility, he should act, look, and dress the part. So he developed MBA cologne to complement the executive's image.

With such a commanding name and price--$100 an ounce--one might think the fragrance would be equally forceful. Not so---it has a subtlety that only hints at the potential that lies within. As Lovell explains, "The man distinguishes his possessions, position, and accomplishments, not the other way around." With each bottle comes a booklet containing thoughtful prescriptions for success from the likes of Drucker, Townsend, Waterman and Peters, Austin, and Kotler.

The cologne is already selling in better department stores in Alberta and BC. Sales have been brisk, but have been mainly to more mature buyers. Preliminary research indicates that many would-be executives (recent graduates of MBA programs) do not know the product exists. To inform potential customers, Lovell will advertise his cologne in MBA Magazine, a professional group publication distributed free to recent graduates. Lovell also intends to sell MBA cologne in bookstores at schools that have graduate programs in business.

Sales to date have returned a respectable 28 percent on investment, Lovell currently controls considerably less than 1 percent of the men's cologne market. Mainstream colognes such as Old Spice and Brut generate sales many times that of MBA, CEO, Wall Street, and Preferred Stock combined. (The latter colognes are MBA's competition in the premium cologne market.)

With the success of the men's cologne, Lovell expects to introduce Ms. MBA later this year.

Questions

1. Identify Lovell's competitive strategy for MBA cologne.

   ____

2. Explain the key to Lovell's success from the strategy identified above.

   ____

   ____

   ____

3. Discuss the potential risk to MBA cologne with the pursuit of the competitive strategy identified above.

____

____

____

____

____

Griffin Industries

Sixteen months ago, Griffin Industries, a diversified plastic manufacturer, announced that it had developed a new material which makes fabrics water repellent, yet breathable. The coated fabric would be ideal for products that not only need to shed water, but also release moisture vapor rapidly. This announcement caused a commotion in the textile business because Griffin would be taking on Herman and Associates, whose HERTRON II has allowed them to become the leading manufacturer of water-repellent and breathable clothing for skiers, joggers, mountain climbers, and other sports enthusiasts.

Perry Humphrey is the man behind the new Griffin coating, called OXFORD IX. He named it OXFORD IX because he received his chemical engineering degree from Oxford University and because he worked nine months to develop the material. Humphrey explained that the coating was developed by modifying a polyurethane film so that when water vapor pressure built up on one side of the film, it would begin seeping through the minute openings between the molecular gaps instead of actual holes, therefore, OXFORD IX remains impervious to liquid water. Thus, through the diffusion process, the product breathes yet remains a barrier to water.

OXFORD IX differs from HERTRON II in that the Griffin product can be sprayed onto any fabric, even single-thickness fabrics, whereas HERTRON II is an ultrathin sheet of material which must be sewn between two fabrics. The sprayability of OXFORD IX gives it several advantages over HERTRON II, including a wider variety of uses and a less expensive method of incorporation into the fabric.

Both companies have since become embroiled in a battle for market share and dominance. Herman and Associates has lowered the price of HERTRON II garments and began promoting itself as the innovator in the industry. It has also mounted a promotional campaign which claims that HERTRON II is the most effective breathable, water-repellent material on the market. Griffin has successfully introduced its own line of clothing for skiers, joggers, and other amateur and professional athletes. It has also begun to market a line of camping tents and sleeping bags. Griffin's latest use of OXFORD IX is for the medical community as a bandage for cuts, burns, and surgical incisions. Herman, not to be outmarketed, is reportedly negotiating with the department of defense to produce foul weather gear for the U.S. Navy.

Questions

_____ 1. Griffin Industries initiated a ___________ attack on Herman and Associates when it began to produce athletic clothing to compete with HERTRON II sportswear.

A. bypass
B. flank
C. frontal
D. guerrilla
E. preemptive

_____ 2. When Herman and Associates lowered the price of HERTRON II clothing and began promoting itself as the innovator in the industry, it was engaged in a ___________ defense.

A. preemptive
B. mobile
C. contraction
D. counteroffensive
E. bypass

_____ 3. Griffin's diversification into the medical products market is an example of a ___________ attack on Herman and Associates.

A. bypass
B. flank
C. frontal
D. guerrilla
E. preemptive

_____ 4. If Griffin Industries initiated a lawsuit against Herman and Associates challenging the claim that HERTRON II is the most effective breathable, water-repellent material on the market, Griffin would be engaging in a ___________ attack on Herman and Associates.

A. position
B. guerrilla
C. preemptive
D. frontal
E. flank

_____ 5. Griffin Industries is best described as a:

A. challenger in the sportswear market.
B. leader in the medical applications market.
C. follower in the military applications market.
D. only (A) and (B)
E. all of the above

Reebok vs. Nike

Sneakers have become an international obsession. Everyone seems to have them and everyone likes them--from the sports enthusiast and the health conscious to the junior executive, the fashion conscious, and the active homemaker. Indeed, according to one analyst, one-third of all shoes sold in Canada are sneakers.

Two giants dominate the athletic shoe industry: Nike from Oregon and Reebok from Boston control approximately 50 percent of the sneaker business. Nike's success was based on creating a performance shoe for the fitness boom, specifically for the jogging craze of the 1970s, while Reebok made it on the new relaxed life-style of the 1980s, recognizing that 80 percent of all sneakers sold are for leisure use. Now both companies make hundreds of styles for both performance and recreational use.

Today in the battle to be number one, it has become Nike substance versus Reebok style. In the mid-1980s, by focusing on a special shoe for women, Reebok roared past Nike, unseating them from their position atop the athletic shoe industry. It was the aerobic shoe that propelled Reebok to number one. although the wrinkled leather was originally a production mistake, management loved it and so did the consumer.

Paul Fireman, Reebok's CEO and founder of Reebok in the United States, was a salesman who once ran a small family sporting goods business. Because of the success of Reebok, he has become one of the highest-paid executives in the nation. Even he is surprised by the success of the business. But Fireman concedes that it is consumers who have made his company number one. Therefore, Reebok will continue to focus its efforts on satisfying the customer. A recent example of this customer orientation is the introduction of hand-painted sneakers for the masses.

Nike was founded by Phil Knight, a runner from the University of Oregon. Knight and his former track coach, Bill Baumann, started the company and rode the running boom to instant success. Knight is the driving force, and remains immensely competitive. While Nike has made concessions to fashion, it is technology the company is counting on to win the war against Reebok. A recent innovation is the Air Revolution, a plastic airbag in the heel of the shoe that is visible. Reebok has developed its own system, called Energy Return, which involves the placement of plastic tubes in the shoes. It may ultimately include a window so that the tubes would be visible.

The competition never ceases. An upstart company called L.A. Gear sneers at research, development, and technology--simply letting people wear their sneakers and then listen to what is said about them. L.A. Gear came from nowhere in 1987 to capture an 11 percent share of the market in the early 1990s.

The industry is cyclical. Today's leaders could easily go the way of Keds, Converse, and Adidas--popular in the 1950s, 60s, and 70s, respectively, and still on the market, but nowhere near number one today.

Questions

1. Explain how Reebok has been both a market leader and a market challenger.

2. Explain why Nike should properly be classified as a market-centred company.

3. Discuss market-expansion strategies that Nike either has used or could use to enhance its market position.

Sources: "Sneaker Attack," *Advertising Age*, June 20, 1988, p. 2; "Treading on Air," *Business Month*, January 1984, pp. 29-34; "Foot's Parade," *Time*, August 28, 1989, pp. 54-55; "L.A. Gear is Going Where the boys Are," *Business Week*, June 19, 1989, p. 54; and "Reebok on the Rebound," *New York*, October 16, 1989, "Sneaker Wars." *ABC News Broadcast*, August 19, 1988.

TESTING TERMS AND CONCEPTS

Part One — To test your understanding of the concepts presented in this chapter, write the letter of the most appropriate answer on the line next to the question number. Answers are at the end of this chapter.

_____ 1. Competitive marketing strategies can be developed for:

A. companies.
B. business units.
C. brands.
D. both (A) and (B)
E. all of the above

_____ 2. Market ____________ are firms whose products serve small market segments not being pursued by firms with larger shares of the market.

A. challengers
B. leaders
C. nichers
D. followers
E. targeters

_____ 3. Dominant firms may do all but which of the following in an effort to remain the market leader?

A. expand total demand
B. protect current market share
C. expand market share
D. reduce total demand
E. both (C) and (D)

_____ 4. Global Industries is promoting its Sparkle brand of liquid dish detergent as an alternative soap for washing automobiles with the slogan, "Sparkle removes dirt and grime without hurting the shine." Global is attempting to expand the total market by looking for ____________ of its product.

A. new users
B. new uses
C. more usage
D. both (A) and (B)
E. none of the above

____ 5. __________ defense is an aggressive defense of market share by actually launching an offense against competitors before they start their offense against the company.

A. Position
B. Preemptive
C. Flanking
D. Mobile
E. Target

____ 6. Market broadening and market diversification are two techniques of a ___________ defense.

A. contraction
B. position
C. counteroffensive
D. mobile
E. target

____ 7. Higher market shares tend to produce higher profits when:

A. unit costs fall with increased market shares.
B. the company offers a superior quality product and charges a premium price that more than covers the cost of offering higher quality.
C. average variable cost increases as the level of production increases
D. both (A) and (B)
E. neither (A) nor (B)

____ 8. In a(n) ___________ attack, the challenger attacks the competitor's weakness rather than its strength.

A. guerrilla
B. bypass
C. encirclement
D. flank
E. frontal

____ 9. In a(n) __________ attack, the challenger launches an offensive on several fronts so that the competitor must protect its front, sides and rear simultaneously.

A. guerrilla
B. bypass
C. encirclement
D. flank
E. frontal

_____ 10. With a(n) ___________ attack, the challenger makes small, periodic attacks to harass and demoralize the competitor, hoping eventually to establish permanent footholds.

A. flank
B. guerrilla
C. bypass
D. encirclement
E. target

_____ 11. Tablerock Industries is a follower in the electronics industry that maintains some differentiation, but follows the leader in terms of major market and product innovations, general price levels, and distribution. Tablerock is pursuing a(n) ___________ market-follower strategy.

A. cloner
B. imitator
C. adapter
D. innovator
E. overt

_____ 12. The key idea in a market-nicher strategy is ___________.

A. specialization
B. distribution
C. pricing
D. product innovation
E. promotion innovation

_____ 13. Market broadening and market diversification are ___________ defense strategies that involve more than defending a current market position.

A. counteroffensive
B. position
C. flanking
D. contraction
E. mobile

_____ 14. There are four basic competitive positioning strategies that companies can follow. Which of the following strategies is the least desirable of the four?

A. overall cost leadership
B. differentiation
C. focus
D. middle-of-the-road
E. none of the above

_____ 15. A(n) ____________ is a group of firms in an industry following the same or similar strategy in a given target market.

A. strategic group
B. audit unit
C. leadership unit
D. tactical guard
E. trade group

Part Two To test your understanding of the concepts presented in this chapter, respond to the following questions by writing the letter T or F on the line next to the question number if you believe the statement is true or false, respectively. Answers to these questions may be found at the end of this chapter.

_____ 1. Competitor analysis is the process of identifying key competitors, assessing their objectives, strengths and weaknesses, strategies and reaction patterns; and selecting which competitors to attack or to avoid.

_____ 2. Customer value analysis involves asking customers what benefits they value and how they rate the company versus competitors on important attributes.

_____ 3. To succeed, marketers must formulate strategies that strongly position their offerings against competitors offerings in the minds of consumers--strategies that give the company, business unit or product the strongest possible strategic advantage.

_____ 4. All firms pursuing the same competitive strategy constitute a strategic group.

_____ 5. According to Michael Porter, middle-of-the-road strategies are likely to yield above-average profits.

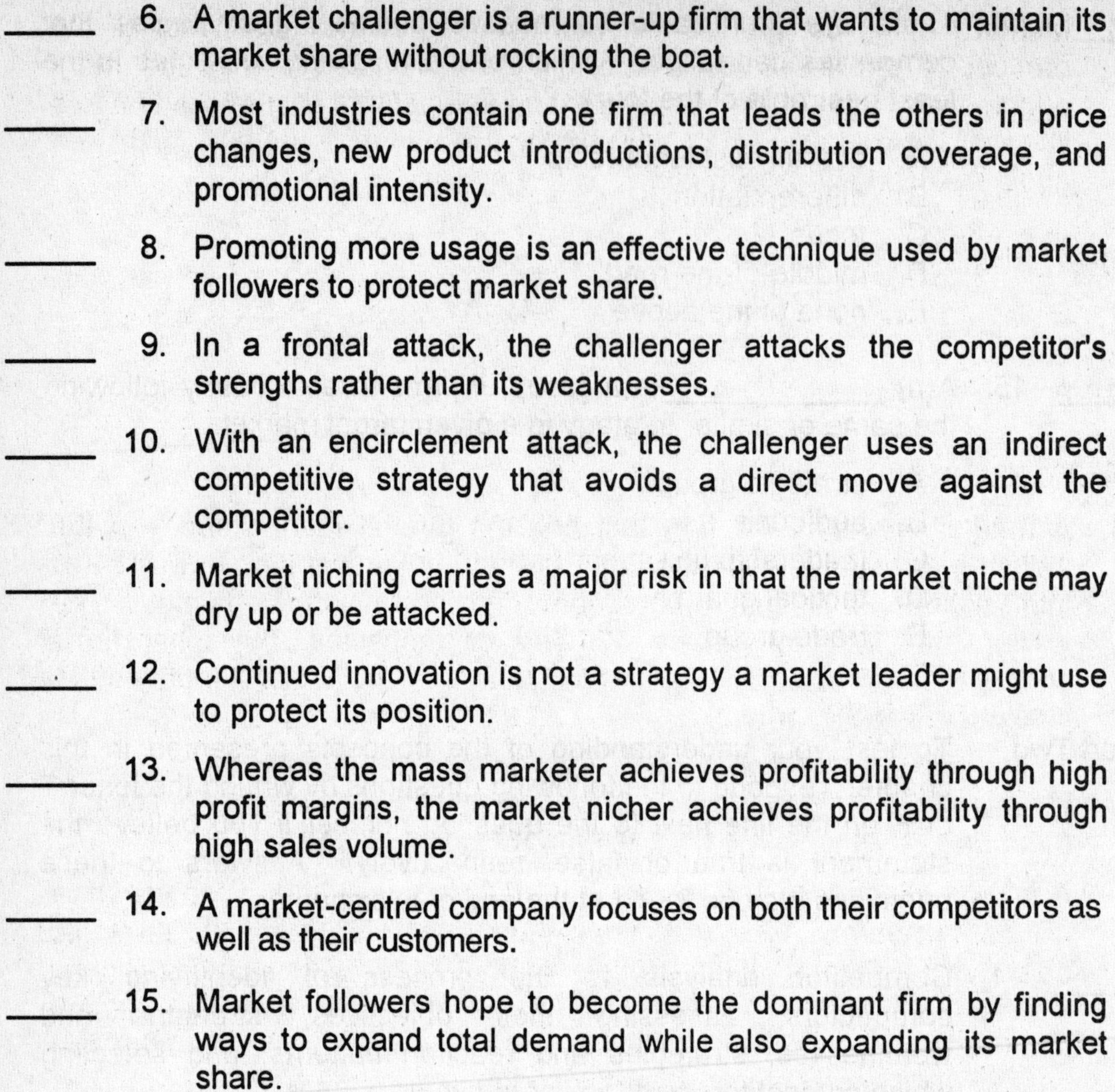

_____ 6. A market challenger is a runner-up firm that wants to maintain its market share without rocking the boat.

_____ 7. Most industries contain one firm that leads the others in price changes, new product introductions, distribution coverage, and promotional intensity.

_____ 8. Promoting more usage is an effective technique used by market followers to protect market share.

_____ 9. In a frontal attack, the challenger attacks the competitor's strengths rather than its weaknesses.

_____ 10. With an encirclement attack, the challenger uses an indirect competitive strategy that avoids a direct move against the competitor.

_____ 11. Market niching carries a major risk in that the market niche may dry up or be attacked.

_____ 12. Continued innovation is not a strategy a market leader might use to protect its position.

_____ 13. Whereas the mass marketer achieves profitability through high profit margins, the market nicher achieves profitability through high sales volume.

_____ 14. A market-centred company focuses on both their competitors as well as their customers.

_____ 15. Market followers hope to become the dominant firm by finding ways to expand total demand while also expanding its market share.

Answers

Applying Terms and Concepts

MBA Cologne

1. Market-nicher strategy
2. The key to the Cologne's success is specialization among customer and marketing mix lines.

3. Market niching carries the risk that the market may disappear (if the product is perceived as a fad) or that the market may be more aggressively attacked by either existing competitors or new competitors such as the mainstreamers who develop a new product and position it against existing competitors.

Griffin Industries

1. C
2. D
3. A
4. B
5. D

Reebok vs. Nike

1. A market leader is the firm that has the largest market share in the industry. It usually leads the other firms in price changes, new-product introductions, distribution coverage, and promotion spending. The leader may or may not be admired or respected, but other firms concede its dominance. The leader is a focal point for competition to challenge, imitate, or avoid.

   Reebok was an innovator when it introduced the aerobic shoe. It was the aerobic shoe that propelled Reebok into the number-one position in the market. Hence, they were the leader in this instance.

   A market challenger is a runner-up firm that is fighting hard to increase its market share. A market challenger must first define its strategic objective. Most market challengers seek to increase their profitability by increasing their market shares. But the strategic objective chosen depends on who the competitor is. In most cases, the company can choose which competitors it will challenge.

   The challenger can attack the market leader--a high-risk but potentially high-gain strategy that makes good sense if the leader is not serving the market well. To succeed with such an attack, a company must have some sustainable competitive advantage over the leader--a cost advantage leading to lower prices or the ability to provide better value at a premium price. When attacking the leader, a challenger must also find a way to minimize the leader's response. Otherwise its gains may be short-lived.

   The challenger can avoid the leader and instead attack firms its own size or smaller local and regional firms. Many of these firms are underfinanced and are not serving their customers well.

Reebok became a market challenger when they developed the Energy Return air system for sneakers. This product introduction positioned them directly against Nike, the leader in this aspect of the industry.

It should be emphasized that a firm might be a market leader in one aspect of the industry, a market challenger in another, a follower in yet another aspect of the industry, and even a nicher in still another aspect.

2. *A competitor-centred company* is one whose moves are based mainly on competitors actions and reactions. The company spends most of its time tracking competitors' moves and market shares and trying to find strategies to counter them.

   A customer-centred company, in contrast, focuses more on customer developments in designing its strategies. Clearly, the customer-centred company is in a better position to identify new opportunities and set a strategy that makes long-run sense. By watching customer needs evolve, it can decide what customer groups and what emerging needs are the most important to serve, given its resources and objectives.

   Nike is properly classified as a market-centered company because their market strategy planning considers not only the competition--Reebok, L.A.Gear, Adidas, and so on--but also consumers--for example, in the development of the Air Revolution sneaker line.

3. Leading firms want to remain number one. This calls for action on three fronts. First, the firm must find ways to expand total demand. Second, the firm must protect its current market share through good defensive and offensive actions. Third, the firm can try to expand its market share further, even if market size remains constant.

   Nike has sought to increase total demand of athletic shoes by attracting new users of the footwear as well as by promoting new uses for it, while also encouraging more usage of the footwear. As a result, people who had never before purchased athletic shoes began to buy several pairs for the various activities they are involved in.

Testing Terms and Concepts

Part One

1. E E
2. C E
3. D M
4. D D

5. B D
6. D M
7. D D
8. A M
9. C M
10. B M
11. B - M The market-follower firms fall into one of the three broad types. The cloner closely copies leader's products, distribution, advertising, and other marketing moves. The cloner originates nothing--it simply attempts to live off the market leader's investments. The imitator copies some things from the leader but maintains some differentiation in terms of packaging, advertising, pricing, and other factors. The leader doesn't mind the imitator as long as the imitator does not attack aggressively. The imitator may even help the leader avoid the charges of monopoly. Finally, the adapter builds on that leader's products and marketing programs, often improving them. The adapter may choose to sell to different markets to avoid direct confrontation with the leader. But often the adapter grows into a future challenger, as many Japanese firms have done after adapting and improving products developed elsewhere.
12. A E
13. E D
14. D - D Companies that pursue a clear strategy--overall cost leadership, differentiation or focus--are likely to perform well. The firm that carries out that strategy best will make the most profits. But firms that do not pursue a clear strategy--middle-of-the-roaders--do the worst. Sears, Chrysler, and International Harvester all came upon difficult times because they did not stand out as the lowest in cost, highest in perceived value, or best in serving some market segment. Middle-of-the-roaders try to be good on all strategic counts, but end up being not very good at anything.
15. A E

Part Two

1. T E
2. T E
3. T M

4. T E
5. F M
6. F M
7. T E
8. F M
9. T M
10. F - D An encirclement attack involves attacking from all directions, so that the competitor must protect its front, sides, and rear at the same time. The encirclement strategy makes sense when the challenger has superior resources and believes that it can quickly break the competitor's hold on the market.
11. T M
12. F E
13. F M
14. T E
15. F M

CHAPTER 20

THE GLOBAL MARKETPLACE

CHAPTER OVERVIEW

Companies undertake international marketing for a variety of reasons. Some are driven by poor opportunities in the home market, while others are attracted by superior opportunities abroad. In looking at the International marketing environment, the company must consider trade restrictions and other aspects of the trade system. The company must also examine the economic, political, legal, and cultural environments of countries they are considering entering. Companies make several decisions in the process of "going global" deciding whether to go abroad, deciding which markets to enter, deciding how to enter the market (exporting, joint venturing, or direct investment), deciding on the marketing program (how to develop the marketing mix for other countries), and deciding on the marketing organization (export department, international division, or global organization).

CHAPTER OBJECTIVES

When you finish this chapter, you should be able to accomplish the following:

1. Discuss the global marketing environment, the international trade system and the economic, political, legal and cultural environments that affect marketing decisions.
2. Define the key elements of deciding whether to go international, deciding which markets to enter and deciding how to enter the market, either through exporting, joint venturing or direct investment.
3. Explain the primary issue of deciding on the global marketing program, whether to use a standardized, or adapted marketing mix or some combination of the two.
4. Distinguish among the three ways companies manage their global marketing organizations trough export departments, international divisions and becoming a global organization.

LECTURE/STUDENT NOTES

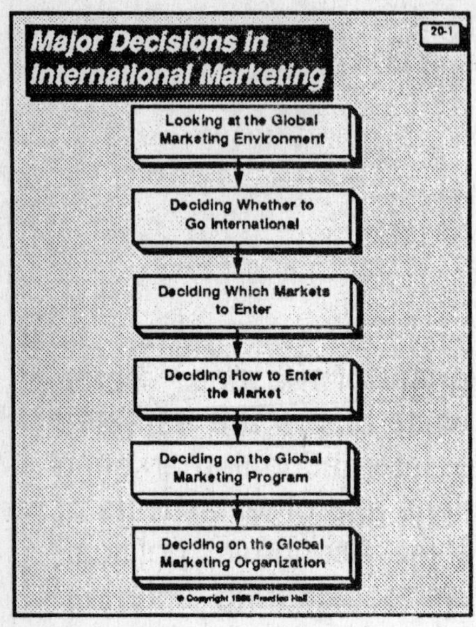

I. Global Marketing into the Twenty-First Century

II. Looking at the Global Marketing Environment

A. The international trade system

1. The general agreement on tariffs and trade

2. Regional free trade zones

3. "Well-behaved" or "disruptive" competitors

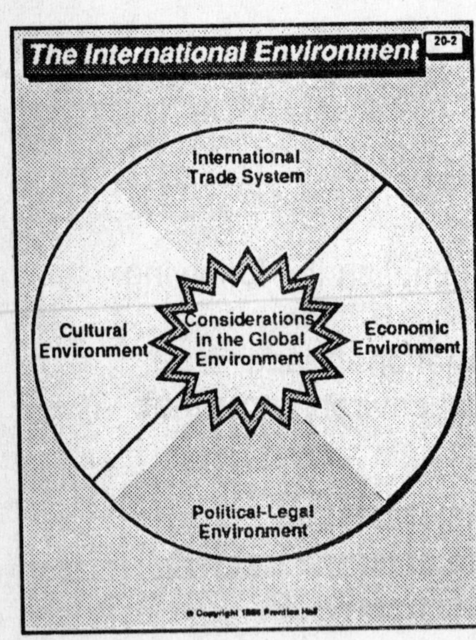

B. Economic environment

C. Political-legal environment

1. Attitudes toward international buying

2. Political stability

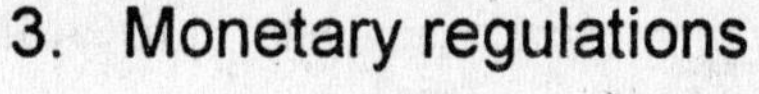

3. Monetary regulations

4. Government bureaucracy

Deciding Which Markets to Enter

Marketer's Checklist for Identifying Markets to Enter

1. Demographic Characteristics
2. Geographic Characteristics
3. Economic Factors
4. Technological Factors
5. Sociocultural Factors
6. National Goals and Plans

D. Cultural environment

III. Deciding Whether To Go International

IV. Deciding Which Markets To Enter

V. Deciding How To Enter The Market

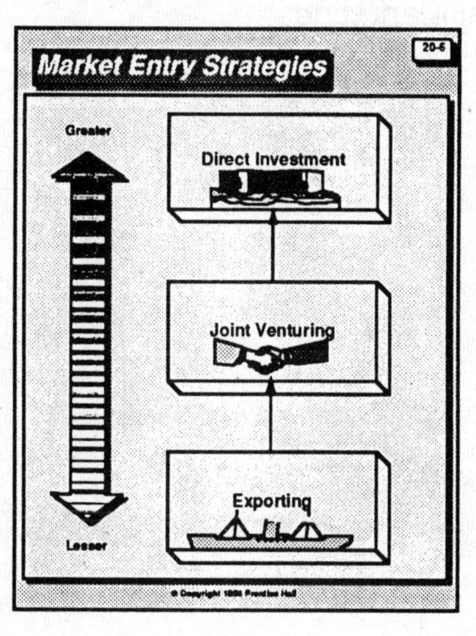

A. Exporting

B. Joint Venturing

1. Licensing

2. Contract manufacturing

3. Management contracting

4. Joint ownership

C. Direct investment

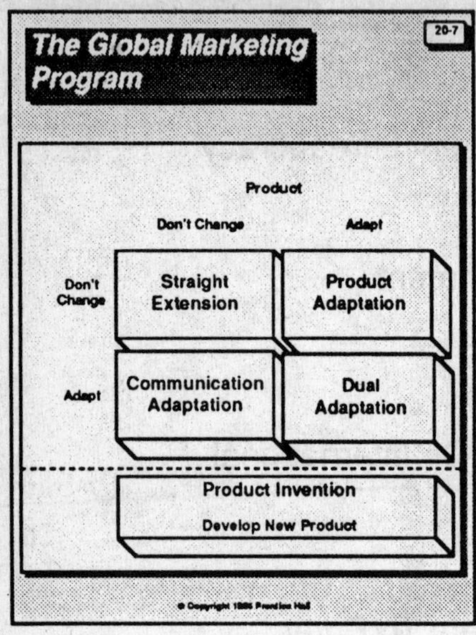

VI. Deciding on the Global Marketing Program

A. Product

B. Promotion

C. Price

D. Distribution channels

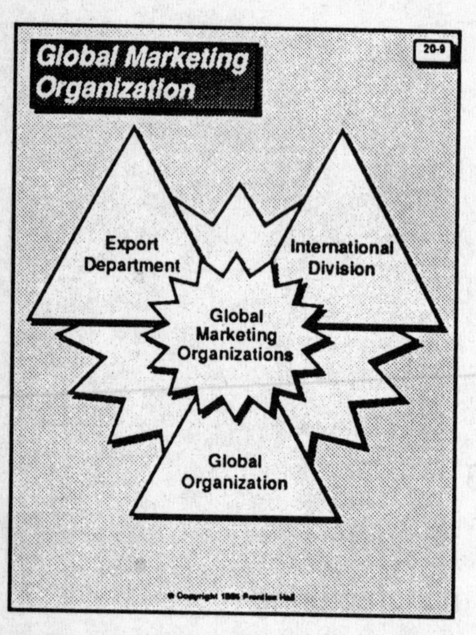

VII. Deciding on the Global Marketing Organization

KEY TERMS

An international marketing strategy for adjusting the marketing mix elements to each international target market, bearing more costs but hoping for a larger market share and return.

Adapted marketing mix (p. 692)

A global communication strategy of fully adapting advertising messages to local markets.

Communication adaptation (p. 694)

Joint venturing to enter a foreign market by contracting with manufacturers in the foreign market to produce the product.

Contract manufacturing (p. 689)

International trade involving the direct or indirect exchange of goods for other goods instead of cash. Forms include barter, compensation (buy-back), and counter purchase.

Countertrade (p. 683)

Entering a foreign market by developing foreign-based assembly or manufacturing facilities.

Direct investment (p. 690)

A group of nations organized to work toward common goals in the regulation of international trade.

Economic community (p. 678)

A ban on the import of a certain product.

Embargo (p. 676)

Limits placed by a government on the amount of its foreign exchange with other countries and on its exchange rate against other currencies.

Exchange controls (p. 676)

Entering a foreign market by exporting and selling products through international marketing middlemen (indirect exporting) or through the company's own department, branch, or sales representatives or agents (direct exporting).

Exporting (p. 689)

A firm that, by operating in more than one country, gains R&D, production, marketing, and financial advantages in its costs and reputation that are not available to purely domestic competitors.

Global firm (p. 675)

An industry in which the strategic positions of competitors in given geographic or national markets are affected by their overall global positions.

Global industry (p. 675)

Entering a foreign market by joining with foreign investors to create a local business in which the company shares joint ownership and control.

Joint ownership (p. 691)

Entering foreign markets by joining with foreign companies to produce or market a product or service.

Joint venturing (p. 690)

A method of entering a foreign market in which the company enters into an agreement with a licensee in the foreign market, offering the right to use a manufacturing process, trademark, patent, trade secret, or other item of value for a fee or royalty.

Licensing (p. 690)

A joint venture in which the domestic firm supplies the management know-how to a foreign company that supplies the capital; the domestic firm exports management services rather than products.

Management contracting (p. 691)

Nonmonetary barriers to foreign products, such as biases against foreign company's bids or product standards that go against foreign company's product features.

Non-tariff trade barriers (p. 677)

Adapting a product to meet local conditions or wants in foreign markets.

Product adaptation (p. 694)

Creating new products or services for foreign markets.

Product invention (p. 694)

A limit on the amount of goods that an importing country will accept in certain product categories; it is designed to conserve on foreign exchange and to protect local industry and employment.

Quota (p. 675)

An international marketing strategy for using basically the same product, advertising, distribution channels, and other elements of the marketing mix in all the company's international markets.

Standardized marketing mix (p. 693)

Marketing a product in the foreign market without any change.

Straight product extension (p. 693)

A tax levied by a government against certain imported products, which is designed to raise revenue or to protect domestic firms.

Tariff (p. 675)

Designing international channels that take into account all the necessary links in distributing the seller's products to final buyers, including the seller's headquarters organization, channels between nations, and channels within nations.

Whole-channel view (p. 697)

APPLYING TERMS AND CONCEPTS

To determine how well you understand the materials in this chapter, read each of the following brief cases and then respond to the questions that follow. Answers are given at the end of this chapter.

International Trade

Canadian furniture manufacturers are lobbying the federal government to curtail imports of furniture. They want the government to totally ban imports while the moderates want the government to either limit imports or impose a tax designed to raise the cost of furniture. In the late 1980's and early 1990's, despite rising demand, dozens of Canadian furniture factories were closed and tens of thousands jobs lost.

Questions

1. The Canadian furniture manufacturers who want the government to totally ban shoe imports are advocating a(n) ___________.

2. A(n) ____________ would limit the amount of imported furniture coming into Canada.

3. The Canadian furniture manufacturers who want a tax to raise the price of imported furniture are advocating a protective ____________.

<u>STP Computer, Inc.</u>

While a number of US companies are looking for ways to move out of Brazil's difficult economy, STP Computer, Inc., is seeking permission from the Brazilian government to start manufacturing its personal computer there. Government leaders in Brazil are expected to give a decision within three months for a licensing arrangement or a joint ownership venture with P.C. of Brazil, STP's current independent Brazilian distributor. In either event, STP plans to produce up to 600 personal computers a month in Brazil in addition to current production of 4,000 computers a month within the United States. STP's Brazilian-made computer will have a unique feature, bilingual capabilities, which should appeal to the Latin American countries.

Miguel Portillo, STP's international bureau chief, sees the Brazilian venture as a model for STP sales in the third-world markets. "Brazil will set the tone for our movement into other countries, such as India, Chile, South Korea, Peru, Columbia, Argentina, and Brazil."

STP must begin to manufacture its computers in Brazil if it wants to maintain its dominant position (68 percent) in the Latin American market. STP is also hoping that the manufacturing plant in Brazil will reduce the number of contraband STP's now entering Brazil. As many as 25 percent of all STP's in Brazil have entered the country illegally. The smuggling of computers is due principally to the high tariffs imposed by the Brazilian government. The tariff, which is designed to produce hard currency for a government beset with a staggering negative balance of trade, has more than doubled the US price of computers.

Questions

1. Which type of joint venture would STP prefer if it wanted to minimize its risk and cash investment in the project?

   ____

_____ 2. Which type of tariff has the Brazilian government imposed on STP Computers?

   A. protective
   B. revenue
   C. quota
   D. embargo
   E. exchange

3. Which product strategy will be practiced by STP when its computers are manufactured in Brazil?

   ____

_____ 4. Which type of marketing organization would most accurately describe STP's international marketing activity after the Brazilian government makes its decision?

   A. export department
   B. international division
   C. global organization
   D. export division
   E. export organization

5. Which type of export was STP engaged in regarding the Brazilian market?

   ____

Cuba

The United States has maintained a trade embargo with Cuba since the early 1960's when Fidel Castro came to power. Canada, Europe and Japan have never taken part in this embargo and have continued to do business with Cuba during this period. Canada has been particularly active in the Cuban market to the point where today Canada is one of Cuba's largest trading partners.

Canadian companies are involved in such industries as tourism and tobacco. In the area of tourism, thousands of Canadians visit Cuba every year for a winter vacation. Several Prime Ministers have even visited Cuba over the years. Most tourists are drawn to Cuba because of its terrific weather, friendly population and low cost. It is far less expensive to go to Cuba than it is to visit Florida or Arizona. In answer to complaints about the accommodations in Cuba, Canadian companies have entered agreements with Cuban firms to build and manage hotels. In addition, business people like tobacconist Thomas Hinds from Toronto are actively importing Cuban products for resale in Canada and the US. Although it is illegal for US citizens to purchase Cuban products, they often buy them in Canada and smuggle them home. Other Canadian companies are also involved in trade with Cuba to improve their infrastructure and natural resource base. The US government has constantly lobbied Canada to stop doing business with Cuba.

In early 1996, the Cuban Air Force shot down an aircraft belonging to a Cuban-American group known as "Brothers to the Rescue." This group consists of individuals dedicated to the removal of Fidel Castro and his communist government. The Cubans claimed they shot the aircraft down because it violated their airspace. Evidence collected by the US government and eyewitness reports placed the aircraft in international airspace.

US reaction to the incident was quick and potentially damaging to Canadian business. The US first tried to encourage other countries, including Canada, to implement economic sanctions against Cuba. Canada's reaction was we would not take part in any sanctions and we would not condemn the Cuban government. As other countries responded the same way, the US Congress passed a bill punishing foreign firms doing business in Cuba. Specifically, it allows US firms that had property seized by the Cuban government to sue any foreign firm currently using it. It also allows for the US government to blacklist businesses and deny entry to their executives, spouses and children of executives, major shareholders, and agents if the company continues to make investments in or improvements to properties expropriated from US firms.

Condemned as "the worst trade deal (law) in history" many countries and groups are fighting the law. Canada claims it violates the freedom-of-movement provisions of NAFTA. Only time will tell what the law really means and how long it will last.

Sources: US fine-tunes anti-Cuba hit list, *Winnipeg Free Press*, Friday May 24, 1996, Canadian Press, p. B8.

TESTING TERMS AND CONCEPTS

Part One To test your understanding of the concepts presented in this chapter, write the letter of the most appropriate answer on the line next to the question number. Answers to these questions are at the end of this chapter.

_____ 1. Which of the following factors helped draw Canadian companies into exporting products to international markets?

A. the weakening of domestic marketing opportunities
B. a very strong dollar compared to other currencies
C. growing opportunities for their products in other countries
D. both (A) and (C)
E. all of the above

_____ 2. The Canadian government has been considering the adoption of safety and emission standards that must be met by all companies that wish to sell automobiles in Canada. Such action would be an example of a(n):

A. revenue tariff.
B. nontariff barrier.
C. quota.
D. embargo.
E. constrictive tariff.

_____ 3. Economic communities usually strive to do which of the following?

A. raise tariffs within the community.
B. expand employment and investment.
C. reduce prices.
D. both (B) and (C)
E. all of the above.

_____ 4. The Cyclops Corporation, a major manufacturer of ore-extracting equipment, would be most likely to find a market for its products in a(n) ____________ economy.

A. subsistence
B. industrializing
C. raw material exporting
D. industrial
E. advanced

_____ 5. Which of the following is not a component of a country's industrial structure?

A. product or service requirements
B. values and norms.
C. employment levels
D. income levels
E. both (A) and (C)

_____ 6. Which of the following is not one of the typical criteria used to rank the attractiveness of potential foreign markets?

A. risk level
B. personalities of national leaders
C. market growth potential
D. cost of doing business
E. both (C) and (D)

_____ 7. The least complicated method of getting involved in a foreign market is through ____________.

A. exporting
B. joint venturing
C. direct investment
D. licensing
E. contract manufacturing

_____ 8. The Chi-Lite Corporation has just completed negotiations to hire middlemen to handle its foreign distribution. Chi-Lite is engaged in ____________.

A. indirect export
B. direct export
C. joint venturing
D. licensing
E. contract manufacturing

_____ 9. The ultimate involvement in a foreign market is investment in a foreign-based assembly or manufacturing facility. This is commonly referred to as:

A. licensing.
B. management contracting.
C. joint ownership.
D. direct investment.
E. contract manufacturing.

_____ 10. The J. D. and B. Company has just completed negotiations to supply management know-how to a foreign company that is supplying the capital for development of a new product. J. D. and B. is involved in:

A. management contracting.
B. joint venture.
C. licensing.
D. direct investment.
E. contract management.

_____ 11. Kieser, Inc., has modified its industrial machine tools for sale in European markets to conform to the metric system. Kieser is engaged in:

A. straight invention.
B. product invention.
C. product adaptation.
D. forward integration.
E. horizontal expansion.

_____ 12. Under a _____________ plan, the seller received full payment in cash, but agrees to spend some portion of the money in the country within a stated time.

A. buyback
B. barter
C. counter purchase
D. compensation
E. sale/countersale

_____ 13. Harley-Davidson accused Honda and Kawasaki of selling motorcycles in the US for less than they cost to produce and/or for less than they charged in Japan. In essence, Harley-Davidson was accusing Honda and Kawasaki of _____________ motorcycles on the US market.

A. saturating
B. integrating
C. price fixing
D. dumping
E. both (A) and (C)

_____ 14. Which of the following is a major problem confronting companies that engage in international marketing?

A. High debt, inflation and unemployment in some countries have resulted in highly unstable governments and currencies.
B. Governments are placing more regulations on foreign firms such as requiring joint ownership with domestic partners, regulating the hiring of nationals and limiting the profits that can be taken from the country.
C. Corruption--officials in some countries award business not to the best bidder but to the highest briber.
D. only (A) and (B)
E. all of the above

_____ 15. A(n) _____________ totally bans some kinds of imports.

A. embargo
B. tariff
C. quota
D. limit
E. exchange control

Part Two To test your understanding of the concepts presented in this chapter, respond to the following questions by writing the letter T or F on the line next to the question number if you believe the statement is true or false, respectively. Answers to these questions may be found at the end of this chapter.

_____ 1. A quota is a tax levied by a foreign government against certain imported products.

_____ 2. An embargo bans the importation of a product.

_____ 3. The European union provides a free trade area for members, but imposes a uniform tariff for trade with nonmember nations.

_____ 4. Subsistence economics offer the fewest opportunities for exporters.

_____ 5. Income distribution is related to a country's industrial structure, but is not affected by the political system.

_____ 6. Political stability and monetary regulations are the only two components of a nation's political-legal environment affecting international marketing.

_____ 7. Direct exporting takes place when the firm hires independent international marketing middlemen.

_____ 8. Joint venturing is a method of entering a foreign market by joining with foreign companies to set up production and marketing facilities.

_____ 9. Straight extension means introducing the product in the foreign market without any change.

_____ 10. Dumping occurs when a manufacturer charges more in the foreign market than in the home market.

_____ 11. The emerging importance of international trade has forced the development of many new marketing principles.

_____ 12. A gray-market exists when distributors buy more than they can sell in their own country, then ship the goods to another country to take advantage of price differences.

_____ 13. One disadvantage of licensing is that if the licensee is very successful, the firm has given up profits and if and when the contract ends, it may find it has created a competitor.

_____ 14. Although some companies would like to stem the tide of foreign imports through protectionism, in the long run this would raise the cost of living and protect inefficient Canadian firms.

_____ 15. Corruption (for example, bribing of officials to gain contracts) is typically not seen as a major problem confronting companies that are moving into international trade.

Answers

Applying Terms and Concepts

International Trade

1. embargo
2. quota
3. tariff
4. industrial

STP Computer, Inc.

1. licensing
2. B
3. product adaptation
4. C
5. indirect export

Cuba

Usually when we discuss the political and legal environment, it is the host country limiting trade. Here it is a third party limiting trade. The political environment in the US may force Canadians doing business in Cuba to choose between continuing their Cuban operations and doing business in the US. For Canada, Cuba has been a stable trade partner over the years. In recent years, Cuba has encouraged foreign involvement through both joint ventures and direct investment. (See the Chapter 5 video case study Cigars for more information on Canada's relationship with Cuba.)

It is US political concerns to secure the votes of the vocal Cuban-American population in Florida that is driving this initiative. Canadian firms must wait and see if the law is actively enforced. If it is, they must decide how to handle the situation.

Testing Terms and Concepts

Part One

1. D D
2. B M
3. D E
4. C E
5. B M
6. B M
7. A E
8. A M
9. D M
10. A - E Under management contracting, the domestic firm supplies management know-how to a foreign company that supplies the capital. The domestic firm exports management services rather than products.

    Management contracting is a low risk method of getting into a foreign market, and it yields income from the beginning. The arrangement is even more attractive if the contracting firm has an option to buy some share in the managed company later on. On the other hand, the arrangement is not sensible if the company can put its scarce management talent to better uses or if it can make greater profits by undertaking the whole venture. Management contracting also prevents the company from setting up its own operations for a period of time.

11. C E
12. C D
13. D M
14. E D
15. A E

Part Two

1. F M
2. T E
3. T M
4. T E
5. F D
6. F D
7. F M
8. T M

9. T E
10. F E
11. F - D In general, this statement is false--the principles of setting marketing objectives, choosing target markets, developing marketing positions and mixes, and carrying out marketing control still apply. But the differences among nations can be so great that the international marketer needs to understand foreign countries and how people in different countries respond to marketing efforts. Therefore, marketers must be willing to modify their marketing strategies to adapt to the unique characteristics of the international market.
12. T D
13. T M
14. T D
15. F M

CHAPTER 21

MARKETING SERVICES, ORGANIZATIONS, PERSONS, PLACES AND IDEAS

CHAPTER OVERVIEW

As has been emphasized throughout the text, marketing is not limited to the sale of tangible goods. This chapter discusses characteristics of the marketing of services, organizations, persons, places, and ideas. Canada and the United States are the world's first service economies, in that a majority of their people are employed in service industries. Services may be classified in many different ways, and they have four important characteristics that influence marketing strategies: intangibility, inseparability, variability, and perishability. Service marketers must manage their competitive differentiation, service quality, and productivity. Organizations must assess, plan, and control their images. Person marketing involves creating a celebrity--a well-known person whose name generates attention, interest and action. Places may be marketed for several purposes. An important form of idea marketing is social marketing, which is the marketing of social ideas, causes, or practices in a target group.

CHAPTER OBJECTIVES

When you finish this chapter, you should be able to accomplish the following:

1. Express the uniqueness of marketing services and the aspects that set them apart, intangibility inseparabiity, variability and perishability.
2. Identify and define strategies for marketing services including differentiation, service, quality and productivity.
3. Discuss organization marketing, including image assessment and image planning and control.
4. Identify the basic elements of person marketing, place marketing and idea marketing.

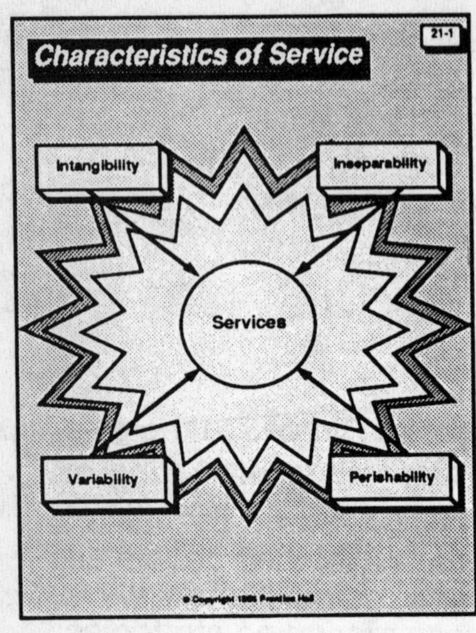

I. Services Marketing

A. Nature and characteristics of a service

1. Intangibility

2. Inseparability

3. Variability

4. Perishability

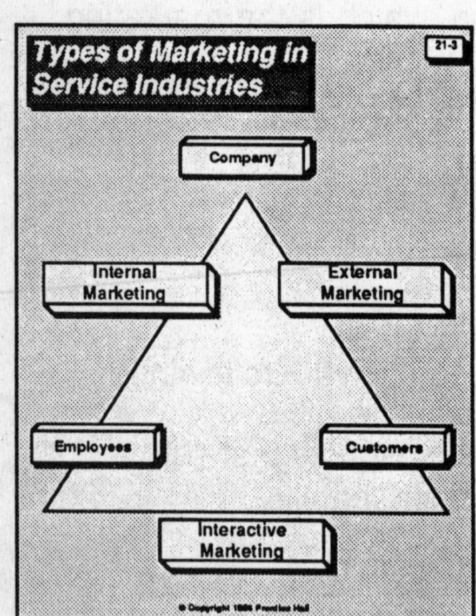

B. Marketing strategies for service firms

1. Managing differentiation

2. Managing service quality

3. Managing productivity

C. International services marketing

II. Organization Marketing

A. Image assessment

B. Image planning and control

III. Person Marketing

IV. Place Marketing

V. Idea Marketing

KEY TERMS

Marketing by a service firm that recognizes that perceived service quality depends heavily on the quality of buyer-seller interaction.

Interactive marketing (p. 719)

Marketing by a service firm to train and motivate effectively its customer-contact employees and all the supporting service people to work as a team to provide customer satisfaction.

Internal marketing (p. 719)

The way an individual or a group sees an organization.

Organization image (p. 726)

Activities undertaken to create, maintain, or change attitudes and behaviour of target audiences toward an organization.

Organization marketing (p. 726)

Activities undertaken to create, maintain, or change attitudes or behaviour toward particular people.

Person marketing (p. 727)

Activities undertaken to create, maintain, or change attitudes or behaviour toward particular places.

Place marketing (p. 729)

Any activity or benefit that one party can offer to another which is essentially intangible and does not result in the ownership of anything.

Service (p. 715)

A major characteristic of services--they are produced and consumed at the same time and cannot be separated from their providers, whether the providers are people or machines.

Service inseparability (p. 716)

A major characteristic of services--they cannot be seen, tasted, felt, heard, or smelled before they are bought.

Service intangibility (p. 716)

A major characteristic of services--they cannot be stored for later sale or use.

Service perishability (p. 717)

A major characteristic of services--their quality may vary greatly, depending on who provides them and when, where, and how.

Service variability (p. 717)

The design, implementation, and control of programs seeking to increase the acceptability of a social idea, cause, or practice among a target group.

Social marketing (p. 730)

APPLYING TERMS AND CONCEPTS

To determine how well you understand the materials in this chapter, read each of the following brief cases and then respond to the questions that follow. Answers are given at the end of this chapter.

Madame Zorba

Madame Zorba, a former fortuneteller, has just opened Yellowknife's first complete occult science centre. Madame offers a complete line of paranormal services. In addition to palmistry, tarot readings, and crystal ball gazing, interested customers can have their aura analyzed, engage in seances, receive training in astral projection, test their powers of ESP, or sample any number of the more exotic occult practices.

Madame Zorba has invested in an unusually nice facility housing a large staff and supported by the best equipment. She expects to enjoy a brisk business, with clientele drawn from "widely diverse socio-economic strata." Like any other businessperson, she is concerned about how best to market her rather unusual "product."

Questions

1. Briefly explain how Madame Zorba might deal with each of the following characteristics which will affect her marketing program:

   A. Intangibility ______________________________

   ____

   ____

B. Inseparability ____

____

____

C. Variability ____

____

____

D. Perishability ____

____

____

2. Madame Zorba should be classified as providing a(n) ____________ - ____________ service.

3. Since the client's presence is necessary in the performance of this service, Madame Zorba is correct to invest in impressive facilities and equipment.

   A. True B. False

4. Madame Zorba's clients are most likely to purchase the services to meet a(n) ____________ need, although some clients will purchase for ____________ reasons.

5. At present, Madame Zorba has little or no competition. What will be the major concern of her marketing program after she opens her business?

____

____

Tours of the Darkside

Dr. Sheila Aniston, a prominent social critic and professor at the University of Toronto, recently introduced a three-credit hour undergraduate course, Soc. 365 - Deviant Subcultures. The course allows students to observe the underbelly of society and is popularly known as "Tours of the Darkside."

The course begins with readings and lectures on sociology and urban history, the class structure, subcultures and deviance. The class takes an unusual twist when the students travel into Toronto's famed "Yonge Street." The tours allow students to observe behaviour typically considered unacceptable and to understand how it thrives and coexists with "polite" society. Interviews with area residents and patrons are included in the tours. Herman prohibits cameras and tape recorders to preserve the desired anonymity and cooperation of interviewees.

Following these experiences, students are assigned a research paper wherein they analyze the motivations of the more respectable patrons who use and have come to depend upon the area's existence. The paper also allows the student to consider the adaptive skills necessary for area residents to survive and in fact thrive in that environment. The student must also evaluate the role played by the area in a larger socioeconomic society.

Aniston, who has studied this area for six years, expects to publish her findings next year.

Questions

_____ 1. The University of Toronto allows only Dr. Aniston to teach and supervise the tours associated with Soc. 365. This suggests the ____________ of the course.

A. variability
B. inseparability
C. perishability
D. intangibility
E. substantiality

_____ 2. The people interviewed and the behaviours observed on a given tour are unique and differ from one to another. This suggests the ____________ of the tours associated with Soc. 365.

A. variability
B. inseparability
C. perishability
D. intangibility
E. substantiality

_____ 3. To protect the anonymity and to entice the cooperation of area interviewees; Dr. Aniston prohibits tape recorders and cameras on the tours. This lack of an actual, unbiased record (film and recording) of the tour would suggest the __________ of the experience.

A. variability
B. inseparability
C. perishability
D. intangibility
E. substantiality

_____ 4. Dr. Aniston is never sure what the students will experience (see, hear, smell, etc.) on a given tour before it occurs. This suggests the __________ of the experience.

A. variability
B. inseparability
C. perishability
D. intangibility
E. substantiality

Woodstock '94

Woodstock '94 - Three days of peace, love and music, not to mention cash machines, metal detectors, corporate sponsors, the Eco Village, the Peace Patrol, mud and 2,800 overflowing portable toilets. It wasn't quite the same as the original Woodstock held some 25 years earlier, but than it couldn't be.

For three days in August 1994, a quarter of a million or so people descended on an 840 acre site in Saugerties, New York. The mainly white, middle class crowd came to the 25th anniversary of the Woodstock Music and Art Fair originally held in Bethel, New York. Such diverse groups as the Band, Red Hot Chili Peppers, Blind Melon, Salt-n-Pepa, Bob Dylan, Joe Cocker and the Cranberries were among the 50 bands invited to entertain the fair goers. Corporate sponsors, the likes of Pepsi, Apple Computers and Haagen-Daz were also there, promoting their wares while also subsidizing the event.

The Eco Village - reportedly there to educate the masses about the environment - seemed more about making money than education. The private security force dubbed the "Peace Patrol" reinforced the 550 State Troopers enforcing the ban on alcohol and drugs, while also maintaining order.

Where the original concert didn't even have an official T-shirt, Woodstock '94 seemed decidedly mainstream. Blatant commercialism caused some idealistic musicians to boycott the event. But most seemed genuinely glad to have been invited--besides the better paid acts reportedly received $350,000 plus a share of the royalties. Promoters of Woodstock '94 reportedly filed a multi-million dollar law suit against rival promoters who wanted to stage an event called Bethel '94--a concert on the site of the original event. Two concerts, commemorating the same event in the same general area, at the same time, would be bad for business.

Some complained the event should have been called Greenstock, not Woodstock. But Woodstock '94 cost $42 million, more than ten times the cost of the original concert. It takes money to stage such a colossal event. This is not to suggest the organizers sold out completely. Other corporate sponsors including alcohol and tobacco companies were politely turned away. Even though profits would have been higher, and ticket prices lower.

Apparently, the commercialism wasn't too much of a deterrent. Over 250,000 people paid the $190 ticket price (compared to the $25 price for the original event) for three days of music, camping, camaraderie and parking. And by some estimates, that was a bargain.

Note: All figures are in Canadian dollars

Questions

Briefly explain how the promotion of Woodstock '94 might deal with the following characteristics of their offerings.

1. Intangibility ________________________________

____

____

____

2. Inseparability ________________________________

____

____

____

3. Variability ________________________________

____

____

4. Perishability ______________________________

____

____

____

Sources: "Field of Dreams," *Rolling Stone*, August 11, 1994, pp. 35-36; "Woodstock," *Time*, August 22, 1994, pp. 78-82; "Lifestyle," *Newsweek*, August 8, 1994, pp. 44-48.

TESTING TERMS AND CONCEPTS

Part One To test your understanding of the concepts presented in this chapter, write the letter of the most appropriate answer on the line next to the question number. Answers to these questions may be found at the end of this chapter.

_____ 1. An activity or benefit that one party can offer another, is essentially intangible, and does not result in the ownership of anything is called a(n):

A. service.
B. asset.
C. consumer intangible.
D. intangible asset.
E. nondurable good.

_____ 2. Services depend upon who provides them as well as when and where they are provided. This service characteristic is known as:

A. perishability.
B. inseparability.
C. variability.
D. intangibility.
E. substantiality.

_____ 3. The Ajax Reducing Salon has mounted an extensive advertising campaign that features before and after photographs of satisfied customers testifying to the ease and benefits of the Ajax program. Ajax is concentrating on which of the following marketing aspects of its service?

A. variability
B. perishability
C. intangibility
D. inseparability
E. substantiality

_____ 4. Which of the following should a well-managed service company have if it wishes to provide high service quality?

A. top management's commitment
B. high service quality standards
C. satisfied employees as well as satisfied customers
D. only (A) and (B)
E. all of the above

_____ 5. Which of the following is not a reason for increased interest in marketing by service firms?

A. rising costs
B. increasing service quality
C. increasing competition
D. production stagnation
E. both (A) and (C)

_____ 6. The Extel Corporation is concerned about the way its public views the firm. Its first step in improving this situation should be to:

A. launch a massive advertising campaign.
B. conduct research to ascertain its current image.
C. carefully plan its desired image.
D. fire its current marketing manager.
E. develop a public relations campaign.

_____ 7. ____________ marketing means that perceived service quality depends heavily on the quality of the buyer-seller interaction.

A. Interactive
B. Internal
C. External
D. Intraactive
E. Hyperactive

_____ 8. Social marketers may pursue all but which of the following objectives?

A. produce understanding
B. change a basic belief
C. change behaviour
D. increase profitability
E. both (A) and (C)

_____ 9. The design, implementation, and control of programs seeking to increase the acceptability of a social idea, cause, or practice in a target group is called ____________ marketing.

A. social
B. place
C. service
D. organization
E. person

_____ 10. The way an individual or a group sees an organization is called its:

A. image.
B. reputation.
C. presence.
D. appearance.
E. sphere-of-influence.

_____ 11. The process of attempting to reduce demand for a vacation spot when the harm from tourism exceeds the revenues is called ____________.

A. retro-marketing
B. intermarketing
C. intramarketing
D. demarketing
E. defacto marketing

_____ 12. ____________ means that the service firm must effectively train and motivate its customer-contact employees and all supporting service people to work as a team to provide customer satisfaction.

A. Retro-marketing
B. Multimarketing
C. Internal marketing
D. External marketing
E. Reverse

_____ 13. One of the best ways for a service firm to differentiate its services is to:

A. promote aggressively.
B. provide consistently higher quality than competition.
C. price lower than competitors.
D. price higher than competitors.
E. avoid sales promotions.

_____ 14. Which of the following have been offered as reasons for the restrictive rules and regulations faced by international services marketers as they attempt to enter a foreign market?

A. The rules are a reflection of the host country's traditions.
B. The rules are designed to protect the country's own fledgling service industries from large global competitors with greater resources.
C. The rules have little purpose other than to make entry difficult for foreign service firms.
D. only (A) and (B)
E. all of the above

_____ 15. Lanark Resorts charged lower prices during off-peak times in an effort to boost occupancy rates. This strategy results from the fact that services are:

A. variable.
B. perishable.
C. intangible.
D. inseparable.
E. substantial.

Part Two To test your understanding of the concepts presented in this chapter, respond to the following questions by writing the letter T or F on the line next to the question number if you believe the statement is true or false, respectively. Answers to these questions are at the end of this chapter.

_____ 1. Developing brand names is one technique to increase the customer's confidence in purchasing a service.

_____ 2. Variability means that a service cannot exist separately from its providers, whether they are persons and machines.

_____ 3. Monitoring customer satisfaction through suggestion and complaint systems and customer surveys is a quality control technique designed to reduce service variability.

_____ 4. Differential pricing attempts to shift some demand from peak to off-peak periods in an attempt to produce a better match between supply and demand.

_____ 5. Since no tangible "product" is involved in service selling, quality considerations are of minimal concern.

_____ 6. The intangibility of a product refers to the fact that a service cannot be stored.

_____ 7. One reason that service businesses have neglected marketing is that they believed it to be unprofessional.

_____ 8. Image refers to the way an individual or a group sees an object or organization.

_____ 9. Periodic surveys of its publics to determine its image do little good for an organization.

_____ 10. A well-managed service firm is only concerned about the satisfaction of its customers and not the satisfaction of its employees.

_____ 11. In a sense all marketing is the marketing of an idea.

_____ 12. Celebrities differ not only in the scope of their visibility but also in their durability.

_____ 13. Since services are intangible, they cannot be branded.

_____ 14. Internal marketing means that the service firm must effectively train and motivate its customer-contact employees and all the supporting service people to work as a team to provide customer satisfaction.

_____ 15. Since customers often compare the perceived service of a given firm to their expected service, if the perceived service meets or exceeds expected service, customers are less apt to use the service provider again.

Answers

Applying Terms and Concepts

Madame Zorba

1. A. *Intangibility* - Madame Zorba should emphasize the benefits of her services. Testimonials from respected customers would be helpful.

   B. *Inseparability* - Madame Zorba should carefully select and personally train her staff. Their experiences, training, and credentials should be matched to their services and publicized.

   C. *Variability* - Madame Zorba should establish and enforce training and service standards to ensure as much uniformity of quality as possible.

   D. *Perishability* - Madame Zorba should consider reservation systems and increased customer participation.

2. people based
3. True
4. personal, business
5. To present an image of professionalism and credibility for both her services and her staff.

Tours of the Darkside

1. B
2. A
3. C
4. D

Woodstock '94

1. *Intangibility* - means that the services cannot be seen, tasted, heard, felt or smelled before they are bought. Organizers gave festival goers an idea of what to expect by announcing the preparations that had taken place. Preparations included offsite parking with shuttle buses, camping areas, a ban on drugs and alcohol, the list of performers and the number of portable toilets along with a host of others. References to the original gathering also gave attendees a sense of what to expect.

   But neither organizers nor attendees knew exactly what to expect prior to the concert. Advanced preparations and the actual event would still be affected by external uncontrollables such as weather.

2. *Inseparability* - means that services cannot be separated from their providers. Because the customer is also present as the service is provided, the outcome is affected by both the provider and the customer.

   This meant that to some extent, the success of the concert would be dependent on the behavior of the concert goers as well as that of the performers, vendors, security force and the organizers. So collectively they, along with other publics, created the event.

3. *Variability* - means that the quality of the services depends on who provides the service as well as when, where and how they are provided.

   Concert organizers hoped to instill confidence in potential attendees by providing information about the concert and their preparations. The suggestion was that a less organized concert would be less enjoyable.

4. *Perishability* - means that services cannot be stored for later use. The point was that one had to be there to truly experience the event. Although there were numerous news broadcasts from Saugerties, MTV televised some of the festival, there was pay per view on cable and there would be the inevitable CD and film, nothing compared to actually being present at the concert.

   The sights, sounds, smells, and tastes cannot be totally captured or recreated during or after the event. Once the event is over--it is over, the experience cannot be recreated. Even another concert-Woodstock '94 compared to Woodstock '69--cannot recreate the event as each becomes its own happening.

Testing Terms and Concepts

Part One

1. A E
2. C M
3. C M
4. E E
5. B M
6. B D
7. A - M In product marketing, product quality often depends little on how the product is obtained. But in services marketing, service quality depends both on the service deliverer and on the quality of the delivery, especially in professional services. The customer judges service quality not just on technical quality but also on its functional quality. Thus, professionals cannot assume that they will satisfy the client simply by providing good technical service. They must also master interactive marketing skills or functions.
8. D D
9. A E
10. A E
11. D M
12. C D
13. B M
14. E D
15. B M

Part Two

1. T E
2. F E
3. T M
4. T M
5. F E
6. F M
7. T E
8. T M
9. F M
10. F - D Well-managed service companies satisfy employees as well as customers. They believe that good employee relations will result in good customer relations. Therefore, management

should create an environment of employee support, give rewards for good service performance, and monitor employee job satisfaction.

11. T D
12. T E
13. F M
14. T D
15. F M

CHAPTER 22

MARKETING AND SOCIETY: SOCIAL RESPONSIBILITY AND MARKETING ETHICS

CHAPTER OVERVIEW

This concluding chapter links the end of the text to its beginning by discussing marketing's role in society. Social criticisms of marketing relate to its impact on consumers, on society as a whole, and on other businesses. From the marketer's point of view, these criticisms relate to unethical and atypical marketing practices, or reflect basic misunderstandings of the forces influencing marketing, consumers, and society. Citizen actions to regulate marketing have focused on the rights and powers of buyers in relation to sellers (consumerism) and on marketing's impact on the environment (environmentalism). Enlightened marketing is consumer-oriented, innovative, concerned with providing value, has a sense of mission, and considers society's long-run interests in making marketing decisions. Guidelines and policies on ethical questions should reflect an organization's social conscience. Public policy toward marketing should be influenced by seven principles that will improve the marketing system's ability to contribute to a higher quality of life.

CHAPTER OBJECTIVES

When you finish this chapter, you should be able to accomplish the following:

1. Discuss social criticisms of marketing's impact on individual consumers, particularly high prices, deceptive practices, high pressure selling shoddy products, planned obsolescence and poor service to disadvantaged consumers.

2. Identify and define criticisms of marketing's impact on society as a whole, false wants and materialism, too few social goods, cultural pollution, and too much political power.

3. Outline citizen and public actions to regulate marketing--consumerism, environmentalism, and regulation--and the way they affect marketing strategies.

4. Explain the business actions toward socially responsible marketing that can foster marketing ethics and lead to different philosophies of enlightened marketing: consumer oriented, innovative, value, sense-of-mission, and societal marketing.

5. List and define key principles for public policy toward marketing.

LECTURE/STUDENT NOTES

I. Social Criticisms of Marketing

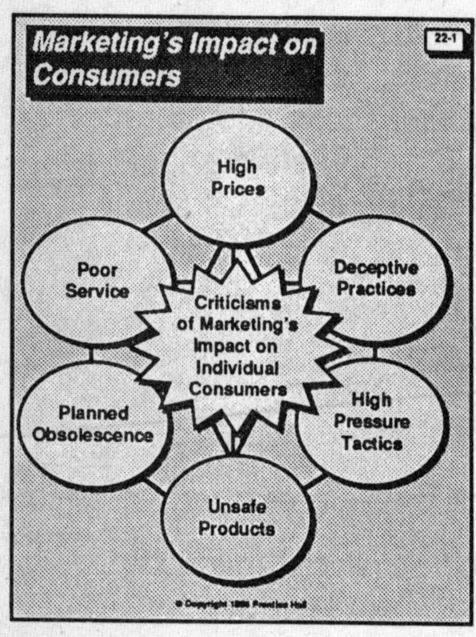

A. Marketing's impact on individual consumers

1. High prices

a. High costs of distribution

b. High advertising and promotion costs

c. Excessive markups

2. Deceptive practices

3. High-pressure selling

4. Shoddy or unsafe products

5. Planned obsolescence

6. Poor service to disadvantaged consumers

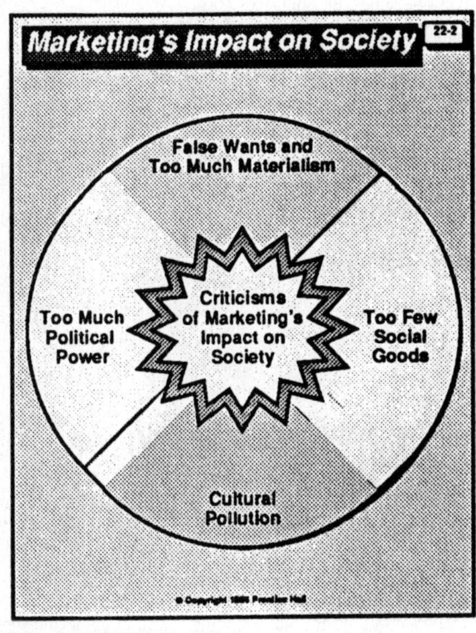

B. Marketing's impact on society as a whole

1. False wants and too much materialism

2. Too few social goods

3. Cultural pollution

4. Too much political power

C. Marketing's impact on other businesses

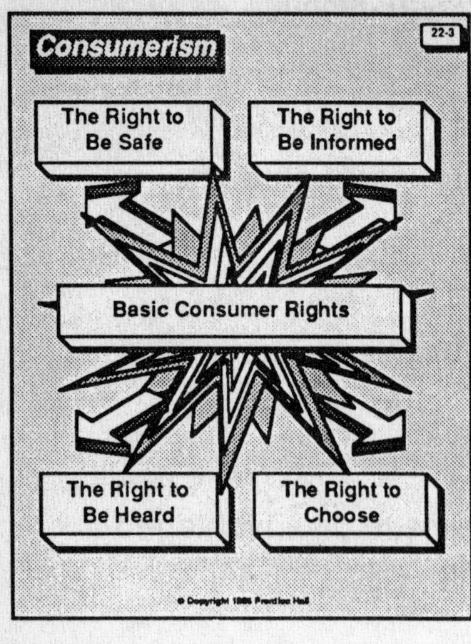

II. Citizen and Public Actions to Regulate Marketing

A. Consumerism

B. Environmentalism

C. Public actions to regulate marketing

III. Business Actions toward Socially Responsible Marketing

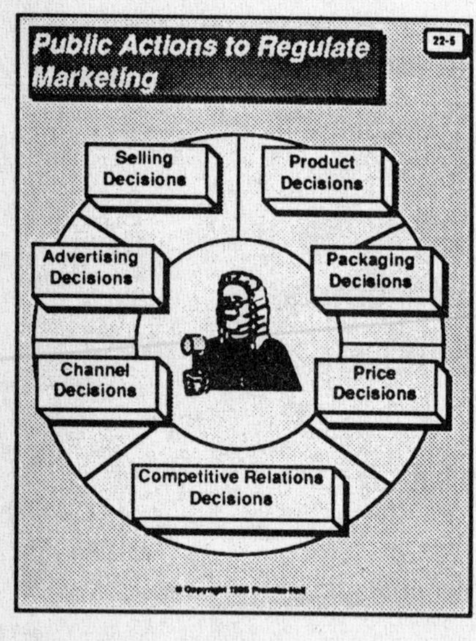

A. Enlightened marketing

1. Consumer-oriented marketing

2. Innovative marketing

3. Value marketing

4. Sense-of-mission marketing

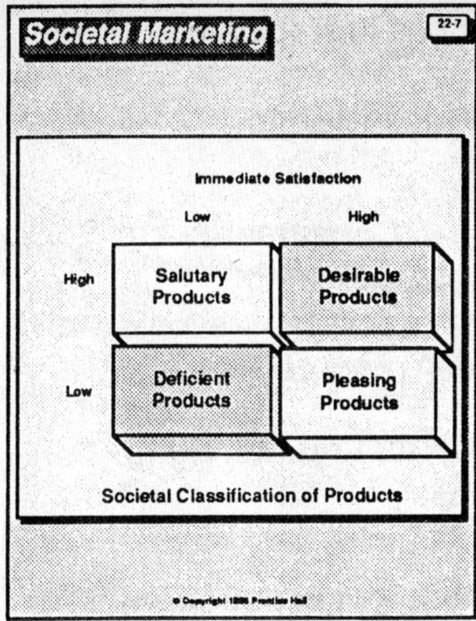

5. Societal marketing

B. Marketing ethics

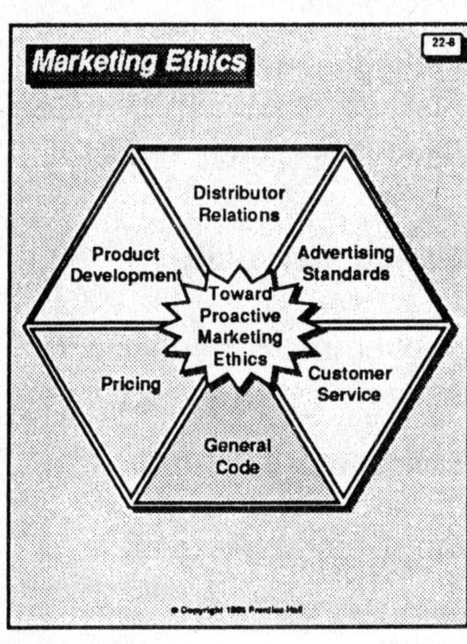

KEY TERMS

An organized movement of citizens and government agencies to improve the rights and power of buyers in relation to sellers.

Consumerism (p. 762)

A principle of enlightened marketing which holds that a company should view and organize its marketing activities from the consumers' point of view.

Consumer-oriented marketing (p. 769)

Products that have neither appeal nor long-run benefits.

Deficient products (p. 770)

Products that give both high immediate satisfaction and high long-run benefits.

Desirable products (p. 770)

A marketing philosophy holding that a company's marketing should support the best long-run performance of the marketing system; its five principles include consumer-oriented marketing, innovative marketing, value marketing, sense-of-mission marketing, and societal marketing.

Enlightened marketing (p. 768)

An organized movement of concerned citizens and government agencies to protect and improve people's living environment.

Environmentalism (p. 764)

A principle of enlightened marketing which requires that a company seek real product and marketing improvements.

Innovative marketing (p. 769)

Products that give high immediate satisfaction but may hurt consumerism in the long run.

Pleasing products (p. 770)

Products that have low appeal but may benefit consumers in the long run.

Salutary products (p. 770)

A principle of enlightened marketing which holds that a company should define its mission in broad social terms rather than narrow product terms.

Sense-of-mission marketing (p. 769)

A principle of enlightened marketing which holds that a company should make marketing decisions by considering consumers' wants, the company's requirements, consumers' long-run interests, and society's long-run interests.

Societal marketing (p. 770)

A principle of enlightened marketing which holds that a company should put most of its resources into value-building marketing investments.

Value marketing (p. 769)

APPLYING TERMS AND CONCEPTS

To determine how well you understand the materials in this chapter, read each of the following brief cases and then respond to the questions that follow. Answers are given at the end of this chapter.

Brown's Department Stores

Helen Mahon is the vice-president of security for Halifax-based Brown's Department Stores. She has become increasingly alarmed at the high rate of shoplifting and employee theft within Brown's store system. The current rate of loss is estimated at $2,600,000 per year.

Mahon is particularly upset because she realizes that everyone is hurt by the losses. Shoplifters, when caught, are prosecuted. Customers must pay higher prices to cover the loss, and cost of the security systems, and store managers are faced with an unpleasant, time-consuming activity that reduces the profitability of the organization.

Mahon was recently approached by Todd Roy Hill, the president of Hill Communications, Inc., with a proposal that has left her in a quandary. Hill Communications produces cassette tapes that contain subliminal messages designed to alter the behaviour of listeners. The listener hears music or "pink" noise such as ocean waves or rushing wind, while the subconscious hears the message (in this situation) "Do not shoplift." Hill explained that the message (any message) is recorded at about 5 decibels below the audible range. In time, the message embeds itself in the listener's mind, thereby affecting behaviour.

Hill produced evidence (studies he had conducted) indicating that losses were reduced by an average of 39 percent in similar settings. With a projected loss reduction of over $1,000,000, Mahon was interested, but she was uneasy because she wondered if it was right to manipulate people in this fashion. She also asked herself: "If subliminal messages can be used to reduce shoplifting, why not use it to stimulate sales at Brown's Stores?"

That evening Mahon came across an article in the magazine Psychology In Action by McGill University psychology professor Rene Alphonse, a specialist in the study of perception, who maintained that subliminal messages do not alter behaviour. Alphonse also went on to state that studies conducted to prove that they do were often flawed and unscientific.

The cost of the system proposed by Hill Communications is essentially what Brown now pays for background music in its stores. Hill has documentation from the provincial government that the practice is perfectly legal in Nova Scotia. He also stated that Brown's would be the first chain of department stores to use the service.

Questions

1. What would Mahon decide if she believed that issues of morality, ethics, responsibility and conscience should be made according to the free market or legal system?

____

____

____

____

2. What would Mahon decide if she believed that issues of morality, ethics, responsibility and conscience should be made according to managers "social conscience?"

____

____

____

____

Palmer Industries

Carl Palmer, President of Palmer Industries, recently startled the beverage industry with the introduction of a self-cooling can. The technology, pioneered by Palmer, allows a slightly modified can to cool itself within 20 seconds of opening. Cooling is accomplished by a carbon dioxide cartridge encased in an aluminum sheath surrounding the beverage container. When the container is opened, the carbon dioxide cartridge is pierced. As the carbon dioxide escapes from the cartridge, it freezes the outer sheath, thereby cooling the beverage. Variations in temperature can be achieved by increasing or decreasing the volume of carbon dioxide in the cartridge. Beer will chill to 3 degrees and soft drinks to 5 degrees, the ideal temperature.

The self-cooling can will have the same outer dimensions as a standard can. However, there will be approximately a 75 ml liquid displacement to accommodate the cooling mechanism. The outer sheath will be bonded to the top and bottom of the can with the inner container wall 2 mm from the outer wall. The carbon dioxide will escape through the aperture created when the can is opened. The self-cooling can will cost approximately $.05 more per unit than a conventional can.

The technology is protected by 16 Canadian and US patents, foreign patents pending. Palmer Industries will license manufacturers to produce the containers and sell them to various bottling companies. Bay Street responded enthusiastically; with Palmer Industries--posting a 12% gain. An additional 6% was posted when the Consumer and Corporate and Agriculture Canada approved the technology as safe for sale.

Palmer plans to start with the beverage industry, but sees this technology applied to any packaged food consumers prefer chilled prior to consumption, including canned fruits, vegetables, desserts and meats. To date, the only group to express doubt about the new technology is the manufacturers of refrigerated soft drink vending machines, who will find demand for their machines declining as the self-cooling cans gain wide-spread distribution.

Questions

_____ 1. Critics may charge that development of a self-cooling can to replace regular cans is an example of ____________.

A. unfair competition
B. planned obsolescence
C. deceptive packaging
D. high pressure selling
E. price gouging

_____ 2. Palmer Industries has utilized patent protection as a(n):

A. barrier to entry.
B. unfair competition.
C. unfair political protection.
D. high pressure selling.
E. planned obsolescence.

_____ 3. Consumers may view Palmer Industries as practicing _____________ marketing.

A. antisocial
B. enlightened
C. production oriented
D. sales oriented
E. product oriented

_____ 4. If, in a promotional campaign, Palmer Industries advertised the self-cooling can would chill soft drinks to 5 degrees when it would only chill them to 14 degrees, Palmer would be engaged in _____________.

A. high pressure selling
B. puffery
C. deceptive advertising
D. creating false wants
E. deceptive pricing

_____ 5. The self-cooling can is best classified as a _____________ product.

A. deficient
B. decadent
C. desirable
D. pleasing
E. salutary

Biodegradable Diapers

Some marketers have been criticized for being so concerned about their own interests that they ignore all others. High prices, deceptive practices, high-pressure selling, and poor service to disadvantaged customers are some of the practices critics bring up when charging that some firms are socially irresponsible. But now several firms have developed what appears to be the correct product for the 1990's--biodegradable disposable diapers.

Over a half million babies are born each year in Canada. They are part of the "baby boom echo"--children of the postwar baby boomers. A baby in the house means bottles, baby food, and lots and lots of diapers. The average baby goes through between 8,000 and 10,000 diapers between birth and toilet training. For the country, that means 1.8 billion used diapers a year, which converts to a half million tonnes of waste filling up landfills and taking 2 to 500 years to dissolve. Concern about the impact of all these diapers has led to a different kind of boom--biodegradable diapers.

Biodegradable diapers are made with advanced plastics, most involving the binding of cornstarch polymers--molecules made up of repeating, identical subunits--with plastic molecules. The newly formed plastic is supposed to be readily broken down in the soil by a variety of microorganisms, such as fungi and bacteria that feed on the starch. As the cornstarch is eaten, the plastic's polymeric chains are broken down into smaller and smaller units, leaving behind only a plastic dust.

The condition of the nation's landfills has also contributed to the growth in the demand for biodegradable diapers. Many municipalities are finding their existing landfills must soon be closed because they do not meet federal guidelines for pollution control. Permits to construct new landfills are difficult to obtain and modern environmentally sound landfills are extremely expensive to build, maintain and monitor.

So far, most of the new diapers have been sold to well-educated parents who are willing to help the environment by paying an extra 5 to 10 percent for a disposable diaper that actually does dispose of itself. Even though the industry is still in its infancy, brands such as Rocky Mountain, Tender Cares, Dove Tails, Nappies, and Bunnies are starting to challenge major brands for supermarket shelf space.

But recently, some people have begun to question just how much disposable biodegradable diapers will do to alleviate the landfill problem. One researcher found that the average landfill contains 36 percent paper, 20 percent yard wastes, 9 percent metal, 9 percent food, 8 percent glass, 7 percent plastic, and 11 percent other materials. And these proportions of materials do not change appreciably over time. Research also indicates that once material is placed in a landfill, it remains virtually unchanged. Decades after it was buried, paper, metal, glass, and plastic remain. Even yard waste and food do not easily decay. It seems that in order for biodegradation to take place, water, oxygen, and sunlight must be present so that the microorganisms can break down the materials. Unfortunately, these conditions are not typically present in modern landfills. Also, the problem with landfills is not so much the type of material placed in them as the volume of that material.

Some researchers suggest that the benefits of biodegradable plastics are illusory and that the solution to our waste problem is a combination of recycling, incineration, composition, and landfills.

Questions

1. Explain why firms that make biodegradable disposable diapers could be said to be following a philosophy of societal marketing.

2. What impact, if any, will biodegradable disposable diapers have on landfills?

3. How are environmentalists likely to view biodegradable disposable diapers?

Sources: "Biodegradable Plastics?" *Country Journal*, May/June 1990, p.25; "The World of Crumbling Plastics." *U.S. News and World Report*, November 24, 1986. p. 76; "Biodegradables That Don't Make Degrade." *U.S. News and World Report*, March 26, 1990, p. 14; "Bagging It." *Scientific America*, August 1987, p. 22; "The Perils of Plastic." *Health*, June 1990, p. 36; and "Natural Plastic." *Natural History* May 1990, pp. 82-84. "Biodegradable Disposable Diapers," Business World, *ABC News Broadcast*, September 17, 1989.

TESTING TERMS AND CONCEPTS

Part One To test your understanding of the concepts presented in this chapter, write the letter of the most appropriate answer on the line next to the question number. Answers to these questions are at the end of this chapter.

_____ 1. The marketing concept is a philosophy of:

A. profit maximization.
B. altruistic service.
C. service and mutual gain
D. invisible competition.
E. cost minimization.

_____ 2. Social critics claim that marketing hurts:

A. individual consumers.
B. society as a whole.
C. other businesses.
D. both (A) and (C)
E. all of the above

_____ 3. Myron Bailey is a social critic who claims that one reason prices are so high for consumer goods is that distribution costs are too high. Which statement(s) could be used to answer this charge?

A. Increased markups reflect an improved level of customer services.
B. Operating costs decrease as sales decrease.
C. Competition has allowed high profit margins.
D. all of the above
E. none of the above

_____ 4. Which of the following is not one of the ways in which consumers have been hurt by our marketing system, according to social critics?

A. high prices
B. high pressure selling
C. new product planning
D. planned obsolescence
E. both (A) and (B)

_____ 5. When a company overstates a product's attributes, it is engaging in deceptive:

A. pricing.
B. promotion.
C. packaging.
D. distribution.
E. sales promotion.

_____ 6. A reaction to high pressure selling is:

A. legislation that requires door-to-door salespeople to announce their purpose at the door.
B. allowing buyers a 7-day cooling off period in which to cancel their contract.
C. buyers complaining to the Better Business Bureau.
D. all of the above
E. none of the above

_____ 7. Critics have charged that the North American business system encourages excessive interest in material possessions. This criticism is known as:

A. false wants.
B. excessive materialism.
C. cultural pollution.
D. insufficient social goods.
E. both (B) and (C)

_____ 8. The false wants and too much materialism criticism states that the interest in things is not seen as natural, but rather as created by marketing. One response to this criticism is:

A. people have normal defenses against advertising, including selective attention, perception, distortion, and retention.
B. the mass media are most effective when they attempt to create new needs rather than appeal to existing needs.
C. the failure rate of new products supports the claim that companies are able to control demand.
D. both (B) and (C)
E. all of the above

_____ 9. Acquisitions can be beneficial to the society when:

A. the acquired company was producing more economically prior to the acquisition than following it.
B. a well-managed company takes over a poorly managed company and reduces its efficiency.
C. an industry that was noncompetitive becomes competitive after the acquisition.
D. none of the above
E. all of the above

_____ 10. When firms use competitive tactics such as pricing below cost, with the intention of hurting or destroying competition, they are engaging in:

A. anticompetitive acquisition.
B. predatory competition.
C. setting a barrier to competition.
D. excessive political power.
E. both (A) and (C)

_____ 11. Environmentalists believe that a marketing system's goal should be to maximize:

A. consumer choice.
B. satisfaction.
C. consumption.
D. life quality.
E. the availability of goods and services.

_____ 12. ____________ products combine high immediate satisfaction and high long-run benefits.

A. Pleasing
B. Salutary
C. Desirable
D. Deficient
E. Socially acceptable

_____ 13. ____________ is an organized movement of citizens and government agencies to improve the rights and power of buyers in relation to sellers.

A. Environmentalism
B. Consumerism
C. Protectionism
D. Conservationism
E. Consumers Union

_____ 14. The most basic and perhaps ultimate responsibility for consumer protection should rest with:

A. government agencies and the legislative process.
B. companies.
C. consumer protection agencies.
D. managers.
E. consumers themselves.

_____ 15. Which of the following is advertising least capable of creating or stimulating?

A. needs
B. wants
C. desires
D. choices
E. images

Part Two To test your understanding of the concepts presented in this chapter, respond to the following questions by writing the letter T or F on the line next to the question number if you believe the statement is true or false, respectively. Answers to these questions may be found at the end of this chapter.

_____ 1. Planned obsolescence is one way in which marketing is hurting competition.

_____ 2. Deceptive practices fall into three categories, including deceptive pricing, deceptive promotion, and deceptive packaging.

_____ 3. Many business people avoid deceptive practices because such practices harm their businesses in the long run.

_____ 4. Marketers would contend that much of so-called planned obsolescence is the working out of dynamic competitive and technological forces in a free society, leading to ever-improving goods and services.

_____ 5. Some people believe that consumers are manipulated by advertisers to serve as the link between production and consumption, with wants coming to depend upon output.

_____ 6. Predatory competition is one example of marketing's impact on other businesses.

_____ 7. Environmentalism is an organized movement of citizens to enhance the rights and power of buyers in relation to sellers.

_____ 8. The maximization of consumer satisfaction is the goal of environmentalists.

_____ 9. According to the concept of consumer-oriented marketing, a company should define its mission in broad social terms, rather than narrow product terms

_____ 10. Pleasing products give high immediate satisfaction, but may hurt consumers in the long run.

_____ 11. The challenge posed by salutary products is to add some pleasing qualities so that they will become more desirable in consumers' minds.

_____ 12. Contrary to what marketers have stated--recent research indicates that consumer needs are in fact determined by advertising.

_____ 13. The principal of societal marketing suggests that an enlightened company makes marketing decisions by considering consumers wants and long-run interests, the company's requirements and society's long-run interests.

_____ 14. The three-day cooling off period was desired by door-to-door sellers to allow them time to check the buyer's credit record before delivering merchandise.

Answers

Applying Terms and Concepts

Brown's Department Store

1. The "Free Market" and "Legal System" philosophies suggest that it is the responsibility of the firm to obey the law as it pursues rational and economic objectives and that the common good is best served when a business pursues its own competitive advantage. Therefore, it is Mahon's obligation to use the subliminal messages as a loss prevention mechanism to legally enhance Brown's competitive advantage and increase Brown's profitability.
2. The "Social Conscience" philosophy suggests that corporations exercise independent, noneconomic judgment in deciding what is morally and ethically right. It also calls for management to apply individual morality to corporate decision. If Mahon was convinced that the system was legal and worked, she could decide to implement it because (a) the potential shoplifter is spared prosecution; (b) the cost of theft does not have to be passed on to the customers in the form of higher prices; and (c) store managers and owners avoid unpleasant situations and enjoy greater profitability. In this decision, her reasoning would be that manipulation of the would-be criminal through the use of subliminal messages is a small price to pay, given the benefits. In essence, the end justifies the means.

   However, Mahon might also decide that subliminal messages should not be included in the background music because it is an act of manipulation and subconscious behavior modification. Even though the act of shoplifting is wrong, the would-be criminal would not be acting of his or her own free will, therefore, the end, no matter how well intentioned, does not justify the means. In essence, it is morally wrong to engage in manipulation and subconscious behavior modification.

Palmer Industries

1. B
2. A
3. B
4. C
5. C

Biodegradable Diapers

1. An enlightened company following the principle of societal marketing makes marketing decisions by considering consumers' wants, the company's requirements, consumers' long-run interests, and society's long-run interests. The company is aware that neglecting the last two factors is a disservice to consumers and to society. Alert companies view societal problems as opportunities.

   A societally oriented marketer wants to design products that are not only pleasing but also beneficial. Therefore, products can be classified according to their degree of immediate consumer satisfaction and long-run consumer benefit. Desirable products give both high immediate satisfaction and long-run benefits. Biodegradable disposable diapers could be seen as a product that meets both of these criteria.

2. The impact will likely be negligible. In order for a substance to biodegrade, sunlight, water, and oxygen must be present, and these elements are typically absent in modern landfills.

   Researchers like Dr. William Rathje, an anthropologist at the University of Arizona, have found that most material put into a landfill does not decay. Decades after it was buried, paper, metal, glass, and plastic remain. Even yard waste and food do not easily decay. This is because biodegradation is accomplished by microorganisms that need sunlight, moisture, and oxygen to do the job.

   The problem with landfills is not so much the type of material placed in them as the volume of that material.

   Some researchers suggest that the benefits of biodegradable plastics are illusory and that our waste problem will only be solved by a combination of recycling, incineration, composting, and landfills.

3. While consumer advocates look at whether the marketing system is efficiently serving consumer wants, environmentalists look at how marketing affects the environment and at the costs of serving consumer need and wants.

   Environmentalism is an organized movement of concerned citizens and government agencies out to protect and improve people's living environment. Environmentalists are concerned about damage to the ecosystem caused by strip mining, forest depletion, acid rain, loss of the ozone layer in the atmosphere, toxic wastes, and litter; about the loss of recreational areas; and about the increase in health problems caused by bad air, polluted water, and chemically treated food.

Environmentalists are not against marketing and consumption; they simply want people and organizations to operate with more care for the environment. The marketing system's goal should not be to maximize consumption, consumer choice, or consumer satisfaction. Rather, it should be to maximize life quality. And "life quality" means not only the quality of consumer goods and services, but also the quality of the environment. Environmentalists want environmental costs included in producer and consumer decision making.

Environmentalists are likely to endorse the marketing of biodegradable disposable diapers over regular disposables since the former are more compatible with their views.

Testing Terms and Concepts

Part One

1. C M
2. E E
3. A - D Marketers could respond to the high cost of distribution system as follows: first, intermediaries do work that would otherwise have to be done by manufacturers or consumers. Second, the rising markup reflects improved services that consumers themselves want--more convenience, larger stores and assortment, longer store hours, return privileges, and others. Third, the costs of operating stores keep rising and force retailers to raise their prices. Fourth, retail competition is so intense that margins are actually quite low. For example, after taxes, supermarket chains are typically left with barely one percent profit on their sales.
4. C M
5. B E
6. D M
7. B D
8. A - D The false wants and too much materialism criticism overstates the power of business to create wants. People have strong defenses against advertising and other marketing tools. Marketers are most effective when they appeal to existing needs rather than when they attempt to create new ones. Furthermore, people seek information when making important purchases and do not normally rely on single sources. Even minor purchases, which may be affected by advertising messages, lead to repeat purchases only if the product performs as promised. Finally, the

high failure rate of new products shows that companies are not able to control demand.

9. C D
10. B M
11. D M
12. C M
13. B E
14. E M
15. A M

Part Two

1. F M
2. T E
3. T E
4. T D
5. T D
6. T M
7. F M
8. F - M Environmentalists are not against marketing and consumption, they simply want people and organizations to operate with more care for the environment. The marketing system's goal should not be to maximize consumption, consumer choice, or consumer satisfaction. Its goal should be to maximize life quality. And "life quality" means not only the quantity and quality of consumer goods and services, but also the quality of the environment. Environmentalists want environmental costs included in producer and consumer decision making.
9. F D
10. T E
11. T M
12. F M
13. T D
14. F M

SECTION TWO

RESEARCH PAPER/PROJECT OUTLINE

This section of the learning guide and workbook contains three outlines for research papers which may be assigned by your instructor. Suggested titles of the research papers are marketing, development of a business plan and development of a marketing plan. The outlines should be viewed as a guide for coverage of the assignment with specific topics added or deleted as appropriate.

The first research paper outline provides an overview of marketing. Its objective is to have you understand that all organizations--whether they are large or small, profit or nonprofit, product or service oriented, public or private--engage in marketing activities. this is a comprehensive paper encompassing information learned throughout the term. The paper begins with a general description of the industry followed by a discussion of a firm within the industry. The suggested outline continues with a detailed discussion of the firm's marketing strategy--that is the target market(s) chosen and the marketing mix designed to serve the targeted market(s). The paper closes with an evaluation of the marketing activities of the firm followed by your recommendations for improvement.

Since many business students have entrepreneurial interests, a second research paper outline,--development of a business plan--has been included in this edition of the learning guide. The objective of this research paper is to have you understand the complexities associated with establishing a business. The outline is very broad and covers many topics, some of which might not be included in a particular business plan. Therefore, you should view the outline as a guide, adding or deleting components as necessary.

The final research paper outline is for the development of a marketing plan. This project is designed to help you understand the challenges associated with developing products and bringing them to market. As was suggested with the first two research paper outlines, this outline should be viewed as a guide for coverage of the topic with specific topics added or deleted as needed.

Following the research paper outlines is a list of publications which may be consulted for additional information. You are also encouraged to consult with the reference librarian at your university library for additional resource material. Business people and organizations such as the Chamber of Commerce, Industry Canada, provincial industry departments and planning and economic development authorities are other helpful resources.

MARKETING
Research Paper Outline

I. Description of the Type of Business Selected

   A. Description of the Industry
      1. Historical development
      2. Current status
         a. sales volume
         b. major competitors
         c. political and legal challenges
         d. major markets
         e. major supplier
         f. publics
      3. Future outlook
         a. threats
         b. opportunities

   B. Description of Firm
      1. Historical development
      2. Current status
         a. statistical information
            (1) size
            (2) sales
            (3) profitability
            (4) market share
         b. microenvironment
            (1) customers
            (2) suppliers
            (3) competitors
            (4) publics
            (5) marketing intermediaries
            (6) organization
         c. macroenvironment
            (1) demographic
            (2) natural
            (3) economic
            (4) political/legal
            (5) cultural/social
            (6) technological
      3. Future projects
         a. threats
         b. opportunities/growth strategies

(1) market development
(2) market penetration
(3) product development
(4) diversification

II. Description of the Firm's Marketing Strategy

A. Selection of Target Markets Served
1. Types of market served (including rationale for their selection)
a. consumer
b. organizational
2. Buying behaviour of target market
a. what buying decisions are made
b. who participates in the buying decision
c. major influences on decision making
d. nature of the decision making process

B. Development of the Marketing Mix to Serve the Target Market
1. Discussion of product
a. product line
b. product classification
c. packaging/labeling/branding decisions
d. new product development process
e. product life cycle
2. Discussion of price
a. pricing policies/objectives and strategies
b. influences on price determination
c. product mix pricing strategies
d. price adjustment strategies
3. Discussion of place
a. nature of distribution channel(s) chosen
b. physical distribution decisions
c. wholesale/retail decisions
4. Discussion or promotion
a. promotion policies/objective and strategy
b. advertising
c. sales promotion
d. public relations
e. personal selling

III. Evaluation of the Firm's Marketing Management Activities

A. Assessment of the relative success of the firm's ability to develop and maintain positive relationships with its customers as well as for other forces in its micro and macro environment.

B. Recommendations for Improvement with Supporting Rationale

C. Discussion How Recommendations for Changes will Improve the Firm's Marketing Effectiveness

D. Conclusion

DEVELOPMENT OF A BUSINESS PLAN
Research Paper Outline

I. General Description of the Proposed Business

  A. Company Name, Address and Phone Number

  B. Identification of Key Personnel

  C. Mission Statement

  D. Brief Description of Marketing Strategy

  E. Financial Projection

II. Description of the Industry

  A. Historical Development

  B. Current Status
    1. Sales volume
    2. Major markets
    3. Major suppliers
    4. Principal competitors
    5. Political and legal challengers
    6. Technological development
    7. Publics

  C. Future Outlook
    1. Threats
    2. Opportunities

III. Description of Business

  A. Organization
    1. Form of ownership
    2. Management and technical experience of key personnel
    3. Mission statement
    4. Planning, implementation and control policies and procedures

  B. Market Considerations
    1. Target markets to be served including rationale for their selection
      a. characteristics of targeted customers

b. influences on buying behaviour
c. characteristics of the market (size, growth rate, estimate of sales potential)

2. Market mix designed to serve the target market
   a. product/service offering
      (1) product/service mix
      (2) major suppliers of raw materials and/or inventory
   b. pricing considerations
      (1) pricing strategy and objectives
      (2) influence on price determination
      (3) costs: fixed and variable
      (4) profit projections
      (5) impact of the economy on the business
   c. place considerations
      (1) location of business
      (2) trade area analysis
      (3) estimate of market potential (estimate of all competitors)
      (4) estimate of sales potential
      (5) type of business district
      (6) store design and layout, if applicable
      (7) pedestrian and vehicular traffic, if applicable
      (8) availability of parking
      (9) accessibility to highways
      (10) zoning
      (11) availability and quality of media
      (12) size and condition of building
   d. promotion considerations
      (1) personal selling strategy and procedures
      (2) sales promotion activities
      (3) advertising strategy and procedures
      (4) public relations activities

C. Differential Advantages Held Over the Competition

D. Financial Considerations
   1. Financial resources needed to commence operations
   2. Pro forma balance sheets, income statements for first five years
   3. Projected cash flow statements for first five years of operation
   4. First year budget - by month
   5. Break even analysis - in units and dollar volume
   6. Projection of costs not detailed elsewhere

a. merchandise inventory
b. production, sales and office equipment
c. salaries and wages with fringe benefits
d. rent and/or mortgage payments
e. insurance, taxes and utilities
f. legal, marketing, custodial, payroll, accounting, consulting, computer services, training, etc.

IV. Summary of the Business Plan

A. Restatement of Purpose

B. Restatement of Why the Business Should Succeed (Reiteration or Differential Advantages Held Over the Competition)

C. Summary of Projected Profit and/or Loss Including Identification of Financial Resources Needed

D. Planning, Implementation and Control Procedures Designed to Achieve Business Goals

E. Concluding Remarks

V. Executive Summary

VI. Non-disclosure Form - This form is critical for protecting new business ideas. Contact a lawyer and have them draw up the form.

DEVELOPMENT OF A MARKETING PLAN
Research Paper Outline

I. Management Summary

A. Mission Statement

B. Marketing Objectives

C. Sales and Profit Projection

II. Macro Environment consideration (Threats and Opportunities)

A. Product Category Demand Analysis
   1. Market potential
   2. Sales potential

B. Economic Analysis

C. Competitive Analysis

D. Political/Legal Analysis

E. Technological Analysis

F. Cultural/Social Analysis

G. Natural Environment Analysis

III. Microenvironment Considerations (Threats and Opportunities)

A. Customer (Market) Analysis

B. Supplier Analysis

C. Marketing Intermediaries

D. Publics
   1. Internal
   2. External

E. Competition

IV. Marketing Strategy

A. Market Segment Analysis
  1. Consumer market
     a. end user demographics
     b. psychographics
     c. decision making process
  2. Organizational markets
     a. buyer demographics
     b. decision making process

B. Market Mix
  1. Product strategies, action plan and assessment
     a. branding and packaging strategies
     b. product service policies
     c. planned modifications over product life cycle
     d. product line decisions
  2. Pricing strategies, action plan and assessment
     a. pricing objectives and strategies
     b. influences on price determination
     c. product mix pricing strategies
     d. price adjustment strategies
  3. Placement strategies, action plan and assessment
     a. distribution channel decision
     b. physical distribution decision
  4. Promotion strategies, action plan and assessment
     a. promotion policies and objectives
     b. advertising activities
     c. public relations activities
     d. sales promotion activities
     e. personal selling activities

V. Action Plan with Time Table of Major Events

VI. Review and Evaluation Schedule

VII. Concluding Remarks

REFERENCE MATERIALS

Broadcasting Cablecasting Yearbook. Washington, D.C.: Broadcasting Publications, 1992.

(marketing)

Delaney, Robert V. How to Prepare an Effective Business Plan. New York: AMACOM, 1986.

(business plan)

Dumouchel, J. Robert. Government Assistance Almanac. Washington, D.C.: Foggy Bottom Publications, 19.

(finance)

Gale Research Inc. Encyclopedia of Associations. Detroit: Gale Research Inc., 1992.

(professional organizations)

Gale Research Inc. Service Industries U.S.A. Detroit: Gale Research, 1992

(background)

Gumpert, David E. Inc. Magazine Presents How to Really Create a Successful Business Plan. Boston, MA: Inc. Publishing, 1990.

(business plans)

IMS Press. Gale Directory of Publications. Detroit: Gale Research, 1993.

(marketing)

Lane, Marc J. Legal Handbook for Small Business. New York: AMACOM, 1989.

(law)

Lesly, Philip. Lesly's Handbook of Public Relations and Communications. New York: AMACOM, 1991.

(marketing)

McKeever, Mike P. Nolo's Small Business Start-up. Berkeley, CA: Nolo Press, 1988.

(business plan)

Mother Earth News. The Mother Earth News Handbook of Home Business Ideas and Plans. New York: Bantam Books, 1976.
(business plans)

Pinson, Linda and Jerry Jinnett. Anatomy of a Business Plan. Fullerton, CA: Out of Your Mind and into the Marketplace, 1989.
(business plans)

Rand McNally and Company. Commercial Atlas and Marketing Guide. Chicago: Rand McNally, 1992.
(demographics)

Ridley, Clarence Eugene and Orin Frederyc Nolting. Municipal Yearbook. Washington, D.C.: International City Management Association, 1992.
(demographics)

Schilit, W. Keith. The Entrepreneur's Guide to Preparing a Winning Business Plan. Englewood Cliffs, NJ: Prentice-Hall, 1990.
(business plans)

Slater, Jeffrey. Rx for Small Business Success. Englewood Cliffs, NJ: Prentice-Hall, 1981.
(accounting practice)

Standard and Poor's Corporation. Standard and Poor's Register of Corporations, Directors, and Executives. New York: Standard and Poor's Corporation, 1992.
(industry background)

Thomas Publishing Company. Thomas Register of American Manufacturers and First Hands in All Lines. New York: Thomas Publishing Company, 1992.
(supplies)

West, Alan. A Business Plan: Planning for a Small Business. East Brunswick, NJ: Nichols Publishing Company, 1988.
(business plans)

The following companies and government organizations offer advice and have resource materials to help start your business.

Banks

Business Development Bank of Canada
- Business Planning Package
- Minding Your Own Business Series

Royal Bank of Canada
- The Source Book
- Starting Out Right

Bank of Montreal
- Developing Your Business Plan
- Cash Flow Planning

Canadian Imperial Bank of Commerce
- Financing an Independent Business
- Franchising in Canada

Toronto Dominion Bank
- Business Banking Services
- Small Business Loans

Accounting Firms

Coopers & Lybrand
- Starting Out in Business
- Financial Statement Services for the Entrepreneur

Price Waterhouse
- Expanding into Exports
- Doing Business in Quebec

Provincial Governments

Newfoundland Department of Development
Prince Edward Island Department of Industry
New Brunswick Department of Economic Development and Tourism
Nova Scotia Department of Small Business Development
Quebec Ministère de l'industrie, du commerce, et de la technologie
Small Business Ontario
Manitoba Department of Industry, Trade and Tourism
Saskatchewan Department of Economic Diversifications and Trade
Alberta Economic Development and Trade
British Columbia Development, Trade and Tourism

Federal Government

Statistics Canada
Canada Business Service Centre

SECTION THREE

CAREERS IN MARKETING

As you complete your first course in marketing, you have learned that marketing is a very broad discipline with approximately one third of all Americans employed in a marketing related field. You have also found that marketing positions provide an excellent career path leading to mid and top level positions within all types of organizations.

To assist you in choosing additional areas to study and or a career to pursue, the following pages contain a representative list of career opportunities in marketing each with a brief job description. Following the list of careers in marketing is a listing of professional organizations and publications you may contact for additional information about careers, employment prospects, educational requirements and compensation. Additional information is presented in the Appendix of the text for developing job search strategies, developing resumes and cover letters, interview techniques and otherwise preparing for a successful career in marketing.

Job Title	**Job Description**
Account Executive	Plans, coordinates, and directs advertising campaigns for clients of advertising agency: confers with client to determine advertising requirements and budgetary limitations, utilizing knowledge of product or service to be advertised, media capabilities, and audience characteristics. Confers with agency artists, copy-writers, photographers, and other media production specialists to select media to be used and to estimate costs. Submits proposed program and estimated budget to client for approval. Coordinates activities of workers engaged in marketing research, writing copy, laying out artwork, purchasing media time and space, developing special displays and promotional items, and performing other media-production activities, in order to carry out approved campaign.
Advertising Copywriter	Writes advertising copy for use by publication or broadcast media to promote sale of goods and services: consults with sales media, and marketing representatives to obtain information on product or service and discuss style and length of advertising copy. Obtains additional background and current development information through research and interview. Reviews advertising trends, consumer surveys, and other data regarding marketing of specific and related goods and services to formulate presentation approach.

Advertising Copywriter (continued)	Writes preliminary draft of copy and sends to supervisor for approval. Corrects and revises copy as necessary. May write articles, bulletins, sales letters, speeches, and other related informative and promotional material. May enter information into computer to prepare advertising copy.
Advertising Manager	Plans and executes advertising policies of organization: confers with department heads to discuss possible new accounts and to outline new policies or sales promotion campaigns. Confers with officials of newspapers, radio, and television stations, billboard advertisers, and advertising agencies to negotiate advertising contracts. Allocates advertising space to departments or products of establishment. Reviews and approves television and radio advertisements before release. Reviews rates and classifications applicable to various types of advertising and provides authorization. Directs workers in advertising department engaged in developing and producing advertisements. Directs research activities concerned with gathering information or with compilation of statistics pertinent to planning and execution of advertising sales promotion campaign. May authorize information for publication, such as interviews with reporters or articles describing phases of establishment activity. May serve as establishment representative for geographical district or department. May transact business as agent for advertising accounts. May direct preparation of special promotional features. May monitor and analyze sales promotion results to determine cost effectiveness of promotion campaign.
Agent	Specialized wholesaler who represents buyers or sellers on a relatively permanent basis. Main function is to assist in buying and selling while performing relatively few other functions. Agents earn a commission for the services they perform. Examples of agents include: manufacturers agents, selling agents, purchasing agents and commission merchants.
Art Director	Responsible for visual component of advertisements. Translates copywriters' ideas into dramatic visuals called "layouts." Agency artists develop print layouts, package designs, television layouts (called "storyboards"), corporate logotypes, trademarks, and symbols. They specify style and size of typography, paste the type in place, and arrange all the details of the ad so that it can be reproduced by engravers and printers.

Assistant Buyer	Performs the following duties in connection with purchase and sale of merchandise to aid buyer: verifies quantity and quality of stock received from manufacturer. Authorizes payment of invoices or return of shipment. Approves advertising copy for newspaper. Gives markers (retail trade; wholesale trade) information, such as price mark-ups or mark-downs, manufacturer number, season code, and style number to print on price tickets. Inspects exchanged or refunded merchandise. May sell merchandise to become familiar with customers' attitudes, preferences, and purchasing problems.
Broker	Specialized wholesaler whose main function is to bring buyers and sellers together and assist in negotiation. Brokers are paid a commission by the parties hiring them. Examples of brokers include: food brokers, real estate brokers, insurance brokers, and marketable securities brokers.
Buyer	Purchases merchandise or commodities for resale: inspects and grades or appraises agricultural commodities, durable goods, apparel, furniture, livestock, or other merchandise offered for sale to determine value and yield. Selects and orders merchandise from showings by manufacturing representatives, growers, or other sellers, or purchases merchandise on open market for cash, basing selection on nature of clientele, or demand for specific commodity, merchandise, or other property, utilizing knowledge of various articles of commerce and experience as buyer. Transports purchases or contacts carriers to arrange transportation of purchases. Authorizes payment of invoices or return of merchandise. May negotiate contracts for severance of agricultural or forestry products from land. May conduct staff meetings with sales personnel to introduce new merchandise. May price items for resale.
Credit Manager	Manages the firm's credit process including determination of customer's eligibility for credit, credit limits, terms of payment, partial and delinquent payments, discounts and allowances and client complaints and inquiries.
Customer Relations/Service Manager	Plans, directs and coordinates activities of personnel engaged in receiving, investigating, evaluating and settling, inquiries, complaints and claims of customers.

Freight Forwarder	Specialized wholesaler who consolidates small shipments from many companies and arranges freight to move at lower transportation cost.
Import/Export Agent	Coordinates activities of international traffic division of import-export agency and negotiates settlements between foreign and domestic shippers: plans and directs flow of air and surface traffic moving to overseas destinations. Supervises workers engaged in receiving and shipping freight, documentation, waybilling, assessing charges, and collecting fees for shipments. Negotiates with domestic customers, as intermediary for foreign customers, to resolve problems and arrive at mutual agreements. Negotiates with foreign shipping interests to contract for reciprocal freight-handling agreements. May examine invoices and shipping manifests for conformity to tariff and customs regulations. May contact customs officials to effect release of incoming freight and resolve customs delays. May prepare reports of transactions to facilitate billing of shippers and foreign carriers.
Inventory Manager	Plans, directs and coordinates the level and allocation of inventory. Maintains balance between amount of inventory and the costs of carrying inventory with goal of providing desired level of customer or client service.
Marketing Manager	Executive involved in planning, directing and controlling marketing activities of the organization. Position involves analyzing marketing opportunities, selecting target markets, developing market mix and managing the marketing effort with goal of creating, building and maintaining beneficial exchanges with target buyer while also achieving organizational objectives.
Marketing Research Analyst	Researches market conditions in local, regional, or national area to determine potential sales of product or service: establishes research methodology and designs format for data gathering, such as surveys, opinion polls, or questionnaires. Examines and analyzes statistical data to forecast future marketing trends. Gathers data on competitors and analyzes prices, sales, and methods of marketing and distribution. Collects data on customer preferences and buying habits. Prepares reports and graphic illustrations of findings.

Media Analyst (Buyer)	Evaluates the characteristics and costs of various media and selects best media for clients. The goal is to reach the desired target market with most effective promotional campaign at a reasonable cost per contact. Negotiates with media for optimal advertising rates, positioning, space and air time.
Physical Distribution Manager	Plans, implements and controls the physical flow of materials and final goods both with firms and through channel systems from points of origin to points of use to meet the needs of customers at a profit. Activities involve transportation, warehousing, inventory control, order processing and materials handling.
Product/Brand Manager	Plans, directs and controls business and marketing efforts related to products or product line. Concerned with research and development, packaging, manufacturing, pricing sales and distribution, promotion, market research business analysis and forecasting.
Public Relations Director	Plans and conducts public relations program designed to create and maintain favorable public image for employer or client: plans and directs development and communication of information designed to keep public informed of employer's programs, accomplishments, or point of view. Arranges for public relations efforts in order to meet needs, objectives, and policies of individual, special interest group, business concern, nonprofit organization, or governmental agency, serving as in-house staff member or as outside consultant. Prepares and distributes fact sheets, news releases, photographs, scripts, motion pictures, or tape recordings to media representatives and other persons who may be interested in learning about or publicizing employer's activities or message. Purchases advertising space and time as required. Arranges for and conducts public-contact programs designed to meet employer's objectives, utilizing knowledge of changing attitudes and opinions of consumers, clients, employees, or other interest groups. Promotes goodwill through such publicity efforts as speeches, exhibits, films, tours, and question/answer sessions. Represents employer during community projects and at public, social, and business gatherings. May research data, create ideas, write copy, lay out artwork, contact media representatives, or represent

Public Relations Director (continued)	employer directly before general public. May develop special projects such as campaign fund raisers or public awareness about political issues. May direct activities of subordinates. May confer with production and support personnel to coordinate production of television advertisements and on-air promotions. May prepare press releases and fact sheets, and compose letters, using computer. May disseminate facts and information about organization's activities or governmental agency's programs to general public and be known as Public Information Officer.
Purchasing Agent	Coordinates activities involved with procuring goods and services, such as raw materials, equipment, tools, parts, supplies, and advertising, for establishment: reviews requisitions. Confers with vendors to obtain product or service information, such as price, availability, and delivery schedule. Selects products for purchase by testing, observing, or examining items. Estimates values according to knowledge of market price. Determines method of procurement, such as direct purchase or bid. Prepares purchase orders or bid requests. Reviews bid proposals and negotiates, contracts within budgetary limitations and scope of authority. Maintains manual or computerized procurement records, such as items or services purchased, costs, delivery, product quality or performance, and inventories. Discusses defective or unacceptable goods or services with inspection quality control personnel, users, vendors, and others to determine source of trouble and take corrective action. May approve invoices for payment. May expedite delivery of goods to users.
Sales Manager	Manages sales activities of establishment: directs staffing, training, and performance evaluations to develop and control sales program. Coordinates sales distribution by establishing sales territories, quotas, and goals and advises dealers, distributors, and clients concerning sales and advertising techniques. Assigns sales territory to sales personnel. Analyzes sales statistics to formulate policy and to assist dealers in promoting sales. Reviews market analyses to determine customer needs, volume potential, price schedules, and discount rates, and develops sales campaigns to accommodate goals of company. Directs product simplification and standardization to eliminate

Sales Manager (continued)	unprofitable items from sales line. Represents company at trade association meetings to promote product. Coordinates liaison between sales department and other sales-related units. Analyzes and controls expenditures of division to conform to budgetary requirements. Assists other departments within establishment to prepare manuals and technical publications. Prepares periodic sales report showing sales volume and potential sales. May direct sales for manufacturer, retail store, wholesale house, jobber, or other establishment. May direct product research and development. May recommend or approve budget, expenditures, and appropriations for research and development work.
Sales Representative	Responsible for sale of products and services to businesses, organizations and individuals at store, office, showroom, or customers' place of business. displays or demonstrates product, quotes prices and terms of sales and prepares sales contracts. Compiles lists of potential customers in developing call schedule and prepares reports of business transactions. Requires knowledge of target market, company, product, competition and territory.
Traffic Manager	Directs and coordinates traffic activities of organization: develops methods and procedures for transportation of raw materials to processing and production areas and commodities from departments to customers, warehouses, or other storage facilities. Determines most efficient and economical routing and mode of transportation, using rate and tariff manuals and motor freight and railroad guidebooks. Directs scheduling of shipments and notifies concerned departments or customers of arrival dates. Initiates investigations into causes of damages or shortages in consignments or overcharges for freight or insurance. Conducts studies in areas of packaging, warehousing, and loading of commodities and evaluates existing procedures and standards. Initiates changes designed to improve control and efficiency of traffic department. May negotiate contracts for leasing of transportation equipment or property. May assist in preparing department budget.

Professional and Trade Associations

Advertising Club of New York
235 Park Avenue, S, 6th Floor
New York, NY 10003

Phone: (212) 533-8080

American Advertising Federation
1400 K Street N.W., Suite 1000
Washington, DC 20005

Phone: (202) 898-0089

American Assoc. of Advertising Agencies
666 Third Avenue, 13th Floor
New York, NY 10017

Phone: (212) 682-8391

American Marketing Association
250 South Wacker Drive, Suite 200
Chicago, IL 60606

Phone: (312) 648-0536

American Society of Transportation & Logistics
P.O. Box 33095
Louisville, KY 40232

Phone: (502) 451-8150

American Telemarketing Association
5000 Van Nuys Blvd. No. 300
Sherman Oaks, CA 91403

Phone: (818) 995-7338

Business/Professional Advertising Assoc.
100 Metroplex Drive
Edison, NJ 08817

Phone: (201) 985-4441

Council of Sales Promotion Agencies
750 Summer Street
Stamford, CT 06901

Phone: (203) 325-3911

Direct Marketing Association
6 East 43rd Street
New York, NY 10017

Phone: (212) 689-4977

Life Ins. Marketing & Research Assoc.
P.O. Box 208
Hartford, CT 06141

Phone: (203) 677-0033

Marketing Research Association
111 East Wacker Drive, Suite 600
Chicago, IL 60601

Phone: (312) 644-6610

Marketing Science Institute
1000 Massachusetts Avenue
Cambridge, MA 0211138

Phone: (617) 491-2060

National Assoc. of Display Industries
470 Park Avenue, S, 17th Floor
New York, NY 10016

Phone: (212) 213-2662

National Assoc. for Professional Saleswomen
P.O. Box 2606
Novato, CA 94948

Phone: (415) 898-2606

National Assoc. of Purchasing Management
2055 East Centennial Cr., P.O. Box 22160
Tempe, AZ 85282

Phone: (602) 752-6276

National Assoc. of Wholesalers & Distributors
1725 K Street, N. W.
Washington, DC 20006

Phone: (202) 872-0885

Public Relations Society of America
33 Irving Place, 3rd Floor
New York, NY 10003

Phone: (212) 995-2230

Retail Council of Canada

Sales and Marketing Executives International
Statler Office Tower, 458
Cleveland, OH 44115

Phone: (216) 771-6650

Women in Advertising and Marketing
4200 Wisconsin Ave. N.W., Suite 106-238
Washington, DC 20016

Phone: (202) 369-7400

Women in Sales Association
8 Madison Avenue, P.O. Box M
Valhalla, NY 10595

Phone: (914) 946-3802

Trade Publications

Advertising Age
Crain Communications, Inc.
740 North Rush Street
Chicago, IL 60611
Phone: (312) 649-5200

Adweek
49 East 21st Street
New York, NY 10010
Phone: (212) 529-5500

Brandweek
49 East 21st Street
New York, NY 10010
Phone: (212) 529-5500

B/PAA Communicator
Business/Professional Advertising Assoc.
100 Metroplex Drive
Edison, NJ 08817
Phone: (312) 985-4441

Business Marketing
Crain Communications, Inc.
220 East 42nd Street
New York, NY 10017
Phone: (212) 210-0100

Direct Marketing
224 Seventh Street
Garden City, NY 11530

DM News: The Newspaper of Direct Marketing
Mill Hollow Corporation
19 West 21st Street, 8th Floor
New York, NY 10010
Phone: (212) 741-2095

Journal of Advertising Research
Advertising Research Foundation
3 East 54th Street, 15th Floor
New York, NY 10022
Phone: (212) 751-5656

Journal of Marketing
American Marketing Association
250 South Wacker Drive
Chicago, IL 60606
Phone: (312) 648-0536

Journal of Marketing Research
American Marketing Association
250 South Wacker Drive
Chicago, IL 60606
Phone: (312) 648-0536

Journal of Product Innovation
655 Avenue of the Americas
New York, NY 10010
Phone: (212) 989-5800

Marketing
777 Bay Street
Toronto, ON M5W 1A7
Canada
Phone: (416) 596-5858

Marketing Communications
Lakewood Publishers
50 South Ninth Street
Minneapolis, MN 55402
Phone: (612) 333-0471

Marketing News
American Marketing Association
250 South Wacker Drive, Suite 200
Chicago, IL 60606
Phone: (312) 648-0536

Mediaweek
1515 Broadway
New York, NY 10021

PR News
127 East 80th Street
New York, NY 10036
Phone: (212) 879-7090

Public Relations Journal
Public Relations Society of America
33 Irving Place, 3rd Floor
New York, NY 10003
Phone: (212) 995-2230

Sales & Marketing Management
633 Third Avenue
New York, NY 10017

Sales & Marketing Management in Canada
3500 Dufferin Street, 402
Downsview, ON M3K IN2
Canada
Phone: (416) 633-2020

Sports Marketing News
Technical Marketing Group
1460 Post Road East
Westport, CT 06880

Stores
100 W, 31st Street
New York, NY 10001
Phone: (212) 244-8780

Telemarketing
Technology Marketing Corp.
One Technology Plaza
Norwalk, CT 06854
Phone: (203) 852-6800